The Art of Industrial Warfare
Amar Manzoor

Revised Edition 2022

7Tao Engineering Ltd

'The Art of Industrial Warfare' (Revised Edition 2022) is available in five individually collectible book covers and subtitles for fans of the 7Tao method. The internal contents are the same for all five books shown below.

The Art of Industrial Warfare

An introduction to Industrial Combat in the US China Trade War

Amar Manzoor

THE ART OF INDUSTRIAL WARFARE

An introduction to Industrial Martial Arts in the US-China Trade War

Amar Manzoor

The Art of Industrial Warfare

Who will win the USA vs China Economic Battle of the 21st century?

Amar Manzoor

The Art of Industrial Warfare

An Answer to the US China Trade War

Amar Manzoor

The Art of Industrial Warfare

The Chinese strategy for global manufacturing dominance

Amar Manzoor

The Art of Industrial Warfare: Revised edition.

Copyright © 2022 Amar Manzoor. All rights reserved

This book is a product of the staff of 7Tao Engineering Ltd www.7tao.co.uk

The 7Tao Logo and 'The Art of Industrial War' and 'The Art of Industrial Warfare' are protected by UK Copyright law under the trademark office.

This book is based on the experiences of the 7Tao team in completing assignments in a variety of corporations, business and institutions across the world. The vehicle for implementation for the 7Tao system are NVQ qualifications and apprenticeships, being used to test the 7Tao systems viability within academia and industry.

The statements and articles conducted within the businesses are produced by the employees of the businesses independently as their own witness testimony and account, and are strictly their own. The references and descriptions contained within this book represent the contributor / article author perception of the results obtained in the 7Tao NVQ effort.

The pictures used in this book are sourced from Wikipedia public commons use, Pixabay, Pexels and donated photographs by the article writers. All references taken from the media organizations stated and are reproduced precisely as they are spoken by the personalities mentioned, including the presidents of corporations, businesses, and countries.

The first edition of this book was released by Shepheard Walwyn Publishers Ltd in 2014 under author copyright, originally designed to investigate the marketplace and create a market stance before the advent of the US China Trade War in 2018. The concept has since been advanced and further investigated to produce this enhanced version of the original publication.

Some of the writing in this book has been shared with Epoch Times media group. Articles can be found published under the authors name in the Epoch Times Newspaper. Some of the articles in the Epoch Times have been included as part of this book.

The materials used in this publication are copyrighted. Copying and / or transmitting portions or all of this without permission may be a violation of applicable law. Users of this book are free to use the contents of this book in such ways as are permitted by international copyright law and the law of the country of use. Any such use of the materials in this book should acknowledge the author and title.

This book comes in five different covers designs as a collector's edition. All five Cover designs created by 7Tao Engineering Ltd using pictures, illsutrations and photo's from Pixabay, Pexels and Wikipedia based common use images with no copyright jurisdiction globally.

Typeset, published and distributed through Ingramspark

Disclaimer

The information provided within this Book is for general informational purposes only. While I try to keep the information up-to-date and correct, there are no representations or warranties, express or implied, about the completeness, accuracy, reliability, suitability, or availability with respect to the information, products, services, or related graphics contained in the printed book and eBook for any purpose. Any use of the methods describe within this Book are the results of the company's research and personal experiences of our customers as they worked through the NVQ BIT system. They are not intended to be a definitive set of instructions for this project of 7Tao. You may discover there are other methods and materials to accomplish the same end result.

'Some of the attack techniques studied' has deliberately been used twice inside this book to emphasise the importance of understanding attack techniques when combined with defensive techniques.

The information contained within this Book is strictly for educational purposes. If you wish to apply ideas contained in this Book, you are taking full responsibility for your actions. It is not recommended you practise industrial martial arts without the correct training program and a dedicated teacher.

The author has made every effort to ensure the accuracy of the information within this book was correct at time of publication. The author does not assume and hereby disclaims any liability to any party for any loss, damage, or disruption caused by errors or omissions, whether such errors or omissions result from accident, negligence, or any other cause.

Dedication

This book is dedicated to all those who fight corruption within all levels of society. Whether its government, corporate, electoral, legal, process, financial, fiscal, climate, information, political, military, business or industrial corruption – our fight is one.

If any good can come from this book in the fight against the growing problem of corruption, then all the credit belongs to God alone. Only the mistakes have been mine.

Contents:

Foreword:	*13*
Introduction:	*26*

Chapter 1: Decline of the Transatlantic Cycle — 31
- Flowing With the Cycles — 33
- The Four-Season Cycle — 36
- The Three-'C' Theory: Colonialism, Communism and Capitalism — 38
- Chinese Dominance and Western Economic Dependence — 41
- The Shift of Trading from West to East — 42
- Defending the Homeland – Protecting factories, jobs and lives? — 43
- United States of America in the year 2000 — 46
- The Art of Fighting, without Fighting — 49

Chapter 2: Industrial warfare VS military warfare — 51
- Asia vs the West — 55
- The power and discipline of industrial warfare — 57
- Ideological Power — 58
- Military Power — 59
- Economic Power — 60
- The Four-Season Cycle in All Things — 61
- The Changing Face of Business: Fourth Generation — 63
- The First Generation (1929-1968): 'Metal Money' — 64
- The Second Generation (1929-1982): 'Mass Production' — 65
- The Third Generation (1982-2000): 'Intense Competition' — 66
- Analysis of the Fourth Generation — 67
- What Will the Fourth Generation Look Like? — 69
- What Lies Ahead for the Businessman? — 72
- China declares battle for Global Growth — 73
- Physical fighting VS Business fighting — 78
- The Rules of Industrial Combat — 79
- The techniques of 7Tao — 80
- Summary of analysis — 81

Chapter 3: Dynamics of the 7Tao — 83
- Defence and Attack — 88
- The Transaction — 89
- The 7Tao Techniques — 89
- Industrial Warfare comes to the US and the EU — 91
- US takes its first pawns in Industrial War with China — 93
- Industrial War has always been around — 96
- Boeing VS Airbus case study — 99
- As the US counter China's industrial war, transactions are key — 111

Chapter 4: Tao 1: Price – Are you Getting and Giving Value for Money? — 116
- Defending Price Strengths — 117
- Attacking Price Weaknesses — 120
- Pricing Starts with the Order — 125
- 7Tao: Case Study 1: Altro Ltd — 128
- Walmart: The foreign and home-based outlet — 133

Chapter 5: Tao 2: Delivery - Is it On Time? — 138
- Defending Delivery Strengths — 139
- Attacking Delivery Weaknesses — 142
- Delivery Starts with the Customer's Order — 144
- Case Study 2: Johnson Matthey, Noble Metals — 145
- Amazon: The best delivery company in the world? — 149

Chapter 6: Tao 3: Quality – Is it Fit for Purpose? — 157
- Defending Quality Strengths — 157
- Attacking Quality Weaknesses — 158
- Quality Starts with Understanding the Position — 161
- Case Study 3: Drury's Engineering — 169
- Adapting to a changing environment is the key to quality — 171
- Flying cars: Product quality leads to improved quality of mobility — 175

Chapter 7: Tao 4: After Market - Do They Come Back for More?	**179**
After Market Begins with the Sale of a good quality product.	184
Case Study 4: The National Skills Academy for Manufacturing	186
After Market: The belt and road initiative.	191
After Market support requires some deep thinking	194
Chapter 8: Tao 5: Customers – Do You Have Enough of Them?	**199**
Defending Customer Strengths	201
Attacking Customer Weaknesses	203
Customers Start with the Order	203
Case Study 5: The Formula One Industry	208
The Regional Comprehensive Economic Partnership.	211
RCEP VS CPTPP	213
Military warfare or Industrial Warfare	214
Universities will become obsolete unless they join the Eurasian landmass.	216
Chapter 9: Tao 6: Shareholders – Do You Make Enough Profit?	**220**
The Argument of Shareholders	220
Defending Shareholder Strengths	221
Attacking Shareholder Weaknesses	222
Shareholder Value Starts with Sustainability and Ends with Growth	223
Case Study 6: Sample Return-on-Investment Receipts	224
A Sample Company Yield Report	231
Talking About a Revolution	233
Asian Infrastructure Investment Bank (AIIB)	238
AIIB vs World Bank, International Monetary Fund and Asian Development Bank	240
7Tao – Attacking corruption	241
7Tao - challenging the oppressor	242
Russia and the alternative to the SWIFT banking system	244

Chapter 10: Tao 7: Employees – Are Your Workers the Best They Can Be? — 247
   Defending Employee Strengths — 248
   Attacking Employee Weaknesses — 250
   Employees are Valued by Knowledge — 256
   The US China Trade War – Defending competitiveness and attacking corruption — 258
   No one wins a fight — 259
   Made in China 2025: Supporting a billion employees — 267
   The rise of expendable jobs and their impact — 270

Chapter 11: The Asian Age – or a New Partnership between Co-operating Cultures? — 273
   Geopolitics of the Eastward Shift — 273
   Education is the Key, Practice is a Fundamental Factor — 275
   China is Back — 277
   Throw Away the Queensberry Rules — 280
   Education and training — 281
   China is in good shape to take over — 287
   Middle East and Iran — 289

Chapter 12: Concluding Industrial Warfare. — 293
   1: President Trump fights back in Industrial Warfare — 293
   2: Unfair trade practices and their origin — 296
   3: Trade War or Tirade War? — 300
   4: Diffusion of the world economy — 303
   5: What lies ahead… the recessions of 2019 and 2026 — 304
   6: Avoiding a kinetic confrontation with Russia, China and everyone else — 312
   7: US China trade war can be resolved but it needs to be understood through transactional spectacles — 317
   The US China trade war morphs into industrial warfare — 320
   Applying 7Tao to China — 321
   7Tao is all around us… it's always been here — 322

Chapter 13: The Art of Industrial Warfare.   324
    1: Initial estimations   325
    2: The 7Tao of industrial conflict   329
    3: The 7Tao of industrial strategy   331
    4: Industrial tactical movements   335
    5: 7Tao energy in the organization   339
    6: Attack and defense using weakness and strength   343
    7: Maneuvering the organization   353
    8: Variation in industrial tactics   358
    9: The workforce on the move   361
    10: The Six business environments   370
    11: The nine situations of business   373
    12: Physical attacks on a corporation, market and country   384
    13: The use of spies in industrial warfare   388

Index   392

Boxes:

1:1 - Destroying Middle-Class Lives   44
2:1 - Burning the House Down?   62
3:1 - Germany – Odd One Out?   83
4:1 - The Big Diesel God   119
4:2 - The Fierce Dragon   122
4:3 - Boys' Toys and Businessmen's Profits   124
4:4 - Some of the Attack Techniques Studied   126
5:1 - Lessons in Stealth and Industrial Warfare   140
5:2 - The Story of Madame Li and Dayang Trands   141
5:3 - The Sneaker War   145
6:1 - Chinese 7Tao versus American Six Sigma   159
6:2 - The F-16 Falcon versus the JF-17 Thunder   162
6:3 - American Creativity or Chinese Creativity?   164
6:4 - Babur and the Tomahawk Cruise Missile   167
7:1 - The Chinese Harley Davidson   180
7:2 - Geely: The Coming of Age of the Chinese Auto Industry   183
7:3 - The Story of Hummer: Industrial Warfare in Action   185
7:4 - Washing Clothes   190
8:1 - The Currency War   202
8:2 - The Renault Saga – It's Called Industrial Warfare   204
8:3 - Sample Tools Used to Correct Mistakes   206

8:4 - The Toyota-Ferrari Formula One Scandal	207
10:1 - 3D Food Printing	251
10:2 - Three-Dimensional Printers	255

Tables:

1:1 - Transatlantic and East Asian cycles	32
2:1 – Comparing cold war economic models 1950 – 1991	51
2:2 – Comparing American and Chinese economic models, 1991 – 2014	53

Figures

1:1 – Industrial revolutions 1800 – 2000	35
1:2 – Rhythmic Oscillation	36
1:3 – The Four Season Cycle divided into 4.5- Year Units.	36
1.4 – Idealised 18-Year Real Estate Cycle	37
1.5 – US Manufacturing employment	46
1.6 – Trading places: China Usurps US	48
2:1 – 7Tao Representation of Power	57
3.1 – Industrial warfare has always been around	96
3.2 – Airbus and Boeing	99
3.3 – Boeing Bubble Burst	109
3.4 – Financial Bubble Graph	109
7.1 – Belt and Road Initiative	194
8.1 – RCEP vs CPTPP	213
9.1 – Shareholder map in AIIB	238
11.1 – World Map of military bases	283
12.1 – The rise and fall of empires by Ray Dalio	299
12.2 – Ascendant strategy and investments	305
12.3 – Nationwide building society house price bubble	310

The Art of Industrial Warfare

Foreword

When Communism collapsed in the Soviet Union, the Chinese Communist party took a different line. Whereas Russia fell under the sway of the IMF and Jeffrey Sachs, China pursued an independent course towards a market economy. Today China has become manufacturer to the world while Russia is mostly reliant on exports of natural resources like many developing countries. The Chinese understood that in 1989, communism was on its way out. Huge changes were about to engulf the world hence the Tiananmen Square incident. Either China changed from communism to capitalism, or change would overwhelm it and the Chinese communist party would lose control of China. They began the change to state controlled capitalism in 1991 just after the collapse of Communism. Slowly but surely, the Chinese have been taking over the global economy in terms of agriculture, manufacturing and services. In 2014, purchasing power parity comparisons between the United States and China showed that the Chinese were now ahead of the United States.

The great power competition between communism and capitalism was the cornerstone of the 20th century leading to the victory of capitalism. This victory would form the basis of the great power competition in the 21st century between the USA and China, rivalry will be based upon competing forms of capitalism. This would result in a ferocious industrial war based upon the ancient principles of the 7Tao. The 7Tao transaction would form essential strategy for market domination – so far, the results of industrial warfare have been phenomenal for China. The question is apparent. Does the 21st century belong to economically resurgent China or the incumbent power, the United States of America?

...

In 1999 while running my first industrial consulting company, I started looking at the possibility of the USA and China beginning to challenge each other and contemplated what that challenge would look like. In my estimation, all signs pointed towards a trade, manufacturing, and industrial war as I scribbled ideas down on throwaway pieces of paper. During the year 2000, when everyone was worrying about the non-existent Y2K distraction, I began thinking about the possibility of conflict between rising powers and declining powers. At that time, many changes were happening in the world. The corporate recession was coming in 2000, also called the 'mid cycle recession' in the 18-year real estate cycle. The Dotcom crash, Enron, WorldCom and many other companies would drive forward what we label an 'earnings' recession. Houses were coming up for sale and no one wanted to buy them because of fear of the inverted yield curve blip that occurs in this particular stage of the 18-year real estate cycle is also called the mid cycle recession. The buyers were already burned from the 1990s house price crash.

Then the world got even worse right in the middle of the 2002 mid cycle recession, the 9/11 attacks had shocked the western world into embarking on a Middle Eastern re-colonization project. This was to enforce what was called PNAC, or the 'Project for the New American Century'. All amusing, utterly confusing and misdirected at the time, I was looking at the changes and trying to see above and over the constant pounding of geopolitical drama's which were dominating the news cycle in the Middle East and the Muslim world in general. One incident fascinated me completely, a very small air collision which happened a few months before the tragic events of 9/11 ushered in military posture review and invasion of primarily Middle Eastern and South Asian territory, a cheap doorway into Eurasia. Half a world away, it was the Hainan Island Incident.

The origin of the 7Tao idea - The Hainan Island Incident.

On April 1st 2001, an EP3 signals intelligence aircraft belonging to the USA collided with a Chinese J8 'Finback' jet fighter about 70 miles away from the Chinese territory of Hainan. The Americans had to land the damaged EP3 Intelligence gathering aircraft on Chinese territory. The 24 crew members were detained by Chinese authorities and interrogated until a statement was delivered to the United States. The exact phrasing of this document was intentionally ambiguous and allowed both countries to save face while defusing a potentially volatile situation between militarily strong states.

I watched the incident very closely looking at details minute by minute. Questions filled every thought that pondered. Why was the USA spying on China? Why are the USA right on the Chinese doorstep in the South China Sea? Why did the signals intelligence aircraft get stripped and sent back in pieces? Why did the Chinese interrogate the 24 American personnel? Why did they make President

Bush say sorry to the wife of the dead Chinese fighter pilot? Where did all that equipment inside the EP3 go? All of the interviews of Chinese ambassadors in Britain indicated that China was not in the same situation it was 100 years ago during its own labeled 'century of humiliation'. They were not taking any threats or intimidation from anyone anymore. The Chinese had power, enormous military power and this led to solving the incident through diplomacy. The Americans only do diplomacy against power's who can hit back, then they revert to economic warfare and using the American designed international financial system against their targeted country. However, with China this was a very difficult option. The sheer size of the country, population, military firepower and its possession of an unknown series of nuclear weapons indicated that there was no hunger for military conflict here. The situation could only get worse and spiral out of control affecting the entire planet.

As soon as the Hainan Island incident ended, China began a rapid military upgrade for Army, Navy and Air force. They were aided massively by the attacks of 9/11 later in 2001 because America was about to be bogged down in an asymmetric fight with known and unknown guerilla forces in Afghanistan, the Graveyard of Empires. As if that wasn't bad enough, two years later they blundered militarily into Iraq as well and meddled with many other Middle Eastern states, dabbling in all sorts of military, diplomatic, financial, religious, government and social re-engineering projects. China saw this invasion with clear eyes and encouraged them, so did Vladimir Putin and the Russian FSB. Both countries knew that if the USA get stuck in that kind of highly complex unrecognizable quagmire, they will never come out – leading to near death of liberalism, western capitalism and possible empire collapse. As the USA invests resources into winning a war that is not even a real war, they will lose control of many other areas of the US Empire. This will force them to fight on all fronts in all parts of the world sustaining an international liberal democracy system which was rapidly collapsing accelerated by the soon to arrive 2008 financial crisis. Slowly but surely, allies began to grow weary of the constant drive to war through colonial conquest masked by liberal democracy. Spinning plates comes to mind.

China had different plans. They wanted industry, factories, manufacturing plants and production centers. They wanted to make China the center of the manufacturing world and so set about pleading to all western countries to use their land as a source of cheap production. China came to be known as the workshop of the world. While America was out and about in tanks and jets, China was busy taking all of the Western factories into the mainland and conducting what I was calling 'an industrial war', previously conducted successfully by Japan and Germany from the 1950's onwards.

I knew as far back as 1994 during the Clinton years that China and the USA were posturing against each other in the South China Sea using naval maneuvers, each side backing off and de-escalating repeatedly. I knew that war between these two would be catastrophic and will involve the use of thermonuclear weapons – both sides were practicing rapid de-escalation strategies on a three dimensional level. All back channels were open, all sides were talking. America knew that China would rise, they either fight them or welcome them into the World Trade Organization. And so, the Clinton administration welcomed them into the World Trade Organization with the hope that they follow world trade rules and rise according to an already established set of international protocols – Clinton would be so mistaken. China readily accepted and took the offer in 2001 WTO talks after a few months of simulated negotiation. That's when it occurred to me that the road to 'Industrial Warfare' had begun. I already possessed a little knowledge of the Japanese rise after the Second World War, which led to major economic tariffs and economic competition during the 70's and 80's, so I wondered how China's rise would affect the planet in terms of competition and geopolitical changes in the future, when China began exports encroaching right on the economic doorstep of the United States just like Japan did in the 80's. Everything was 'Made in China'.

My background used to be one of studying ancient Martial Arts, engineering and reading ancient Eastern texts. I loved the East, I travelled, met with eastern people, was inspired by their cultures, absorbed by their diversity and was fascinated by their religions. So I looked into their trading styles. In Pakistan, India, China, Indonesia, Malaysia and areas of the Middle East, the story was the same. Everyone just traded everywhere with whatever means they had - their own rules system was not yet hardened into rule of law. They sold anything to anyone and cared for just one thing – The Transaction – one at a time.

Then I had my 'flux capacitor' moment and I wrote it down on a napkin from a Thai restaurant. The napkin read "The Art of Industrial Warfare". For months I thought about the title, repeatedly, until a vision formed in my head about what I wanted to do. I had to create something; to do this I had to write down what this title meant. Instead of trying to find the meaning to the title, I turned to Engineering and created a framework for achieving my task ahead. Reading Eastern versions of Philosophy, Engineering, Martial Arts and Japanese Continuous Improvement I set about designing what I would lovingly call 'An Industrial Combat Method', because that is exactly what is was - A Martial Art specifically designed to function within industry which I eventually published in 2005.

Two decades ago, I figured out that there would be an economic conflict between the USA and China in the form of a trade, industrial, economic, manufacturing and financial war. Two decades later, my forecasts were proven correct. In April 2018, the US-China Trade War was announced and it was based around the manufacturing industry. Within six months, the stirring economic conflict was dominating every global news channel every hour of the day. Within eight months, the conflict began to infect the bloodstream of the global economic system. The US-China Trade War was a factor that every government, company, employee and global corporation had to consider before estimating business. The US China trade war will affect the entire planet, in every product, with every Dollar, Yuan, and other global currencies and with every business community in the world. And this conceptual book would form the cornerstone for me understanding this conflict with the 7Tao as my very own central guiding light in the trade fight between these two superpowers.

It's not just a question of making a prediction. Everybody makes predictions, everyday, in every workplace, in every country across the world. The power is in intricate preparation—preparing for an event to come and being completely ready for it, as best as you can. After years researching, teaching, discussing and practicing industrial conflict through various incarnations of the 7Tao industrial engineering company, the 7Tao idea was crystallized in 2000 giving me the motivation to prepare for a seismic paradigm shift. I realized that China's high growth trajectory would have huge implications in every global sphere for the next century: diplomatic, geographic, military, economic, financial and cultural. The 7Tao system was to be designed by me and for me as a successor to Six Sigma, Lean, Continuous Improvement and Agile Manufacturing. 7Tao was designed to take business from the third generation of competition and embrace the ideas of a fourth generation set of disciplines. 7Tao is all about embracing the East as we journey into the 21st century – But I had to build it. How do you build something so immense for a conflict that will not arrive for another two decades at least?

2000 – 2005 – Creating the 7Tao concept.

The concept of 7Tao is partially based on the ancient principles of Sun Tzu's *Art of War, the book of 5 rings, Lau Tzu, 36 stratagems, Seven Military Classics and the Tao of Jeet Kwon Do*. The practical application, however, is focused on Industry, so the system is written in industrial literature with ample signs of Sun Tzu in its written form. The Industrial concepts borrow from Six Sigma, Lean Manufacturing, Total Quality, 20 Keys, and other engineering texts spanning Manufacturing and Production Engineering. 7Tao looks like an industrial policy and strategy document and its readers are of all types, CEO's, statesmen, politicians, engineers, business leaders and workforce personnel. The customer will be absorbing the culture of Sun Tzu without knowing that they are moving towards Eastern thinking. In this six-year period of writing, building and simulating industrial warfare, the internal tests on the 7Tao were being tried out with many students from numerous companies contributing to the testing process.

These students were all involved in locally based companies within a hundred miles of where I was working. We would all convene in one academic based 'simulation room' in Barnfield College to test out the new techniques. The students would then take each technique and test it in their respective workplaces when they went back to the sites. This incubation period was perfect both for me, the objectives which I wanted to achieve and for the students, as they got to test each 7Tao technique in their workplace. It was a learning curve for all of us and one that we all enjoyed. We did it because we loved to do this, not because we wanted to get paid … a labor of love between the teacher and students who wanted to discover their own talent. Many of the students at this age are passionate about their learning and will experiment with little thought about the results. This is where innovation lies – with the youth.

Each one of the techniques contained within 7Tao is both independent and intertwined. You can use them individually, or you can start combining them into multiple arrays of Defense and Attack. The 7Tao system is built on the martial / Sun Tzu principles so it becomes easy to use once you know how to practice the system. Like any martial art, specialist field, sport or any other competitive discipline, it all comes down to practice – the more you practice, the better you get at it. The final product looked like a set of training manuals, reflective of the job I was doing, the place I was teaching in and the field that I was practicing. 7Tao worked like a dream inside the college. Now to take it on the road…

2006 to 2015 – Proving 7Tao.

How do you prove something no one believes in? How do you sell something no one wants? How do you make someone read a document which seems so unique and so different, that it's not something people recognize? How do you make someone buy the product when they don't want to buy? How do you make them accept a set of results which are so outlandishly high performance that they simply don't believe in them? How do you tell a customer that the US-China Trade War is coming and that they will face some very difficult times down the road in 15 years time? How do you make people believe that you are prepared for this event – which has not appeared yet and is so far on the horizon that it is practically invisible? How do you avoid being discarded, scoffed, belittled, rejected, ignored and sidelined as the industrial conflict between the USA and China is forming right in front of your eyes? The biggest hurdle was me! Why would anyone believe an upstart drop out from a small town in England? – An immigrant from Pakistan? – An ex martial artist? – A classic American car loving Brit who can't drive very well? Why would anyone believe a first time author who had never published before? Why would anyone even accept me in any way other than a lovable rogue? The Janitor in Good Will Hunting comes to mind. But I wasn't doing it for them, I was doing it for myself and needed the help of God if I was to succeed.

These were ***massive hurdles*** that I had to cross. The British National Skills Academy for Manufacturing were visiting Barnfield college, their representative at the time, John Bradley was recruiting for people and I asked him for help to move forward. I told NSAM straight up, "There will be a US-China Trade War in the future and I want to get ready for it". They laughed out loud at me at first, but we must remember, they are British. The British do not turn an idea away just because it seems different and wildly unfamiliar. They have the foresight to stand by logic and see through the noise of hearsay and sales hype to inject logic and reason into their decision making.

The British have an amazing capability of recognizing talent and nurturing it to embrace the future. They take care of their people, they take care of their country and they take care of their decisions. The British are quite strict when it comes to encouraging entrepreneurship, they will do what it takes to remove the barriers stopping creativity and encourage new business. Most of the world's education systems are based on British principles. From BSc, MSc and PhD... even the titles reflected British Universities.

NSAM knew immediately that there was something there, that portions of it would work even if it was not all 100% relevant at this particular time in 2006. 'Give Amar a chance to function and let him work out his ideas. He knows what he wants to do and he knows how to do it. Apart from anything else, it's fascinating what he has done so far.'

The proving process began in 2006. Proof of concept means testing, and this means finding failures and fixing them within the 7Tao system itself. Over this ten-year period, I found all of the failures and fixed them on a daily, weekly, monthly basis and annual basis by rigorously testing the 7Tao system within industry – and I am constantly adapting the system as the world changes. Improvement came as I tested in client sites over the coming decade.

7Tao began to improve its performance. The more exposure it gained in plant environments, the more it fused itself into the variety of customers who embraced it. The more powerful the customer became, the more they wanted of 7Tao. This process repeated itself over a ten-year period and each time the results were exactly the same – unbelievable performance every time. The *external* on-the-road testing process was repeating the results of the *internal* incubation testing process which occurred from 2000 to 2005. 7Tao shook up the decision-making systems of every company it touched and the performance yields that each class returned were beyond expectations every time. The beauty of the system was that it was being guided by the British government education seal – that made it a slightly easier sell. When a customer saw it, they would look at the possibility of trying it knowing that NSAM had recommended the system – with the NSAM seal of approval, the quality mark would ensure to the customer that it was a product which they would not be disappointed in. The customers had a process. Look, touch, taste, swallow and then gorge on 7Tao as they feasted in profits. All while their employees gained valuable qualifications in apprenticeships and national vocational qualifications comprised of both certificates and diplomas provided by EAL (Engineering and Marine Training Awards Ltd).

2014 – 2018 – Promoting 7Tao.

Once near the end of the proving stage, the promotion cycle kicked into gear. This was the hardest part of getting 7Tao to the world. The first edition of this book was written and published in 2014 by Shepheard Walwyn supported by Anthony Werner. Newspapers, social media, radio stations and magazines were approached in an attempt to get the word out that this system existed to take on the challenge of the *'not yet arrived'* US-China Trade War. 7Tao was something that could resolve this $500 billion a year problem before it became cancerous, affecting every country, every product and every transaction in the world. Many hurdles and many difficulties were faced in this torrid road to promotion. Wall after wall had to be scaled and in most cases, I fell flat on my face when I got over the other side. The best opportunity came when a reporter named Joshua Philipp in the USA began reading into the system and we both decided to get in touch with regards to what I had achieved so far. The *Epoch Times* newspaper and International Media Group began to take an interest in what had been achieved to date in the UK. 7Tao's main aim was simple: to move the concepts, (which systems like Six Sigma, Lean Manufacturing and Total Quality had established so successfully in the 1980's, 1990's and 2000's,) forward to a new level to face the changing circumstances of the world economy, thus staying relevant to future needs and honoring all the achievements of Shingo, Deming, Juran and Ohno of the past. 7Tao was relevant to the past philosophies the Japanese had pioneered and had a forward future vision into what the US China competition would look like. 7Tao was designed to be used in the context of a US-China Trade War.

The Epoch Times newspaper struggled with me during 2015 to 2018, helped me at every turn, they lifted me up when I had fallen down and provided me with all of the encouragement and support that I needed to keep going until the US China Trade War actually turned up. The Epoch Times team never gave up on me as the 7Tao system began its entry into the global marketplace… they helped me all the way.

During 2016 election cycle, the Trump Administration, who never even wanted to win the election, managed to get hold of the Art of Industrial Warfare book through Peter Navarro and Casey Fleming. The 7Tao system was in Trumps mind and in his closest political advisor's decision-making process. Is this at all possible? Did this even happen?

Only God knows where 7Tao would go now. It was churning around, interpreted, and mixed up in Donald Trump's mind. He was bellowing out proclamations throughout the 2016 election. Most of what he was saying made sense – especially in the rust belt, this is where the voter would put him into power. The message of Industrial Warfare resonated in the heart of the American manufacturing worker.

Then the most shocking event of the 21st century took place. *Donald Trump won the 2016 Election and became the 45th President of the United States of America.*

Was this book, the Art of Industrial warfare; at the core of the 2016 election and at the epicenter of the US China Trade War? The 7Tao system had gone global and no one knew, *not even me.* I'm still not sure today.

Donald Trump Picture: Wikipedia commons. Public use.

2018 onward – Embedding 7Tao in the US-China competition.

The US China trade war was announced in 2018 across every media platform available. Every TV station across every continent in the world was talking about the problem with excitement.

So how do you solve the most complex problem in the world for the next 100 years? The answer is simple. You learn about the industrial problem, design a solution which grows with the problem from the year 2000 onwards, 20 years ahead of time. The key is not in answering, the key is in learning and adapting… constantly.

You know what to fight for and you know what to fight against. Most importantly, you know when not to fight, because that is 99% of fighting. Knowing when not to fight…

How do you prove the power of 7Tao in front of a global stage? I began to notice segments of my books industrial warfare language appearing in Donald Trump's election campaign – I was quite certain he had educated himself in the practice of industrial warfare with the help of his advisors, but I didn't know if it was with 7Tao. Did the 'chosen one' choose my book? This was the ultimate question of the 21st century?

Donald Trump wiped out the competition, in every way possible, at every turn, overcame every challenge and each hurdle to win the 2016 election. A large portion of his election campaign was based around a US China Trade War which had been brewing under the radar since 2012, when President Barack Obama began taking the Chinese to the international courts under the WTO rules. It was ineffective, ignored by the Chinese, Russians, Indians, and everyone else- but it was the start of the 'Pivot to Asia'.

During the course of the Presidency in April 2018, Donald Trump began the largest trade war in history against China. The US China Trade War was based around manufacturing, industries, plants, factories, supply chains, transactional competition, imports, and exports. I believe that the Chinese and the American administration had one thing in common – both understood the 7Tao and both of them were intrigued with the 7Tao secret. Both parties understood that the transactional conflict played out for the marketplaces of the world would require understanding the differences between the USA model of Capitalism and the Chinese model of Capitalism. The American or western model is based on Queensberry rules capitalism and the Chinese model is based on their own eastern capitalism with a different set of Asian rules. The negotiations would last forever because they will never agree with each other. They are two completely different types of capitalism – and it is this difference that houses the eternal philosophy of the 7Tao.

Donald Trump was asking the Chinese not to be Chinese. Donald Trump was asking them to change their laws. Donald Trump was asking the Chinese to abide by a certain set of American administered rules and regulations. The Chinese didn't give a damn what Donald Trump was bellowing about. When he started a Trade War, they just fired back. So we have disagreement between two superpowers and it's based on one subject, the rules of the level playing field or as I like to call them, The Queensberry Rules.

The Biden administration announced further that they would be engaging in 'extreme competition' as they grouped together the fractured Quad and an indecisive Europe to create some kind of a unified group against the growing might of China. The Quad is more military option based, while the European partnership is more trade based. The Democrat administration led by Joe Biden is perplexed as they face a China which is creating trade groups like RCEP, CPEC, global FTA's, Belt and Road Initiative and an Islamic countries pact across the world. The Chinese want the world's Island. They want Eurasia. They want to supply 5 billion 'third world' people with everything they need for centuries to come.

Here lies the central question of this book, the Art of Industrial Warfare. Will the future of capitalism be based on the Chinese or the American Model? One uses Queensberry WTO rules and the other uses non WTO ancient eastern principles. Who will win the battle of the 21st century – The USA or China? As we head towards a confrontation with these two superpowers, we can see the confrontation building in legal, industrial, technological, trade and political formations. This confrontation was now morphing into military in the South China seas, and in Eurasia. Where-ever China has an economic footprint, military problems turn up and strife appears. Someone wants to stop China.

Pictures: Wikipedia commons use.

When two opposing models meet, there will be conflict. The question arises 'what will the fight look like?' I believe strongly that it will be an industrial war – a competition between American Industry and Chinese Industry – and the world economy is the prize. A fight between plants, products, factories, assembly lines, markets, and customers – the cornerstone of this fight will be the 7Tao transaction – He who gets the most transactions wins. Each competitor will have to fight for every transaction, for every buyer in every corner shop on the planet.

Is 7Tao the central question of the 21st century for all those involved in the US China Competition? Did Donald J Trump use this 7Tao book to win the 2016 election? Is 7Tao a core component in the US China Trade War? Is 7Tao a primary question behind every decision-making process in every corporation of the world?

Every product, service, community, shop keeper, logistics move, production line, in fact - every job in the world will be affected by the US China Trade War – and they are all looking for an answer. With this challenge in mind, I present to the reader my journey into discovering what I believe is a central component in the 'extreme competition' of the 21st century between the US and China: 7Tao – The Art of Industrial War.

Introduction

In spring 2009, Politico magazine reported that the Pentagon sponsored 'the-first-of its-kind' economic war game in Johns Hopkins University. Apparently, participants were told it was the first time Pentagon staff were conducting such an exercise. Three years later in the State of the Union speech, President Obama announced the creation of an international trade enforcement centre (ITEC) to investigate unfair trading practises.

These were the government's first responses to a growing realisation and concern that the industrial base of the United States was being eroded by competition from China.

More than a decade earlier, a small British company, 7Tao, had realised that the 21st century would be dominated by industrial war between an emergent China and a declining USA, and that the old Western rules would no longer apply. To understand the growing Chinese dominance, 7Tao began researching, learning, recording, practising, and teaching the Art of Industrial Warfare ® through the beginnings of a Sun Tzu and martial arts based methodology commencing in 1999.

To the Chinese, competing in the global economy is a martial art – applying Sun Tzu's Art of War with industrial capacity, so what better way of dealing with the situation than using their tactics? This book reveals some of the most inspiring secrets of the Chinese arts of industrial warfare so that the West can compete again on a different level playing field. We show how factories, markets, and whole economic regions can benefit from applying a mindset of industrial warfare.

7Tao have been conducting business to business, team to team and individual to individual industrial combat sessions across a large number of companies for two decades, implementing the industrial combat system and preparing companies for what will be a difficult future of constant economic struggle between the US and China. The results have always been fascinating watching customer battle against other customers in the practise of industrial warfare. The Pentagon, The Chinese and the Whitehouse do not realise that there is more to industrial warfare than using tariffs and creating new regulations specifically designed against imports. Industrial warfare means that entire industries must learn how transactional dominance affects them individually and how they must learn to survive in a world which regards the international rulebook of trade as a slight disruption to be swiped away as a relic of the 20th century.

Class by class, industrial combat is being practised through a powerful, yet simple methodology called 7Tao®. The aim of the game is simple: To win in a fourth-generation industrial war against a world which does not play by the rules steeped in the 20th century. How to win is explained in everyday language that can be used in any business, trade, or enterprise. Perhaps if we can practise the concepts of industrial warfare, China and the USA may be able to work together to design the next generation of rules that they can both agree upon. The alternative is war between these two economic and military giants. This option is inconceivable, devastating and horrifying for all life on the planet.

To appreciate the scale of the change that is required, it is useful to look at the historical context. During the first half of the second millennium, while Europe languished as an economic backwater, China had reached a high level of civilization and become a powerful trading nation. However, about the middle of the millennium China lost its way and began to stagnate and fossilise as the West is today.

As the sun was setting on Chinese dominance, so it was rising in Western Europe where the 'new learning' of the Renaissance was changing people's mindset and sparking discoveries in science and exploration that were to lead to European domination of most of the globe over the next 500 years, effectively creating a global economy, with America superseding Britain as the dominant partner after the second world war. The tables, however, are now being turned on the transatlantic bloc, whose corporations appear to have no answer to the competition from the East.

This is a dangerous and intolerable situation which will affect downing street and capitol hill in decades to come, which needs to be remedied without further loss of time.

Unfortunately, the West's policy makers are gridlocked. There is a poverty of philosophy, driving the Transatlantic nations further into debt to be washed away with induced inflation in the decades to come, and exposing those enterprises as hostages of fortune to the cash rich Asian corporations and their sovereign wealth funds. The industrial bases of entire economies are being depleted as transactions move ever Eastward. What Europe and North America took for granted forty years ago is no more.

China has not just taken the lead, she has taken on every product the West used to dominate and is producing exports which reach every market in the world. The growth has been astonishing rather like that witnessed in Europe after the renaissance.

In four decades, China has grown from an agricultural backwater into a globally centred industrial giant. China has power: economic, military and, most importantly, industrial. Industries in the West which have been starved of orders may never recover. Unless, that is, either China disappears, or the West changes the way in which its value-adding enterprises operate. Change entails new ways of thinking, and acting, all the way from the shop floor to the CEO's. We have no choice but to get a grip on destiny and realise that we have to learn how to navigate a world in which the East, and specifically China, will be king.

The Transatlantic economies wasted the last four decades by sustaining activity on the back of property speculation and price inflation. Eventually, this led to a banking crisis because people could not afford to pay back their astronomical debts. This false economy fell flat on its face in 2008, first with the shock of Lehman Brothers, and then with the implosion of the whole banking sector. Governments had to bail out the banks at Taxpayers' expense, forcing some countries to seek bailouts themselves and resort to austerity measures, cutting wages, jobs and pensions, accelerating the downward spiral. The Transatlantic nations are still in deep trouble as they went right back to drinking from the punchbowl which depends upon inflation of land values tempered by extortionate inflation in general as the West begins to retry the inflation based remedy of the early eighties to offset the collapse in industrial might.

The policy of austerity, direct and indirect taxation is cutting deep into the finances of every family, student, and pensioner. Tragically, this is fostering the discontent that is driving people to protest in the streets. The risk is that these protest movements will morph into organised rebel groups mobilising against their governments in search for an equitable economy.

I fear that the longer the economic downturn persists, the more likely governments are to turn to repressive methods to maintain order. Repressive methods such as labelling, immigration control and fascism will begin to rear their heads. Heavy policing will be used to control a restless population who will be dividing into opposing factions leading to an almost certain recipe for civil war in many Western countries. This will be divisive and weaken western economies. The solution is to restart growth, but this time on a more inclusive and sustainable basis.

The Chinese on the other hand, have mastered growth ahead of their competitors. They have focused their entire development around manufacturing industry, leading to gaining the title 'the factory of the world'. They have a ferocious method of thinking which overpowers the opposition. This thinking is based almost entirely around the capturing of the 'transaction'. They will do what it takes to shift the product. The system of thinking which guides them requires manoeuvres that have defensive and offensive constructs, the impacts of which enables them to drive any global competitor out of existence, whether that competitor resides in the first world or third world.

I have studied their methods and assembled the Asian logic into a new system based on the ancient principles of the Art of War by Sun Tzu, which have served their culture and civilization for 3 millennia. This is 7Tao – The Art of Industrial Warfare ®.

7Tao is a business improvement system that bridges the chasm between the dynamism of post-communist China and the floundering economic paradigm on which Western enterprises rely. 7Tao deploys the ancient arts and philosophy of warfare which guide China's manufacturers in their assault on global competitors and marketplaces.

7Tao opens the doors to the secrets of China's success to those organizations that wish to survive by understanding the ruthlessness of the Asian intrusion. 7Tao's methods are designed to revamp the practises of Transatlantic businesses of all sizes, and in any area where obsolete managerial practises are threatening profits and market share. 7Tao's secret of success lies in the way all employees of the firm are mobilised to fulfil the purpose for which their enterprise exists – tracking and completing the transaction, from the first customer order to the cash till.

The traditional monetary instruments employed by Western governments, which are supposed to stimulate growth, are not working. Nor will they, as long as central bankers pour yet more debt and inflation into their economies. This is geopolitically very dangerous. It can lead to the dismantling of the international legal system; it can render entire blocks of countries irrelevant as 'might is right' becomes the organizing principle of globalization.

This will lead to the formation of two blocks competing against each other in legal, military, political and economic struggles consisting of the Transatlantic alliance of US and Europe against Eurasian block led by China, Russia, Middle East, Central Asia and India. We need to avoid the stresses that could lead to direct confrontation between powers which command massive military firepower.

In my view, the only way to restore stability to the global economy is to ensure balanced growth for all nations, so that no one is left behind in the pursuit of prosperity. This will require a change of culture, a new way of thinking and operating. Above all, it requires a rejection of the obsolete management theories that once populated the corporate world of the West. And so, as my contribution to rebuilding and sustaining the great Western enterprises, I offer the reader insights into the methods of 7Tao.

...

CHAPTER 1

Decline of the Transatlantic Cycle

For 350 years, the Transatlantic economic cycle reigned supreme. Powered by industrial revolutions that began in Britain and spread to Western Europe and America, it came to dominate over the rest of the world industrially, educationally, and militarily. It established the terms and conditions of international trade and banking, the rules of the game.

The modern world was built during those 350 years. For much of the time the British Empire reigned supreme so that the characteristics of the Transatlantic cycle have a strong British input in law, governance, and education. British inventions harnessing steam power to drive machinery, ships and trains transformed the cost of manufacturing, transport costs and the distance goods could travel, laying the foundations for the modern global economy. For much of the 19th century Britain was the workshop of the world and the City of London its financial hub. During the second half of the 19th century Western Europe and America industrialised, creating the Transatlantic economic sphere which dominated the world economy.

The peoples of Asia looked on the West in amazement. The difference between the two was enormous in every area that mattered. Wanting to catch up and enjoy the same standards of living, they strove to emulate Western technology and corporate organization. The dynamism which once gave rise to the transatlantic sphere has now shifted to the Asian sphere. The tables have turned. Dominance is moving from the Transatlantic cycle to the East Asian cycle. The security and prosperity of Western nations will in future depend on how the East Asian economic challenge is confronted. Western multinational corporations must reappraise the economic landscape.

So far, the complacent West has failed to read the signs. Asia began its ferocious rise in the sixties with the Japanese driving their brands into the global marketplace. In the last four decades, Toyota, Nissan and Honda have grown from scorned and belittled brands into international powerhouses with a reputation unparalleled among car makers. In comparison, General Motors, the Western giant of car manufacturing, has been wounded almost to the point of destruction, losing most of the brands it once controlled. Scattered across the USA are empty shells of abandoned factories littering the rust belt. Understanding how this happened is essential to the survival of the Western corporation.

But the West has more to contend than the Japanese giants. Many Eastern companies – from South Korea, Taiwan, Thailand, Malaysia, India, and others – have worked hard to emulate the West's success. And then, hard on their heels, has come the transformed China. She arrived in the global markets four decades ago and since then, by introduction into the World Trade Organization in 2001, has intruded into every area of commerce, deploying its huge geographic presence, a population of 1.4 billion and a mastery of the tools of economic and industrial combat. The network of economic power has changed dramatically.

Table 1:1: Transatlantic and East Asian Nations.

Transatlantic nations	Eurasian Nations
875 million people	3.942 billion people
12.5 % of world population	56.3 % of world population
Rigid, pugnacious, governed by law	Dynamic, assertive, driven by trade
16.3 % of Earths land mass	14% of Earths land mass
Separated by Atlantic Ocean	Eurasia largely single land mass
GNI: $42,131 billion	GNI: $19,975 Billion
58.3% of World GNI	27.6% of World GNI
14.4% of oil reserves	2.2% of oil reserves
7.6% of gas reserves	5.6% of gas reserves
34.5% of coal reserves	21.5% of coal reserves

The Transatlantic bloc comprises the European Union, Norway, Switzerland, the United States and Canada. The East Asian bloc consists of Pakistan Eastwards to Japan, Korea and Mongolia including Indonesia and the Philippines. Sources: World Bank, (Population and GNI 2012), Wikipedia (Landmass), BP statistical review (Coal, Oil, Gas 2012).

Flowing With the Cycles

The rise and decline of geopolitical areas is cyclical in nature and within these longer cycles are shorter ones. The Transatlantic cycle is characterised by the industrialisation of production, but the development has not been a straight-line progression. The first phase of the Transatlantic cycle began with the Industrial Revolution in Britain towards the end of the 18th century with the development of steam driven machinery and transport. This was brought to an end by the speculative railway mania about sixty years later. At the nadir of the first phase, a new cycle opened up with the repeal of the Corn Laws in 1846. A new era of free trade was ushered in, and Britain became the workshop of the world, exporting manufactured goods all over the globe. This cycle came to an end as Britain faced stiff competition from manufacturers in America and Europe. The third phase was powered by the discovery of electricity and the internal combustion engine, but the centre of gravity for industry moved across the Atlantic to America as Europe tore itself apart in the First and Second World Wars.

The fourth phase, beginning after World War II, is characterised by the automation of production and electronics. In this period America emerged as the world-dominating, hegemonic power, its powerful corporations operating globally but still essentially on the British model. This gigantism, however, has proved a liability as it failed to see competitors arising. No heed was paid to scientists and engineers who warned corporate heads of US businesses to change their ways. The biggest organizations in the world dismissed the theories of Dr Joseph Juran and Dr W. Edwards Deming. So this new breed of scientists, trail-blazers in the art of production-on-time and quality management, went to Japan to teach the theories they had developed.

The Japanese listened carefully and adopted their production processes. As a result, Japanese corporations like Toyota began to outdo their American competitors, slowly but surely, month by month, year by year. That was the beginning of the East Asian industrial revolution. Today, Japan's automotive industry has matched and, in some cases, overtaken General Motors, Ford and Chrysler. Multiply this redeployment of economic power by the population of East Asia and you will start to appreciate the sheer scale of the challenge facing the West. The spell of Western supremacy has been cracked. Korea, Malaysia and Thailand were next to pile into the global marketplace but the West's supremacy remained as long as the Chinese dragon slept, under the spell of communism. Once the Communist Party decided to adopt 'Capitalism with Chinese characteristics' everything changed.

Figure 1:1 traces with particular reference to America how the industrial cycles unfolded as Kondratieff waves (named after Nicolai Kondratieff, the Russian economist who identified the cycles from the long swings in commodity prices).

Each Kondratieff wave lasted between fifty to seventy years. Each contains certain industrial patterns which follow a spring, summer, autumn and winter pattern. The timing of each season is determined by an 18-year cycle in land prices, which rise for fourteen years and fall for about four years. The recessions and depressions have followed these patterns right through to today. I will focus on these four industrial revolutions, three of them British and one American. What we are now witnessing is one of the most important changes in the last five centuries: the eclipse of the Transatlantic cycle and return to the East Asian cycle. This will be a watershed event, greater than anything which has challenged the West in the modern era. If the West is going to survive this tectonic shift of economic power, it will have to understand the dynamics of the business cycle.

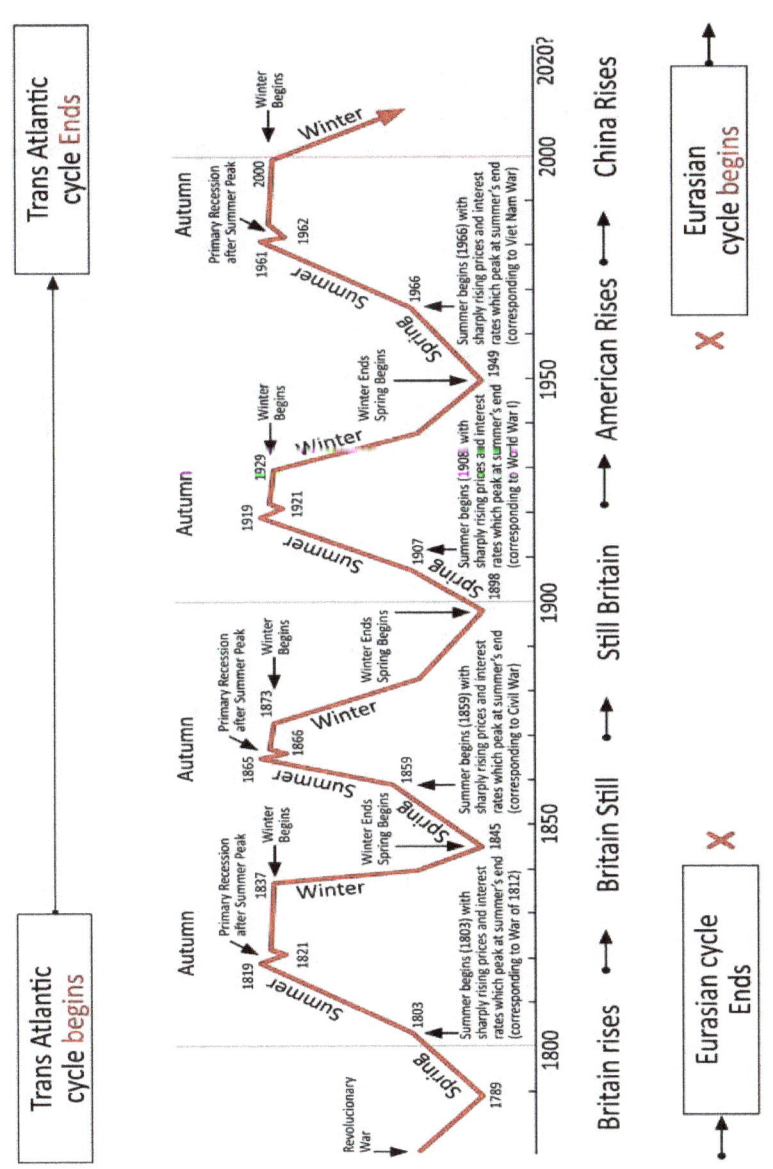

Figure 1:1

Source: Adapted from www.kondratieffwavecycle.com/kondratieff-wave/

The Four-Season Cycle

The four-season cycle, consisting of spring, summer, autumn and winter, is detectable in everything in the economic landscape. The 18-year real-estate cycle can also be broken up into four seasons, each of 4.5 years. Figure 1.2 illustrates the rhythms oscillating within the trends tracked in Figure 1:1.

Figure 1:2 Rhythmic Oscillation

Source: http://ray.tomes.biz/ed-real.gif

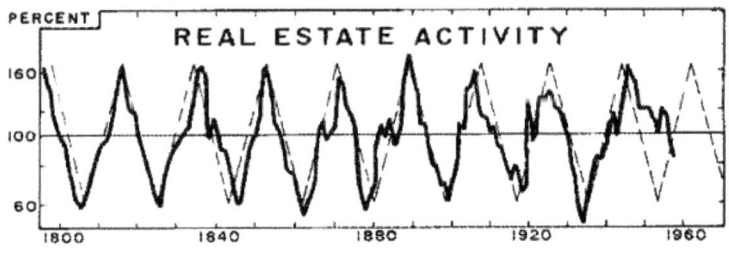

Figure 1:3

The four-season cycle divided into 4.5-year units: *Source:* 7Tao

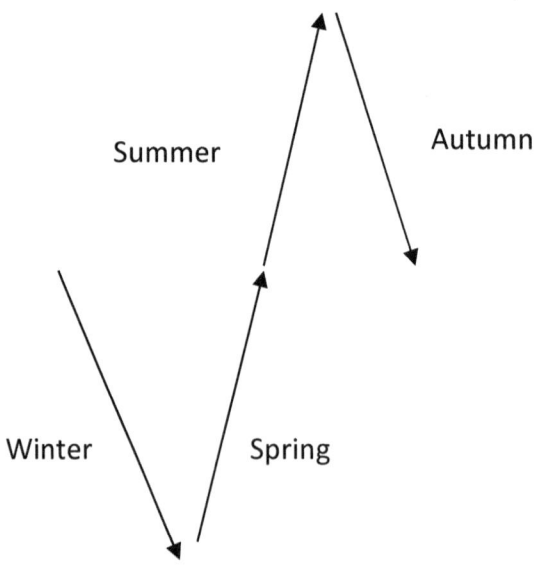

This real estate cycle is a consequence of the way in which the economic system was designed 350 years ago. It contains an unstable boom-and-bust mechanism predicated on property rights and methods of taxation enshrined in the political systems of Western Europe in the 16th century. These rhythms will continue into the future for as long as the rules of engagement in the economy remain the same.

Figure 1:4

Source: Roy Wezlick, Research Corporation, St Louis, MO, USA.

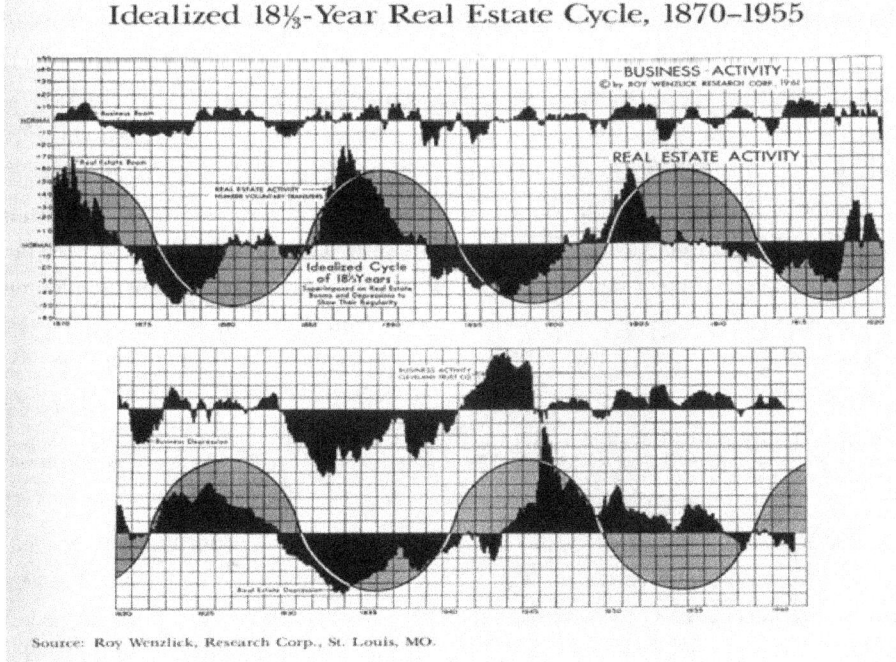

Figure 1:4 illustrates how real estate cycles correlate with business activity. Note the greater amplitude of the real estate cycle and how downturns in business activity lag behind the collapse in the property market and upturns tend to precede property booms. The real estate waves are repetitive and consistent, though their intensity varies according to the way in which intricate day-to-day events in the different cycles play themselves out, just as some winters are very cold and others mild.

The Three 'C' Theory: Colonialism, Communism and Capitalism.

During the 20th century three economic ideologies competed for dominance:

        1 Colonialism
        2 Communism
        3 Capitalism

Colonialism

The beginning of the 20th century was dominated by rivalry between the European empires scrambling to lay claim to as much territory as possible, culminating in the First World War which knocked Russia and Germany out of the race. The basis of the colonial system was for the colonies to provide food and raw materials for the workers and factories of the imperial power and to be a market for their manufactured goods. If the likes of India, China or the Middle East wanted cars, they bought them from Europe or the United States. The factories of the UK overflowed with orders. Production lines were crammed to meet global demand. In South Asia, 'Made in England' was a phrase associated with quality. In Pakistan and India, all products came from factories operating within the UK, and the cultural patterns of colonialism did not end with the retreat of the empire. People continued to act, think and buy along colonial lines. Everything there was – and still is – British: the air force, the army, the navy, the medical system, the bureaucratic administration – and, of course, the English language still dominates the Indian sub-continent and much of South-East Asia.

    American corporations, however, seized the initiative after World War II and expanded into every area as the American empire rose to dominate the global economy. Some observers called it the 'benevolent empire' as the dominance was more commercial than political, but the United States did exercise considerable political influence through the International Monetary Fund and World Bank, the so-called 'Washington Consensus'. Moreover, as colonialism began to recede, the masterly manufacturers of Japan and Germany came from the ashes of their military defeat to carve out their share of global trade. American era was defined by oil. All inventions were based around oil consumption and transportation throughout the 20th century, making the Middle East very wealthy. The colonial era was still being carried forward into the middle of the 20th century as the old ways of colonialism were being discarded and new more presentable and digestible methods of colonialism were being introduced to continue the process.

Communism

After the Russian Revolution communism, with its so-called 'non-imperialist' designs on world domination, emerged as a competitor ideology which the Soviet Union sought to spread to developed and the developing countries after World War II. With an ever-expanding agenda of land growth and domination, communism became known in the West as the 'Red Peril'. The Russians produced and exported tools designed for superpower dominance, but their chief victory was the proxy war fought in Vietnam. This was the height (and, as we now know, the twilight) of communism. Its bureaucratic, state-run industries did not prove a credible alternative to the equally aggressive march of industrial capitalism. The command economy was doomed to fail and communism was abandoned in 1991, two years after the Soviets left Afghanistan. The socialist paradigm was discredited. The Transatlantic cycle had triumphed. You had to be capitalist to succeed in this world.

Predictions of the failure of communism began as early as the mid-1970s. Surprisingly, the most accurate prediction came from inside the Soviet Union itself, from Dmitry Orlov [1]. He witnessed the Soviet collapse in 1991 and the descent into a social and economic nightmare. He later predicted that the United States would go the same way. He did not offer a precise timing but was convinced that calamity was on its way. Others jumped onto the bandwagon, predicting the fall of America as China's economic power grew, threatening to replace the United States as the primary economic power on the earth.

1 Dmitry Orlov, *Reinventing Collapse*, New Society Publishers, 2008

Capitalism

The capitalist hegemony reigned supreme from 1991, it was 'the only game in town', or so the analysts in Washington believed. In the years leading up to this, ideologies and political relationships had been predicated on the basis of a bipolar order. No longer. Suddenly, the
whole planet had to change the way it thought, aligned its armies and perceived everything, from education to pension systems.

America found that its Cold War industrial architecture was redundant. It had no longer had the same need for its F16s and other fighter/bombers. But the same logic applied in other countries, so at the moment of its ideological victory the US empire found its economic flanks vulnerable. How would it survive if no one wanted to buy what it made? The solution was developed within the framework of political strategy. *If you control the oil, you control the world economy.* The US moved aggressively into the Middle East to ring-fence the oil supplies which had been taken for granted over the past century. The threat of Iraq's weapons of mass destruction (which did not actually exist) mobilised much of the rest of the world in support of President George W. Bush's project of democracy in the Middle East and the Islamic world in general. American capitalism achieved its first surreal victory since the Vietnam failure in Iraq. Little did we know that this empty victory would result in unpredictable changes in the Islamic world twenty years later.

Meanwhile the whole world was buying into the capitalist growth model. Everything, both good and bad, was emulated. Other countries built manufacturing, agricultural and service industries on American models. The victory, however, was bitter-sweet. Some of the latecomers to capitalism decided to out-compete the West.

Asia focused intensely on developing its manufacturing industries. The number of containers being shipped around the world from Asia shows the extent of growth within the Asian sphere of business. This has created a massive shift in expectations within China and its allies. The Asian tigers were eclipsed by the dragon as it rose to prominence in Asia. But China was fighting for industrial dominance, with the entire world as its battleground. It outplayed every competitor in the ensuing industrial warfare. It didn't need to invade with soldiers, tanks and aircraft, it could do something much simpler: sell its goods to everyone who wanted to buy them and buy what it needed from them. Theirs was the most ferocious industrial fighting force to be seen in the last two centuries.

The result is the revival of a now cash-rich East Asian cycle blessed with relative economic stability. The Transatlantic cycle is burdened with economic crisis and debt. The world has swapped the old lopsided global economy for a new one. How did it happen?

Chinese Dominance and Western Economic Dependence

China fully understood the concept of industrial warfare. It can be summed up in a brief statement by the Communist Party leader, Deng Xiaoping, in 1992: 'The Middle East has oil and China has rare earths'. Through a policy of restricting rare earth exports and acquiring US based supply-chain operations and relocating them to China 'to receive a reliable source of rare earths' needed for automated manufacturing and guided missiles, Chinese dominance in a crucial sector has been established.

More generally, its strategy has been to make products of an acceptable quality but cheaper, which could be produced and delivered to market quickly, thus becoming the workshop of the world. Their many shareholders found they had lost control of the businesses in which
they invested. Employees, lulled into a false sense of security by the boom years that followed the recession of the early 1990s, rediscovered their expendability. Jobs were no longer for life.

The 3 billion inhabitants of the rest of the East Asian continent followed the Chinese. This has led to the biggest industrial revolution the world has ever seen – a global economic earthquake. They have mastered the capitalist process and their adaptation of it has been brutal. Theirs is a no-holds-barred, no-mercy form of capitalism. They have begun to suck the life out of their competitors.

To succeed, China realised that it had to set the standards. The formula is simple: don't worry about the product, just make the transaction appealing. The mandarins of Beijing calculated that, if they could put enough effort into manufacturing, they could create an industrial revolution right across East Asia that would generate such an explosive force behind their growth curve that it would leave the West reeling.

In an attempt to survive, many Western corporations moved much of their production to China. Their logic was, 'If you can't beat them, join them'. The Chinese laughed all the way to their banks. They aimed to absorb capital and enterprise invested in Western factories, and Western corporations obliged them! This was an exquisite twist in the art of industrial warfare.

The West was asleep. Its financial sector had been bloated by the property market, and it convinced itself that value was being added to the Transatlantic economies by flipping houses and selling bits of paper in the City, playing 'pass the parcel' with toxic fuse-lit financial instruments, leveraged on the very mortgages taken out on those unaffordable houses. In reality, it was a game of acronyms, and these represented nothing more than pieces of paper being shovelled from one 'financial centre' to another. When the property market succumbed to the effects of the 18-year cycle, the house of cards fell. The bankrupt world monetary system collapsed.

The Bank of England, which had never before in its three-hundred-year history resorted to printing money to get it out of trouble, embarked on quantitative easing – a fancy term for just that: printing money. The collapse of the financial architecture was devastating, there were bank runs and monetary collapses, and the bankruptcy of Greece and Ireland as Europe followed the United States. Piece by piece the Western economy was falling apart.

The end of colonialism and communism, and the rise of a new form of capitalism, has empowered India and China. 3 billion people with an aggressive, survival of the fittest work ethic, important natural resources, and armed with nuclear weapons, are building vast networks of raw material supply chains across the developing world. They follow no rules, no western trade laws, no 18th century gentlemen code of morality and no ethics; they just want to 'sell, sell and sell' and don't care who they sell to. This supply-and-demand magnetism is destroying old relationships and building new ones.

The Shift of Trading from West to East

I believe that there is still time for the West to recover. However, responsibility for rescuing the economy rests not in the hands of governments, but with the industrial infrastructure. Unfortunately, the people responsible for that infrastructure have little knowledge of how
to influence a world which has already changed beyond recognition. They face the most competitive environment mankind has known in the last five centuries yet approach the new challenges as if it's business as usual!

Many questions, much uncertainty, few answers … Ask any of the established economic consultancies and they will offer you, for a very high price and in an eloquent but predictable manner, explanations that bear little relation to the realities of the emerging future. All the solutions offered rest on the experiences of the past. Consultancies offering no real new solutions, just making the customer feel better through intricate and well-presented analysis of the present. But the past is dead. Current theories were constructed by the previous three generations of business leaders.

Success in the future will depend on principles synchronised with the new world order. That world order is not capitalism based upon Western principles. We now need to come to terms with a new kind of capitalism based on East Asian models.

Footnote: 2 Fred Harrison, *Boom Bust*, Shepheard-Walwyn (Publishers) Ltd, 2005.

Defending the Homeland – Protecting factories, jobs and lives?

During the 1960s competition from the East Asian cycle was weak. Engineers in Birmingham (both England and Alabama) took their jobs for granted. In the 1970s competition opened up a little and people started developing what was called the total quality approach. During the 1980s competition increased, and attention was focused on new approaches such as Just In Time:

> Price: Cost cutting
> Delivery: Just in time
> Quality: Total quality
> After Market: Customer care

In the 1990s these principles were enshrined in corporate methodologies such as Six Sigma, which focused on the quality of process and number of defects per million opportunities. Six Sigma was first widely used in the AlliedSignal Corporation; it broke into mainstream methodology with the help of the late Jack 'Neutron' Welch of General Electric. Both Larry Bossidy, CEO of AlliedSignal and Honeywell, and Jack Welch, CEO of General Electric, were idolised. Six Sigma was a huge success, becoming a 'must have' in any business. People built their careers around Six Sigma doctrines, which were applied to every process in industry. Jack Welch responded to the economic environment, cutting bodies out of the General Electric Corporation. He called it cutting waste, but there was another way of viewing this strategy: by axing jobs he was destroying middle-class lives (see Box 1:1).

Enterprises that arrived in this new economic landscape found local populations that did not fight by the Queensberry rules. Western corporations struggled to adapt. Some, deploying their sheer size and weight, survived. The trickle of outflow from the United States turned into a flood as firms flocked to India, China and the other growth centres in Asia, such as Vietnam. The migration was stunning: 'Catch the Chinese train while you can' was the motto.

Box 1:1: Destroying middle class lives.

AS General Electric penetrated the rest of the world, host countries found that they had to compete with this goliath of industry or get mauled. Competitors emerged to threaten GE. Jack Welch's response was to dominate by throwing American capital at each country and exploiting its markets. GE grew from a market value of $14bn to $410bn. Welch achieved this by firing the lowest 10% of his managers and rewarding the top 20% with bonuses and stock options. The number of employees was cut from 411,000 in 1980 to 299,000 in 1985. Employees whose corporate employers emulated the GE strategy either had to move with Globalisation or lose their jobs. Most of them lost their jobs. Only the higher level employees were secure.

In interviews with the *Financial Times*, just after the financial crisis, Jack Welch said, 'On the face of it, shareholder value is the dumbest idea in the world. Shareholder value is a result, not a strategy... your main constituencies are your employees, your customers and your products.' Many CEOs have distanced themselves from him, stating that he would not have made this statement while working for GE.

Francesco Guererra, *Financial Times*, 3 December 2009

Factories owned by the Western corporations, such as the British car manufacturer Rover were moved to China. They will never return unless it is to China's advantage. The Chinese don't conform to the rules in which the West is steeped, on copyright, litigation, royalties, and libel. They operate in a completely different world. They operate entirely upon the principles of Eastern industrial warfare. He who makes a transaction wins. They have land, they have population; nothing holds them back. They are truly ferocious in industrial warfare. They want to extract factories from the West and place them in the East. We in the West talk about 'positive migration', 'up-skilling', 'the post-industrial economy'; we have many complicated rationalisations for the capture and relocation of value. They talk about factories and jobs.

For us this is de-industrialization, though the process is spun with terms like 'positive growth'. Apologist's claim: 'These old jobs are going to go and we are going to create new ones which add more value.' Translation: 'We are in deep trouble because everything we created has just disappeared and we are going to have to find you something to do because we simply can't compete with these people.' The state has failed to protect the capital base accumulated over 350 years of invention and sacrifice.

Governments have responded by replacing the muscle of manufacturing (value added exports) with the fat of public service (non-value added), much of it funded through debt. One indicator of this debt was the massive explosion in house prices. Everything possible was done to keep the bubble floating. This was the age of hedge funds and Masters of the Universe, 'Much for the few and nothing much for the many'. The bubble of 2008 has now burst. Few people realised that this false economy was subject to the 18-year property cycle. In 1997 Fred Harrison warned successive governments that this collapse was about to take place but of course they didn't listen.

The British failed to understand that the world was changing. This was not a conventional credit crunch (three months) or a downturn (six months), nor was it a recession (two years). It was not even a depression (six to ten years). This was the beginning of something far more horrific. This was a *depletion*: an event which sucks out the value of an economy and places it somewhere else, leaving 'Detroit-like' desolation behind it.

A depletion is permanent. Yet the people with their hands on the levers of power failed to comprehend what was happening to the fabric of their societies, let alone take action to put firewalls around their people. Once depletion sets in you can't recreate the economy.

You have to run for your life. The edifice created out of thin air was celebrated by commentators such as Charles Leadbeater, who wrote a book called *Living On Thin Air: The New Economy*. (4)

That economy collapsed around them. They saw bank runs, riots and mass protests in the streets of Athens and Madrid, and the return of soup kitchens to Dublin as businesses died from the shock of the financial collapse.

The Bank of England and the Federal Reserve panicked. In their disregard for the value of their currencies, they started to print money. The result of the economic collapse was catastrophic. They were flying on vapour: there was no fuel in the tanks of the Western countries.

Footnote: 1 London, Viking, 1999.

United States of America in 2000: Top of the world.

When the USA inherited the British Empire after WWII, it also inherited the economic system and the economic demands of every country in the world. The US had just set up factories to produce munitions during the course of World War 2, industrialists such as Henry Ford, William S Knudssen and Pierre Samuel Du Pont were the leaders of the massive drive to equip the forces of the Allies against Germany, Japan and Italy during the course of the conflict.

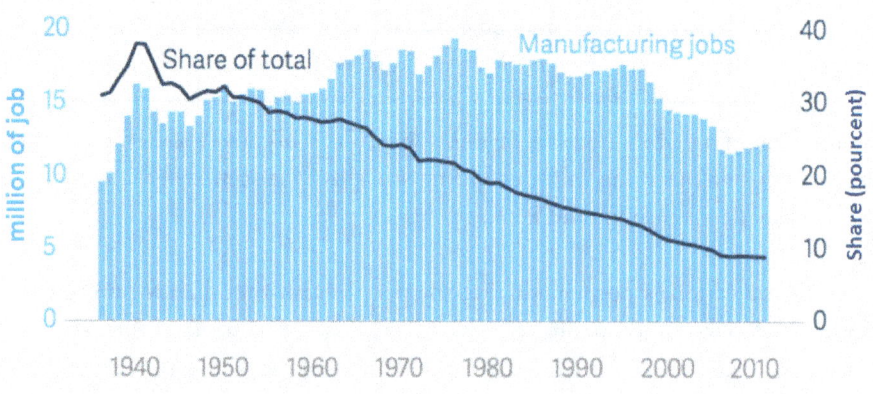

These were the men under whose leadership, America was transformed from a war economy into a peacetime industrial giant. Corporations such as General Motors and General Electric were exporting American made goods to every country of the world. Over the course of two generations, the share of manufacturing in the American economy has been reduced by 70% as factories migrated elsewhere in the world and automation replaced many of the hands-on workers who depended on making things with their hands.

The U.S. could have kept these jobs, and kept these factories within the shores of the West but cost cutting due to inefficient transactions forced moves to China. The question arises quite clearly "Why did they move all of their factories to China?" It was not just America moving factories to China … Europe, India, South Asia, Japan, South Korea, South America and the Middle Eastern states all moved factories to China.

Suddenly, due to Chinese leadership in the manufacturing industry, China became known as the 'factory of the world'. For every Western firm that landed in China to manufacture their goods, 20 new and unknown Chinese brands would appear close to them fighting for the same market and competing in the same area. Over a short amount of time of three decades, the effects would be devastating to the manufacturing industries of the West. The world map below displays the world economy showing the American domination of the world economy in the year 2000 as compared to the world economy in the year 2019.

This massive growth curve and almost total eclipse of the manufacturing industry of the world has resulted in gasps of amazement from the West and a fear of a rising superpower who will increasingly dictate the way in which leadership is conducted on the world stage. This has resulted in tumultuous changes inside the United States as it struggles to adapt to a civilization based historical power who has suddenly reclaimed its position in the world that China has traditionally held over at least, the last two millennia. The small 400 year blip of Western domination of the world economy triggered by colonialism has dramatically come to an end. Eurasia, the world's Island has formed right in front of our eyes and it is impossible to stop its further development into a political and military based sphere of influence dominating the planet. This begs the question, "What does the future hold for the West?".

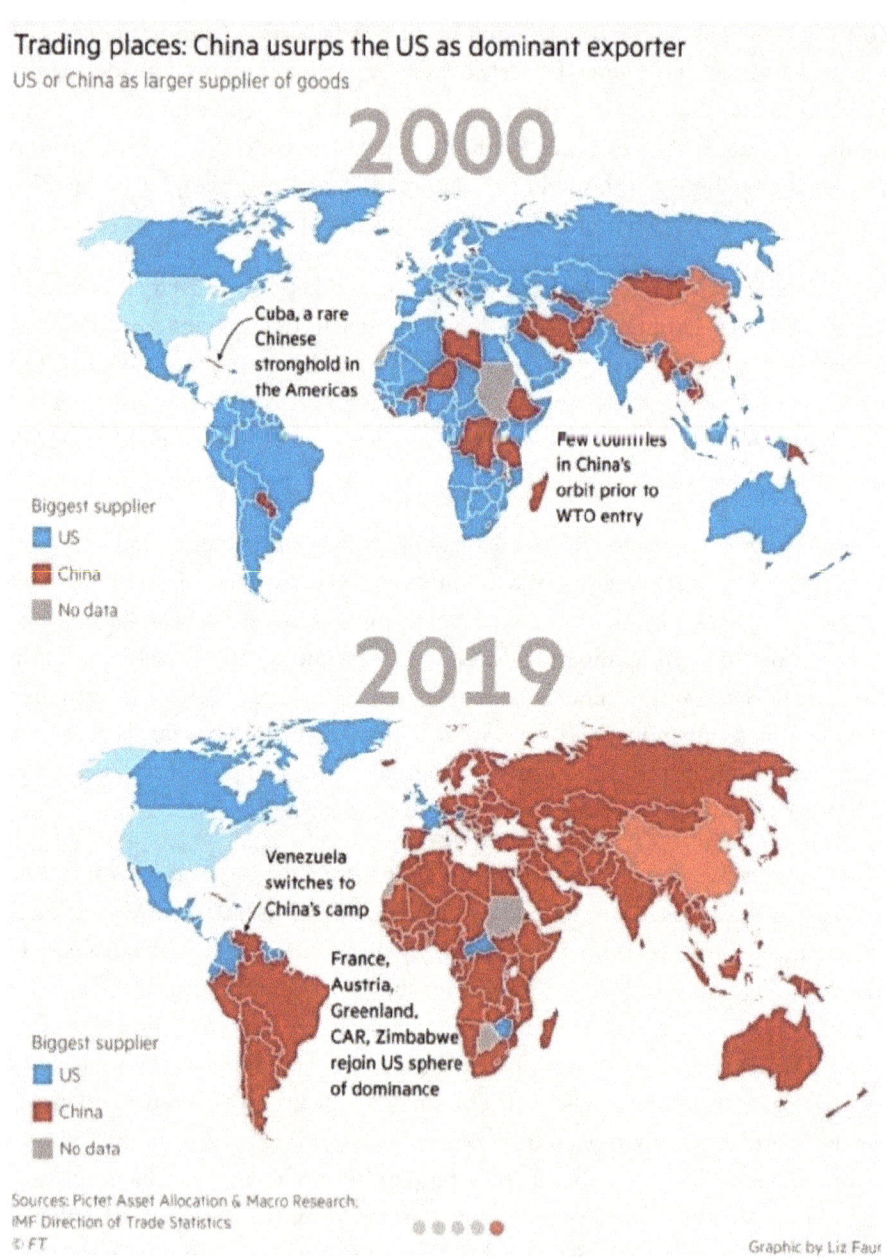

Footnote: Graphic by Liz Faunce: Pictet Asset allocation and Macro research. IMF Direction of trade statistics. Financial Times: February 28 2020, Lucy Colback.

The Art of Fighting, without Fighting

Bruce Lee quoted one of his enemies on the Chinese Barge in Enter the Dragon (Warner Bros: 1973) that he practised the Art of fighting without fighting.

As the USA engaged in the protracted War on Terror, dragging on for 20 years since 2001, the primary strategy was military – boots on the ground and flag in the air. America chose to send its forces into the heart of Eurasia by using the Middle East and Afghanistan as entry point steppingstone into the centre of the world's Island. This was the wrong move to make because the nature of the war was not military, rather, it was an economic war. Moreover, and specifically, this was an industrial war which required deep thinking into how to arrange and measure the ways in which industrial wars are fought.

Industrial wars are being fought in all shapes and sizes since the beginning of business. World War 1 & 2 were focused on industrial warfare. Industries that we inherited today had their grounding supporting the armed forces of WW2. However, these industrial wars did not end with the end of these conflicts, the industrial wars continued long after military operations had ended. Military support-based industries and factories were transformed to produce peacetime civilian goods again to dominate the worlds markets. The only power which was civilising the industrial wars were the rules of engagement. A legal system built by the British primarily, to protect the rights of business owners, manufacturers, tradesmen, and financiers and control the ways in which countries can be administered. These laws were designed to ensure peace and security in the land. When the businessperson spots peace and security in the homeland, he will very quickly set up shop in that place and begin operations to trade with the people of Britain and then eventually the world. This gave rise to repeated industrial revolutions driving the British people forward to economic, industrial, academic, and intellectual excellence for which they are today renowned.

The complaints which the West is registering with China revolve around these facts. Constant ear wringing about 'China does not play by the rules' dominates the airwaves in business circles. There needs to be some clarification here, and the truth needs to be told.

'China does not play by Western rules'. This is a fact that we must learn to accept. China has its own set of rules, ones which have been baked into the existence of this civilization for thousands of years. As the weight of the transaction frequency moves further Eastward to the centre of the Eurasian landmass - meaning Beijing; it is about to settle where the transaction weighting has been stable for the last 3 millennia.

China will become the dominant power in Asia and will hold the leadership position in Eurasia with countries flocking towards its policies over the next millennium. Instead of fighting them using obsolete military drives originating in World War 2 thinking like the failed wars of Iraq and Afghanistan, perhaps it is wiser to consider adapting to a reality which has formed before our very eyes within just two decades. For our businesses to survive, we must embrace the concepts of industrial warfare. Tanks and planes are not going to navigate this challenge. Only critical thinking will. This is a business problem, not a military problem.

China is **defending** herself militarily with some of the most capable weapon systems in the developed world. It is impossible to attack China without risking total annihilation and mutually assured destruction in the South China Sea and at home. China is **attacking** industrially and economically to overtake the worlds industry one transaction, one product, one market at a time. It is inevitable that China will grow to dominate every market for every manufactured product in the world. Without firing a single bullet, China has eliminated 350 years of Western market domination and is still building to dominate markets across Europe and Asia for the next millennium.

The Russians have learned this valuable lesson from China as they carve their way into the European heartlands to be part of the new Eurasian silk route with Ukraine, the Black Sea and the Eastern European region as their new area of control. They are expanding industrially through the lands overlapping the new Belt and Road Initiative silk route and defending militarily using their enormous conventional and nuclear capability to umbrella their expansive efforts. This is the way of intelligence. This is the Art of Industrial Warfare. This war will be completely different to the Cold War of the 20th century. That was an ideological battle between communism and capitalism. This will be a straight fight between two opposing forms of capitalism which operate by different rules.

CHAPTER 2

Industrial Warfare vs Military Warfare

IN ANY WAR, *you engage* using straight line symmetric warfare (Military-kinetic); *you win* by circuitous, asymmetric warfare (Economic). This is basic Sun Tzu, 'the greatest exponent of Chinese martial arts and author of *The Art of War.*' This is exactly how the West defeated the Soviet Union in the Cold War. The more efficient production systems in the West effectively forced them into admitting that their command economy was no match. Here is a table I use in lectures to illustrate the point:

Table 2:1 Comparing Cold War Economic Models, 1950-1991

Country	USA (1950 – 1991)	Soviet Union (1950 – 1991)
Economics	Dynamic Market economy with strong domestic manufacturing base	Sluggish command economy with shortages of basic consumer goods.
Politics	Democratically elected.	Unelected Authoritarian government.
Driven by	Profit motive to become rich.	Economic plans, no personal incentive.
Tax revenues	Multiple source revenues from thriving economy	Standard Tax rates based upon equal pay across careers
Morale	Strong personal economic incentive	Little personal economic incentive
Competition	Strong competitive spirit	Planned economy, no competition.
Airplanes	F14 Tomcat - F15 Eagle - F18 Hornet	Mig 29 – Sukhoi 27
Missiles	Peacekeeper ICBM	SS18 ICBM.
Manufacturing	High efficiency based on strong consumer demand and thriving export markets.	Inefficient manufacture, unresponsive to consumer demand, export focus on military hardware and oil

Stock Market	Hugely profitable, constantly growing.	No stock market.
Property Market	Housing dominated by 18 year real estate cycle. Boom bust present in economy.	No real estate cycle. No land price fluctuations. No boom bust.
R & D - innovation	Very strong. University based leadership since 1945.	Average, but directed primarily by government and military strategy.
Population	250 Million	140 Million

When a weaker economic model is pitted against a stronger one, the weaker is bound to lose. It's just a matter of time. The alternative was mutually assured destruction (MAD). There was no hot war, just a war of economic attrition.

As Sun Tzu points out in his attack stratagem: *'to fight and conquer in all your battles is not supreme excellence; supreme excellence consists in breaking the enemy's resistance without fighting'*.

If you are forced to fight an opponent by his terms and conditions, this will make the competitor have the advantage position. If this is the case, each one of your objectives will be three times larger than you would want them to be; and it will be harder to achieve your aims in winning the war. When someone corners you without fighting, your efforts may be the ones which place you in a losing position. Before fighting, always think carefully about the outcomes of any confrontation. Now let's compare the same criteria in the coming war between China and America and see what correlations are in the same scenario we are facing today in a repeat of the superpower tussles in the 21st century. We can immediately see that the situation remains exactly the same as it was in the 20th century. It is two economic systems fighting in the background while nuclear weapons protect the nation and its boundaries. Further to this, it looks like the same dangers are being faced in this struggle as they were in the last struggle. 1991 was a pivotal year during the last struggle. 2026 will be pivotal year in the coming one… why will this be the case? Because this is the end of an 18-year real estate cycle, just like 1991 was in the end of a real estate cycle.

Country	USA (1991 – 2022)	China 1991 – 2022
Economics	Decline of older industries, increasing regulation, production moving offshore. Gently coming to the end of the Kondratieff wave.	Communist command economy has now been abandoned. The rise of an aggressive market economy with few rules replaces communism.
Politics	Increasing corporate control of democratic system.	One party communist state.
Driven by	Financial sector, inflated house prices and rent seeking.	Unrestrained entrepreneurship and an uncontrollable building boom.
Tax Revenues	Tax receipts weakening.	State capitalism tax system strong.
Morale	Dampened by loss of factories and growing rich poor divide.	High – century of humiliation is over. China is back into its natural state.
Airplanes	F22 Raptor – F35 Lightning – Very expensive and quickly obsolete.	J20 Mighty Dragon, J31 Gyr-Falcon, J10 Vigorous Dragon. Very expensive and quickly obsolete.
Missiles	Hypersonic Nuclear Weapons	Hypersonic Nuclear Weapons
Manufacturing	Industrial base hollowed out by outsourcing, exports no longer competitive.	Out competes the entire world, massive exports – everything in the world is made in China.

Stock Market	Very strong – Growth rate over a four decade run.	Very strong – Growth rate over a four decade run.
Property Market	Broken by 18-year cycle – Lehman brothers collapse. The real estate driven recession of 2026 will collapse the entire global banking and property system.	Broken by 18-year cycle – Evergrande collapse. The real estate driven recession of 2026 will collapse the entire global banking and property system.
R & D – Innovation	Very strong – University system exceptional.	Very strong – University system exceptional.
Population	332.4 million in Feb 2022.	1.448 billion in Feb 2022.

The West is faced with a huge challenge, involving so many factors. To even begin to deal with it, there needs to be some serious, clear thinking. One thing is certain: the West beat the Soviet Union through economic attrition. The Chinese are beating the West through economic attrition. It is staring us in the face. Barack Obama, Joe Biden and Donald Trump are facing a very difficult decision: Do they try to make 5 billion people abide by Western norms? Or do they accept that the world has changed, and that the West has to adapt to the world? If we have to adapt, how do we adapt? What is the process of adaptation?

In order to answer these questions, you have to be exposed to several important forms of knowledge; the first being manufacturing; the second is warfare, particularly Chinese based thinking on war. Finally, a product which can be harnessed to come up with a set of answers, which will lead to the next generation of products, allowing us to compete again. This is what '7Tao: The Art of Industrial Warfare' attempts to address.

It has been accepted that China will not be following our rules established in the 20th century. However, if those rules are not adhered to… then does this amount to corruption? It seems as if there will be two ecosystems operating in two different cultural spheres and both of them will be accusing each other of corruption. Interesting times indeed.

Asia vs the West

Major geopolitical changes are taking place as the Asian cycle forms. Russia, China, India, the Middle East, South Asia are going through seismic military and economic changes as the Asian cycle gathers momentum.

• Russia is building a pipeline to connect its huge energy reserves to the Chinese market. Russia has even lifted the ban on supplying weapons to Pakistan and other Islamic countries.

• China is revitalising the ancient silk route by engaging Pakistan to help goods move quickly towards the Middle East and the warm waters of Gwadar port. Pakistan will become a logistical pivot. This will be the main gateway politically and culturally to the Islamic world.

• China is developing economic relationships with India to benefit from its market of 1.2 billion people. The Chinese will be helping to calm relations between India and Pakistan.

• China is moving towards South Asia and destabilising Japan and South Korea's trading relations with these countries. Japan and associates are concerned with China.

• China is investing heavily in missile technology to complement its 'anti-access' strategy of denying the United States Navy the freedom to roam in the seas off its coast. China can attack the United States with a large array of weaponry which it is rapidly developing to protect its economic interests. She can even attack America with hypersonic nuclear weapons.

China is now in position to take over the world in economic terms. It is in pole position rapidly rising and becoming the primary pinnacle of economic partnership for every country. She can choose her relationships, she can choose her strategy, she can choose to abandon the dollar. The entire world is at China's feet. China will partner with the rest of Asia, harness the energies of 5 billion Asian people and will be conducting an industrial and economic war against the West for many centuries to come.

This confrontation between these two superpowers will be on many fronts, and it will be felt in every community of the world. The fronts that need to be considered from both sides are, industrial, financial, political, community based, racially applied, geographical alignment, military based, economic, alliance based, trade deal alignments, export based, capital investment and even sea based. The changing order will affect the globe.

The Future of War will go either of Two Ways

1: The West fights China and Russia militarily. The tools involved in this war will be firstly conventional and then nuclear weapons at a later stage. This will be an extinction level event, will involve many countries and will be over in about a week Russia and China have the capability and self-reliance to eliminate all of Europe and the USA within hours.

2: The West fights China and Russia industrially and economically. A possible tool for this war will be the 7Tao Industrial combat fighting method. This will be a protracted economic war lasting many centuries with two spheres of influence. The Western sphere of influence and the Eastern sphere of influence; The West will play by the rules and the East will say 'whose rules, your rules?'

It is expected that these two scenarios will develop concurrently. There will be a massive build-up of a diversity of weapons across multiple platforms. These will include Land, Sea, Air and Space based weapons systems. However, they will probably not be used just in case a chain reaction of events is set off, leading to an exchange of such destructive capability that all life on earth is wiped out by the players in this war, namely: China, USA, Russia, Pakistan, India, and the European Union.

An industrial war will take the form of competing styles of capitalism, mercantilism and manufacturing, producing friction in many different countries. It is likely that these styles of competition will involve 7Tao and the lowest common denominator of trading warfare – the Transaction. These industrial conflicts will involve movement of goods, people, energy, skills, information, and profit-driven enterprises across borders and into markets never ventured before.

The Power and Discipline of Industrial Warfare

Industrial war is by far the most competitive element in the structure of power. If the Western economy is to survive the great depletion that is now taking place, corporate leaders need to come to terms with the concept of power. The component parts are identified in Figure 2:1, which offers a unique insight into what warfare has always looked like it has not changed throughout the past millennia; it will not change in the future.

To understand this position, *we have to understand the concept of power*. This is very important as this forms the basis of what I am attempting to address. We will begin by taking a bird's eye view of power and then focusing down onto the core thesis of Industrial Warfare. The main aim of this book is to gain an insight into Industrial Warfare, but in order to understand where it fits, we need to hover around the other nodes of power to build patterns around how four generations of change are affecting the world. These changes have always been taking place, waxing and waning from when nations are born until nations die and are taken over by other nations in historical perspective.

FIGURE 2:1   7Tao Representation of Power

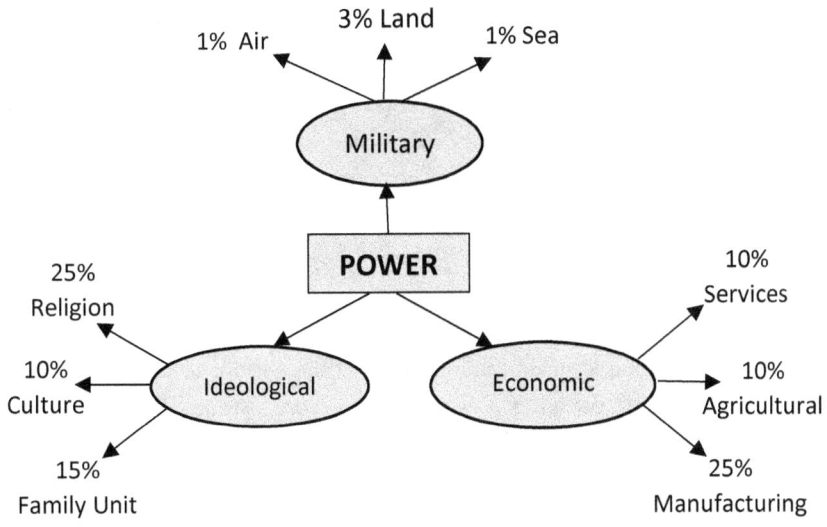

Source: 7Tao : 2003

Before we dig deeper into the economic branch of power, we must first understand the roles of the other two. The ideological and military branches of power comprise 55% of the above power model.

Ideological Power

This represents 50% of a nation's power. If you lose faith in the ideology, you die a death similar to that of the Soviet Union.

Religion (25%)
Half of ideological power takes the form of religion. Religion provides the moral fabric of the nation; it is a divine thermometer with the ability to identify an illness before permanent damage is done to society. Religion also acts as glue: it binds the family unit to the culture. It is a God-sent natural antidote to excess, hedonism and self-destruction. Without a major religion guiding the affairs of state (excluding fanaticism or extremism), the state will self-destruct within two generations. *Yardstick: How many people go to Church, Mosque, Temple, or Synagogue?*

Culture (10%)
Culture makes up 20% of ideological power. It reinforces good practice in ways of living, eating, greeting, dressing and healing. Culture is what softens our souls and makes us appealing to mankind. A poor culture can do much damage to a nation. For example, a drug culture may break down the next generation, affecting the way we will live in the future. Other examples of destructive cultures involve pornography, guns, racism, hedonism and consumerism. A poor set of cultural dynamics can undermine the fabric of society within two generations. *Yardstick: How many people in the country have severe physical, sexual and mental health problems?*

Family Unit (15%)
The family unit, the biological building block of the nation, contributes 30% to the power of ideology. It provides a seamless structure through which religion and concepts of ethics, integrity, unity and fairness can be transmitted through the generations. The family unit is the physical tie that binds the three ideological powers together. It is the generational bridge which bonds parent and child. The preservation of the family unit is paramount: without it, the social fabric of the nation implodes. Family unit destruction can bring a country to its knees within

two generations. *Yardstick: Is the divorce rate over 50% yet? How many single-parent families are there?*

Military Power

Although the most talked about type of power, this is in fact only 5% of the power model. This is because, for a nation on the economic and ideological growth path, the role of the military is defensive. It is only when a society is in decline that military power becomes intrusive and oppressive, expanding to sustain a system that is disappearing. When military success is at the forefront of a nation's foreign policy, that nation is about to die a violent and protracted death. This process explains the facts of history, the rise and fall of nations.

Air Power (1%)

Air power, the most celebrated form of military power today, represents just 1% of power. Many weird and wonderful machines light up the skyline: F-16s, F-15s and F22's from America, Euro-fighters and Mirages in Europe, Mig 29s and Sukhoi 35s in Russia. Incredible machines, incredibly expensive to maintain, they are the air tools used to defend land or to attack enemies before they can strike. If you do not have an air force, your borders are vulnerable to invasion. *Yardstick: How many of our planes did we lose? How many of our enemies' planes were lost?*

Land Power (3%)

Land forces, essential for defending the nation, contribute 3% to the power structure. Land forces win wars. They protect our interests, help us collect our booty, and leave a controlling footprint wherever they go. Without the toughest land forces, your people will suffer in the long term. You will be marginalized and colonized. The land forces of invading armies will capture your economic treasures and humiliate your people and their ideology. *Yardstick: How many of our men were killed? How many of the enemy were killed?*

Sea Power (1%)

Sea forces (1% of the total) protect coastlines. The sea is mankind's most important highway, the trade carrier of the world. Whoever dominates the sea, dominates the globe. To protect this interest, we need a navy able to challenge any other navy in the waters and protect shipping lanes. It should move without hesitation to protect the industries the shipping lanes serve. *Yardstick: How many of our navy's ships were sunk? How many enemy ships were sunk?*

Economic Power

This is 45% of the total power model. Without an economy, we starve. In the capitalist world, economic power may look like the only power. The economy gives a nation hope and fosters the creativity we need to survive. The more they are able to better themselves economically, the more people will secure their ideology and preserve their place among the nations of the world. There are three segments to the economy.

Agriculture (10%)

We have to eat and agriculture provides a route to survival based upon tilling the land. By becoming an agricultural nation, we build a base on which our children may survive in the future. Their hopes of shelter, food and family are fulfilled, and we can export the excess to build a better infrastructure for our lands. *Yardstick: Are we exporting food or are we importing food?*

Manufacturing (25%)

A nation is identified by the products it makes and supplies to other nations. When a nation is exporting goods, it is attracting value, creating value, and trading in value. This makes the nation itself 'valuable'. Manufacturing supplies the tools needed to survive to all the other power nodes: agriculture (tractors, combine harvesters), service industries (computers, telephones), the military (tanks, ships, planes), cultural institutions (artefacts, equipment, music, film) and the family household (cookers, microwaves). Everything that enables power is manufactured. Without manufacturing, there would have been no industrial revolutions, no economic development, no higher standard of living, no easy communication. Military power is heavily dependent on manufacturing the highest quality tools for combat. *This book is about the importance of fighting a manufacturing and industrial war. Yardstick: How many manufactured goods do we export? How much do we import from our competitors?*

Services (10%)

Services allow efficiency of consumption and the spread of value to the consumer. The service economy is of direct importance to local, national and international communities. The service economy supports manufacturing and agriculture in the direction of the economy; it supports the ideological reinforcement of the community. But the service economy cannot replace manufacturing. Service economies are very easy to displace, and even easier to replicate. Service industries can escape borders much more easily than manufacturing. *Yardstick: How many service industries do we export to other countries? How many overseas service industries are competing with us in our nation state?*

We are now ready to examine shifting patterns in the structure of power. In particular, we will examine the ideological, economic and military changes that have followed 'four-season' waves into the present.

The Four-Season Cycle in All Things

The ideological, military and economic aspects of power all possess a four generation pattern of change. We have seen above how the four season cycle, in conjunction with the Kondratieff wave, shaped the emergence of the Transatlantic nations as the dominant power over the last 350 years, through a sequence of industrial revolutions. The four-season Kondratieff wave, which 7Tao has identified as an indicator of changes to come, has huge implications for the power structure. The changes that occur in these economic cycles have an impact on society and the way in which problems manifest themselves in everything we do. The timing and effect are never exactly the same, but a pattern is evident.

We need to appreciate that the military, social and economic cycles have their own DNA structure. It is worth noting that each cycle has its own timing: although they are all divided into four phases, they conduct themselves according to their own timing. The cycles are not interrelated. They operate independently of one another. However, the one fact they share is the four-season pattern. It is difficult to predict exactly when changes will come, but we can be sure that they will always come. It is equally difficult to forecast how the military, ideological and economic cycles will behave because there are too many factors which influence and complicate them. The behaviour of these cycles, the way in which they operate, may be influenced by factors such as the internet, population, and the behaviour of other cycles.

They will form massive, complicated networks within each of the waves of change as they wax and wane into their own formations. The one thing that we can be certain of is that they will be related to the Kondratieff wave and to the way in which this particular economic cycle plays itself out. Much of this data relates to Chaos theory. Although cycles have predictable patterns in isolation, when a number are interwoven a more complex and irregular pattern emerges with their own cause and effect. Like water, they will find the best place to settle and the most efficient way of getting to their resting point. Much of these changes will be the old superpower coming to terms with a destroyed currency through inflationary policies and a shift of power to a challenger nation. In this case, the Middle Kingdom of China will regain its old position of the previous millennium's past.

From the characteristics analysed, we are able to conclude that we have a serious 'winter' problem on our hands, and one that current monetary policies are exacerbating (see Box 2:1).

We need to think carefully about how our businesses and nations will survive. We need to know what we are facing to understand what lies ahead in the

> **Box 2:1 Burning the House Down?**
>
> The Western winter has been seriously worsened by the money-printing mania of the US Federal Reserve and the Bank of England that began in the early part of 2009. They are burning the house down to keep themselves warm for a season. Western leaders understand that we are in drip-feed mode. If we don't print money, the recession returns; if we do, the economy survives while we figure out what to do next. The more the East Asian cycle grows, the more Western central bankers increase the money supply to offset the effects of depleted value. But more and more plants are moving to the East. How do we replace this value? By competing with the East Asian cycle or by printing money? Something has to give.

near future. We must study the economics of a fourth generation and decide how we can successfully navigate the depletion process.

Let us look closely now at the challenge which we face: the rise of China and the depletion of the western economic cycle. The pivotal point for consideration here is one thing: how does this affect the Corporation and the leadership of the corporation? How will the leader of the corporation face and survive the fourth industrial revolution? How will the CEO deal with fourth generation competition?

The fourth industrial revolution is coming with fourth generation challenges. In economic terms, we can call this winter period. This is where the down cycles force the trend back to its original position where it began. It is where recession and depressions are possible, made up of many mini downtrends in commodity and land based cycles. If we are to be able to navigate these shallow waters to come, we must first understand where we are in the fourth generation of industrial revolution.

The Changing Face of Business: Into the Fourth Generation

The chief executive officer's principle task during the ascension of a business is to prepare for its later decline. He must be able to anticipate the challenges as the business experiences its descent. At one time a business leader could be reasonably certain that the future would resemble the past and present. He could use what he'd learnt from the strategies, tactics, and operations of the past as he planned for the future. Today's business leader does not have this luxury.

The Key Issue

Modern business must take account of three earlier, distinct generations which have built on each other. In the West, agriculture, manufacturing, and service industries are still learning third-generation business techniques. These techniques, however, were developed in the 1960s, at a time of market growth. This growth model is now more than forty years out of date. Is it not time for a fourth-generation business technique to surface? If so, what might it look like?

These questions are of central importance to what I would like to explain. Whoever is first to recognize, understand and implement a generational change in the business environment will gain a decisive advantage in the marketplace. Any business that is slow to adapt to the winter portion of the cycle will become irrelevant to the marketplace and lay itself open to catastrophic collapse. My purpose here is to outline this powerful generational shift now occurring in the globalized business community, to signal the direction of change and discuss how we should embrace it. Our starting point is historical perspective.

Three Generations of Business

Businesses need to evolve and re-appraise themselves on a continuous basis. The modern era has witnessed three watersheds in which change has been qualitative, three distinct generations of change in the past hundred years. These conditions overlap as progression is a slow process from cities to villages, cultures to cultures and systems to systems. It is important to get a general sense of these generational changes, but to appreciate that the timing was not the same across the globe.

The First Generation (c.1850-1968): 'Metal Money'

The first generation of industrial development covers the expansion of international trade made possible by improved transport, Britain's adoption of free trade and the policing of trade routes by the British navy. In this global trading economy metal money, especially gold, was the accepted means of exchange between different currencies, with sterling the dominant currency till it was replaced by the dollar after the Second World War. Economies were local, significantly based on agriculture, and each transaction involved a high degree of trust by both customer and businessman. The economic cycle of the village was dominant.

People knew each other and knew what was expected of them. The rules of business were simple and trading was essentially clean. Manufacturers were small enterprises by today's standards. The made-to-measure principle was king, based on meeting the needs of the individual customer rather than supplying mass markets. Mortgages were relatively rare. Trade represented the way communities were interlinked. Communication between one area and another was via travelling salesmen.

People found it hard to copy one another's secrets due to barriers of entry and other difficulties such as obtaining an engineering education. However, the copying of products did occur. Branding was a new concept. Respect was achieved by producing high quality products which were delivered on time at an agreed price. There were few, if any, mass pricing strategies. Prices would change as each customer turned up onto the doorstep of the supplier, the supplier would take as much as possible from each customer. Each trade was individual along with each product.

The Second Generation (1908-1982): 'Mass Production'
This generation of industrial development spanned the Kondratieff wave (see p.4) from winter 1929 to summer 1982. It began with the Model T Ford, which first came off the production line in 1908 and the management principles involved continued up till the end of summer cycle of the American Industrial Revolution in 1982. The second generation benefited from advances in technology and the development of mass production and took advantage of the infrastructure established during World War II.

The new manufacturing generation had reached maturity and was fighting fit. From the Churchill era to the late 1980s, we experienced a paradigm shift of innovations beyond the linear development of previous cycles. Huge industries came to dominate our way of thinking and our way of life. Banks became international and were no longer restricted to the localities in which they originated. Mass production resulted in a complete culture change and the growth of export-driven economies. The shift away from the physical (gold connected) money era was signalled in 1971 when the US Federal Reserve abandoned the gold standard established by the Bretton Woods Agreement.

The manufacturing boom attracted huge amounts of foreign exchange and external interest in the pioneers of American industrialization, people such as Henry Ford and Walter P. Sloane. The changes were enormous. Agricultural output as a proportion of the nation's income declined and cities began to expand. The modern manufacturing economy based on the consumption of oil was making workers of the old school increasingly redundant. Culture changed. The kitchen became a utensil-driven rather than a labour-driven unit. The car became a necessity rather than a luxury. The communications industry was given new life through the expansion of telephony, radio and television. The legislation that governed trading patterns was becoming increasingly stressed.

Accordingly, changes were made to the laws of trading and their associated rules affecting the ways in which businesses were governed by the political establishment. Competition increased between businesses, though car companies were still well placed to sell everything they produced. Then, in the late 1970s, the

Japanese established themselves in the trading environments of the West. The era of intense international competition was about to begin.

The Third Generation (1970 to the present): 'Intense International Competition'

The third generation gave us our first view of what 'well governed' global competition would look like. This generation began in earnest in the mid seventies and was primarily led by Japanese and German enterprises. The primary driving force was 'new ideas for existing factories'. The industrial strength of the Japanese overwhelmed many Western industries. They were able to add more value to their products. They embraced the concept of the 7Tao of business transactions with religious intensity. They aimed to dominate markets by attacking the competition, and effectively buried the competition. This had far-reaching effects. The 7Tao elements – Price, Delivery, Quality, After Market, Customers, Shareholders and Employees – were meticulously scrutinised. As a result, they destroyed the British motorcycle industry, closed down competitor electrical appliance companies and cut the number of competitors' factories by 70%.

The Japanese had effectively launched themselves into the first phase of an industrial war. They had demonstrated how it was possible to close down 'enemy' industry. Astounded and demoralised, the West was left to pick up the pieces of their manufacturing operations.

The Japanese ended up dominating the electrical and mechanical markets. Everything they made had a buyer and each buyer respected their ability to give them what they wanted. During this era, the foundation stones were laid on a global scale for the 'increased competitive advantage' of the future. The phenomenon of the internet arose. Marketing was directed at younger and younger consumers.

Diversity was the order of the day: people were given control of demand, and everybody wanted something different. This was said to be the era of the electronic nation. The dot.com bubble grew and burst. Electronic simulation was reflected in music and entertainment, and also in bringing up children and the education of the next generation.

Analysis of the Fourth Generation

In the previous three generations there were seven major catalysts which resulted in an increasing rate of change and rising levels of market force. What perspective do we gain from these earlier shifts as we look towards a potential fourth generation of business? Earlier generational shifts (especially the shift from the second to the third generation) were marked by a growing emphasis on several central ideas. All seven of these are likely to be carried over into the fourth generation. These seven catalysts had always existed in all of the previous generations. However, their importance grows each time the competitive forces around the globe increase.

Catalyst 1. The 7Tao of the Transaction

This will be the model for businesses of the future. The elements were present in all previous cycles of business, but business managers did not focus on them. Workers will be judged by the value they can deliver. Jobs will no longer be of the 'do this', 'finish that' kind. The worth of employees will be judged in terms of the value they can add to the business. That worth will be defined by the Transactional vectors of Price, Delivery, Quality, Aftermarket, Customers, Shareholders, and finally, the seventh, Employees. Training the employee to 'adapt' will be the cornerstone of the business, because it will be the 7th Tao employee that drives the remaining 6Tao of gaining transactions. It is fundamentally important to train the employee to adapt to the constantly changing conditions of the marketplace which only respects transactions.

Catalyst 2: Innovation

Innovation, and dominating new markets for as long as possible before the competition catches up, is central to success. Markets will be 'very short' in terms of time cycles. The 'on demand' world requires immediate customer satisfaction. Some call this the 'customer delight process'. Being able to give the customer what is new and exactly what they want is one of the most important factors in the survivability of a business.

Catalyst 3: Conflict

Industrial conflict is growing, as Japan demonstrated in the previous generational shift. Increasingly competitiveness will turn into conflict as corporations battle to preserve the status quo. They will need to move into their neighbours' territories.

They will want the 7Tao to drive them to perfection through growth. This conflict will be economically bloody: there will be many business casualties. Uncertainty will reign and forecasting will become very difficult. A combination of military and industrial warfare will be used to take over territories which will be important in the trading lanes of the world economy.

Catalyst 4: Globalization

Fourth, and most important, is globalization. The number of competitors is set to increase from the third generation by a factor of 100 to 1. The third generation was about competition between individual corporations. The fourth generation will be about corporations battling for supremacy on a continental basis. Competitors will emerge from everywhere, wielding different levels of force. Containing these conflicts may become difficult for global lawmakers as corporations bend and twist the rules. Service, manufacturing and agricultural units will stretch a nation's moral boundaries to breaking point. For the working class, uncertainty will be the order of the day.

Catalyst 5: Rules of the road.

In the fifth catalyst, the established western rules will be broken, and the international norms will be side-lined. Established systems such as World Bank, International Monetary Fund, Asian Development Bank, the SWIFT system of international transactions, the routes of global trade, the sea lanes and shipping ports, road movements and control routes and finally the ways in which fair trade is governed will also change. Enormous pressure will be placed on the old system of trade which will bring it to breaking point. These old systems, policies, rules and regulations will have to be updated to reflect the fact that Eurasia has risen, and business looks different now.

Catalyst 6: Economic cycle broken.

The 18-year cycle, which drives global trade will align into one global boom and bust cycle; this current cycle will finally explode in 2026 bringing the entire global economy down with it. Last time in 2008 they papered over damage done by the 18-year cycle. This time in 2026 however, the 18-year cycle will smash the global economy to pieces.

Catalyst 7: Picking up the pieces.
Just as the Soviet Union broke in 1991 in the depths of the last of the 20th century 18-year cycle, so the new 18-year cycle will usher in new realities for the next century. The combined residue effects of the 2008 financial crisis carried over into the 2026 economic crisis will bring about monumental changes for the next century. Civil war will take over the Trans-Atlantic cycle as America reverts back to its origins of Democrat vs Republican. This will allow the Eurasian economic landmass to grab the torch of the global economy and revert to the original leadership position of China leading the world just like it was back in the 15th century. This means that the rules will be different, and the world will look more like it did back in the previous millennium. This also means that borders will change and countries will have to change their whole policy to accommodate the reality of the new superpower arriving.

What Will the Fourth Generation Look Like?

Considering all the characteristics of the modern business world, the emerging picture of industrial competition will not be pretty. Any organization will have to refocus sharply its view of how to operate on a strategic, tactical, and operational pattern in order to survive. And the key word is *'survive'*.

There are seven important factors to consider in fourth-generation business.

Factor 1: Placement
Organizations will be lighter than ever before. They will be able to shift their operations from one country to another. They will have no geographical allegiances: their allegiance will be to the 7Tao. One Tao will be played against another to make ends meet. Corners will be cut to meet the organization's needs. Corporations will not bow to governing bodies in their bid to survive. They will search for countries that can offer them the best exit strategies or incoming placement strategies. In short, governments will be at the mercy of corporations. Business centres and business parks rather than government buildings will be the centres of power. Governments will actively try to recapture their power and will try their best to make sure that they benefit from the corporation, this will lead to tax wars between governments and corporations.

Factor 2: Corporate warfare

Corporations will become cornered tigers that will fight with their last ounce of energy to survive. They will enhance their chances of survival and growth by understanding that they are in a fight to the death. These battles will cost the loser his life in the marketplace. To survive and find space to breathe in the next generation of business competition, businesses will have to embrace the economic fighting arts. If the world cannot protect you in the coming century, you have to learn how to protect yourself.

Factor 3: Deregulation

Established laws of trading will become irrelevant to businesses. The less law a business is tied up in, the more options it will have in its quest for profitability. Law will simply become one tool in the arsenal of weapons employed by businesses to attack competitors. The business will pay scant attention to the needs of its host country and its people. Only the strong will survive. This will be seen in the growth of mergers and acquisitions, and increased destruction of weaker competitors. Governments will have less control over corporations, which will increasingly dictate the way in which countries are ruled for their own benefit. The removal of legal restraints will be the only cause for concern for directors. 'What can you offer me?' is the question every CEO will ask before moving his business to a country. If governments do not accept the criteria laid down by the marketplace, they will not get to host the corporation. Every town will be asking, 'Will the corporation land here?' Market forces will become the 'be all and end all' in the considerations of governments at every level.

Factor 4: Destruction of the Economic Cycle

Many industries will either die or move to where they will be most competitive. This will destroy entire communities. The economic foundations of cities will crumble and communities will be left to pick up the pieces. In the UK, people of the West Midlands recently experienced this with Rover, the last British-owned car manufacturer. When prized jobs disappear, huge distortions of wealth develop in a community. Families are wrecked and lives change. Derelict buildings scar urban landscapes, ruins of a once glorious industrial past. Detroit's fate today will be the future for many other urban centres if their corporations fail to adapt to the 7Tao.

Factor 5: Changing disciplines and styles
Many methodologies today have different sets of survival tactics, and many are making progress in the new era. Six Sigma, Lean Manufacturing, 20 Keys, the Toyota Production System, Total Quality Control and Just In Time are some of the survival strategies adopted by leading corporations. But these are all geared to third-generation (1970 to the present) competition. They served the third generation very well but the fourth generation will demand more ... much more. Necessity must become the mother of invention once again.

Factor 6: The increase of protectionism.
As countries increasingly embrace conflict of exports against each other. They will be placing barriers at the borders and increase tariffs to protect indigenous manufacturers from being assaulted by outside competitors who do not play by the established western rules. These tariffs will not just challenge China, but will also address India, the European Union, South America, Japan and ASEAN region. The USA will position itself against its competitors in every region of the world as it embraces the fighting arts of industrial warfare. This set of actions will begin with tariffs, but will escalate into every industry as trade war morphs into industrial war. The lowest common denominator will be the transaction as each industry backs the government and the government backs each industry. The complexities of industrial conflict will increase as the USA and China entrench themselves in defining the battlespace of the 21st century. Each step forward will contain a transactional element of 7Tao and whichever side masters this, will win the transactional, trade and industrial war.

Factor 7: Training, education and adaptability.
In any complex scenario, the key is your fighting force. Whoever has the best trained workers will win this battle between the USA and China. The Chinese economic war fighters are ferocious, equipped with 3000 years of history, an ability to take pressure and endurance levels never before witnessed by the fighters in the West.

The workers in the factories of the plants doing battle will need training to develop their understanding as the battle lines become greater and more demanding. Training will only be available through the corporations and the government offices as this involves the life of the plant and the future of thousands of workers both within the plant and spread throughout the supply chain. Entire supply chains will be affected as they struggle to adapt to the US - China industrial conflict which will morph, wax and wane as it progresses into the 21st century. Whichever government invests in its training systems is the one who will win the war.

The US China Industrial War is a chess game of wits and a constantly changing battlefield. This will be the most important development of the 21st century.

Training to adapt to multitudes of cultures, new laws, new ways, new peoples, seeing losses in a different way will become the norm as our current system adapts to a world not seen since the 15th century. The rise of the East will test every salary, region, country and continent in the world. Companies will have to be adaptive to survive, constantly training their people, constantly equipping their workforce with the abilities to change and adapt to difficult climates. If they do not understand the new globalisation, they will not be a part of the new world economy that is forming right in front of our eyes.

What Lies Ahead for the Businessman?

As complexity increases in our multi-cultural world, it will become necessary to simplify things through business realignments. We need to remove the complexities of the current environment which will not fit into the context of the fourth-generation business environment. The fourth generation business strategy of the future will accord with the current culture of defining success. *This means placing business on a war footing.*

Already, methodologies are appearing which seek to embrace change. 'Out with the old and in with the new' is what is happening every day as corporations and employees struggle to remain relevant in the age of the 7Tao of business. If you are not bound by the market requirements of 'competitive price, speed of delivery, defect free quality, requests of the after-market sale, in tune with the needs of the customer, fulfilling the needs of the shareholder, and securing the performance of your employees' *you will be rendered irrelevant in the global market.*

For corporation employees, the struggle is particularly acute. Not only are you fighting the ravaging effects of economic inflationary pressures. If you lose your job, you lose your ability to stand on your own two feet – you lose your house, you lose your mortgage, you will very likely lose your wife and children too. She may search elsewhere for security; her children will need to eat. It is increasingly happening. Economic battles weigh down heavily on the family unit. Each node of the power model is inter-connected; you cannot separate the effects of one from the other.

There is no easy way out of this future. The weaker corporation cannot run from the battle. It must fight or change will overwhelm it. There are many questions for the corporation to answer: How do we fight? Where do we learn how to fight? Who do we fight? Who among us will fight? When must we fight? What do we fight with? What happens when we fight? Where do we go after a fight? One question in particular is very important: *What does economic fighting look like?*

As we see in cities like Detroit and states like California, where derelict buildings scar the landscape, economic war is not like military war: it *looks like* economic war. The rules of economic warfare are completely different from our current understanding of conflict. The economic war models of the past are as obsolete as the infrastructure that served them. Economic warfare has changed. We no longer 'look down' upon the markets, as we did in the Transatlantic cycle, but 'look across' at markets which are dominating the East Asian cycle. To embrace the changes of the fourth generation, we need to learn how to fight for our transaction. In the next section, we will cover the similarities between a martial artist attacking and confronting his competitor in a physical fight, and a corporation attacking and defending against a competitor in a business fight. Here, our aim is to get to the essence of 7Tao.

China declares a battle for global growth.

In February 2016, China declared in its National Congress that there will be a battle for growth. This battle will consist of nation states fighting for global market share. As nations align themselves with the Eastern Eurasian cycle or the Western Trans-Atlantic cycle, the global playing field is changing into a full-scale economic competition.

Recession and Disruption

The global marketplace is shrinking. The transactions of the past are changing, as they are increasingly demanding better price, faster delivery, advanced quality, supportive aftermarket services, increased customer satisfaction, increasing shareholder returns, and more capable employees. The pressures on business to adapt are becoming intolerable.

Training demands increase daily as obsolescence within the business and the marketplace haunts the CEO at every turn. A head in the sand approach doesn't work anymore. Threat levels increase daily with hydra-headed disruption coming from all directions. Small nimble competitors are appearing from all geographies and start-ups with little or no experience are taking on global corporations from nowhere and fighting for an efficient transaction.

As the market shrinks, so does the need for employment. Employees can find themselves without a job overnight. This then leads to recession as buying power evaporates and large numbers of people find themselves without a stable income. This anger at the changing world economy leads to frustration and guilt, which turn to voter apathy, lethargy in leadership, and demands for change. This is why Donald Trump, the insurgent candidate, gained the Republican Party nomination and eventually the 45th presidency. His message of nostalgia and manufacturing industry from the 70's and 80's rung home with the voter, and what he promised was the utopia of industrial dominance that the USA used to have over the world during the 1950's and the 1960's.

Battle for Growth

In preparing for a battle for growth, China is getting ready for something that hasn't appeared in the last 250 years. What the Chinese like to call the Dragon War environment.

All economies around the world are going to fight for growth in a decreasing transactional landscape. Take TATA steel in the U.K. as an example of what the future will bring. The Chinese are clearly fighting an industrial war here. Dumped Chinese steel exports at ridiculously low prices are meant to kill any possibility of doing business with other companies.

Because of the need to shore up shareholder value, there is constant pressure to cut costs. Any wrong move by a company competing with the Chinese may result in a loss in stock ratio, leading to a greater calamity of the share price falling. This is what the Chinese are hoping for.

Once the Chinese sell to distributors at prices marked down because of excess inventory in the Chinese marketplace, they will be looking to either shrink down their competition or eliminate it completely. This will allow ease of entry into the market at a later date.

Customers will have no choice but to buy from China because there won't be any other competitors. The British know that when Tata steel closes down in the current crisis, imports of steel will have to be taken from outside the country. This then becomes something completely different, a matter of national security. Why? Because it takes decades to build up the infrastructure of an efficient steel industry, and once the foundation of these industries go, they never come back.

This Has Happened Before

You don't have to go back too long to see these effects. The electronics industry in Silicon Valley, the motorcycle industry in the U.K., the automotive industry of Detroit, the aircraft industry and Boeing plant in Seattle, the textile mills of the past, the record industry of California. People speak of these changes as positive news, as if these jobs will go and better ones will come. Maybe. But these plants will not come back.

When Japan industrialized, it became a threat to the established U.S. brands in the 70s. The rest of the Asian economic tigers followed them in household goods production and automotive industry dominance.

This time however, the situation is different. The sheer size of the industrial giant stalking the world's marketplace makes us quake in our boots. This is not Japan who follows our rules, or other competitors who play by the rules. This is China, which has dominated the world economy for 18 out of the last 20 centuries. They are returning to the number one spot, and they intend to make the world in their own image, just like the Japanese and Germans have tried to do before them with their respective drives for manufacturing dominance over the world economy.

The Battle for the Transaction

Indeed, disruption has always happened throughout history, whether in scientific, military, innovative, or social ways. Disruption is just another word for change. The key thing to remember about disruption is that it is based upon two concepts, defence and attack of the existing transaction.

The speed of the transaction in agriculture, manufacturing, and services is increasing. It's not on-time delivery that matters any more, it's now emotional delivery or instant delivery that matters. Can I get what I want with the swipe of my phone? Can I place one finger in the air and have a taxi turn up to take me where I need to go?

Disruption means one thing, can you attack a competitor's transaction and compete with them on the elements of the exchange of goods and services? This is what Uber, AirBnB, and the Chinese steel industry are doing now.

They are disrupting the flow of finance from the customer to the supplier—in its basic form they are attacking supply and demand. You do this by analysing exactly what makes up a transaction in its basic form and then you out qualify that transaction using whatever weapons in your arsenal you have designed, purchased, assembled, and created from scratch.

Overnight, competitors are disrupted using the basic attack strategy of a better transaction. Everyone in the marketplace is thinking about it right now.

It's open season among nation states as well. In a recent infamous battle between America and China, Britain was in the centre. America wanted Britain not to join the AIIB (Asian Infrastructure Investment Bank, a Chinese initiative that competes with the U.S.-dominated World Bank and International Monetary Fund), but Britain ignored the warnings and went ahead and joined anyway. And then Western nations followed them. The customers and countries flocked to the AIIB because they need to be involved in the economic **development** of Eurasia.

Essentially, Britain disrupted the World Bank and the International Monetary Fund by joining AIIB, which took the wind right out of the sails of the two previous banking flagships. So suddenly, the IMF and WB found that they were disrupted and had to change the way they operate in order to survive. If they don't change the way they do business and become competitive, they could easily lose out to entire countries, regions, and even continents as they become increasingly irrelevant to the smarter competitors who have attacked their previous nation of transactions with more value, capability and reach to the populations they intend to supply.

The British people followed suit and voted for Brexit, reinforcing the employment independence of the British people and Britain's own preparation for the battle for growth.

Preparing for Battle

So how do you prepare for battle in such an uncertain and unpredictable world, where a competitor can spring up from anywhere? When a trusted ally will just abandon you in the blink of an eye? When time has no boundaries and time to prepare doesn't exist anymore? What do you do when there are absolutely no geographic boundaries to business and no interests except short term interest because of the enormous pressure balance sheets and uncertainty brings in the marketplace?

This is a very difficult proposition for every lawmaker, CEO, or shop floor employee who has pressures hanging over their head that they simply have not seen before. Each country, corporation, and enterprise will have to create their own plan to adapt to the world of disruption, depletion, and the rise of unrestricted warfare which everybody in the world is facing right now. We live through interesting times indeed. Understanding your own battlefield is paramount to success, this means that you have to know your marketplace, who your competitors are, what strategies they have against you, the pressures in the economy, the pressures of the bigger competitor, the pressures of the smaller competitor, the economy to come, the environmental changes to come and the different ways in which your business can be bought down by forces you do not expect.

You plan as best you can. You cannot control those factors outside of your organization or your business boundaries. All you can do is prepare for these changes in case they cross over your demarcation line in business. If this is the case, you must have a self-defence technique which will serve you in your time of need. Like any other self-defence method, you never know when you will need it to defend your business when the time comes. 7Tao focuses on this issue, solving problems and being able to articulate them so that they can resolved with minimal effort and investment. The battles will be fierce and the competitors will be preparing from many different angles.

Physical Fighting vs Business Fighting

When a competitor fights, he fights using the seven senses. When a business competes, it competes using the seven senses of business. These are listed below in the table. In either case, if any one of these seven senses is impaired, it will affect the outcome of the fight.

#	Physical fighting	Business fighting
1st sense (Tao 1)	Sight – eyes	Price – sells for something – currency
2nd sense (Tao 2)	Sound – ears	Delivery – deliver on time
3rd sense (Tao 3)	Smell – nose	Quality – perfect quality
4th sense (Tao 4)	Touch – body	After Market – supporting the customer
5th sense (Tao 5)	Taste – tongue	Customers – provision of goods/services
6th sense (Tao 6)	Balance – body	Shareholders – return on investment
7th sense (Tao 7)	Fear and hope	Employees – the most valuable asset.

A - When a physical competitor fights. He does two things:

• He defends against attack into his physical area, which is his body.

• He attacks and defends against the competitor in order to ensure his own safety (7Tao defends the user's transaction and attacks the competitor's transaction to ensure the business's safety).

B - When a martial artist strikes a competitor. It effect's all seven senses. Sight. Sound. Taste. Hearing. Touch. Fear. Balance.

• He will feel the pain, his ears will ring, he will smell blood, taste the strike's effect, get misty eyed, lose his balance, and he will feel fear. If you hit him hard enough: game over, knockout.

• When a business attacks a competitor, it will have a similar effect. It will earn less money, downsizing of delivery operations will take place, quality will suffer as costs are cut, after market reduces in effectiveness, customers will leave, shareholders will withdraw support as lost profits affect psychology, and employees will lose hope and begin to abandon ship.

C - The physical competitor has an array of attack techniques to overcome his opponent, kicking and punching to attack his competitor's seven senses. 7Tao has over 256 attack techniques to attack a competitor's transaction.

D - The physical competitor has an array of defence techniques to defend himself from the opponent. He defends his own seven senses. 7Tao has 256 techniques to defend our transaction.

E - In order to attack his opponent, he has to reach out into the opponent's area using his tools and techniques that he has mastered through practise. 7Tao invades the competitor's marketplace.

The Rules of Industrial Combat

First things first: there are **no rules** in industrial warfare. You either win or you lose. Barack Obama can complain as much as he likes about playing by the rules as he did in his state of the Union speech in 2012. I don't think anyone is paying any attention Mr President ... you had better adapt or die. All your speeches look like they want to calm the voter down and make it look like you are doing something when you are not.

- The attacker and defender have one thing in common: they are in a fight for survival.

- Whoever is best trained and best practised has the best chance of survival.

- The attacker and the defender will be using:
  - Long Range Techniques – Strategic.
  - Medium Range Techniques – Tactical.
  - Short Range Techniques – Operational.

- For every defence technique, there is an attack.

- For every attack technique, there is a defence.

- When a competitor strikes you... you can use single or multiple defence methods to defend your transaction. The 7Tao.

- When you strike a competitor, he has to use single or multiple defence methods to defend against your strike.

The Techniques of 7Tao

- Each technique is connected between attack and defence. All talk to each other independently and with synergy at the same time. (See Box 4.4 and Box 8.3)

- The nature of attack is to reach out into an opponent's territory. The nature of defence is to stop the attacker from achieving his objectives of attack.

- The student immediately recognises his problems when he is studying 7Tao because *all his organizational problems* are handed to him from an operational, tactical and strategic point of view. All he has to do is find solutions.

- Each technique reflects the other. The aim is simple, to defend our transactions. To increase our transactions, primarily by engaging in industrial warfare against our competitor. Don't run or complain just take him on ... head on if need be!

- You do this by two philosophies in business: This is the sole aim of business – to remain efficient and effective. One is *saving money*. The other is *making money*.

- This is what makes any business successful: you have better transactions and more transactions than anyone else.

Summary of Analysis

The first two chapters have outlined the wide range of factors involved. All are interlinked in different ways and all are connected to the economic cycles, waves of change, and generations of adaptive development. It is indeed very difficult to tie them all together. The only thing I am trying to do here is to paint a picture of what the world looks like, and where I think the future will go. The following facts are evident when corporate leaders looks around them:

- Competition is extremely fierce. This ferocity will increase over time. Companies that can't sell will downsize and then eventually close. See Detroit like desolation.

- China is a millennia-old competitor, over three thousand years of history and a population of 1.4 billion. These people can fight, and they are bright! They can fight in any way, form, territory, geography, environment, and method. The Chinese leadership are well informed, they have size, unit, organization, territory and are militarily aware and prepared. To challenge them militarily, you have to go to their territory. They don't need to come to your territory in the USA.
- A new bloc is forming right in front of our eyes: Russia, China, India, Middle East, parts of Europe are getting together to trade against the dominant Western hegemony. Their market alone consists of 5.5 billion people.

- Analysis of the waves indicates that we have an uphill battle. The economic cycle is against us. We are on a downward trend and up against a fierce competitor – China.

- Our Western economic system is not supporting the industrialist. Rather, it is supporting the rent-seeker. They can't fight industrial wars – industrialists fight industrial wars!

- No one follows rules anymore. It is survival of the fittest that counts. Banks can't print their way out of this downward cycle. The Industrial problem needs to be tackled head on with Industrial Warfare. The old methods of efficiency and effectiveness are either obsolete or becoming obsolete as the rate of change increases in at a pace unseen before.

- The future of warfare will go one of two ways. The first is military warfare, the second is economic warfare. The crucial question is: if all competitors are arming themselves to the teeth with tools and methods of mass destruction – including hypersonic nuclear weapons, which way will conflict go? It is my analysis that warfare will become industrial and economic because military conflict offers no outcome other than mutually assured destruction.

- In order to confront in economic conflict our competitors who do not play by our old economic Queensberry rules, we have to learn non-Queensberry methods. This means we must carefully analyse the future options of warfare. If they don't play by the old rules, neither will we. If the major part of warfare is economic, then we must learn to recognise the fact that 7Tao, or more importantly, understanding the 7 parts of the transaction, is a primary weapon in the economic conflict which is taking place.

The essence of 7Tao is based around the principles of Eastern conflict. 7Tao is nothing less than a 'full on' economic and industrial combat method designed to operate in a world where the above-listed facts are a daily occurrence. In the remaining chapters of the book, the 7Tao technique is introduced and each Tao is explained in sequence with its own chapter and a case study illustrating its application.

CHAPTER 3

Dynamics of the 7Tao

The future depends on our coming to terms with the fact that we will be confronted by unique challenges. We will need to re-skill ourselves and re-tool our enterprises. Political leaders must embrace a future based, not on austerity, but rather on a new kind of prosperity in preparation for industrial warfare.

If the Chinese, Japanese and countless others can bring industrial warfare to everyone else's shores, can the West not send its best industrial commanders to dominate the rest of the globe in a way that will preserve our people's prosperity? Britain, the first industrial nation, ought to offer leadership. The formula which I offer prescribes an alternative to the age of austerity and permanent depletion.

Box 3:1 Germany – Odd One Out?

While the UK abandoned manufacturing during the Thatcher years, Germany continued to invest in a manufacturing sector perfecting the art of making products. Brands such as Mercedes Benz, Audi, BMW, Volkswagen, Siemens and Hugo Boss grew and became increasingly confident even during the recent downturn.

BMW Confident of prospering during downturn. Chris Byrant in Munich, *Financial Times*, 9 September 2011. Chris Byrant notes that 'BMW reported it would not make a loss if the auto sector experienced a repeat of the 2008/2009 financial crisis,' underscoring the confidence of German car makers in being able to sustain a strong emerging market for premium vehicles."

German manufacturers focus on brand excellence, quality and the good reputation of their products. This makes the products attractive even in the heart of Chinese dragon territory.

Ninety-nine per cent of warfare is economic. Every time a housewife goes to the supermarket she is at war with her purse. She has to fight to survive, to keep to her budget and get her work done in the time available. All the shops in her area compete for her transaction. The same contest is taking place in every supply chain right across the globe.

Any corporation that wants to survive into the future needs to be sceptical about governments that have pulled the wool over their eyes during the financial crisis. The force, the momentum, the sheer pace of events now unfolding shows that the struggle for economic survival will not end soon. Governments are trying to buy time by inflating their currencies. This is known as a currency war. Ben Bernanke, Chairman of the US Federal Reserve (the central bank) is trying to blame 'emerging economies', particularly China, for America's financial crisis. He claims that the Yuan is undervalued, which gives China's exports a price advantage in world markets. It is unlikely that the Chinese will change their position. They will do what is best for their nation, just like the Americans are trying to do what is best for them. This leads the USA back to quantitative easing again causing inflationary pain to all of their people.

Western governments are trying to inflate their sovereign debts away by printing money, hoping this will pull the system out of its death spiral. But third-generation capitalism is dead and it is just a matter of time before that realisation explodes in the public consciousness. Meanwhile, if Western governments like those of the US, UK and the EU continue to abuse the purchasing power of their currencies, they could be seriously devalued with the ensuing inflationary spiral which evolves from QE.

The economic system needs to be seen to represent true value. If it loses that reputation, it may end up like that of Mugabe's Zimbabwe or Germany's Weimar Republic. Once a run on the banks turns into a run on the currency, it will be a question of survival of the fittest, in business, in the population, and in the country in general. At this point in time, in the aftermath of the depletion of 2008, it is very tempting to devalue currencies to the point of oblivion. Except for a few countries (like Germany), most governments in the Transatlantic orbit are relying on credit creation. At current rates, the only medium that will retain value is gold. Couple these factors with relentless oil depletion, the energy and water crises across the world, localised wars and the threat of climate change, and we have a good idea of the challenges confronting the human race for many generations to come.

Where will the sense of confidence come from? When customers buy, they have seven ideals (the 7Tao) in mind:

1 - I want to pay as little as possible for the product.

2 - I want to get it on time.

3 - I want it to be of good quality.

4 - I want good customer service.

5 - I am the customer, I want to be respected by giving me what I need and want.

6 - I want return on investment.

7 - I want to know that the people who made my product are well trained, have a good reputation and observe the above six ideals.

These are the 7Tao principles that the Chinese define as a sale. Together they make up the *transaction*. A transaction is when a mutual exchange of goods and services takes place. Defined in the dictionary as: 'A **transaction** is a completed agreement between a buyer and a seller to exchange goods, services, or financial assets in return for money.'

We can see two distinct economic models and points of view in the world today:

A: To satisfy demand, you must supply products with the above seven elements in mind (China, Japan, Germany). Market driven Capitalism. These seven elements come alive as soon you take currency out of your pocket to buy a product.

B: To satisfy demand, we have to create stimulus packages which enhance the economy and keep transactions moving. (USA, UK). Government driven capitalism.

In A you don't have to pay for additional costs on top of production. You don't have highly paid employees working to pay off expensive mortgages, gut-wrenching loans at compound rates of interest and the unreasonable taxes the government hangs round your neck to sustain a warped economic model. You don't have to pay for the mistakes of banks which lent to people in order to sustain an 18-year cycle which goes bust repeatedly. There is no value in a transaction in a country which has a warped inflated currency and expensive economic boom bust cycles. The costs for the Western manufacturer are huge because of the nature of the Western economic system.

In model A you just have to pay for the product. Therein lies the value, and the customer can immediately recognise value. B is obsolete. In B the people are left with nothing; the country is depleted. If corporations can't sell in such circumstances they will go somewhere else.

A is the Eurasian model, adopted with intensity by the Chinese and designed with great intricacy by the Germans and Japanese (who lost World War II). B is the Western, Transatlantic model. In order to free ourselves from B we have to fight power with power. We must reject the regime which is enforcing this system, we must move against our so-called 'rulers'. This is called 'revolution'. As the world turns to the Eurasian model, the Chinese and surrounding countries will free themselves as the Western power base weakens beyond repair. The gutting of industry will lead to depleted value in countries like the UK.

The Chinese didn't go into their targeted countries with tanks, bombs and threats. They just opened businesses. They are recovering the pre-eminent position they held in the centuries before their defeat in the Opium Wars humiliated them. They are now more prepared than ever to reclaim their original position as economic power of the world.

An example: Why should I buy a Western combat jet for $100m when I can buy twenty Chinese jets for $100m? The Chinese salesman says to the buyer: 'It does 80% of what that Western jet does, and it's a hell of a lot cheaper. There you are buying just one aeroplane sir, here I am selling you an air force squadron!' Let's calculate this in value terms:

1 Western plane = $100m = 100% firepower = 100% = 1 Jet.
20 Chinese planes = $5m @ 80% x 20 firepower = 1,600% = 20 Jets.

That is value for money! The numbers rule. 'Hi-tech?' you ask. 'Quality?' Well, the only use for these planes will be to decorate some airfield in the middle of nowhere for decades, or possibly they may be used against their own population. Very rarely will they be used in international combat. That sort of war is now fought with missiles and rockets, as the Hezbullah ruthlessly displayed in 2006 in the Lebanon-Israel conflict. As Russia displayed recently in Ukraine. And as the USA displayed in Iraq, Iran, Afghanistan, Pakistan, Syria, Yemen, Sudan, Somalia, Algeria, Libya, Nigeria, Eritrea, Indonesia, Malaysia, Kashmir, India and any other Muslim country I haven't mentioned in the War on Terror from 2001 to 2021. The fact of the matter is that these wars still continue, and western powers still invest and supply arms to wars in the Middle East for decades to come.

Economic warfare has evolved into industrial warfare, and it is critical that industrial warfare is understood properly if the West is to compete in world markets. Old-school economic warfare was good in its time, it suited Victorian thinking, colonial prestige, high-tower organizations and nine-layer management systems. It suited a promotion-based culture in the second- and third-generation industrial wars.

The economic markets of the future will be flat. That great equalizer, the internet, has made it possible to sell directly into an English home from China using Alibaba to see the product and Alipay to buy the product. Industrial warfare is a truly democratic form of economic power.

Defence and Attack

What do we defend and what do we attack? As we have seen, there are seven parts to any transaction:

1 **Price:** This needs to be competitive in the markets which are being served.

2 **Delivery:** It must always be on time, without fail.

3 **Quality:** This should be 100% – or at least 99.7%.

4 **After market:** Support must be offered from use to non-use of the product or service.

5 **Customers:** They are vital – they buy the product.

6 **Shareholders:** The Shareholders or owners of the business count the profits.

7 **Employees:** They actually do the work required to win the transaction.

Every business in the world embraces these 7 Ways (7Tao) **whether they know it or not**. These factors are what make up the transaction; they are what makes the business viable. Let's take a simple example.

The 7Tao of Potato Chips

Price: £1 per bag.
Delivery: No more than ten minutes frying time.
Quality: Not too raw, not too burned. (Frying chips is an art!)
After market: Supply salt, vinegar and ketchup.
Customer: Pays £1.
Shareholder: Makes 30p profit on each bag of chips.
Employees: Someone has to do the frying to complete the transaction.

This transaction takes place in a local marketplace. The competition is the fried chicken shop down the road, the fish and chips shop up the road and the takeaway pizza place across the street.

The potato chip shop owner must ask the following questions: What must I do to attract customers to my shop? What can I add in each segment of the transaction to increase the number of transactions? To achieve such outcomes, what weaknesses in my transactions must I eliminate and what strengths must I build on?

The Transaction

The seven principles of the transaction apply to every business, whether it makes cars, ships, satellites or potato chips. The 7Tao already exists in the DNA of supply and demand, we must understand and implement it thoroughly. It will prepare a modern corporation for the new generation of economic combat. This is what it is designed to do. 7Tao will reveal the truth about our modern economic environment. It will defend the transactions that one needs to defend and actively attack competitors' transactions. This is what I designed it to do. There are no Queensberry Rules in fourth generation business!

Defending the businesses transaction: Defence involves protecting the transaction. An organization is sustained by its cash flow. This cash flow is sustained by customer relationships established in the marketplace. The marketplace is a product of the 7Tao of the transaction. How do you stop a competitor from taking your customers? This is the primary question which 7Tao asks. The key words in the answer are 'relevance and value'. If the product or service is relevant to the marketplace, the organization will thrive. An organization becomes irrelevant when it starts to evade its responsibilities. The marketplace only respects responsible and valuable transactions, nothing else. 7Tao empowers the businessman with over 250 transactional defence tools which help to increase value in their products and services.

Attacking the competitor's transaction: When we successfully attack a competitor, we are basically taking their transaction by defeating it. This is achieved by removing its relevance to the marketplace. Relevance involves getting things on target, at the right time, at the right place and connecting with only as much force as is necessary. 7Tao empowers the businessman with over 250 transactional attack tools. When different tools are combined, billions of combinations of techniques result with which to create a powerful industrial fighting system which attacks the competitor's transaction by exploiting the competitor's weaknesses and defends our own.

The 7Tao Techniques

The issue at stake is style. Defensive postures are good, but attack is the best form of defence. My fear is that Western corporations, schooled in the Queensberry Rules, are losing the will to win. I have studied Chinese practices on the shop floor and know that they have one aim in life: to replace every competitor in their path. They show no respect for Western regulations, courts of law or ethics. All they want is the transaction, and nothing less. Their business ethics are their own, their regulations serve China and their laws are Chinese and Eastern based.

The techniques involved in combat are both orthodox and unorthodox. 7Tao is a modern system which takes today's economic world as we find it; it does not waste time on dreams of economic heaven. The real world is raw and deadly, but whoever takes it on could win the economic battle and destroy the competition. But of course the prize rose has a thorn. Most people don't like the prospect of economic battle and find it alien. However, those who have experimented with it, perhaps without knowing what they were taking on, found it the best corporate system they had ever tried when applied in the 2008 financial crisis and perhaps further into the future in the coming financial crisis in 2026.

My students have engaged in economic corporate battle simulations and have never looked back. They learned what to do and what not to do, who to fight and who not to fight, when and when not to fight. Their decision-making ability was honed within a month and they felt good. Confidence and a sense of being in control came over them as they discovered something in themselves that they never knew existed. This wasn't boring statistics, or Cost Cutters Incorporated; there were no mantras like 'May you lose your job today so that I may keep mine tomorrow.' Working in teams, they grew united and started to take care of each other responsibly. The systems of the simulated company grew tighter as they learnt to throw out what was not required. Almost overnight, they became successful fighting units.

When customers were brought in to interact with them, something changed. No two competitor styles were the same: every one that came through had a different approach in combat. Some were harsh, others timid, but all were touched by the system. The T'ao system was working well in every area tested.

> **1:** Customers could book a week's course at a time and be trained for industrial battle.
> **2:** They first studied the techniques and systems they would be confronting.
> **3:** Competitors from other 'companies' then challenged them (identities were not revealed until after the battle).
> **4:** They fought for a whole day. This involved building toy-scale production lines of cars, boats, trains, planes and other vehicles to test their managerial, production and financial competence. In a short time and small space they were forged into economic fighters.
> **5:** After the 'high' of economic battle, they were assigned projects so that they could apply what they had learned. The environment was so pressured that students came in as 'soft perception' and exited as 'Iron vision.'
> **6:** They were assessed and rewarded according to the system once they had graduated.

The one thing all the customers enjoyed was the *battle*. Each time they entered the *dojo* (the economic fighting arena), they would be trained to fight a different 'company', in a team comprising fifteen people. Day after day I watched them spar, some winning, some losing. Some losers took it well, others argued to their last breath, trying to justify themselves and unable to accept losing to another company. The losers learned more than the winners. They carried their failure home and were forced to analyse the reasons why they had lost to their competitors. The techniques they learned brought out the best and worst in all of them. The weaker competitors were isolated. There is no place to hide in 7Tao, you either play your part successfully or your team loses. It's pure industrial warfare – accepting losing and winning with intelligence.

The reason why the techniques were so well learned is that they *had* to win, and to win they had to ensure that they were prepared. They learned every one of the defence and attack techniques required in the bouts that were taking place. It wasn't pressure imposed by their superiors that induced them to prepare, they applied the pressure themselves. They simply did not want to lose the battle. This motivation, this feeling of empowerment, instinct for survival and willingness to play as a team is seen in global players. It is what is *forging* (not training) them into superior workers. They fight like cornered tigers or like sharks going in for the kill.

Training is regarded as a necessary evil but 7Tao is different. The 7Tao student is forged in the intense heat of competition. He learns by his mistakes and comes to understand loss; he has to be on his toes all the time. He doesn't concentrate on being taught, but rather on learning and survival. The student is thrown into the deep end – sink or swim. Losing would cost him the title. The 7Tao system speaks to his instinct, his sixth sense, his sense of direction and understanding of balance. Most importantly, it opens up the real world and shows him what he is really facing in the change from the Transatlantic to the Eurasian economic cycle.

Industrial Warfare Comes to the US and the EU.

President of the European Union Jean-Claude Juncker told an audience in Hamburg on March 2, "We can do stupid as well." Juncker was referring to President Donald Trump's threat of imposing import tariffs on certain goods coming from the EU.

"So now we will also impose import tariffs," Junker said. "This is basically a stupid process, the fact that we have to do this. But we have to do it. We will now impose tariffs on motorcycles, Harley Davidson, on blue jeans, Levis, on bourbon."

In reality, however, the EU has already put disproportionately high taxes on U.S. imports. When America imports cars from the EU, the tariff is 2.5 percent. For a U.S.-made car going into the EU, the tariff is 10 percent. That tariff ensures that Europeans drive European cars. We all know that there is a lot more to selling a car than just tariffs, but Trump wants America to export, and to do that, we need to have a level playing field, and this is Trump's main concern.

In response to Juncker's statement, Trump indicated that the United States might start increasing taxes on imports of European cars such as Mercedes-Benz and BMW. If one looks at the strategies employed in global industrial warfare, we have merely scratched the surface. The complexities of industrial warfare go far beyond the trivial argumentative language. Industrial warfare is happening constantly, in all geographies and in all industries.

Even when there is peace between enemies and allies, a competitor will be looking to outsmart his rival, whether a nation-state, industry, supply chain, or product. The key is understanding how it takes place, and which blows to absorb, which ones to block, and how to engage the enemy.

Only around 10 percent of industrial warfare actually shows itself on the surface, in the form of actions such as tariffs, which can be seen as defence mechanisms. Ninety percent of the strategies, tactics, and operations involved in corporate attack and defence manoeuvres are actually under the surface. These are far more discreet and much more damaging to the economy.

Underlying pressures dictate the direction of global battle.

The motivation for industrial warfare does not just rest upon Trump's shoulders. Every country in the world is involved—whether on an international, national, regional, or local level. All competitors are competing and taking each others' intellectual property. In the business world, this process is sometimes described as "benchmarking." With benchmarking—spying, in business terms—questions are asked and gap analysis is done. What is competitor A doing that we, competitor B, are not? Sometimes, visits to plants are even arranged to see the systems, take pictures, create videos, and buy products to take apart.

That's the very first thing Lexus did when they started. They bought a BMW, a Mercedes, and a Rolls Royce and took them apart before creating the Lexus model range. Today, Lexus has taken a large chunk of the high-end luxury car market. No one complained when they did it. And Lexus never complained when their latest car was bought by their competitors BMW, Mercedes, and Audi. All of these competitors know that when we build a product, competitors will take it apart and find out what we have been doing.

Competitors are usually the first to buy the new product, before other customers can even get to it. This is common practice. The Global competitor does it all the time. It's called the learning process, and it takes many forms in the precision involved in executing the 7Tao of the art of industrial warfare. The lesson here is very simple. The key is to learn about the process of industrial warfare and be aware and informed about the strategies that competitors across the world will take.

The issue at hand isn't "stupid" tariffs, as Juncker described them, but instead the nature of an industrial war that has been ongoing for decades, and of which the EU has been just as much a part.

As this battle grows between the three main economic geographies of the world, it is a matter of time before the EU, the USA and China are locked in industrial battle for decades to come. As we move forward, let's see how the USA has engaged China and the EU in industrial warfare.

US takes its first pawns in Industrial War with China

Your first moves in a fight are never the main ones. They are designed to feel out the competition, to engage, and to get a feel for an opponent's speed, power, response, penetration, and reflex. Once you get an idea of your opponents' strengths and weaknesses, then you launch an attack on them with the intent to try to knock them out, push them back, scare them away, or—if you are bold enough—incapacitate them.

On March 22 2018, the Trump administration slapped $50 billion to $60 billion in tariffs on Chinese goods entering the United States. This indicates that the United States is very serious about repairing the $375 billion trade deficit with China and ending Chinese economic theft. This first retaliatory shot in the industrial war with China is likely designed to feel them out, to get an idea of how to strike them, and to counter their strikes.

The Chinese retaliation was comparatively light and placed a $3 billion tariff on American goods going into China. It was basically a block against the first strike—and that's what you do when someone reaches out to your export area: You intercept the strike, instead of attacking the opponent's body.

After the initial blows, the conflict went to the negotiating table, and senior officials with the Chinese delegation have reportedly begun working with the United States to reach a new trade agreement. Initial reports said that China may cave on several U.S. demands.

Yet, as the Roman general Vegetius once famously stated, "If you want peace, prepare for war." If negotiations are inadequate, or if the conflict grows into an open industrial war, both countries would be fighting for their economic lifeblood. With this in mind, we can benefit from gaining a better grasp on how industrial wars are fought on an international scale.

The Workings of Industrial Warfare

Let's take a look at aircraft manufacturer Boeing as a case study in industrial warfare. The Chinese competition was already working to replicate aerospace technology and was partnering with foreign aircraft manufacturers like Boeing while quietly taking steps to replace these same companies in the global market. All of Asia wants technology transfer.

One in every four jetliners that the Chinese buy are from Boeing. As soon as the U.S. strike came, pressure was applied to Boeing immediately, by sourcing other supply chains and holding back financial payments. The Chinese government then levied a second strike of cancelling orders on existing aircraft, rather to produce its own Comac C919 aircraft.

It is obvious that China is creating its own airliner from the technology transfers originally created in the Boeing deals, most of which have already been transferred. China can replace those contracts by contracting other suppliers around the world, with Airbus, Embraer, Sukhoi and Yaklovev being natural examples.

On the surface, it would appear that Boeing was suffering from attacks on Chinese trade, while in reality, it would merely be a hiccup in a longer-term strategy of the Chinese to replicate, then replace, the companies it is competing with.

As the Chinese struck deals, the partnerships it formed with companies were not based on American business culture. These deals were based on the business culture of the Chinese Communist Party—and there is a significant difference.

American companies have complained about this model of Chinese business culture, because it is such a powerful form of industrial warfare, and if taken to court would unlikely survive the ramifications of U.S. law. But the world does not adhere to U.S. law, and, until now, China has played by its own rules in global trade.

The Economic Fight

An industrial war needs legal backing and protections from the government, but it also needs industries to engage in the fight themselves. It is the industries that must take up the gloves and be able to fight for themselves in the area of industrial warfare. Government can nudge them into the market battlefield through funding, education, and support.

With China, in particular, after the U.S. government employs tariffs and laws, and sets the battlefield, it will be on the industries to fight the war. It's on the industrial battlefield where the orders are being taken, where the manufacturing is being done, and where the money changes hands.

For businesses, this means finding out the exact points where products are being supplied to countries, and then engaging with those countries for the same product market.

When a customer goes to a shop, they should be able to see a product on the shelf of that shop. Is it made in America, China, or Japan? The customer then needs to decide whether to hand over money for that product or not. This is what the tariffs can be used for—to keep your product out of the shops, to keep it off the shelf, or to limit your exports down to a trickle. The decision then becomes, "Shall we bother to engage this country in the first place, or shall we go somewhere else we can sell?"

The first shots in the new industrial war have been fired, and we need to analyse the first moves made, where we need to sharpen up manoeuvres, and how we can industrially strike a competitor without getting six punches, two kicks, three knees, and two elbows in the Western economies' face. Industrial warfare is a very complex game, and if you don't know how to play it, you may end up doing damage to yourself.

Industrial War has always been around.

Industrial warfare has always been happening for centuries, both in front of our eyes, in the courtroom and behind closed doors in ways few of us have seen or witnessed. Here are a few examples of industrial battle constantly taking place between competitors:

Competitor A	*The Battle / Product*	Competitor B
Ford Motor Company	*Automotive*	General Motors Corporation
Ferrari	*Sports Car*	Lamborghini
Revell	*Model Plastic Kits*	Air fix
Tesco	*Supermarkets*	Asda
Coke	*Soft Drinks*	Pepsi
Boeing	*Aircraft*	**Airbus**
Lockheed Martin	*Defence*	Boeing
Apple	*Telecommunications*	Huawei

COMAC C919	*Aircraft commercial airliners*	Airbus A320
Supermarine Spitfire	*World War 2 Aircraft*	Hawker Hurricane
Chevrolet Camaro	*American Muscle Cars*	Ford Mustang
Kawasaki	*Motorcycles*	Ducati
Redrow	*House builders*	Barrat
Ali-baba	*E-commerce*	E-bay
Lenovo	*Computers*	Apple
Fedex	*Logistics*	UPS
Harper Collins	*Books*	Simon and Schuster
Corn Flakes	*Cereals*	Weetabix
General Electric	*Manufacturing*	Honeywell
Ford F150	*Pick Up Trucks*	Dodge Ram 1500
F35 Lightning	*Stealth Aircraft / fighter*	J20 – Mighty Dragon

These brands will fight and compete in multiple arrays of fighting styles. In existing industrial battles such as Dodge Ram vs Ford F150, the battle is mostly controlled and actions are contained within a legal framework which limits the amount of industrial warfare competition taking place. Essentially, both competitors are wearing gloves, jaw pieces, elbow protection, knee protection and have a trainer and eagle eyed watching judges in their corner ensuring that the rules are followed. Any below the belt punches are picked up immediately and the rules of competition are quoted. However, these rules are Queensberry based. They serve boxing very well, because the limited amount of movement is constrained to the fists only.

What we have not considered is what happens when completely different type of fighter turns up for battle. What will we do then? Its fine competing with players who all operate within the ring, with boxing gloves, jaw pieces, a stool in the corner with a bucket of water and a towel. What if a competitor turns up who knows how to rip your throat out – using two finger removal thrusts?

If a fighter uses his knees, feet, fingers, eagle grip, elbows, heels, palm, fists, locks, breaks, pull, tears and backs that up with a fighting style that is all brains, how do we engage the competitor?

This is what we face not just with China, but the third world in general. This is what Trump is facing as he takes on the greatest competitor the USA will face in a stiff battle for competition. Donald Trump calls it trade wars, Joe Biden calls it 'extreme competition'. I have labelled it Industrial warfare. At the end of the day, this is a battle for the transaction and its source of victory lies at the heart of the consumer. The consumer wants 7Tao whether they know it or not. Whichever competitor has the best 7Tao will win this war for the 21st century. Will it be America? Or will it be China? Practising the arts of industrial warfare as they have always done in the last 3000 years?

To paint an example of how important transactional warfare has become, we will use the Boeing vs Airbus study to show how the battle between these two commercial aviation giants has played out in the past 5 decades. I have been studying industrial battles between corporations for the last two decades and looked into as many angles as I could process. Industrial warfare has always been going on. It has been happening in every marketplace and with every product in the world and nothing has changed, the game still remains the same. All that has changed are the tools and techniques used to fight these industrial wars. The number of players has increased as more nations have industrialised which has made competition heavier than it has ever been.

Case study: Boeing VS Airbus:

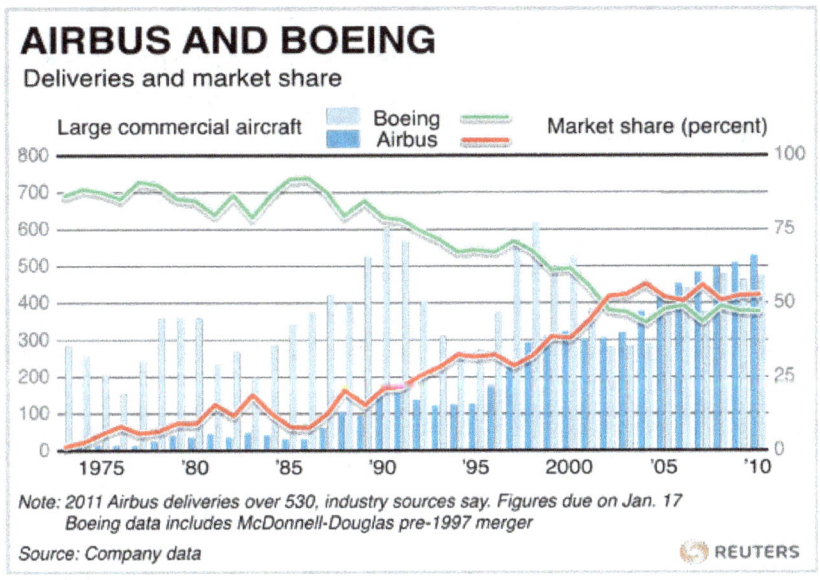

Figure: 3.2 Source: Boeing Company data. Reuters Jan 17th 2011.

Boeing lost two 737 Max airliners. Lion Air of Indonesia lost an aircraft in 2018 and Ethiopian Airways lost an aircraft in 2019 due to defects in the MCAS system.

The fault of the crash was first blamed on air crew, then pilots and then the airlines themselves. None of these airlines did anything wrong, in fact, the pilots and the airlines did everything right. They switched the MCAS system off, they fought the aircraft when it did not perform according to the way the pilots understood. They asked for training in the simulator. They complained when they found that this is dangerous for the passengers.

Boeing did not listen to any of the complaints from both the airlines. In fact, they mocked the air crews, the airlines management and the engineers who were maintaining the aircraft. This resulted in the deaths of all passengers and air crew on board both 737 Max airliners. All of this was shown in the Downfall documentary on Netflix in March of 2022.

What was the cause of the crashes – according to the 7Tao Transaction Analysis process? According to the principles of 7Tao, both sides of the transaction can be seen to create significant footprints inside the Boeing organization. In the table page 102, we analyse the way in which the problems were manufactured because of the corporate culture which served the shareholders of wall street rather than the customers of the world's airlines.

Boeing and McDonnell Douglas merged in 1997 to create a new organization existing under the brand name of Boeing. This led to dramatic culture change in the top management who wanted a performance based approach in manufacturing aircraft. Boeing only had one competitor so far, and that was Airbus from Europe. Airbus had been slowly encroaching Boeing's market dominating position since the Mid 1970's and gently supplying a more diverse and larger number of aircraft as they grew the organization to global level performances. This had massive effect on the way in which Boeing was run. Ever since World War 2, Boeing did not have any competitors, it solely dominated the global marketplace and built solid aircraft and could charge whatever they wanted for price. They had no international competitor so they competed internally on the quality in the job. They had no large military supply chain. With the creation of the 747, which was originally designed as a cargo aircraft, but turned into an airliner, they dominated the skies of every country in the world with the 747 Jumbo Jet.

With Airbus slowly gaining grounds in market share since the mid 1970's, so suddenly, they began to feel the pressure to change. This impacted their company, and the customers began to shift over to Airbus. The transaction parameters of 7Tao started to change, once the pressure was beginning to mount on the company – both internal transaction pressures and external pressures began to show in the way the company was being run.

The Boeing strategy was simple. Take an existing design for the 737 which is now over 40 years old. Put some new fuel-efficient engines on it and sell as many cheap aircraft as possible on the world markets placing airbus under severe pressure to perform. They sold over 5000 units of the 737 in many formations around the world. The workhorse of the world's airlines was about to become the workhorse of the company share price. This lifted the share price to astronomical levels never seen before and made very large amounts of cash for the company.

They could now invest in new aircraft and create a brand-new strategy to expand, diversify and extend offerings throughout the world.

The strategy seemed to work… and then something happened, which affected one product line, the 737, and could affect every Boeing product line. Process changes were for the shareholders; the customers and employees took a back seat. Two of the three entity-based Tao were given no importance and the shareholder Tao was given more attention. This resulted in the massive leap of share price growth as shown in the Yahoo share price chart (shown on page 118).

Internal and external 7Tao transaction impact analysis.

Internally, the pressure which was being placed on the process inside the organization resulted in effects seeping out and affecting the product outside of the organization. As we are aware, product and process are tied together as Yin and Yang. Products are made by processes and the process is the product. The analysis clearly shows how the 7Tao Transaction was affected by the changes in the way the company was run and how this affected the marketplace. We won't go into deep analysis into every single process cause and effect. Rather, we will list down a few of the actions taken from an academic point of view to look at how 7Tao can solve a difficult problem of corporate change within a company.

Transactions must be designed for the customer. The customer cannot take the place of the shareholder or the employee in importance. They all have their place in the transaction and giving more importance and weighting at the expense of the other is a recipe for disaster. Many large corporations have been rendered obsolete in the past simply due to the fact that they did not understand the 7Tao of the marketplace. He we complete a sample analysis of *what the author thinks* happened between Airbus and Boeing and where mistakes were made according to the principles of 7Tao. According to research done on the internet and watching the actual documentary 'Downfall' on Netflix in 2022, 7Tao harnessed the following interpretation of events through our manuals in Industrial Warfare. These are 7Tao findings and we share with the general public in good faith and public interest. The 7Tao transaction analysis provided in the following pages is interlinked through the 7 Tao elements. Each of the Tao connect to each other and the effect of one will affect the other. All 7Tao must be perfect for the transaction to succeed. If one Tao fails, all Tao will fail, then the business will fail.

Defending competitiveness	Tao	Attacking corruption
1: Lower costs by extending the life of the 737 40-year-old design. Add 2 fuel efficient engines to replace the existing ones. 2: Reduce the amount of training required for the airline thereby saving them money and Increasing chances of an order. No training required existing 737 training will suffice. 3: Make large sections of workforce redundant. 50,000 jobs targeted to be cut in 1998. 4: Simplify planes, reduce components and processes. 5: Reduce documentation and signoff & stamping processes. 6: Reduce employee benefits on the shop floor and increase top level performance driven bonuses. 7: Reduce the amount of exposure to quality, documentation and review processes to reduce accountability.	Tao 1: Price	1: Deception was being practised by management to cover up mistakes and push through orders. 2: Quality inspectors were reduced dramatically. Instead of 15 Quality Inspection officers per line, reduce the numbers down to 1 quality officer per line. 3: Complete the quality signoff process by the next officer, rather than a quality officer. 4: Apply automotive lean processes to aerospace and create a high output simple planes process, thus creating a fragile manufacturing process instead of a strong manufacturing process. 5: Push FAA to allow the planes to be stamped and approved. 6: Threaten employees who speak up with 'extreme hire and fire' practises. 7: No writing down, no accountability of the crime. Reduce the amount of writing down.
1: Reduce amount of manufacturing actions, thus increasing output. 2: Reduce quality monitoring actions, thus increasing output. 3: Reduce components, shortening production lines.	Tao 2: Delivery	1: Quality suffers as a result, thereby affecting customer safety. 2: Increasing passenger numbers creates stuffed discomfort aircraft for airlines.

4: Reduce workforce and increase overtime payments. Add temp staff for dips and troughs. 5: Decrease supply chain, ordering from fewer suppliers. 6: Increase subcontracting and subassembly opportunities. Push manufacturing into the supply chain. 7: Redo all of the deals with suppliers. Get more from them for less. Thereby passing the problems into supplier's hands. 8: Increase output targets for employees by reducing focus on quality and reliability process parameters. 9: Reduce airplane hours of work from 11 days to 8 days per plane. 5500 unit hours of work down to 4000 unit hours of work. 10: Put an automotive production line based assembly rather than one spot create and deliver.		3: Increase payload capacity creating heavy planes with more power. 4: Product design specifically for airline profits thereby increasing sales of aircraft quickly. 5: Reduce weight of airplane coupled with more lift and carry capability not suited to an old 1967 design. 6: Source new materials, structures and processes to allow for efficient aircraft design and build shorter production lines. The old 737 structures were not capable of handling the changes to an adapted market. 7: Increase number of Work in Progress aircraft on the production line creating more processes in line, stretching employee hours and stress. 8: The next process has to be reached, because the aircraft moves 2 inches per minute on the production line. This decreases ability to check and increases 'move it on' actions. 9: Increase production of aircraft from 31 a month in 2005 to 57 a month by 2019. Trying to make Boeing into Toyota.
1: Use other quality process based tools such as Six Sigma rather than the sign off processes used by the FAA for decades in the past. 2: Focus on fixing statistics rather than fixing problems representing	Tao 3: Quality	1: Non use of FAA processes effected the structural integrity of the plane by using automotive philosophies and corporate quality check tools.

better graphs rather than good quality. 3: Shareholders own the airplane. Quality of delivery involved planning for per flight return on investment. 4: Increase stress analysis on existing structures to handle performance changes. No new components to be made, just existing designed to be strengthened. 5: Increase supplier quality performance parameters, replan design and pass the stresses to the supply chain. Reduce the component inspections coming in. 6: Reduce inspectors from 15 per shop floor to 1. Signoffs now done by employees. 7: Reduce amount of failures to be recorded to lower levels. 8: Reduce the sensors on the outside of the aircraft reducing costs while maintaining performance process.		2: Pretty charts rather than shop floor employees proud of a job well done. 3: Employees and customers own the airplane. A strong link between customers and employees of Boeing needed to be broken. 4: Flight return on investment weakened the old design. These kinds of massive performance changes needed a brand new aircraft design. 5: Deceive the FAA into thinking standards were being maintained. 6: Conceal stress breakages, employee stresses and broken shop floor processes. 7: Do not record incidents of quality failure. 8: Increased allowance and descriptions of minor incidents and reduced major quality incidents allowing for greater capability of failure. 9: Fewer back up systems creates larger failure modes and effects. Increase in foreign objects debris.
1: Relax descriptions of standards to customers on aircraft. 2: Reduce amount of training needed for new aircraft. 3: Create reduced characteristics about the MCAS systems.	Tao 4: After Market	1: Test pilots deceived customers and regulators in tests. 2: Cover up training requirements for MCAS leading to fatal failure modes and effects catastrophe.

4: Create good press about the airplane. 5: Sell capability and more cash flow to customer. Thereby selling the airline a transaction rather than an airplane. 6: Restrict the number of complaints and lower the noise levels of customers to minimal. 7: Move as much stock back into customers hands from Original Equipment Manufacture and from Repair and Overhaul processes. Keep it flying. 8: Increase rotables, repairable and consumable parts.		3: Deceive the FAA and conceal the danger of the system to FAA AEG processes. 4: Leave MCAS problem for later, fix it in 2020 when we have space and more money. 5: Ignored and mocked customer complaints and failure reports as 'stupidity'. 6: Possible dangerous issues were called irresponsible analysis by Boeing thereby bullying customers. 7: Keep old parts passed as much as possible. Increase new parts supply into old parts inventories.
1: Focus on costs, competition and shareholder value from Mcdonnell Douglas rather than engineering excellence and safety from Boeing. 2: Create cheaper more capable aircraft to sell them cheap and make them do more. This gets the airline greedy for more money by investing in Boeing trust accumulated over the last 70 years. 3: Change priorities at CEO and board levels. James McNerney became the first Boeing CEO not to be an engineer running from 2005 to 2015. McNerney Harvard MBA originating from McKinsey. He increased revenue, cut costs and was infamous for strategy and marketing. 4: Make customers a part of shareholder strategy rather than a	**Tao 5: Customer**	1: Retrofit an old 737 rather than create a new aircraft. Airbus had the advantage here because it created the A320 from scratch in 1988. 2: Airlines were sold a transactional solution and not an airplane. The customers and the passengers suffered as a result. Temporarily, they did make a little extra profit from the old design. But the price they paid as a result of safety nearly collapsed each airline along with Covid 19 temporarily suffocating all demand for 2 years from 2019 to 2021. 3: James McNerney and Dennis Muilenburg pushed sales and marketing watching competitors airbus rather than customer demands.

Tao in their own right. The transaction process and shareholder process reaches right into the customer processes. 5: Look at customers from an order point of view rather than a customer expectation point of view. 6: Offer all Airbus customers a cheaper option and look for demand orders in marketplace through airlines competitors, air shows and customer relations. Focus on beating airbus to get the order rather than meeting customer needs. 7: ask what the customer wants. This means listening to their concerns and adapting aircraft delivery to airline problems and not aircraft building. This will mould Boeing to look at the world through airline lens and not through aircraft manufacturer vision.		4: As customers became a part of shareholder strategy, their rights and values were removed to become a performance value rather than a delivery of expectation. Both these processes are merged creating confusion in employees and ignorance in customers. 5: Major safety parameters missed, concealed and ignored. 6: By focusing on the competitor Airbus, transaction parameters were stretched for the customer through existing platforms rather than creating new platforms. Fear of losing was driving sales rather than meeting expectations through investment and product planning. This cut many corners from employee concerns and customer needs thereby reducing product performance and increasing customer transaction performance leading to a product elastic snap.
Shareholders want the following: 1: More Aircraft from less people. 2: More aircraft with less components. 3: Cheaper aircraft with less investment. 4: Faster production lines with less rigour of testing materials.	**Tao 6: Share holder**	Shareholders got the following: 1: Weaker plane manufacture based on automotive principles. 2: Aerospace and automotive principles do not mix. One flies in the air and one rolls on the ground. 3: Aircraft are about wing and air flow. Cars are about tyres and road grip.

5: Less quality coverage because most of the 737 design has already been tested. 6: Wider product applicability. 7: More market availability with wider application. 8: More shareholder returns with greater means of doubling the stock. 9: Doubling the stock means reinvestment into the company.		4: Justifications of economics will lead to possible quality problems. 5: Wrong manufacturing systems can lead to product failure. This will lead to breakage. 6: All Boeing transactions will collapse as the centre of the company implodes. 7: Aircraft breakage is lethal.
1: Reduce quality checks by inspectors. 2: Reduce number of quality inspectors. 3: Reduce number of employees by making 100k redundancies over a decade of mass layoffs. 4: Reduce the time taken to build the aircraft. 5: Increase output of the production line. 6: Increase speed of manufacture.	Tao 7: Employee	1: Make 100k employees redundant. 2: Lose decades of expertise on the shop floor. 3: Lose key workers who go to other industries like Airbus. 4: Lose facilities such as educated skilled employees passing valuable lessons to new employees. 5: Lose training centres. 6: Lose customer facing employees who are trusted by the global customer.

So what happens next to the Boeing Share price?

We are currently going through the return to normal phase for Boeing stock price. But this will begin to go down further if the 737 Max problems continue to plague the company. This will lead to a larger sell off coming in the later part of the curve. As this impending problem hits the Boeing stock price, the selloff will worsen leading to the stock price hitting lower levels and affecting the company in negative ways.

A possible scenario for Boeing could be as follows: Boeing will begin to place counter strategies to arrest the collapse by making even more redundancies, collapsing product lines and offering strategies to service customer lines. This could lead to a breakup of the company as McDonnell Douglas is sold off to become an independent company and Boeing is sold off to becoming its normal mode of existence going back to be headquarters in Seattle where the culture can be returned back to normal before 1997. An engineering culture will take over servicing an existing Repair and Overhaul operation stemming back to its original engineering operations. Boeing will begin again, servicing its current Airline customers and going back to the drawing board on original equipment manufacturing.

Meanwhile, Airbus will clean up the global market and become the dominant competitor until Chinese company COMAC can take over Boeing's position to become the main challenger to Airbus.

Lessons will be learned and applied as COMAC try not to make the same mistakes as Boeing did. This will be vital to surviving the competition against Airbus.

As Boeing bows out of the future, the Boeing VS Airbus battle will come to an end and the COMAC vs Airbus battle will just be beginning. It is possible that COMAC takes over Boeing and becomes the dominant supplier inheriting the Boeing supply chain and customer marketplace. It's what happened in the 70s when the Airbus corporation entered the market.

COMAC are now developing multiple route and range aircraft for through routes across Eurasia as they ramp up to challenge Airbus and Boeing for domination of the global markets. If their cash flow is strong enough, it is likely that they will be strengthening across the 5 continents as their numbers increase and their market penetration grows deeper. COMACs research and development will increase and their innovation rates will become much more developed. They will also be catching up to innovation from the West as well, constantly honing their transactional capability and increasing market relevance as they grow more supportive and embraced with their customers. The constantly tightening relationship across 3 dimensional metric measurements will create stable relationships with countries in the future.

Boeing Bubble Burst.

I'm forever blowing Boeing bubbles … pretty bubbles in the air.

Figure: 3.3 Source: Investopedia, Tradingview.com (BA long term chart – 1987 to 2020.

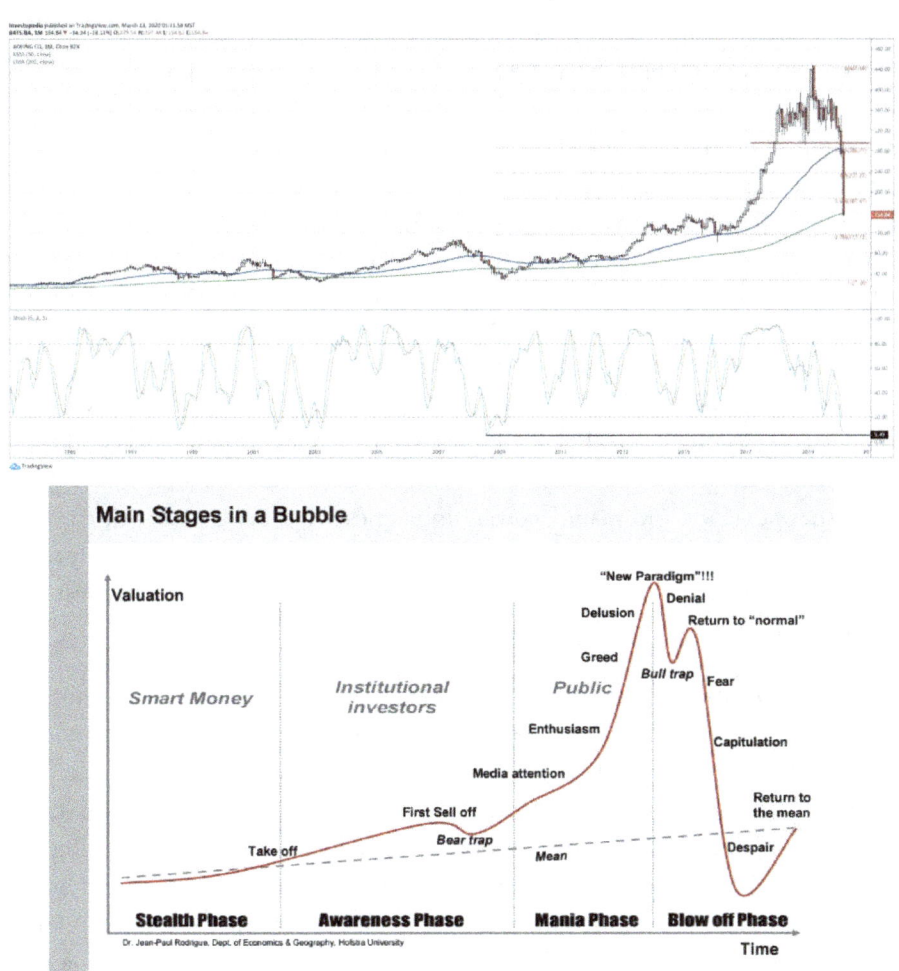

Figure: 3.4: Source: Bubble chart: Dr Jean Paul Rodrigue. Hofstra University.

It's ironic when you actually look at the chart. But bubbles always burst the same way. In hindsight it's an easy thing to see, its knowing when the bubble will burst and how to respond, that's the hard part. You have to get out at the right time. The big bubble burst to come is the 2026 depletion. This one is the one that everybody thinks will not come... so how do you know that this will actually happen?

Dr Jean Paul Rodrigue really has nailed the bubble graph philosophy by reading into tulip mania and analysing exactly how bubbles form, bubble up and then pop. The academic version of the bubble graph is quite uncanny when you compare it to Boeing graph from 1995 to 2021. The bubble has burst in exactly the same way all bubbles burst. In the authors view, the 7Tao equation at Boeing became unbalanced, shareholder returns instead of employees and customers, reduced prices, compromised quality, overzealous delivery targets and layoff after layoff since 1998 has produced a shell of a company which sacrificed the needs of the factory to give to the needs of Wall Street. Main street lost as it always did.

Every time, the story was the same. American Factory closes down, Wall Street loves China, invites them in to compete in the United States. The American people were being robbed of jobs, land, stability, housing and security. Something had to give, something had to break, people were so fed up that they turned to the most unlikely president that they could choose to represent them, Donald J Trump. Trump knew that the old manufacturing industries were being sold off, closed down, moved abroad, broken up and rehashed as smaller entities. He promptly put the blame squarely on China, just like he put the blame squarely on Japan just as he did in the eighties.

Boeing suffered at the hands of incompetent management running at the behest of Wall Street. These managers tried to turn Boeing into Toyota. Instead of taking those pieces of the Toyota Production System which would work for Boeing, they instead tried to shoehorn the aircraft industry into an automotive driven production line. This cannot be done in Aviation, the lead times are simply too high because of the nature of the parts and components. Aerospace is a high investment - high inventory industry, with large inventories to support maintenance and repair. That is the nature of the industry, you can't change its nature. You can't turn a gorilla into a lion and you can't turn aerospace into automotive. If you try, you will end up killing the company and destroying the American presence in the marketplace.

China has been watching, learning, thinking and reflecting upon the actions of the Boeing executives in cahoots with the fund managers in Wall Street. The Chinese will not repeat these mistakes. They will do this by limiting the stock market, placing fund managers and speculators such as the Wall Street boys into ball and chain environment. They will create laws that ban these actions, but they won't be able to stop the biggest bubble that will affect the whole world. The 2026 depression and bubble burst.

Until then, the US China trade war will turn into industrial war and we will keep watching the board change in the chess play of industrial war between the US and China. It is then that the real industrial war will begin, when the reality of the factory is all that remains, and when everybody is on the floor with a collapsed trading system. You will only be as good as the tools in your hands.

As the US counters China's industrial war, transactions are key

Trade warfare is just a tiny part of industrial warfare. In physical terms, it is the scream before the fight. There is a lot more to industrial warfare than meets the eye.

The West needs to understand that to fight China in an industrial war, you had better know what you are doing. This is a completely different opponent altogether. There are no Queensberry rules here. That means no gloves, no referee to stop the fight, no throwing in the towel, and no medical staff to tend to your wounds.

The aim of industrial warfare is not to win according to a set of rules, or to win a game of some kind. It is designed specifically for one thing: to put the opponent out of business. And it has been working very well for the last three decades that China has been using its own version of industrial warfare—the effects of which have depleted American manufacturing, sapped natural resources out of Australia, and allowed the Chinese economic domination of Latin America and Africa.

Industrial war is the fight for manufacturing, and this extends to the fight for natural resources, shipping channels, intellectual property, skilled employees, and a long list of other assets.

The United States is now entering this fight, after allowing the Chinese relatively free reign for decades. President Donald Trump may place $60 billion in tariffs on Chinese goods, and this may help establish a set of enforceable rules in this domain. But the Chinese are unlikely to agree without testing the boundaries of the ring.

As the United States enters this field, it must first understand that in any conflict, the key is in preparation. Those who are more prepared, who have made more calculations, who understand the terrain that they are engaging, who understand the enemy, who understand the moves the enemy will make and counter with—who understand the nature of the battle—are the ones who have the better probability of being the winning side.

The key word here is "probability," as things can be uncertain even when the battle may look as if it has been won. A single unlucky strike can render your entire effort useless.

In a kinetic war, the type most nations are used to fighting, the main weapon looks like a projectile: a bullet, missile, bomb, or arrow. During the war, you fire as many as you can against an opponent until you defeat their army, forcing them to yield to your terms of surrender.

In industrial warfare, the projectile looks like a transaction. The more transactions you make, the better your chances of winning the conflict.

Transactions Are Key

There are thousands of attack and defence techniques in industrial warfare depending upon which industry you operate and with countless combinations for forming actions and responses. This creates massive potential to build complex strategies.

Yet, within all of these techniques, the most important objective in industrial warfare is based on one thing: transactions. And this is the objective that the Trump administration has taken head-on. The more transactions you have, the bigger your business. The fewer transactions you have, the smaller your business. This rule applies to anyone in business since most people are in business to make money. Nothing else.

A transaction can seem more complex than it immediately appears, however there are only 7 measurements to any transaction, and these apply to the seven methods of securing a transaction. These are price, delivery, quality, aftermarket, customers, shareholders, and employees.

When all of these seven elements of a transaction are firing on all cylinders, the business senses are sharp, and the machine that drives it is well-oiled, in tune, and ready for growth. After transactional growth has been achieved at home, the industrial war fighter will be looking for growth abroad—in other lands and among the economies of other nations. That's when it becomes very serious.

Attacking and Defending Transactions

In order to secure transactions, we need two simple directions: one that moves into the territory of a competitor, and another that defends our territory.

The defensive system in industrial warfare is designed to save money and keep it inside the demarcation battle line—which means in your own country, or, in China's case, within China.

The attack system is designed specifically to invade a competitor's territory and to take their transactions. If this is taken to an extreme—as the large nation states have been doing—entire geographies can be depleted of their industry, ecosystems starved of transactions, and the local populations depleted of their livelihoods, leaving economic devastation in its wake.

The state of the current battlefield is a big part of why Trump was elected. The United States has been on the receiving end of global industrial warfare for more than five decades, and the results are showing in cities like Detroit where industrial depletion has rendered the working population redundant. This Detroit effect is spreading right across the nation as the waters become more shallow and competition in everything becomes so endemic that people simply cannot make a living anymore.

Under the effects of an economy depleted by foreign industrial war, like a starved body, the local economy begins to cannibalize itself, and the targeted country will be forced to sell off its resources and assets to survive.

Not understanding industrial warfare has a massive effect on a population, will make the voter base change their approach to politics, and will suffocate the civil service, which is run by taxpayers. If its effects are not curbed, the instability resulting from economic depletion through industrial warfare can even lead to civil war. This reared its head on January 6th 2021 where republican voters suspected wrongdoing in the American elections.

While it is technically nonviolent, the effects of industrial warfare can be just as devastating as conventional combat. Thus, it is vital that the United States understands the nature of the war in which it has been engaged, and which the Trump administration has begun to counter.

This tussle between corporations of American and Chinese origin will be the focus of the new war between these two Superpowers. China does not even address herself as a superpower, she feels that this name is steeped in a bygone era of the past 20th century, long dead with the Soviet Union. The basis of the battle will be simple, the American government must help US corporations win by providing support to their aims. The Chinese government must help their corporations win by supporting them. The battlefield is the entire planets marketplace. In most cases you have an entrenched established competitor who plays by 20th century Queensberry rules, and on the other side you have an up and coming competitor who does not play by Queensberry rules at all. China feels suffocated and unable to innovate by these rules of trading emanating from the 20th century. If China wants to increase its global footprint, it must fight according to its own rules.

This is going to be fascinating to watch as a new set of rules is developed by the US and China as they fight to dominate the planet. Will they agree on terms and principles? Will the Chinese trust the Americans after the debacles of the past? Will America or China survive the 2026 recession which will be 100 times worse than the 2008 recession? Will they break even more rules just to stay alive and allow their corporations to breathe? How will smaller countries engage the US and China as they try to make the best deals from this fight as each superpower will be targeting smaller countries geographically?

In the next 7 Chapters, we look at each of the 7Tao in order and understand the work that has been done in this area of economic competition between these two superpowers. Creating a simple process, we will go through each of the 7Tao chapter by chapter, ensuring that the reader has exposure to the concepts of this critical form of thinking and philosophy which challenges the Western world of 20th century rules and regulations.

Once we have completed the analysis of the 7Tao by analysing each Tao in its component form, we will summarise and then introduce the concept of the Art of Industrial Warfare in Chapter 13. Here we will go through all of the industrial warfare related concepts in its poetic and Sun Tzu based form. This final thirteenth chapter lays down the world of industrial warfare in its most basic form. Understanding how industrial warfare can be written in Sun Tzu terms, provides us with a viewpoint on how to function and navigate in a new world of conflict where battles will be fought on territories which we do not recognise.

CHAPTER 4

Tao 1: Price:

Are You Getting and Giving Value for Money?

How much should you charge the customer for the product or service that you supply? If a business fails to equate price and value, it fails.

Entrepreneurs ask several questions. Is there enough work in this product to keep the business going? Will it deliver a good profit? Will it attract further business in the future? The 7Tao approach reduces such concerns to one issue: competition. What is the scale of the threat from the competition? Am I doing enough to stay ahead of the pack?

7Tao makes a great deal of competition. The art of competitive strategy is more wide ranging than is assumed in the West. It holds accountable every single process that leads to the delivery of a product or service. There must be complete control over the process from initial order to final delivery. After all, it is in every process that you are in competition with your rivals. After all, the product will be made up of similar processes for similar products.

In most organizations, once employees are attuned to the day-to-day job it becomes mundane. People don't see that the world has changed because all they see is the four walls that enclose them. They interact with the same people every day and their conversations are repetitive. Being oblivious to changes taking place around you can be fatal.

This happened in Britain in the 1970s and 1980s as competitors caught up. Too many British people believed that strikes would help their cause. This cleared a space which the Japanese marched into. Their products were cheaper and of better quality; they were delivered faster into the marketplace, and they came with excellent after-sales support. The result was happy customers, smiling shareholders and well-trained employees. While Britain was disunited, the Japanese were united in triggering the cascading downfall of the UK's manufacturing industry. And the Japanese are still here, running profitable plants in Swindon

(Honda), Derby (Toyota) and Sunderland (Nissan) during 2012. Where I live, in Luton, the General Motors Vauxhall plant has closed down a decade ago in 2002.

Defending Price Strengths

Defending the price of a product requires a critical step-by-step examination of all of the pressures involved in holding down costs and raising the price as high as possible. In between cost and price lies the yield needed to keep the business alive. There are two approaches to this conundrum. The first is to pass the costs on by charging the customer a higher price. This would prove fatal in a highly competitive environment: your business would be crushed by cheaper competition. If others can offer the same or more for less money, they win.

The 7Tao objective is yield. Yield is by far the most important element of any operation. The focus should not just be on cutting costs: a firm can cut itself to death. This has been the error of many companies which have tried to survive by cutting so much out of their operations that they end up not being viable. This is what happened with Rover, the British car company. Pushing profits up starts on the shop floor. It starts with the transaction. Each and every process completed by every single worker is a transaction. The measure of any organisation is how strong it is on the shop floor, where hands touch the product. The greater the intelligence with which the hands touch the product, the more money you will make from the added value that this brings to the product via the manufacturing process. True, there are support services within the management structure which are essential to the operation. Fundamentally, however, a car company is measured by the number of cars it sells, an aeroplane company by the number of aeroplanes. Profit is an accumulation of yields collected through all the processes that go into making that particular product.

7Tao begins the process of transactional accounting by measuring the workers' production processes on the shop floor. We study the factors that affect that particular job. The workers have to be trained to international standards reflecting the fourth-generation world in which we now live. This requires critical thinking, but the 7Tao system arms us with useful techniques. We need to look at ways in which price can be controlled and in doing this every single detail of the way in which workers operate needs to be assessed. We don't just look at labour costs, material costs, energy costs … we look at something far more basic: the profitability of every individual process which each worker completes. Profitable processes are essential if a product is to be saleable.

The primary power of China, or anyone else starting up whether as a nation or as a company is to begin on Price. I constantly go to the supermarket and see new entrants who offer the same quality as established brands beginning their journey into the marketplace, ushering themselves a market presence. Almost every single one fights on price to begin with, this allows them a foot hold into the marketplace while they navigate the different forces they must engage.

Their competitor will be watching them and thinking their main steps to counter their growth strategies one they have entered the market. Usually, this means buying them out and buying out their market share. This will add their brand into the portfolio of the bigger competitor and remove any threat the smaller competitor was presenting. This is common practise in the marketplace when you are working in the West. In the East however, the culture and the economic landscape is different. The aims and objectives of the competitor will also be different leading to a direct confrontation in the global marketplace.

The Eastern trader's culture is completely different from the Western trader. As they have no legal apparatus to observe, they have to rely on their wits to survive which means they have to educate themselves in a hectic marketplace which resembles more street environment than the law office. Much of their experience comes from street trading and getting beaten by a chaotic system where there are no rules at all. This means that it is survival of the fittest from the word go. Animal kingdom instincts come into play as the trader is pushed from pillar to post in games he does not understand at an early age. This is a common story in China and everywhere else in the third world. Business people meet deception when they begin transactions and have to start from the bottom up with no legal recourse other than the bribes they can pay to win a court case which has very little effect on the outcome of their business. How do you navigate an environment where there is little direction, where the waves are higher than the boat your in? You have to turn to transactional analysis and know your environment in exact terms. Measuring your competition and being in a group of traders allows them to survive as a group. It is then in the interest of the group of traders to look after each other because if one of them goes down they all go down. They can then group together an focus on keeping their prices under control.

Box 4:1: The Big Diesel God

Here we have a prime example of China's fighting prowess. One of these vehicles is an established US brand, the other an upcoming Chinese brand. One manufacturer is going to complain about Queensberry Rules not being followed, the other is going to shake that off like water from a duck's back. Some will call it cheap imitation which hits below the belt, others will call it flattery and say it is fair game. Some will go on about copyright, others will just accept what the world has become.

Can you tell the difference? **Pictures taken from Wikipedia commons usage**.

The Chevrolet Silverado is an instantly recognisable truck in the United States. It has been part of the staple American automotive diet since the country began its journey on the road to 20th-century industrial dominance. Let's get a measure of these two vehicles. One is 5.7 litre petrol, the other 2.2 litre diesel. One is made in America, the other in China. They are around the same size. One has been around for generations while the other is its company's first real offering. One costs around $50,000 new, the other $17,000. One is a proven durable vehicle used by millions, the other is an upstart. One is powered by the famous GM V8 engine, the other has a Toyota engine. **So, which is better?** Let's take you down somewhere where there are poor people. They've seen these things on TV, there are so many American TV shows running all over the world. They like the truck, they want the truck, but they can't afford the truck. Then they see this BDG offering. Which one do you think they will buy? Would you buy the cheaper one, or would you stay loyal to the brand and buy the more expensive one? Or perhaps buy five for the same price? This is what the world was like before all the legal underpinnings took over the West. It is what the world looked like when China was king. *There is no copyright. There are no Queensberry Rules!* The art of industrial warfare is the most important subject any manufacturer in the West can study. It is a fundamental strategy for fundamentally challenging times. *Choices... choices... choices...*

Introducing a new approach into the workplace will create instability. Dealing with that transition is the responsibility of management. They can reassure employees that the intention is not to cut jobs. Quite the opposite. The intention is to strengthen a particular role, to gear it up to international standards. This is the key challenge: How do you get someone to change? Managers may fear resistance, as in 'Joe Bloggs in Block C won't accept anything I tell him.' But there is a way to engage employees. You have to appeal to their competitive spirit, and also stress the well-being of the community in which they live and work. The objective is not just to change the individual, but to change the entire community. This means involving everyone in the activities that complete the transaction. You have to use language that Joe Bloggs understands, *the language of competition.*

That is why 7tao encourages employees to participate in effective team-building strategies that use competitive activity to achieve targets. They are trained by facing the sort of intense competition that is unique to the marketplace. 7Tao does not confuse them with complicated statistics or 'management speak'. Motivation exercises presented as 'development' are avoided. Our aim is to secure 100% results from every worker we train.

The employee, whatever his place in the organization, whether in tier one management or tier five on the shop floor, almost always achieves a 1:10 return on investment. For every dollar the organization puts in, it gets ten or more back. Usually more. Once the ball starts rolling in an organization, it goes on and on. Process by process, worker by worker, yields start to improve, and this is reflected in the bottom line. The pressures of the fourth-generation world of business are built into these dynamic training sessions. At every stage, workers become more aware of their position, what they do and how they operate. The key to the survival of a business is taking them away from the four walls that surround their daily jobs and introducing them to the reality of the modern world. The pressures management face when they have to make decisions are revealed to the shop floor; in this way unity is achieved across the organization. These pressures must be shared equally if the organization is to succeed.

Attacking Price Weaknesses

Within everything there is good and bad. Recognising and promoting the good and reducing the bad is fundamental to creating a position of strength. Within any transaction there are strengths and weaknesses. Eliminating transactional weaknesses and promoting transactional strengths is fundamental to creating good yields in the workplace. It's not easy to recognise strengths and eliminate weaknesses in a process. You have to learn how to recognise and isolate them first.

One of the most powerful features of 7Tao is its capacity to *attack weaknesses*, to destroy any weakness in a company before it festers and becomes endemic in the workplace culture. Any weakness left long enough to turn economically septic will spread and attack a company's yields, undermining that part of the organization's process, making it obsolete in the marketplace. A process dies when weaknesses overtake it. This can lead to product death, and finally corporation death. A business will go stale very quickly if not invested in innovation daily. As the number of competitors heats up, the speed of innovation will inevitably quicken too. Keeping up with these changes is fundamental for any company.

Understanding Price changes depends on many factors, internally within the organization and externally from the economic environment. Internally, one can control costs as best as is possible using process analysis of each of the 7 Segments of the transaction, externally there are two main factors which we need to consider influencing the right price. Competition and economic environment.

The nature of economic competition however has changed beyond the limits which any western legal system can handle, making the laws of the Western world largely irrelevant. For us to be able to challenge the growing power of Eurasia which is 10 times larger than the transatlantic nations in most ways possible, we first need to accept this fact. Complacency and depending upon rules which do not serve us comfortably any more is the first stage to recognising that the world has changed. All third world countries and their citizens see the Western world as a soft touch and ignore the rules and norms we consider daily routines. There are two way we can go in this particular situation. Either we force people to follow the rules and end up destroying our nations through 'double down' stubbornness, or we adapt to a world which is rapidly changing in exponential terms into one which is Eurasia centric. Immigrants who come into the western world looks at the west from a 'soft touch' point of view. They come to earn money, complete difficult laborious jobs and rarely assimilate into the indigenous population. They form communities within communities, cultures within cultures and increase their population. Price is their primary concern from start to finish.

Box 4:2 The Fierce Dragon

Experimental aircraft have been stars of the aviation industry for decades. Trust between the Israeli and American aircraft industries was a great source of pride for both countries. And then this happened...

Pictures from Wikipedia commons, November 2010

They look amazingly similar, don't they? How come? Official lips are sealed, but it has been suggested that the J10 programme is somehow related to the cancelled Israeli Lavi fighter programme.

What the Chinese said: In an interview, the general designer of the Fierce Dragon, Mr Song Wencong, stated: 'Our nation's new fighter's external design and aerodynamics configuration are completely made by us and did not receive any foreign assistance; this made me very proud. Our nation developed the J9 in the 1960s, this adopted the canard configuration. So, those statements that said J10 is a copy of Israeli Lavi are just laughable.'
source: http://military.china.com/zh_cn/news/568/20070105/13858504.html

What the Israelis said: As the Americans were investigating the possibility of this technology falling into the wrong hands, the then director general of Israel's Ministry of Defence said in an interview that 'some technology on aircraft' had been sold to China and that some Israeli companies may not have 'clean hands'.
Source: David Isenberg, *Asia Times*, 4 December 2002

What the Russians whispered: In May 2008 Janes Information Group reported several Russian sources claiming to be involved with various Chengdu military projects. A number of engineers, designers and technical specialists described visits to Chengdu and other areas of China in the 1980s. One source alleged that high-level Chengdu officials claimed to have a single Lavi prototype at one of their facilities.
Source: Janes Information Group, 19 May 2008

What I think: Well, I certainly think there is a resemblance. Just a little ... But you make your own mind up! I'm quite sure some sort of ferocious industrial battle has been going on here. Who won and who lost? China, Israel, America...? Who were the winners and who are the losers?

Competition will result from two types, internal competitors, and external competitors. Internal competitors, e.g. Ford and GM competing with Chrysler will retain prices approximately within the same bandwidth as your price because the same pressures that go into building your product go into building their product. External imports, however, are another thing. Companies like Walmart actively discuss the competition and look to attack competitor retail outlets through pile them high sell them cheap strategies. The nature of the industrial war is fought at retail levels, and this is where Chinese made goods will gain a foothold and turnover on the shelf space. If the shelf space is stocked with multiple goods from internal and external environments, external imports and internal home-made goods. It is primarily the price that will dictate the speed of the product going off the shelf. The rest of the sales process will be a conversation about quality and warranty support. Therefore, the home-based manufacturer must stress on the strengths of the product being homemade brands, made in the USA.

If however, the home made brand builds in China, does little assembly in labelling inside America and distributes through similar channels, they may be able to match the foreign competitors pricing power. This is what brands are doing today in general. They build in China, ship back over in the USA, label their product as Made in the USA, and shift product across the nation. So that's how they get around it…

Recent examples showed that Tyson foods factory in the United States had shipped their chicken cutting operation to China. They had lowered their cost of cutting and packaging the chicken into saleable portions. This was slightly incorrect, what actually happened was that a wrangling negotiation indicated that China wanted to export its chicken processing plants to the American market and compete directly on price terms, making China the largest poultry exporter in the world. If they could achieve export into the American market, they could export to every market in the world after that achievement. It's the license they are after, and they will use price as a spearhead to achieve that license. 7Tao identifies weaknesses in an organization before they can proliferate. If we attack them before they damage the yield of each process, we can end the threat of process obsolescence before it begins to infest the operating environment of the workplace. This requires diligence and understanding; it requires the employee himself to face the fact that he may not be part of the profit-making process.

Box 4:3: Boys' Toys and Businessmen's Profits

Children's toys and models is the area of manufacturing that industrializing countries try first. Hong Kong began by making Dinky 'hot-wheels'-type cars for American companies. China has followed hot on the heels of countries like Malaysia, Hong Kong, Japan and South Korea, making exactly the same things. However, the Chinese were different: they didn't just produce for someone else. They produced for themselves and directly supplied overseas customers with their own brand of a similar product. What is the difference between these two buggies? There is none. Both work exceptionally well. Both are radio controlled, one metre long and can go at 70 mph. And both look good. Ah, one difference: the price of the Chinese copy is substantially lower.

Pictures sourced from Pixabay

The Industrial Warfare Element

Whether you play with the Chinese copy or the original HPI Japanese model, a toy is a toy, an hour of playtime is an hour of playtime. The question is, how much are you willing to part with while you wait for the 'I want it' fever to wear off? This is the big question for parents. The child will play with the new toy for a week, then they'll store it away somewhere for years. When the child's grown up they'll realize what a lot of junk is left to sell at car boot sales and yard clearouts, including this buggy.

Here come the Chinese. 'Why do you want to pay $2,000 for that truck when you can pay $300 for ours? If you contact us directly via the internet we'll deliver it right to your door from China? How much loss do you want to take? You could save $1,700 to spend on something else.'

> **How Do They Do It?**
>
> They spend more time on assembly processes than we do because they rely on manual labour and our processes are automated. They have to pay their employees; we have to pay for electricity to run the machines. They have to assemble the same number of pieces as we do and pay for the same materials. They have to produce *exactly* the same truck as we do. So why is theirs so much cheaper? How can they lower their costs and still keep their workers happy? The answer lies in their economic model. Their economic system is not yet as mature as the Western one, and they are free to design it differently, to suit their economy. The difference lies in what they tax and how they tax it. Their aims are the same as ours: they want Chinese companies to dominate the world; they want people to have jobs and to enjoy the new freedom they have as consumers because this will ensure the stability of China while the rest of the world is plagued by youth unemployment. The stability of China depends on their ability to win the economic war. China and the Chinese people come first. Period. No negotiation.

7Tao relies on intensive training and project allocation. We arm employees with as many tools as possible for the attack. Once they have learned how to use the correct tools for one or more of the 256 attack methods (see Box 4:2), they begin the process. Anything they identify as unnecessary to the marketplace is isolated and eliminated. It is necessary to trust the workforce, communicate the objectives of the organisation and engage them in activities which will make a difference. Until they are trusted to go out into the shop floor and defend their product, you will not be able to win in the economic battlefield against competitors who do not play by the rules.

Pricing starts with the order

So where do you start to improve the yield process? The answer is with the order. Once you obtain an order, you immediately start to defend the strengths and attack the weaknesses so that the yield is achieved as soon as possible. As there are many tools to choose from when defending strengths and attacking weaknesses, you must learn which to use and when. These are key parameters to improving performance. The worker needs answers to the questions, 'What do I do? When do I do it? How do I get there?'

> **Box 4:4**
> **Some of the Attack Techniques Studied**
>
> Here are some of the attack techniques studied by 7Tao students as they figure out how the modern-day industrial world operates.
>
> Attacking customers – Attacking shareholders – Attacking employees – Attacking the ideals and culture of the company – Attacking suppliers – Attacking logistics – Attacking management – Attacking finance – Attacking information – Attacking ideas and concepts.
>
> Using deception – Employing spies – Manipulation of information – Sabotage: orthodox and unorthodox techniques – Trickery and deceit – Delay tactics – Creating fear in organizations – Removing motivation – Destroying unity – Using laws against a competitor – Exploiting arrogance – Exploiting business environments – Removing strictness – Attacking the plans of a competitor – Ranking and isolating terrain – Attacking the manufacturing process by using over-production – Attacking the company using waste arising from time in hand – Inducing transportation waste in an enemy's business – Increasing processing waste – Installing extra stock on hand to increase waste materials – Creating unnecessary motion and extra movement – Increasing defective goods throughout the plant chains – Attacking leadership systems – Weakening long-term strategic planning through constant destruction – Attacking customer and market focus – Attacking information – Attacking human resources – Attacking the management of processes – Attacking business results – Attacking workers – Attacking materials – Attacking machines – Attacking manufacturing methods – Attacking the measurement system – Attacking places – Attacking procedures – Attacking policies – Attacking agility – Attacking partners – Attacking innovation – Attacking legitimacy – Attacking the culture of an organization – Pre-emptive attacks – Attacking brands and brand identity – Attacking protocols and standards – Attacking the 7Tao consumption criteria. Many more attack tools and techniques can be combined to produce devastating patterns with which to understand and defeat your competition in any part of the world.

Two figures are combined make up the yield. You add the value of defending the process to the value of attacking weaknesses in the process to achieve the desired yield. The return on investment is measured by subtracting the amount of money the company invested in the 7Tao process from the amount of returns measured in the yield calculation.

To understand this, look at the diagram below.

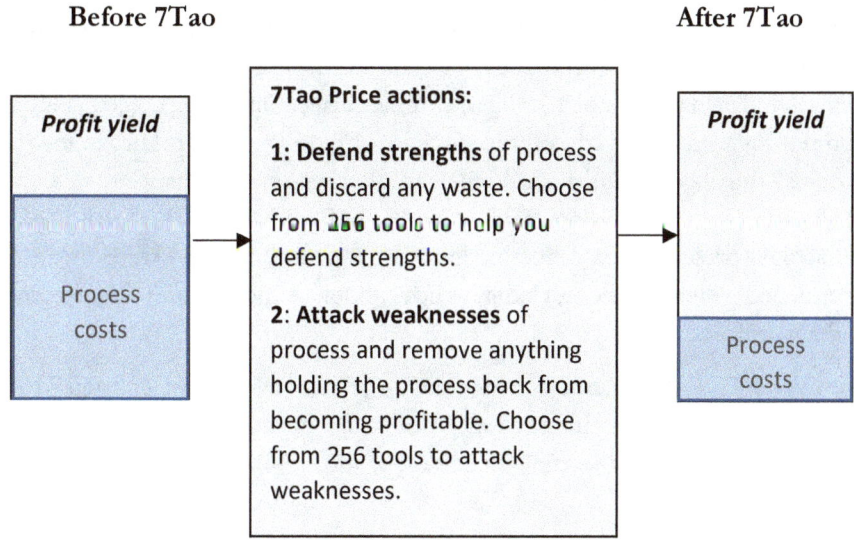

The process yield is larger in the after diagram because clotting in the system has been eliminated. This is fundamental, to improve process flow as well as to remove any gaps within the process. When we defend strengths we are eliminating waste. When we attack weaknesses we are removing anything which is stopping that process from producing a larger yield. It's like clearing arteries in a medical procedure: we not only thin the blood but also remove any obstacles that impede blood flow. We not only make the process responsive but also actively remove any difficulties that slow it down.

Having applied the 7Tao principles to price, we now have breathing room in which to manoeuvre the business into a competitive global marketplace. We can now choose either to lower the price, without going into debt, or to raise it if this is made possible by the absence of competition. If the competition is heavy, pricing must fall into a band or belt where the competitor can survive. If price becomes irrelevant or is too high, the customer will not come to purchase the product.

7Tao: Case Study 1

Altro Ltd

Altro Ltd is a leading manufacturer of flooring who wanted to improve its workplace environment in the face of increased global competition. The company knew what it wanted. Cheaper rivals were nibbling away at its market share. Altro called in 7Tao who practised improvement understanding using the Business Improvement Techniques NVQ qualification. The results speak for themselves: yield returns of 1:10 were commonplace. On some projects massive yield returns were achieved as these students of the 7Tao method began to recognise the huge potential within their plant. They saw the chance to get involved in top level decision making processes. By the end of their training course their projects were delivering impressive returns and they were reconfiguring the shop floor, changing how it looked and felt, and was perceived by the workforce.

Pat Patel, the manufacturing training officer at Altro Ltd, enlisted 7Tao to improve the firm's basic transaction process and measurement system. Here he explains how he found the implementation of the 7Tao system on the Altro shop floor.

"Altro is a Times 100 company which has repeatedly received awards for being 'the best manufacturing company to work for in the UK'. It has in fact received many awards in multiple categories for the development of human resources and for becoming the best company in its field of manufacturing flooring, walls and resins for markets across the globe." Says Pat Patel.

"7Tao approached Altro, offering training in their economic and manufacturing system. At first the sheer size and complexity of the 7Tao system was daunting. The Master came in and explained what training would be offered and what benefits the company could expect. I could see the advantages that it had over Six Sigma. What I didn't understand was what economic combat actually looked like and how it could help the company. I warmed to it because of the excitement it offered. I hadn't seen anything like it before, in spite of having a degree in manufacturing and working for several other companies. Several of the officers from the shop floor also came along and they found the same. What was this and how did it work? We were curious to find out how it could be related directly to the transaction which Altro was completing. Everything was being looked at from a transactional viewpoint and from a competitive angle. We were excited enough to try it and to see how much of a difference it could make to the company. Trying new things was embedded culture in the company. No one had tried this before, so we wanted to make a go of it.

The 7Tao system: The course was going to be five to six days long and it would explain some of the most powerful concepts that we had ever seen. The 7Tao system had tools which were being used to control:

Price: Tools for attacking price competitiveness and tools for defending our price.

Delivery: Tools for attacking delivery problems and tools for defending our delivery times.

Quality: Tools for attacking defects and tools for defending our quality.

After market: Tools for attacking after-market service competitiveness and tools for defending our after-market strategies.

Customers: Tools for attacking established markets and tools for defending our customers.

Shareholders: Tools for sustaining the share price and tools for growing the share price.

Employees: Tools for attacking weaknesses in employees and tools for growing strengths in employees.

The whole system was based upon these Seven Tao principles. Everything was looked at from this one middle transactional point of view, we are being on one side and our competitors on the opposing side. We listed all the intelligence we had about our competitors to run it through the system. The 7Tao system started to build a comprehensive picture of where we stood in the marketplace and how we should operate as a company to increase our growth. We took it very seriously because everything being discussed was real. It was based on our own knowledge of what was happening in the marketplace and how this was being reflected in the workplace. It was very exciting asking questions from every competitive viewpoint. Everybody was racking their brains saying, 'How can we beat them here?' In everything, we were looking at the weaknesses and strengths of our transaction and selecting from the huge combination of tools provided by 7Tao to find out what our position was in the marketplace compared to our competitors. Every training day was fascinating because, as the teacher of the system explained how markets work, and which tools were to be applied to each one of the 7Tao, we slowly came to understand where we would fit into the full transaction. This dominated our thinking every course day. It was massively competitive and asked us challenging questions. Slowly but surely, with the accumulation of knowledge, we started to understand where we were sitting in relation to our competitors and how we should be thinking to dominate the marketplace.

Training: The training was tough. Everything we had learned in theory had to be applied in practice to the economic combat simulation. Three teams of five people were asked to compete against each other in the building of a racing car. The racing car came in pieces which we had to build within five hours. It wasn't as easy as just building the racing car, we also had a budget which we had earned in the course through our performance in applying the tools to our business. Each team had to compete against the other two teams, which would be actively attacking us and defending against us. In the class we had learned how to combine and apply attacking and defending tools and so we had some idea of what was coming when the other teams attacked us – we knew how to defend ourselves against their attacks. We had all learned to use forty tools in defence and forty tools in attack in order to create a balanced system, so no one team had an unfair advantage in any form over the other teams.

This simulation was purely designed to test our operating capability in the marketplace allowing us to visualise our strengths and weaknesses in operating in a world where people would not respect the laws under which we were operating. Even if they did not attack us directly in our homeland, they would definitely attack us on the international marketplaces where our laws do not apply or are ignored because of irrelevance to their culture. We had to see where we stood. This meant understanding the terrain of the transaction and being able to predict where our competitor would come from, what direction the attacks would take place and how ferocious the attack would be. Sometime, the opponent would feign an attack on us and then attack the other team instead forcing us to reveal our transactional position. This was devastating to our teams cohesion and capability.

Nobody trusted anybody else on the build day. The economic combat was brutal – the teams went out of their way to win the marketplace and manipulate the different stages of the build strategies to dominate their competitors. A furious competition emerged with teams engaging in all sorts of behaviour to try to outwit their competitors in every way possible. It was striking how much knowledge the employees had absorbed in a short time. If they didn't, they would lose, and nobody wanted to lose. Everybody wanted to win, so they learned as much as they possibly could to ensure that the system served them and gave them an advantage in building the production line. The simulation brought out the best and worst in all the people who were taking part in the competition. Everything we thought we knew about each other had to be revised. People we thought were weak came out strong and people we thought were strong came out weak. It was simply amazing watching the pressure and the excitement of this formula-one-level event tearing everyone's weak points out and bringing out strengths they never knew they had. We had never really been exposed to the marketplace in this way before, it was so brutal, competitive and close to the truth. With so many different people trying to gain an advantage over the others, each round of economic fighting was exhausting. It was the speed of the event which took us by surprise. That was easily the fastest day we had ever lived – five hours went like five minutes. The day had gone before we even realised it, and each of us was exhausted at the end. However, we still wanted more; we didn't want it to end.

The results: The results at the end of the course were astonishing. With Six Sigma, all we were looking at was quality (Tao Number 3), through a statistical eyeglass, and that became tedious, repetitive and quite frankly boring. Here with 7Tao, we were looking directly at the transaction in all its forms and within a balanced attack and defence framework. The three-dimensional view of the transaction showed us exactly what the market looks like, firstly in terms of establishing the transaction of a process, secondly in defending that transaction, and finally in attacking the marketplace. 7Tao had a vision of where we were, where we should be in terms of market leadership and what we needed to do to get there. 7Tao understood the velocity of the transaction and what this meant with regards to the strength of the company. What really shook us was the rate at which it could increase the speed of a transaction as products travelled through the factory. The result was amazing. We achieved an average return on investment of 1:24 right across all of the students we applied the system to, and who in turn applied it to their workplaces.

7Tao put all of the other courses we had completed to shame, making them look weak and irrelevant with regard to achievement and, more importantly, excitement. This is the key word, *excitement*. I could not stress this word more than is necessary. This is the best word to describe 7Tao.

Conclusions: It was the best decision I made for the company and was well received by the leadership of the company in the final presentations. It blew us away when we saw how much impact it had achieved in such a short time for Altro. The factory was changing at an alarming rate physically. Many of the students who went on the course were stunned at how much was achieved in just six days.

I had taken a risk in choosing 7Tao, a slightly more advanced system than others being offered to me, but my hunch was proved correct. This was truly different to anything I had ever learned, and it ended up turning everything we had thought of on its head. The relevance was what got me in the end, the way in which each problem has already been described for you, the effect it has on the organization and how easy it really is to fix it. Problems are not so bad when you are actually able to solve them using the 7Tao method. I can understand why it is thoroughly Chinese in its design and implementation. It does not waste any time at all, just gets in and out of your transaction, cleans it up and shows the way in which the East looks at us in the West." Pat Patel. Training manager in Altro Ltd in 2009.

Walmart: The foreign and home based outlet.

Inbuilt obsolescence is killing the Walmart business model. According to market principles and the demand changes of the transaction, Walmart is out of date, out of touch, and out of depth in understanding the way in which the transaction culture has changed.

The Walmart model was built upon real estate, square footage of space and the yield that each square foot of space can yield a return on investment. That is the basic style of trading that Walmart was built on. In order to drive transactions, Walmart opted for a pile them high, sell them cheap approach with goods being sourced from US, EU as well as China, India, Vietnam, Malaysia, and many other Asian countries. It was the outlet for manufactured goods being produced in the East.

The corporations that owned the goods manufacturing plants closed down the factories in the United States and sent them to China to create even greater yields for the holding companies that were eating the yields for these goods. Transaction costs were the target and part of the plan was to release these goods through established retail brands that contained natural scalability and large goods holding capacities. Walmart fits this description down to the last nut and bolt.

The logistics that supported this transactional design allowed massive throughput of products, effectively suffocating indigenous manufacturers across the United States. This produced layoffs affecting large portions of the U.S. population as manufacturing industry jobs trickled down to a tiny selection of products that consisted of military products and high barriers of entry products such as aerospace and defence. These were the only products that were not sold at Walmart. After all, where do you store an airliner or a jet fighter?

Although China has been blamed on many fronts, the truth of the matter is that it was the U.S. holding companies, business owners, and shareholder voting systems who opted for this to happen and effectively encouraged its growth as the sell-off took place over a 22-year period since the year 2000. This model of outsourcing has been done before, with Japan, Malaysia, Thailand, and many others. The process is labelled globalization. It has changed the very nature of work itself.

Change of Transaction Logistics

Delivery of very low prices, quality acceptable to legitimate standards, warranty-based aftermarket, customers who were happy to part with little money for a standard product, shareholders who were happy at the thought of massive return on investment, and Walmart employees who were becoming the go-to place for lifelong employment ensured that the transaction continued for as long as possible.

The Walmart model transaction did not just deplete the manufacturing industry of the United States, it also literally wiped out the mom-and-pop stores that littered the North American landscape. Now that Walmart had an effective model, the rest of the world's large retailers watched carefully, and simulated and emulated this style of trading. These types of stores came from everywhere to surround the waterhole and drink in the same way that Walmart was drinking.

Here in the UK, Sainsbury's, Marks and Spencer, Aldi, Lidl, and countless others are doing the same thing as competition increases, and the increased heat being produced by this retail war forces each retailer to start turning to cannibalization in order to survive. At every corner each retailer turns, melting returns on investment rates are forcing shareholders to put pressure on the company to produce the yields they require.

Any form of loss produces massive downswings on the share price as the losses multiply and cascade into all areas of the firm. This then produces even more pressure on management to pass and relay even more pressure on the employees to come up with good ideas, suggestions, and improvement schemes disguised as cost cutting to produce results for the shareholders of the firm.

This is not just in Walmart. It's everywhere, all over the world, in every retailer and in every high street with boarded up outlets that used to house businesses. All retailers are sourcing from China India and South Asia to source the cheapest goods to place on their shelves just to survive.

Where Do We Go Now?

We understand that the supply chain has produced these results, and yes, we also understand that blame is being channelled up to the leadership of the country resulting in proclamations based upon divisive politics. The immigrants who enter the United States and Europe are feeling the same pressures as they flee poverty based upon the business model described above. President Donald Trump has nailed the problem very well, and it is not just the Trump administration that is telling the truth. This is also showing up in Italy, Spain, Britain, Germany, France, and throughout Europe. Fascism could return in Europe as people struggle to contain the overspill of pressure associated with each family that is being dragged through this set of very difficult economic circumstances. The pressure that this is producing on the public services and any unions that the EU was developing is breaking unity and annihilating plans for the future.

Changing for the Better

What must be done is very simple. Bring the factories home and do everything to avoid a kinetic war that encroaches upon the world as it enters an environment of international exchange levels. The problem lies with the family, giving them their freedom back and the chance to make a living just like they used to. No amount of sexualization of the youth can replace the fact that the system is broken and does not function anymore. Future generations of our nations will be like deer in the headlights, paralyzed as they fall into the trap of internal and external strife and very possibly civil conflict.

Yes, it began with a transaction that suited Walmart, snowballing into something unrecognizable in today's market economy. Transactions have been seized from the family and this is producing massive undercurrent pressures in society that have shown up in the voting system. It is likely that in the future this will lead to increasingly tense political environment leading to clashes and conflict in the streets.

Trump, EU convulsions, and Eurasian nationalism are not the problem. The problem is figuring out how we got here and what should be done to improve the situation. We either do it peacefully or we do this violently through war. If we do this violently through war and throw our problems on Asia's doorstep, and Eurasia responds in kind, this will produce an inevitable nuclear war involving Russia and China.

If we don't fix the problem internally, the pressures spilling onto the streets could produce the environment for an incremental path toward civil war over the coming decade. This will be exacerbated by the advent of the 2019 recession and the massive 2026 recession which are threatening the very existence of the West itself. Times might be good now, but the chickens are about to come home to roost. It is completely within perception to think about what the governments will do to cover up the 2019 to 2021 recession. The last time it happened in 2000 to 2002, it was Y2K, 9/11 and the War on Terror. What spurious incident will cover up the steep drop about to happen in the stock market when the inverted yield curve turns up on our doorstep in 2019?

Another big worry is that after Afghanistan has ended – same as with the Soviet Union, the spooky return of inflation could lead to run away hyperinflation leading to economic collapse. It will be absolutely vital that the central bankers raise interest rates to counter the effects of runaway inflation which will occur after 2021. If inflation is not controlled, we could be looking at the destruction of the USA during 2026 when a financial crisis 100 times the size of 2008 forces governments to choose between house prices vs treasury bonds. My estimation says that they will choose to raise interest rates thereby collapsing the property market to levels where owning a house will be relatively easy.

Those who take great pride in saying 'I have 23 houses' as a measure of wealth will suddenly find those properties dragging their economic position down as they seek to cut their losses and exit the marketplace. How do you sell that many depreciating properties when no one is buying, and everyone is selling? Better think of fire sale strategies now.

In the spirit of Walmart, new property websites will crop up specialising only in discounted, repossessed and foreclosure properties. These will dominate the headlines as the governments choose between national and country debt and people's personal debts. First time buyers, landlords and property speculators will be hit out of the field. This begs the question, what happens to the financiers who are pushing all of this? Last time it was Lehman Brothers, AIG, Royal Bank of Scotland and many others. This time in 2026, the objects of worry will be deeper, the targets will be Bonds and Currency and other financial instruments. If they decide to point their frustrations at the Russians and the Chinese, this will result in possible nuclear conflict and definitely conventional conflict in selected countries where the superpowers and economic regions have political and economic borders. They may retarget the Middle East; however, this will just result in another 20 years of tiring protracted war like Afghanistan – this hasn't served the West since 2001, it will not serve the West now. However, the 2026 crisis recession will affect the currencies of the world which will have direct pressure on the populations of the West. Will this turn into multiple versions of January 6th, 2021? This remains to be seen as protests around the world increase daily as the cost of living goes further out of reach of most families on the planet. Prices of all products then will be out of reach because the money printing spree that has lasted since 2008 has now turned into a tidal wave of liquidity which will sweep any form of value out of the reach of customers. If there is no value for money, then why should there be money? BITCOIN and other digital currency strategies have been designed to counter this argument, so the message is clear. We either protect our currencies, or we won't have any currencies. Once alternative stores of value begin to rear their heads, we know that there is a problem. Value is trying to find a home, and if we don't give it one, it will go elsewhere in search for stability. Just like water, value finds a stable place to settle. The Euro, Pound and Dollar better start thinking about their positions.

This is where the crisis will reach an absolute pinnacle of worry for everyone on the planet. 2026 comes beckoning. The tide will go out. And the future will show who was ready and who was not.

CHAPTER 5

Tao 2: Delivery: Is it On Time?

How many times have you heard words like these? 'They want it done yesterday … rush order … The customer is complaining that we're not on time … late delivery … We'll have to increase our overtime hours to fill the order …'

This happens when a business is not managing its time properly. Overcoming the problem is vital in a marketplace where new competition is emerging from all over the world. One bungled order can mean the permanent loss of a customer. You lose revenue which should have been passing through your accounting system, and this can make the difference between remaining open for business and shutting down. At the very least you may have to reduce the workforce as business ebbs away.

Many delivery methods have been developed in the past three decades, among them Lean, Just in Time, Lean Sigma and 20 Keys. They all aim to get the product delivered on time, in response to the demands of the customer. Too often, when a delivery is due, your people are still dashing about the factory looking for what component goes with what and ending up making a part delivery because the resources are not available to complete the order.

Many SMEs (small to medium-size businesses) do meet their delivery dates, so why is it that you can't complete yours? In addressing the problem, we must start by understanding how to prepare for the dangers in the marketplace caused by late delivery.

The first thing to remember is that 'time is money'. If you can't organise your time you will undoubtedly lose money in the long term. 7Tao takes a firm stand on time-based elements. The sooner your products are in your customers' hands and out of yours, the more profitable your business will be.

This isn't a new idea. You are probably already doing it to some extent. The Toyota Production System, for example, aims to adapt shop-floor processes to overcome situations in which sub-assemblies hold up production. The key to solving the problem is attitude. People on the shop floor tend to resist change. Faced with complicated tasks, they prefer routines with which they are familiar.

They tend to think that pressures on the business are management's problem and nothing to do with them. The top management wants more capability, more action, more competitiveness, higher yields and more profit. You are left reading management report after management report as the number of new ideas proliferates. You become almost numb to all the fads, which makes it easy to retreat to familiar methods in your search for solutions in response to pressure from above. That's what corporate survival in the modern world is like. If delivery is to be on time every time, it is important that the customer understands the strengths and weaknesses of your delivery process. Better methods of defending strengths and attacking weaknesses can then be formulated.

Defending Delivery Strengths

7Tao is different from other methodologies in that it does not seek to embed itself in the corporate culture with mantras. 7Tao delivers customer targets, not a philosophy. Defending the delivery of a product requires thinking about the process step by step. The aim is to eliminate problems on the production line which obstruct the completion of output. To achieve this, we have to look at products at the 'work in progress' stage. There will be processes within your operating structure that are strong, and these must be identified. These processes will include different assets – people, machines, suppliers, knowledge, attitudes. Garnering these strengths and separating them out from weaknesses is the starting point in trying to improve the implementation process. Once we have defined what you are good at, we can examine what you are not good at and reveal the weaknesses that are clogging up the delivery process.

It all starts with examining the process at the most basic levels and following it through to final delivery. We must then break each component process down into practical elements so that we can get to grips with the length of time it takes for a product to work its way through the production system. You may say, 'But we are already doing this, using Six Sigma' or such. The problem is saturation. With current methodologies you never reach saturation point. The saturation point is reached when the system, the philosophy, becomes embedded in the workforce, when the method is used every day to solve problems and moves on to the next generation of problems.

Box 5:1 - Lessons in Stealth and Industrial Warfare

F35 – Julius Delos Reyes: Wiki commons   J-20 – Alexandr Chechin: Wiki commons

Chinese test pilot Xu Yongling called the J-20 a 'masterpiece' of home-grown innovation. He said the F-117 technology was already 'outdated' when it was shot down: it could not be applied to a next-generation stealth jet. BBC, 25 January 2011

United States House Committee on Armed Services Chairman Howard McKeon said of the J20: 'My understanding is that they built it on information that they received from a Russian plane that they were able to copy'. *Straits times, 19 January 2011*

Russian military commentator Ilya Kramnik conjectures that China is still ten to fifteen years behind the United States and Russia in fighter technology and may not be able to manufacture all the advanced composite materials, avionics and sensor packages needed for such aircraft, and could instead turn to foreign suppliers. However, he speculates that China may be able to produce the J-20 at a cost 50% to 80% lower than US and Russian fifth-generation jet fighters.
RIA Novosti military commentator Ilya Kramnik, 29 December 2010

What the press said: Balkan military officials told Associated Press that China and Russia may have adopted some stealth technology from a Lockheed F-117 Nighthawk which was shot down by the Serbian military in 1999 during the Kosovo war.   Associated Press, 23 January 2011

What the author of *The Art of Industrial Warfare* says: Eighty per cent less than the competition! The competitors' aircraft will be made, put into the desert, covered in white plastic and left to rot there in Amar C, G and F desert storage facilities in Tucson, Arizona. The aim is not to use them, the aim is to sell them! Don't bother making them if you can't sell them.

Unit cost of the American F35 on the left: $132 million. *Aviation Week*, 10 March, 2011
Unit cost of the Chinese J20 on the right: $50 million. Estimated by Amar Manzoor
Delivery time: China 10 years; America 30 years. Estimated by Amar Manzoor

> **Box 5:2 - The Story of Madame Li and Dayang Trands the biggest suit maker you have never heard of**

Li Guilian, or 'Madame Li' as she is called by her employees and Warren Buffet, was a simple farmer's daughter when she started her business thirty years ago. She began with just one sewing machine. Her aim was to ensure that poor peasants had decent clothes to wear. She made work trousers, shirts and new sleeves for existing clothes.

When China's economy opened up in the late 1970s, she took a trip to Japan to learn how suits were made. Little by little the company began to make more complicated garments as they advanced towards the design and manufacture of high class, high quality clothes. It took Madame Li time to learn the complicated art of suit-making but with patience and endurance she mastered high quality tailoring and began the arduous process of exporting suits back to Japan. Her company Dayang Trands now makes fifteen million garments a year and exports to all four corners of the globe. She supplies clothing to Banana Republic, DKNY, Calvin Klein and Marks and Spencer.

The company grabbed every opportunity to promote the sale of its suits. No chance was written off with 'It will never work'. They always aimed for it, and hit their target. Madame Li sought out Warren Buffet of the internationally famed Berkshire Hathaway when he was opening a metals factory in China. He was measured and a bespoke suit was produced and delivered to him the next day. Impressed, Buffet decided to invite her to one of his board meetings, which then turned into an opportunity for Madame Li to suit him in the best production she could design. (Later Warren Buffet claimed that some of his business partners were wearing Trands clothing too.) 'Warren Buffet has given the company a major boost,' said Madame Li.

It didn't end there. Bill Gates also became a customer, and Chinese President Hu Jintao wears Dayang Trands. As opportunities arose, Dayang Trands expanded into every market they targeted, and all areas of clothing manufacture. The growth curve has not just been phenomenal, it has been electrifying. And the key to seizing every opportunity was delivery of product quality and delivery of a quality reputation for every suit wearing individual in the world.

Word of mouth in delivering quality is always the best.

If the results of a system are really to take effect, you have to be able to answer the following questions positively:

- Is the workforce defending the company against the competitor?
- Do employees know that there *is* a competitor?
- Are they involved in the defence process?
- Are they doing what is required for us to stay competitive?
- Are they actually applying the method to the workplace, or are they using it just to get us managers off their backs?

This is where the 7Tao defence method scores. The 'buy-in' that gives it the advantage over other methodologies is that 7Tao doesn't force-feed the shop floor, it just encourages them to respond to a ferociously competitive environment. It empowers the workforce to deploy their skills. The only time a 7Tao student will sit in class is when he wants to recuperate, and to contemplate the lessons he has learned through the intense economic fighting in which he has been engaged. *7Tao uses the intense heat generated by the economic combat process to bring about changes in attitude, process or return on investment.* Through induced confrontation, the business can be raised to its optimum level of performance.

The purpose of meeting a delivery target is to maximise profit. If the time taken to produce is reduced, this will improve a project's return on investment. This adds more value to the yield. Once employees understand the firm's delivery strengths, they will begin to recognise weaknesses in the delivery process. The end result is a reduction in the time it takes to produce the required results.

Attacking Delivery Weaknesses

Weaknesses occur when people do not know how to manage a set of new problems, or recurring problems, in the cycle of production. Problem's fester and proliferate until they infect the whole plant, causing it to become uncompetitive in the marketplace. Competitors strike when these weaknesses become a corporate disease. Competitors can smell them in a business. In no time they will attack your market share, taking as many customers as they can away from you. You will end up with products you cannot sell. In extreme cases, whole industries can be taken out, as happened when the Japanese attacked the British motorcycle industry in the 1970s.

The search for weaknesses in delivery should be unremitting. They must be terminated before they expose the firm to its competitors. Weakness is revealed by the market and by competitors.

The first step in attacking weaknesses is to identify when and how they occur. This involves exploring their effects on the business.

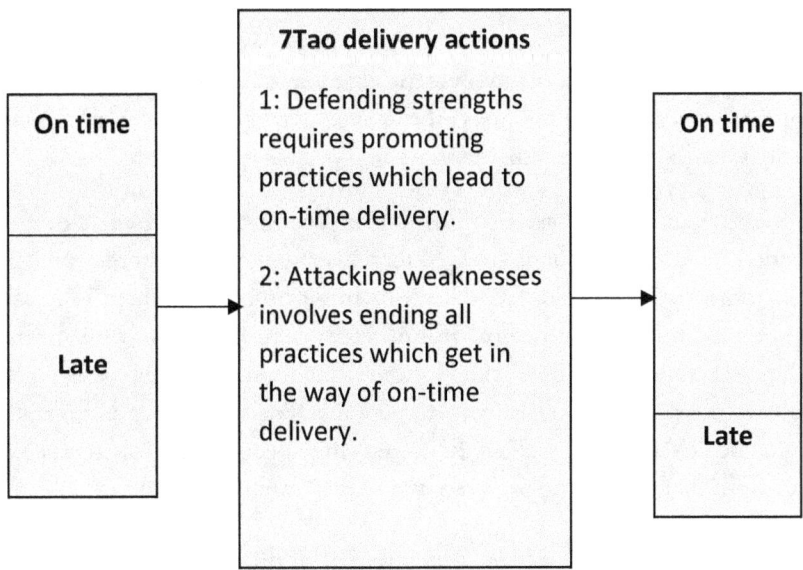

This is not as easy as it looks. You may be saying, 'I've tried everything to end these time problems, but I just can't get rid of them.' Racking your brains and blaming others gets you nowhere. The challenge is to unify the workforce so that everyone works together to solve the problems.

To do this you have to secure the empathy of the workforce. This is probably the biggest difficulty you are facing. You know what to do, you may even know how to do it, but time is running out. Your bosses don't care how you get it done, *just get it done!* The difficulty is getting the workforce to act. How do you motivate them?

The 7Tao approach is based on *forging the student*, not training him. This works because it encourages 'buy-in'. Its beauty is the process of performance.

Students judge a learning programme by the degree to which they enjoy it, not by its mantra. The more they enjoy it, the more involved they get. Motivation requires breaking away from the norm, doing something different, putting effort into the process of change in ways that have not been tried before.

Delivery starts with the customer's order.

Who calls '*Go!*'? Some will say the customer when he says he wants something. Others will say you, when you get the first lot of supplies in to start the manufacturing process. Delivery starts with the delivery date and works backwards from that point. Achieving it involves production scheduling, one of the most difficult challenges. Management sets the delivery date but they may take away the inventory required to achieve that target.

You may have to pacify half the workforce who are idle, while others are overloaded. The supply chain is stressed to deliver something yesterday which was ordered tomorrow. How do you deal with these problems? There is no single answer because only you know how complicated the problems get when pressures like these accumulate. The 7Tao solution involves spreading the pressure throughout the plant by ensuring that everyone across the floor participates in achieving the delivery process. Success comes when people work together, creating a momentum that is fulfilling for everyone as the target is achieved.

7Tao achieved this within Johnson Matthey by using powerful economic fighting systems to create a 'burning platform', which students use to power the business. Achieving this 'burning platform' involves getting workers to respond to problems so that they are connected to them day by day. This is by no means an easy task.

It basically translates into understanding all of your processes in your workplace and enable change processes both above your station in management and below your station where workers are functioning for you. Further to this, you will also have to communicate process changes by engaging your co workers who are on the same level as you in the organization.

Box 5:3: The Sneaker War

Pictures from Wikipedia commons

Nike has over 180 factories producing sneakers for the American market. The last time I checked Alibaba.com, there were over 112,000 suppliers of sneakers in its database.

Hang on ... this is one serious marketplace. There are eight billion people on this earth and almost all of them get through at least one pair of training shoes in their lifetime. Eight billion people on this planet – that's a lot of sneakers! Sneaker wars Continued over the page…

Case Study 2:

Johnson Matthey, Noble Metals: By Grieg Sneddon

Johnson Matthey PLC, an international powerhouse of manufacturing, supply precious metals to producers of catalytic converters and speciality chemicals. At the time Greig Sneddon was continuous improvement manager and, although he was nearing his retirement in 2009, he decided to implement the 7Tao system through the BIT NVQ approach. Our approach was standard 7Tao practice: get the students sparked up and motivated, get them to believe in themselves (rather than making them believe you); through competition and play watch them immediately improve their performance. During 2009 **Greig Sneddon** was witnessing the remarkable impact of 7Tao as he played one interaction after another in the design of the Transaction in Johnson Matthey improvement projects. These resulted in improvements across the plant as students linked money directly to work and understood how business was conducted in the engineering department through a transactional interface.

Sneaker wars continued... When I was growing up I used to take my trainers with me when I went to Pakistan with my mother and father. The visits were forced on us; we had little interest in going there but we were encouraged to find out about our roots (later on in life we tried to forget as much as we could about our roots). The kids there were so impressed with our shoes that they'd ask us if they could have them when we were leaving for the UK. None of them could afford such shoes. They cost £45 back in 1986 – well over 1,000 rupees; basically translated, that was a whole month's salary. I'd hand the shoes over when I left and buy cheap sandals to wear on the flight. I never gave the shoes to a kid who asked for them, I gave them to the kid who was the quietest, the one who everybody picked on, the one who was called the worst names because he was poorer than the rest of them. Usually this was the Pashtun fleeing persecution from the Soviet Union.

The last time I went back to Pakistan, in 2004, what I saw surprised me. All the kids were wearing high class sneakers and Levi jeans. 'How much do they cost?' The little Pashtun kid I used to give sneakers to was now a practising doctor. He used those very shoes I gave him to do the work that no one else was able to do because they didn't have the right footwear. With the money he earned he learned English and was awarded a scholarship for poor children by the Red Cross/Cresent. Eventually he became a doctor. He was delighted to see me when I went back after nearly twenty years. He took me to a shop that was offering sneakers for sale at 100 rupees or 200 rupees – the most expensive were 300 rupees.

How was this happening? Everybody wanted to buy such shoes. They all liked Western dress and wanted to be seen as Western. The programmes on TV were Western; even the women were becoming Westernised. The American dream was being delivered by the Chinese! The demand was huge. The delivery of product to marketplace was faster than any Western competitor could have achieved. The Pakistani kids wanted the American dream and they wanted it fast. Chinese suppliers were delivering it fast. They were dominating the market before their competitors arrived.

Affordability and matching product image to an area where they cannot achieve consumption is the key. The kids want to be seen as a certain style or fashion and the Chinese supplier gives them what they are looking for. In certain terms, the mentality of the consumer counts as the Eastern trader recognises exactly what the consumer wants through sharpened instincts.

In the following report **Greig Sneddon** describes the remarkable impact of 7Tao. Written in 2009.

"Having used improvement philosophies like Juran, Crosby, Six Sigma and Lean in a wide variety of manufacturing companies throughout the UK and at all levels of the organization, I was fascinated when the subject of 7Tao appeared in the UK. From what I initially understood, it was said to be a new manufacturing methodology developed within China. The government's National Skills Academy helped me to trace down the technique. I needed to look at this methodology. I was about to retire, so I knew I would never get this chance again.

I was working with an $8bn (in 2009) manufacturing corporation in the south of England, in Hertfordshire. We were investigating the possibility of implementing a continuous improvement programme combined with the opportunity for shop floor personnel to gain a qualification. After examining a number of possibilities we decided that the National Vocational Qualification (NVQ) – Business Improvement series of qualifications suited our needs. With this in mind we contacted John Bradley of National Skills Academy for Manufacturing who subsequently introduced us to Amar Manzoor.

From our first meeting, Amar came over as a great enthusiast for his subject. He outlined the 7Tao philosophy and how it could be integrated with the NVQ qualifications. I became excited at the prospect of working with him since the training material included a large number of improvement tools which were new to me and, I believed, the manufacturing industry.

We decided to run a pilot programme using fifteen people from the shop floor. The participants were from nearly every department of production and were chosen, after interview, from a list of volunteers.

The pilot training took place over seven four-hour sessions and individual projects in the work areas of the participants. The training sessions were instructive and delivered in a participative and humorous style, which made the experience enjoyable for the participants. The final session brought the training to an exciting finish. It consisted of forming the participants into three competing teams who each had to build a miniature petrol-driven racing car. The teams had to use a specified number of the 7Tao defence and attack tools and techniques which measured the degree of knowledge within the individuals and the teams.

The projects were individually based and were targeted at improving the key business processes within the departments of the participants. The projects that were made were quite challenging, in that they were aimed at making significant changes in the work area and in the organization itself. At their conclusion, the participants delivered presentations to senior management illustrating the various improvements and the results derived.

Outcomes: The pilot was very successful in that:

a) Every participant gained the qualification being offered by 7Tao through the government who supported 7Tao in the implementation of the programme.

b) The participants became extremely motivated and most of them became 'agents for change' in their respective departments.

c) Every project resulted in impressive improvements in the key business processes and the key measures of 7Tao, such as price down, increased delivery speed, responsive quality improvements as a result of the effort, after-market support increases, customers were very happy, shareholders were shocked at the power of the system to give them exactly what they were looking for, and, for the employees ... bonuses began improving as a result.

d) The qualification became a 'must have' for anybody in the organization who wanted to improve their work area and process and, indeed, their career prospects.

e) It proved to the precious metals company that this was the vehicle which could deliver major positive change to the organization. With this in mind, a second course was planned about six months later. The next course was delivered in the same manner as the first and produced even more impressive results. Massive improvements resulted as the 7Tao system started to sweep the problems of the organization away.

Conclusions: The 7Tao philosophy has delivered outstanding results whenever it has been implemented. It goes far beyond all of the major improvement strategies being used in industry today in the sense that it is more demanding, much more exciting, and it is driven by the nature of the transaction which occurs through any business 'process by process' throughout the plant's operation. If you consider the fact that it is Chinese-based, it tends to crush the waste out of the system of the company through productivity increases and huge changes to the way in which *business* is done, not just the way in which *work* is done. This is what makes it powerful; it looks at business and connects the transactional value of the business from the start of the order process to the end of the delivery process.

The range of tools and techniques is huge; however, what must be remembered is the fact that these tools combine and form their own structures depending upon the situation that they are placed in. If a certain situation within a business demands a certain set of tools, the process owner, or the job holder, will naturally be attracted to those tools through the sheer power of the descriptions within each of the techniques being displayed. Each technique contains the DNA of each problem within the organization. Every job holder can instantly recognize the problems facing them every day because... they face them every day. This is the beauty of the technique. it is instant in its application and its decision-making ability. All of the organs of the business are included within the tools. Like going to a chemist or a doctor, you tell the doctor your symptoms and the medicine is provided for you immediately, which then helps you on the road to recovery. This is exactly what took place. We were stunned at its accuracy, at its ability to find the core issues, and its ability to change as the organization changed. There was no one approach in its implementation, but all of the answers were right!"

Amazon: The best delivery company in the world?

President Donald Trump is going after Amazon and its business model. Here is a battle brewing based on the significance of one main feature, the Transaction. It asks just one question: How come Jeff Bezos gets to keep all of those billions, dodging various taxes with online business, while the common man in the United States is struggling from one day to the next? This is the crux of the matter.

To understand how we got into this situation, it is very important that we look at the history of the transactional development. In one line, Amazon has wiped out entire chains of economy with its powerful understanding of one main action: undercutting. This is Bezos's main aim as he marches ahead with a huge growth of shareholder returns.

The more Amazon eats up the competition in its carnivorous style of industrial combat, the more the share price grows. The more the share price grows, the more money Amazon has to eat up even more competition—until eventually, Amazon becomes the only store in the United States.

This is classic industrial warfare. Bezos's drive to take over global markets is a case in point of how important industrial warfare thinking is in this modern day and age. He has some very smart people who have been infected by this style of thinking in his boardrooms. This is not a company anymore. It is a war machine designed for just one thing: devouring. They don't compete anymore; they eat competitors. That's the main aim of the growth process. Every day, we shop at brick-and-mortar stores and say to ourselves, "Can we get it cheaper from Amazon?"

As we make decisions in our mind and click around the internet for our desired consumption of goods, Amazon is busy thinking of how to dominate and maintain relevance. It has probably produced learning engines that scan and analyse buying patterns and changes in the competition culture as the market moves forward, swaying violently from left to right.

Only the most responsive steering and the most aware driver who has the best tire grip can stay on the road in this one. Amazon is a flat aerodynamic machine: the downforce gripping the marketplace is strong, the spoilers are doing what they are supposed to do, and the transactional engine performs very highly with few fuel stops, all as the share price keeps growing ever larger, giving them even more power and ability to pass the competition. In fighter jet terms, it is a MiG-87, something from the future to be marvelled at. You just can't get away from the fact that this transaction design is so carnivorous and vicious toward anything that stands in its way that it will end up devouring anything that comes against it.

Seeds of Destruction

Yet the seeds of death have already been planted. Like any other entity, Amazon has the seeds of destruction already inbuilt into its DNA, just like General Motors did in the late '90s, and similarly to the banking sector just before the catastrophic collapse in 2008. We all know the statements "This is too good to be true" and "Something is not quite right here." Like the disease of cancer, the problem is already within us, and it is just a matter of time before it comes out. The question is, what are seeds of destruction and what do they actually look like? The answer lies in the current model of operation and the change in the environment of trading. When things are on the up, everything looks good, and when they suddenly change, what looked good just two years ago can suddenly turn to "I better get out now while there is still time."

For Amazon, the seeds of destruction are the shareholders and the relationship they have with the share price. This is the exact point from which the cancer will grow and metastasize. Bezos likely knows it and worries about it every day. It's staring him right in the face and sitting opposite his desk as he studies the daily financial reports and thinks to himself, "How do I keep this going?"

It's not just Bezos who worries about this; it's every CEO who is facing this disease. They can't keep running from it for long because the more the competition increases, the more threats pile up in every corner both internal and external, and the worse the situation gets. Anything can take this transaction down: competition, price changes, currency changes, logistics cut outs, international politics, trade agreements, recessions, depressions, and fluctuation in management thinking. In the digital landscape, smaller, more vicious competitors can act like velociraptors. These small-business competitors may even hunt in packs and be better able to adapt to the environment precisely because they are smaller, faster, have bigger claws, and are looking for just one thing: to eat the big guy. They are just waiting for that illness to set in so the big entity can stumble just a little. They are always in the grass, plotting, planning, circling their prey—and Bezos's management structure likely knows that they are there. Amazon can try to step on them or eat them using its big management style, but at each turn, another one pops up. Then there is Trump, who is inducing hatred for this company. He openly dislikes Amazon, and Amazon dislikes him. All Trump must do is point out the big monster that is Amazon, increase pressure upon it, and immediately its share price will go lower. Trump knows this: He just wrote a couple of tweets and the share price for Amazon went tumbling. New competitors were born, new pressures were created, new fissures appeared, and as predicted, the share price was affected. The question is not whether Amazon will die, but how and when. It looks like the answer is only a few years away. In industrial war, the transactional model Amazon is using has its limitations. From a banking point of view, it looks like 2004, and in 2022 only three years to go before the 2026 great depletion reckoning. It is when the depletion comes that the greatest changes will take place anywhere there is money or value. The 2026 depletion will change everything in the economic horizon of the world.

Delivering CEO's who prosper in a harsh economic environment.

The CEO of any company in the world is under severe pressure. The primary forces the CEO is facing are built directly on the forward-moving nature of business and the sheer number of walls he must scale as he struggles for transactional relevance in a marketplace. To understand the causes of worry for CEOs, we must look at the increasingly diverse challenges that the uncertain global business environment is forcing on his leadership systems. In any environment, the world is changing so rapidly and with such speed that it can be impossible to keep up. This fragmentation process of technologies, global competition, and divisions of people is the force behind this rapid change. The only way to keep up with the change process is by diversifying the work structure to be able to embrace and adapt to the current world and see what is coming market.

It is worth looking at a sample of the different types of forces as they break into cellular formations that are causing knock-on effects in multiple environments. The list is long, and each force has additional relations, which sometimes connect to each other and at other times do not. This makes for difficult forecasting as actuaries struggle to make sense of a world that is not one, they recognize from their training.

A Hostile Environment

The forces against the CEO are many: finance, currency, recessions, depressions, social change, human capability, emerging technologies, competition from every part of the world, disruptions, increased requirements for performance, ethical standards being reduced, and employees who are being reduced to the next workday as uncertainty forces them to take ever more risky decisions to break themselves out of a perceived downward cycle. This environment is everywhere, and problems that should be handled by the organizational structure are constantly rising to the top as people try to make heads and tails of the daily appearance of new challenges, which need to be understood and then tackled. The CEO must deal with all these diversified pressures and be always held accountable for them. He must delegate responsibility and accountability to his management, and either put them in positions of management internally or hire outside consultants and management agencies to perform these tasks, all while reducing costs.

Becoming Obsolete

Yet the CEO's greatest difficulty is obsolescence. As soon as one issue is dealt with, it is already obsolete—whether this comes in the form of technology, skills, finance, economic issues, pricing, products, designs, delivery problems, or any other issue with the health of the organization.

This overwhelming force of obsolescence is what is currently powering the changes in the world. Look at the military: fighter pilots are becoming obsolete because of the advent of drones and the increasing obsolescence of flight based military systems becoming counterproductive. This likewise affects every CEO who produces fighter jets as they scramble to sustain a business built on the back of Cold War technological thinking. No matter how much they upgrade the aircraft, pushing even more technology into the existing platform to try to make the existing aircraft even more high performance, it makes no difference. The primary force that is driving the change is transactional obsolescence. In a world of warfare, obsolescence is the fact that military warfare as defined in the past is completely obsolete and has become counterproductive. The more you use a tool like the military in counterproductive situations, the worse it is for that tool.

Taking a bird's eye view of the situation, we come to realize that warfare has changed, and this is my point here. When we look at an aircraft manufacturer, we begin on the shop floor by asking, "What's bothering you?" The next stage is to get to the plant manager and say the same thing, "What's bothering you?", and bring it to the next stage up in the business unit, and then to the CEO.

Grasping the Changes

But when all is said and done, it doesn't rest with the CEO. The real change comes from understanding the environment and accepting that things have changed. Then we can see the simplicity of the truth that guides our decisions. With the aircraft industry, the question should be, "If warfare has changed, and if the environment has changed whereby these aircraft are increasingly obsolete, becoming irrelevant and counterproductive units, what can we do to remain relevant?" The issue is always a higher one than we expect, and the questions always go into a historical, philosophical perspective with a deep cyclical underlay involving multiple measurements of the forces of change.

The questions a CEO must be asking may not be hidden in the management section of the organization. The questions the CEO needs to ask are quite obviously on the production line and the delivery process to the customer who may be confused about what he wants. This is where the CEO finds the truth about his marketplace, and where research and development need to be directed. Delivery is not just about delivering the goods, it's also about delivering the results. The pressures are increasing, and delivery is becoming even more difficult. If results are not delivered, internal fracture of the management team is a sure result. Leadership shifts and broken motivation constantly plagues the corporations of today. Leaders must focus and watch all their minions and command total respect from executives who may not have any loyalty to a company other than to warm a seat. It is vital that delivery of results becomes a process and a system rather than a management pursuit.

Business models based on constant cost cutting.

The only constant is change. When you look at any business, you don't look for sustainability; you look for the changes that will make the business obsolete. As change ensures that businesses go obsolete, it comes in the form of transactional relevance. A self-defeating cycle of cutting is now eating into the heart of every business in the world. This is affecting the economies of the world as they struggle to adapt to the forces of change.

Obsolescence is haunting the very nature of every product, service, and farm good in the world. The forces are many, but a key one is artificial intelligence. The effects of artificial intelligence, which mean less manpower is required for doing the same jobs, are increasing unemployment in every business in the world. In every field, AI starts by learning and doing mundane work, "helping" the lower jobs. Then it creeps up, gently growing as it reduces the need for staff support services. This is exactly what happened in the travel and tourism industry 15 to 20 years ago. High-street firms that used to book flights for you and had internal connections to find you cheap flights were no longer required. Now you can simply open a website, search through a database, and complete the transaction using a credit card.

At first, the number of travel agencies reduced by 10 percent. This figure grew over the years to 50 percent, resulting in the consolidation of existing travel firms, which became larger conglomerates with new business models. Along the way, they shed thousands of jobs, retaining only that talent that could push the new vision ahead to stay relevant in the marketplace. Now this process has slowly begun swallowing the legal field in the United States, and larger firms in the UK, under conditions of heavy competition, are now taking the same approach of cutting costs, shedding bodies, shoring up the balance sheet, taking profits, and becoming fat cats laughing all the way to the bank. All of this AI technology simply means one thing: Monetary value is pushed to the top, at the expense of those at the bottom.

Increasingly, lawyers are becoming smaller, more independent entities who run their own offices or work for specialist concerns, supporting only businesses and people that require their specific set of skills. In 15 years', time, it's possible that 90 percent of people working within the legal field will become obsolete and redundant. We must define competition within its correct terms. Today, the competitor does not look like just another business entity who is trying to compete for your business. Instead, it is the customer and the sheer amount of cost-cutting choices available to him or her. It is the fleeing shareholder who is trying to minimize losses and maximize gains to keep money working for appropriate rates of return on investment. It is the employee who is actively trying to survive in their field, where they are forced to innovate when they see that the writing is on the wall. It is the product itself that is desperately trying to find innovative ways to circumvent the middlemen and reach its targeted consumption audience.

Snatch and grab have become the trademark economic activity of these times as this cannibalistic environment becomes ever more encroaching. But the economy is rising fast. There are more jobs now than ever before. Unemployment is at its lowest rate since the 1950s. Really? This has happened because dangerously low interest rates have forced up the land cycle performance. Money printing has made huge amounts of surplus cash looking for a place to settle. Where is this money settling? Back into house prices, property speculation, and financial instrument exchange. This will now come to a head when the next set of central bank-led recessions rear their ugly heads around 2019 to 2021 and in 2026 to 2035.

This begs the question, if 2008 was this bad and nearly choked the entire world economy, what will 2019 to 2021 and 2026 to 2035 be like? To answer that, we need to consider how the effects of a classic recession will be magnified by the previous low interest rates and quantitative easing, by a possible bond market collapse, by rising taxes, and by interest rates raised by 10 percent to prevent currencies from collapsing. Competition will be much more intense, cannibalization of the economy will become a free for all, and strife will be found in the streets of countries all over the world as societal degeneration takes a turn for the worse, infecting every competitor.

Yes, we have some time, but it is only a short amount of time. In 2019, the tide goes out with the banking boom-bust cycle, and we will see who has their underwear on. The only piece missing in this puzzle is - what excuse will the governments of the world use to cover up the recession? Will it be a military, terrorist, financial, technological or medically based set of circumstances which will be used to cover up this extremely deep coming recession? Its impossible to see the future from here, however, the patterns of the past reveal an emerging scenario which does implicate a set of difficulties is about to turn up. Ah, it was the Covid-19 pandemic… now it all makes sense. Every time there is a mid cycle recession, something or another will turn up to cover it up in the background. Is this conspiracy theory or just a matter of fact when you consider the timings of the mid cycle recession and all the other facts mentioned.

CHAPTER 6

Tao 3: Quality: Is it Fit for Purpose?

Corporations in the consumer-led economy of the West place product quality high on their list of priorities. The Chinese assign equal importance to all seven Tao factors in the production and supply process rather than stressing quality. Quality is Number 3 in the 7Tao system.

What 7Tao aims for is a balanced consideration of the requirements in the transaction which involve quality. If you simply stress the necessity of quality, the price of the product goes up. Costs escalate. You may end up with a perfect product that few people can afford. With this in mind, quality requires careful consideration. The quality standard must be that the product is fit for purpose. That fitness will range from very low in some countries and markets, to very high in other countries and markets.

Defending Quality Strengths

Hundreds of tools associated with quality and statistical process control are used to improve the quality of the product. The aim is to sell more units of the product. The logic is simple: 'Our product is the best so buy our product.' A whole industry of consultants and quality-control champions has grown up round the principles of quality.

The 7Tao doctrine takes into account the needs of the marketplace. It sees quality in relation to the transaction that is being sought. If a product can be marketed at $300, and that is the right price for the particular marketplace, don't invest another $600 in quality improvement: the customer doesn't need it and won't pay $900 for the product. The customer is prepared to pay only $300 whether you like it or not. Customers are naturally attracted to a good price. To 7Tao, 'fit for purpose' means 'fit for the nature of the transaction'. Depending on only one of the 7Tao is too risky: it distracts you from the other six important elements in the transactional process.

The key is *affordability*. Customers must get the quality at a price they are willing and able to pay. Defending this concept requires a balanced approach to quality. The Chinese tailor their prices and products to suit the global market. In

Africa they sell sneakers at prices which secure sales; in America they sell sneakers at prices that correspond to that market's expectations. Quality varies, and prices reflect the realities.

The difference between the 7Tao approach and other approaches to quality is that 7Tao aims for market share based on the principle of achieving a transaction. To achieve market dominance in *all* geographical locations, if you focus on quality, you must make sure that you justify that emphasis in relation to price, delivery, after market, customers, shareholders, and employees, so that quality is not given priority at the expense of transactional cash flow. Defending the quality of the product requires eliminating as many defective examples as possible so that you retain your position in the marketplace. 7Tao tolerates only 0.0000007% of defects for every product sold. This means that, for every million products sold, you are allowed seven defects. Very few will achieve this standard. The most important thing in this exercise is to learn lessons. All poor-quality products must be scrutinised until the quality problem is solved. Defective items should be carefully stored and used as examples to show trainees what poor quality looks like. Mistakes must be physically demonstrated to the whole workforce, so that they know what to look for and how to avoid them. Training must be provided for each error. The drive to improve quality must unite the workforce. It is crucial to identify a defect while it is developing. If it travels down the manufacturing process, it can become very expensive to resolve later.

Attacking Quality Weaknesses

To attack quality weaknesses, we must attack defects internally. 7Tao uses all the tools available to the marketplace to ensure that defects do not become endemic in the manufacturing system. Certain tools evolved by third-generation methodologies (like Total Quality Control, Just in Time and Six Sigma) are incorporated into the 7Tao system.

The difference is in the cleaning process. 7Tao determines the value of a process and assigns time and effort to it based upon that value. The process is broken down into its component parts and appropriate tools are deployed (such as the 80/20 Rule, the seven quality tools and process capability). Attacking the problem involves reducing the number of defects and calculating the savings thus

Box: 6.1 : 3rd Generation Six Sigma vs 4TH Generation 7Tao

Everyone knows about Six Sigma. It is the international standard used by nearly every Fortune 500 company. Its strategy is simple: reduce defects per million opportunities. It is a simple ruler-based scale used to complement the corporation's strategy. Very few know about 7Tao. It's new and it's Chinese. People laugh at it just as they laughed at the Japanese when they started out on the road to excellence.

There are fundamental differences between the Six Sigma method and the 7Tao method. One is a statistically based measurement system used and developed in the West, the other a profit-driven economic fighting method used and developed in the East. Six Sigma represents America, 7Tao represents China. They are poles apart in their thinking and their application.

Six Sigma talks about statistics, bell curves, SPC charts and central limit theorems, and has various ways of eliminating corporate mistakes using statistics and conversation. Six Sigma has over one hundred tools and uses mathematical software to make complicated calculations. Six Sigma is a graphically represented system.

The 6-Sigma system is brash – a lot of noise is made about its use within a company. Shareholders applaud it. The more you practice it, the higher up the Sigma scale you go, the fewer defects in the business. Trainees listen to lectures on statistics and are taught the application of statistics in the business environment. They work their way up the ladder by earning a series of 'belts'. The highest one is the Master Black Belt. The focus is purely on quality, quality, quality. The target is the reduction of defects; student projects always involve defect-reduction procedures. Six Sigma is complicated and engaging at the engineering level. At the shareholder level it is about proving the excellence of the product or service. *It is a common qualification in the West.*

7Tao talks about defence and attack. How much money did you make and who is your competitor? 7Tao has over five hundred tools. The system is quietly practised within a company. The talk starts and ends with the transaction.

The more you practise 7Tao, the more you will be able to dominate markets. How many customers do you have and how much do they buy? 7Tao is an economic fighting method. The classes are economic fighting sessions with students practising corporate battle from the word 'go'.

The lectures are about breaking into new markets and defending against competitors in markets where you currently dominate, and about understanding the weaknesses of the competition. The focus is on profit, profit, profit. You work up the Master scale according to the number of companies you defeat. The highest achievement is the Grand Master qualification.

7Tao is attractive to shareholders because it is about growing the number of customers and transactions. It uses engineering knowledge as a main element in growth. It starts with the transaction, and it ends with the transaction. *It is a rare qualification in the West.* Which one would you choose? Do you want to learn about the way things are done in the West, or in the East?

The cost of achieving a Six Sigma Black Belt is $10,000. The return on investment can be anything between $1,000 and $1,000,000. The more Black Belts you have, the more your savings, and the more you focus on the next generation of quality problems. Knowledge, respect, and satisfaction in a job well done are the returns. Your motto is, 'We are a Six Sigma company.' Practised openly and candidly, it is a herbivore method with defensive horns on its head.

The cost of achieving a 7Tao Operational Master qualification is $5,000. The return on investment can range from $10,000 to a dead competitor and an open marketplace to feast on. The more 7Tao Operational Masters you have, the more ferocious your company will become in the marketplace and the more the competition will fear you. Your motto is, 'We are going to eat you alive.' Practised quietly and in secrecy, it is the method of the carnivore.

The growth rates of China and the rest of Eurasia should give you the answer to which to go for, the 7Tao carnivore or the Six Sigma herbivore. Which method is more tuned to facing the challenges of the future? Which system introduces us to the challenges we will face as the world changes? Choices, choices, choices...

made in attempts to achieve perfect quality transactions. What is at stake is the survival of the business. Good quality is the bedrock of a good manufacturing process. All too often a shoddy product is offered at a premium price. In resolving quality issues, however, costs have to be kept down. Let's look at an example.

Product A is manufactured with a 5% profit margin. The workforce unknowingly introduces a defect into the chain, which travels down the line and is identified only in the final stages of the production run. If a defect is not caught until near the final stage, the product will be basically unsaleable. The resources used to make it – materials, skill, labour, machines, fuel, logistics, supply chain, management – will all be wasted. 7Tao rigorously exposes awareness of the implications all the way down the chain to the point of delivery to the customer. It uses hundreds of examples to ensure that quality is effectively controlled. By understanding the nature of poor quality, a firm can identify and exploit the poor quality of its competitors' products. This is achieved by acquiring samples of those products and analysing them on a daily basis. This is a fundamental step towards success. By measuring the strengths and weaknesses of competitors, you can develop the most effective strategy for attacking them.

Quality starts with understanding your current position

There are several steps to understanding the significance of quality in an organization. The journey starts with causes and ends with solutions. First, priorities must be established. Then you must compare your organisation's quality performance to that of the competition. This means figuring out where you are in the marketplace. This is not easy to achieve as you have to benchmark your competition in the product sphere or the process sphere. The product sphere means you buy the competitors products and dismantle them. The process sphere means that you buy the people in the competitor company… that can cross into illegal. But hey, that how the world works these days right? What will you do?

Change happens all of the time. It only gets faster and more hectic.

The only constant is change. When you look at any business, you don't look for sustainability; you look for the changes that will make the business obsolete. As change ensures that businesses go obsolete, it comes in the form of transactional relevance. One of the best ways to stay relevant to the marketplace is

Box 6:2 The F-16 Falcon versus the JF-17 Thunder

Industrial warfare is an unpredictable game. You can start out with the best of intentions and end up in deep waters.

When the Soviet Union invaded Afghanistan, the USA was so worried in its cold-war thinking that it gave the first batch of its F16s to Pakistan in 1983. Pakistan was ecstatic at the time. The war plane was in the Pakistani nation's psyche. Every truck transporting goods in Pakistan was decorated with an F16, such was their love for the aeroplane!

Before the Soviets retreated from Afghanistan in 1991, Pakistan decided to upgrade its air force. So, suddenly, the ties that had bound Pakistan and the USA were broken. Pakistan called the years 1990 to 2001 the 'lost decade'. It had an ageing fleet of aircraft, diminishing in number, and sanctions were to make it very difficult to get spare parts for them. The country had been abandoned militarily. The situation deteriorated when both India and Pakistan tested nuclear weapons in 1998. The sanctions regime hurt Pakistan much more than India, it being the smaller country.

Pakistan decided to go it alone. Fed up with being rejected and charged extortionate prices for aircraft (the weaker and more desperate they got, the more the price went up), they created the JF-17 with Chinese help. The initial development cost of this very F-16-looking plane was a paltry $150 million. The R&D was to create a platform on which they could build their future strategies. They produced a prototype of the aircraft in four years (1999 to 2003) and it flew for the first time in August 2003. By February 2010 they had inducted their first squadron of Black Spiders with fourteen aircraft.

The JF17 is now so combat capable, that it is attracting buyers from all five continents including from first world countries. This has added to Pakistan's capability and appeal as an engineering and manufacturing country.

> Industrial warfare is unique. What looks like a supply-chain black hole may be filled with indigenous technology. The most important element is confidence. People used to say, 'We can never do this – we simply can't compete and build the fighters the West is building.' An inferiority complex ran from grandfather to father to child for many a generation. However, when they tried they realized they *could* do it: it wasn't that difficult, they weren't any less capable than the next person on the planet. It was just a matter of organization, innovation and motivation. The Chinese helped them a lot. 'Why are you worried? Why do you tell yourself you're less than the people you admire? Learn to respect yourself and your own capabilities! Stop thinking like peasants and start thinking like engineers!'
>
> So they did it, they produced their own aircraft. The enemy over the border, India, started its LCA programme in 1983, and it was still being tested in 2010. The design was obsolete by 1989, but national pride keeps the Indians going. They are so afraid of being seen as failures that they simply will not give up the LCA programme. The Pakistanis are now confidently supplying just about every military technology all by themselves. They take great pride in the fact that they are achieving something at last. If the Pakistanis can produce their own fighter aircraft, anyone can!

to increase quality and sustain quality in a constantly changing environment. A self-defeating cycle of cutting is now eating into the heart of every business in the world. This is affecting the economies of the world as they struggle to adapt to the forces of change leading to frustration, unemployment, redundancy, and irrelevance. Protests across the rust belt will increase unless quality jobs are not found for these people who have lost their livelihood. Obsolescence is haunting the very nature of every product, service, and farm good in the world. The forces are many, but a key one is artificial intelligence. The effects of artificial intelligence, which mean less manpower is required for doing the same jobs, are increasing unemployment in every business in the world. In every field, AI starts by learning and doing mundane work, "helping" the lower jobs. Then it creeps up, gently growing as it reduces the need for staff support services.

MIT: Source: Wikipedia: Madcoverboy   Peking University: Source: Wikipedia: Galaygobi

Box 6.3 : American or Chinese creativity

'Ah, but the Chinese are no good at invention. We have all the ideas. We are innovative. We produce men like Thomas Edison, Steve Jobs and Bill Gates. The Chinese can't invent anything so they just copy, and they can't even do that well! They can't possibly rival our education system. We own the most patents in the world. Our business leaders tell them what to do and how to do it.'

I hear such statements constantly when I lecture in different countries. But right now the Chinese are learning the creative arts, design and expression, and research and development. The money is there. It's just that the institutions need to be fired up and the products need to be created as fast as the economy is growing.

Let's take an example, the new J20 stealth fighter. In January 2011 it was taken out of its wraps and was received with surprise by US defence attaché Robert Gates. It was a shock. No one had expected China to roll one off the mat so quickly – these things take years to design and develop. They were left shaking their heads over how quickly China was catching up.

Then they muttered, 'Well, it's probably just a show piece that doesn't even fly.' The J20 flew – quickly, safely and came back down to earth. And again. They kept quiet. Then they pointed out that the Chinese had picked up the pieces of an F117 stealth fighter and probably managed to copy it. The Chinese denied this.

They are clearly not behind the West. They have been catching up very fast indeed and in most respects they are already ahead of us. In fact the Chinese are miles ahead of the game, so far ahead that they do not have debt. They have a controlled, subservient and passionate population. They have ideas too because they have good brains, and the more opportunities there are of a cross-pollination of technologies, the more ideas they'll have. Guess what? They have 1.3 billion ideas. They have enlightened, fearless risk-takers, fighting ethics, strong manners, a good diet and five thousand years of history. The Chinese people know who they are. Do we any longer know who we are in the West?

This is exactly what happened in the travel and tourism industry 15 to 20 years ago. High-street firms that used to book flights for you and had internal connections to find you cheap flights were no longer required. Now you can simply open a website, search through a database, and complete the transaction using a credit card. At first, the number of travel agencies reduced by 10 percent. This figure grew over the years to 50 percent, resulting in the consolidation of existing travel firms, which became larger conglomerates with new business models. Along the way, they shed thousands of jobs, retaining only that talent that could push the new vision ahead to stay relevant in the marketplace.

Now this process has slowly begun swallowing the legal field in the United States, and larger firms in the UK, under conditions of heavy competition, are now taking the same approach of cutting costs, shedding bodies, shoring up the balance sheet, taking profits, and becoming fat cats laughing all the way to the bank. All this AI technology simply means one thing: Monetary value is pushed to the top, at the expense of those at the bottom.

Increasingly, lawyers are becoming smaller, more independent entities who run their own offices or work for specialist concerns, supporting only businesses and people that require their specific set of skills. In 15 years', time, it's possible that 90 percent of people working within the legal field will become obsolete and redundant.

We must define competition within its correct terms. Today, the competitor does not look like just another business entity who is trying to compete for your business. Instead, it is the customer and the sheer amount of cost-cutting choices available to him or her. It is the fleeing shareholder who is trying to minimize losses and maximize gains to keep money working for appropriate rates of return on investment. It is the employee who is actively trying to survive in their field, where they are forced to innovate when they see that the writing is on the wall. It is the product itself that is desperately trying to find innovative ways to circumvent the middlemen and reach its targeted consumption audience.

The industrial economy is different to the asset economy. The asset economy is about exchanging already established sores of wealth and moving them around from one holder to another. This is how the speculation based economic environment has unfolded right in front of our eyes. The young do not even have a chance to prosper in this type of asset driven nightmare. Those who got in first, either accidently or by design, in the housing and financial markets are seen as the lucky ones. Those who stuck to their trades, lived their lives in measured means and struggled like their father before them are the ones who are suffering as the average price of house goes 1000% higher than it used to be.

If this bubble bursts. The effects will be devastating for decades or even centuries to come. This bubble bursting coinciding with the rise of an industrial power like China will produce pressures which have never been witnessed in the last millennium, let alone century. This begs the question, 'how do we get ready for such a scenario?'

Competition will be much more intense, cannibalization of the economy will become a free for all, and strife will be found in the streets of countries all over the world as societal degeneration takes a turn for the worse, infecting every competitor. Yes, we have some time, but it is only a short amount of time. In 2019, the tide goes out with the banking boom-bust cycle, and we will see who has their underwear on. Or am I wrong? Well, time will tell.

Sacrifice of the worker is fundamental to the survival of the firm. As quality increases with constant automation and artificial intelligence. Old quality systems are being slowly relegated to history and workers who built quality skills to complete their jobs find themselves on the street unemployed. The quality targets which are developed by Artificial Intelligence systems are completely designed by the robots who now make cars. There is no room for human error as humans are completely pushed out of the economy. In 2022, when this book was updated, it was impossible to imagine a world where this kind of environment could even exist, but by the time the 2026 depletion is well underway, the knowledge contained within the 7Tao system will become more relevant than ever. It is now impossible to see what the future will look like in 18 year cycle terms, however, we only have to look at the effects that previous economic cycles have had to realise that mushroomed and exploded cause and effect happens every time. You don't have to look too far to see governments and industrialists such as Elon Musk worrying about the effects of AI and robotics. As the labour force is rendered increasingly redundant, quality will improve as AI replaces the manufacturing process and production plants. Cheap robots can now produce products such as missiles with great ease as AI enables manufacturing plants across the world to achieve the same quality as plants in the West. This process has been happening since the 1950's and quality has been at the centre of the change.

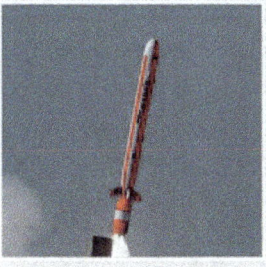
Image: Wiki: Raza0007

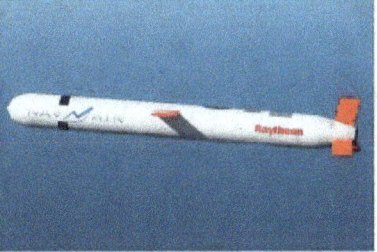
Image: Wikipedia commons

Babur vs Tomahawk Cruise Missile

Amazingly similar, don't you think? On the left is the Pakistani Babur cruise missile, on the right the famous US Tomahawk cruise missile.

The speculation continues today. Six Tomahawk missiles crash-landed in Pakistani territory after the US launched air strikes against Afghanistan in 1998. Was the Tomahawk simply copied by Pakistan? The basic design of the Tomahawk and the Babur – the propulsion system, the general fuselage, the fold-out wings, the weight of about 1,500 kilograms, the length of six and half metres – is the same. There is, however, no confirmation of this theory. The Pakistani missile organization NESCOM has rejected it outright.

My interpretation: The industrial warfare technique suggested here is called 'scrounging'. This is a common ploy used in every part of industry. The opposition scour rubbish bins, waste deposits and scrap metals facilities for any clues that will help them develop a similar or better product. It is an effective technique, deployed by the Soviets and the Americans during the Cold War, and even Hitler used similar methods. You find a product, take it apart and – hey presto! – you make a new one just as good or better

When change takes place, it usually leaves a trail of evidence behind it so that you can piece together what technology has been used and how it has been applied. Brainstorming such situations is the key, learning how to detect technology trails, how to pick up and buy evidence. Technology spreads round the world in this way. Most countries have at least a dozen spies in every area of the world where they think they can pick up useful technologies and disappear with them. Industrial warfare is definitely more important than military warfare! Now that the Pakistanis and the Chinese have reverse engineered a missile, increasing its range, quality and reliability, who do we think really won the battle of the cruise missile tactical strike? Its not just Pakistan that has copied the cruise missile, there is a version of the Tomahawk cruise missile scattered across many countries in the world. Nowadays it has even been improved upon.

```
┌─────────────────────────────────────────────────────────────┐
│ Benchmark yourself. Find out where you are in relation to the│
│ competition. Pick seven competitors you share a market with  │
│ and find out where you are on that list. Who is at the top   │
│ and who is at the bottom?                                    │
└─────────────────────────────────────────────────────────────┘
                              ↕
┌─────────────────────────────────────────────────────────────┐
│ Prepare your 7Tao defence manuals to figure out a defence   │
│ strategy. Implement the operations, tactics and strategies  │
│ in the defence folder to ensure that you are capable of     │
│ sustaining the 7Tao in your business. Defend the 7Tao       │
│ *value* in your business. Do not allow it to be taken away  │
│ by a competitor in the marketplace.                         │
└─────────────────────────────────────────────────────────────┘
                              ↕
┌─────────────────────────────────────────────────────────────┐
│ Measure the impact of your defence and attack. Is your 7Tao │
│ growing? If not, get back in for the next round. Battle him │
│ hard and ensure that you are able to reduce him to a size   │
│ you can manage. Check your 7Tao monitoring your growth      │
│ process.                                                     │
└─────────────────────────────────────────────────────────────┘
                              ↕
┌─────────────────────────────────────────────────────────────┐
│ Engage the 7tao attack manuals to figure out an attack      │
│ strategy. Implement the operations, tactics and strategies  │
│ in the attack manual to make sure that you are able to      │
│ exploit every chink in your competitor's armour. Attack the │
│ 7Tao value in your competitor's business. Once you take his │
│ 7Tao, you will grow.                                        │
└─────────────────────────────────────────────────────────────┘
                              ↕
┌─────────────────────────────────────────────────────────────┐
│ Benchmark yourself.                                          │
│                                                              │
│ Is your price the most competitive?                          │
│ Is your delivery the fastest?                                │
│ Is your quality of products and services the best in the     │
│ marketplace?                                                 │
│ Is your after-market service the most supportive?            │
│ Is your customer happier with you than with your competitor? │
│ Is your shareholder richer?                                  │
│ Is your employee the most productive and creative?           │
└─────────────────────────────────────────────────────────────┘
```

Case Study 3

Drury's Engineering

Drury's Engineering is a specialist UK engineering firm operating in the sphere of oil, gas, Formula One motor racing, defence, and the aerospace industries. The firm was purchased in 2008 by Richard Dunn. In 2009 it began its journey through the 7Tao method through the NVQ BIT process. By 2011 Drury's Engineering had grown to five times its purchase price in the middle of the most violent recession in eighty years. How did they do it? How did a small 26-man operation grow its value by 400% in just two years? The key lies in understanding the yield of the transaction. We can divide the transaction into three stages, as illustrated in this table:

Cost	Process transaction	Yield
Price: How much must I pay for what I have to do?	**Price:** I pay for getting the work out, not for doing it.	**Price:** How much profit did I make from each process of work?
Delivery: How quickly can I get it into my process area from the supply chain?	**Delivery:** How quickly can I get the processed product out of my door and into the customers' supply chains?	**Delivery:** Did I beat the deadline or did it beat me?
Quality: Is the quality perfect or will I constantly be sending back defective goods to be replaced by perfect quality goods in my supply chain?	**Quality:** Is the quality perfect or will my company produce defective goods against my order?	**Quality:** How many items came back for reprocessing and by how much did these reduce my profit margins on the whole job?
After market: Will I be supported in my purchase of equipment and services?	**After market:** Will the customer come back or will they go away for ever?	**After market:** How many complaints did I receive as the problem travelled right up to the end customer point? How much did each complaint cost me?

Customers: Will I be respected as an individual customer or will I be treated as a number?	**Customers:** Will they grade me, sustain me, keep me as preferred supplier or am I a one-off?	**Customers:** How much did they pay me? Did they pay me enough for the work I did for them?
Shareholders: Can I save money on my purchase?	**Shareholders:** How much money did I make getting those goods and services out of the door?	**Shareholders:** How much did I get to keep in the end?
Employees: Will my employees be working or will they be idle?	**Employees:** Do my workers smile at the end of a job or do they hate the work?	**Employees:** Are my employees secure, well trained, growing in their personal and professional lives? Are they happy in my workplace?

Richard Dunn, Managing Director and 2010 CEO of Drury's, explains how 7Tao helped him to understand the transactional business environment when they were called in to improve Drury's workforce skills. This is what he wrote about his 7Tao experience.

"What you need is the nerve to engage with such a [7Tao] methodology. An unnerving approach when first encountered, but the focus you achieve is immeasurable.

Aggressive? Only in the text, not in the approach. Through the intense training, you will win, you will survive, and you will want more of this revolutionary ideology. You will have many more tools in your arsenal when the training is complete. My business is richer in knowledge, richer in confidence and richer in profit through the 7Tao approach. Believe me when I say, 'Without nerve you will not survive,' 'Without an open mind you will not survive' and 'With an unblinkered approach you will become stronger.' 7Tao will give you the nerve, the open mind, confidence and energy to survive the enormous economic pressures put upon your business. These economic and business pressures are not going away, and neither is 7Tao. My recommendation is to engage with the 7Tao methodology and ride the storm."

Adapting to a changing environment is the key to quality.

Many understand the sheer force to which the Japanese entered the marketplace during the 1973 oil crisis. They had 2 angles of attack in the marketplace that yearned for their products so suddenly when the oil crisis produced gas lines in the fuel stations across the West.

The first was that the car produced by Toyota, Nissan and Honda was fuel efficient. The second was that it started up every time. 'It will never let you down 'was the message which the Japanese manufacturers were trying to get across.

Not only were the Toyota's reliable, the fit and finish was also very good. Sure, they had teething pains when entering and adapting to a new marketplace, but generally, the cars were coming along just fine. As the Japanese learned about their target market, they adapted their quality systems to that market thus producing appropriate solutions to the problems which the products experienced in the country of sale.

They did this by eliminating not only mistakes, but even the possibility of making a mistake. If you eliminate the possibility of making a mistake, you have no mistake to fix and you have no problems which to return to re-manufacturing stations. This was where they made the greatest gains, in systems like Poke Yoke and other forms of fool proofing, they were able to out produce their competitors in the United States.

When the Japanese started their drive to excellence in the United States, their cars imitated the originals. Toyota Celica's shouted at you "I want to be a Ford Mustang". But pretty soon, the imitations were better than the real thing. This was entirely to do with the quality of the product. The best part was that Toyota didn't emphasise quality. The customer automatically knew that they were buying a quality product when they bought a Toyota. They didn't have to explain why the car was good quality, because if you had to do that, you were obviously missing something.

The Toyota Land Cruiser began as a competitor to Land Rover. In Australia, sales were dominated by Land Rovers, when the Toyota Land Cruiser came out, it outsold the Land Rover to near extinction in the marketplace. In September 2019, it was revealed that the Toyota land cruiser had sold more than 10 million vehicles globally becoming another one of Toyota's best-selling vehicles on the planet.

The Toyota Camry has been the best-selling car in the US for 20 consecutive years. The reason why is because customers love it. Customers have demands for everything including safety and security, quality and reliability, performance, and appeal. Toyota Camry gives the customer the exact product they are looking for and this pure adherence to quality builds the one thing which customers are looking for – Trust. Can I trust that this car will give me the product that I need and the performance I need to achieve my life's objectives? America is made up of families and the Toyota Camry becomes the third adult in the home. Mother, Father and then Toyota Camry. The Camry is part of Americas staple diet now, it is featured in every household menu and has become part of the furniture of the household. This is the trust which Toyota has built with pure dedication to quality of delivery of product and service to their customer.

There are many reasons why quality is important for your customer's, some of them are as follows:

1: Quality builds trust.

If a customer trusts good quality work and good quality products. They will keep coming back. When you have good quality products, this allows you to raise your prices or retain your prices allowing you to stay in business. If you cannot keep good quality products or services, you will lose your customer starting with one, two and then before you know it sales have been cut in half. It is important to measure your quality in your organization. Make sure that you can look at all of the product and services which require customer loyalty. Ask the customers for the information required to complete better quality questions and metrics.

2: The customers will recommend you.

When a customer uses a brand to show how much better their product is, you have achieved excellence. Recommending brands is a much-desired way to get more sales though your door, but to achieve that, you must beat your competition. The best way to get the quality required to sustain excellence is by having no defects. The Japanese have a phrase called Zero defects. Although they never achieve the aim of zero defects, they are always targeting that metric to get as close to it as possible. If they can achieve 3 defects in a million, usually, they are quite happy in product manufacturing performance.

3: Less customer complaints and less returns.

When less products are being remanufactured or repaired, you know you have a quality product. It is important that quality products lead to less customer complaints in product or service because it allows a seamless relationship of supply with the marketplace. Customers will keep coming back for more product or using your service when they learn that you are a reliable source of supply for their needs.

4: Concentrate on 7Tao senses.

People like the way a product looks, feels, sounds, tastes and smells adding confidence of brand and the assurance of reliability. This makes them naturally inclined to purchase because they have a strong appreciation of results of the product. If a product or a service can allow them to engage in all of their capacity with a product, they will immediately be inclined to form a relationship with that product. This results in a long-term sales process with regards to achieving customer client relationship. The 7 senses dictate exactly which direction a product will go.

5: Return on investment.

Good quality products and services create a better yield than poor quality products and services. When a customer sees that a product will last them a very long time, won't let them down, creates an excellent vibe and feel for them, they will undoubtedly purchase leading to a greater return on investment for the company. This ROI will be in tangible returns in monetary terms and also in intangible terms in good will from the customer and the marketplace such as recommendations of the product or service. Over time, intangible measurements can lift tangible measurements such as increase in sales across the company.

6: Growth results.

Growth a product variety will result as you increase quality performance. You will naturally begin to ask can we operate in this area too? Can we build products in this area too? Can we invent something new? Can we fulfil a task which no one else can fulfil? Can we build a product or a service for a future which has yet to arrive? This where R&D, product development, visionary concepts and new forms of physics come in to drive results forward.

The key about growth is the ability to ponder and ask questions about the future which do not matter yet but which may matter in the future. Flying cars used to be a consideration many years ago but in the coming years, flying cars may well be a normal sight on our roads and in the skyways that are being considered to direct them. When quality of questioning combines with excellence in production, that is a sure way to increase innovation in process and product. This is point where out of the box questions are asked. If you come to the end of the road on one line of innovation, you begin to think of other ways of innovation. This is exactly how the flying car is being developed. It started with the electric car, then combining different methods of transport, then propellers and duct fans. Before anyone knew, a flying car had been built. The refining process had begun along with the diversity of the product.

Flying cars: Product quality leads to improved quality of mobility.

What if we can go up too, not just left right back and forth? This is the question many manufacturers are asking today as they consider the impact of electric flying cars. Innovation doesn't just come in small incremental movements; it comes in paradigm shifts, as well. When innovative capability can cross platforms and combine different technologies to embrace those environments, we really have a globally relevant economic cycle. Innovation appears to be pointing toward road-air-sea crossover vehicles, with power sources that range among electric, gasoline, fusion, hydrogen cells, and many other power combinations. It's worth looking at the ways in which these innovations will change our lives in the years to come.

Air-Road Crossover: A new line of innovation

Many designs for air-road crossovers are being conceived. The research and development for this type of vehicle is now so easy to apply that the number of products coming out is becoming vast and their applications unlimited. Take Yves Rossy, and the jetpack he designed in his garage. This ex-pilot had an idea about a jet wing. He made one, strapped on four gas-turbine engines from model airplanes, embedded a fuel system into the wing and, voila!

The new developments in cars will change the landscape, as well. The new flying cars and bikes, which are based entirely upon the drone idea, are now becoming reality. As these new flying cars become commercially available, people will come to use them in all sorts of ways, thus affecting everything around them from safety, navigation control, commercial uses, military uses, and even criminal uses.

If there are 1,000 of these cars flying about in the years ahead to come, the police will need one as well to catch any criminals who do 'bad stuff' inside them. This means that helicopters and various other flight-based vehicles will likely hit the road to obsolescence too. Regulation will have to change as well, to allow for control and licensing of these types of products as they transform the very nature of our lives.

Home-Based R&D

The R&D signs are everywhere. Economic atomization and R&D home-based capability are leading people to go out on their own and discover what they are capable of, leading to innovations and intelligence levels being applied throughout the world, as people say to themselves, "I've got an idea, and I think I can make it."

The most important factor is the industrial effect of these types of innovations. What is the cause and effect on established industries as they become increasingly left behind, with obsolescence sneaking up like a Cheetah seeks its prey? Well, the fact of the matter comes down to industrial warfare, it's all about transactions. If an inventor makes a flying car in a small shed in his back garden, industrial unit or R&D laboratory somewhere in the country and obtains 1000 orders for his invention. He then removes 1,000 transactions across a range of established brands, leading to 1,000 fewer orders on their order books for small older planes built upon research established from the 1920s.

This will lead to cutbacks, layoffs, and closures among weaker competitors who have plodded along for decades. When others realize that the one who got there first with his passenger drone car is making money, they will pile into the emerging market, as well. Before you know it, there are 20 different offerings for the same product, leading to even more transactions; supply and demand changes as the economy morphs to secure customers who want to buy something different. If it's all about buy and sell, then it's about competition and money. If it's about competition and money, then it's about industrial warfare. That is the crux of the matter.

Any innovation is guided by industrial warfare attack and defence methods, no matter where you look, or what you make or what you do. If you are dealing with money, manufacturing, production, and sales, industrial warfare will be a vital element of your study structure.

Many companies are pushing to be the first in this line of innovation. If you can remember where Tesla was in 2008, you will find a company that was in

the middle of nowhere with Electric cars, on its way to becoming a working company with a few R & D ventures with Lotus looking into the possibilities of making a usable road worthy electric vehicle which can stay within the laws and regulations of the land. They were so small that everyone ignored them, dismissed them, relegated them to crackpot inventors, with Elon Musk belonging in the space age. 15 years later, Tesla is dominating innovation on all technological plains. Today Tesla has the largest Market Cap of any vehicle supplier in the world. They are the biggest automotive company in the automotive field. Further to this, they have forced every other vehicle manufacturer to produce a line of electric vehicles which makes Tesla even more respected and investor friendly. Tesla started out using discovery and innovation journey as their guiding light, meeting many close shaves with bankruptcy and closure. A lot of the smaller companies that began in support of the main Tesla brand met with that fate. Many of their competitors now meet with that fate as they simply cannot duplicate the success with which Tesla has dominated the marketplace.

This is exactly what is taking place with flying car manufacturers. All new industries begin with experimentation and a show of new technologies and capabilities. 90% of these companies will die in their first decade of operation. The ones that survive to change the world are the ones who starved their way through the obstacles that are thrown at them by the consumer, marketplace competition and governments who have vested interested in keeping the status quo the same. But they do get through, just like Tesla, Television and the Internet, they go on to change the way the world works for many decades to come. These are the people who go down in history as the celebrated leaders of their nations. People like Nikola Tesla, Albert Einstein and Isambard Kingdom Brunel, Leonardo Da Vinci and the latest additions to global change makers, Elon Musk, Jeff Bezos and Jack Ma.

It's not just the Chinese who know this about innovation. All companies must study where they fit in the world of competition, whether they have an existing set of products based upon the old designs, or a new set of products based upon future designs. You have to sell them in the marketplace, and that is what really counts. It all comes down to the acceptance of the transaction. The flying car will become the corner stone of our existence just like the car did in the 20th century, it will change the way in which new houses are designed to accommodate flying cars, how energy is distributed and how commerce is completed. This innovation will not just change the way in which we live and move, it will change the entire infrastructure of living and moving to accommodate this new living and moving space in the decades to come.

CHAPTER 7

Tao 4: After Market: Do They Come Back for More?

Making a customer come back to you is the hardest trick. You have to make sure that your price is affordable, delivery is on time and the quality of the product is unmatchable. Then there is a good chance that the customer will come back for more. You must offer a service to the customer which allows him to feel secure in his purchase. You need to earn his loyalty. You are not just selling a product, you are looking to win customer approval through excellence in your manufacturing, production and distribution processes.

Choices, choices, choices... There is so much competition in the world, in every field, in every job, in every phase of life, in everything we do.

Competition is measured by the number of products from which a customer can select. When competition becomes lethal, the purchaser becomes numb to offers. The lifetime of a business is curbed. For it to survive, the number of offers it needs to make rises dramatically. Cash flow is king. How do you grow new fields of business in a ruthlessly expanding business environment? How will your competitors react when you intrude into their customer bases? Will they make counteroffers? Will they cut costs to steal your customers? Unrelentingly, the questions keep coming.

Defending the aftermarket requires a deep knowledge of your customers. You need to build relationships with them to understand their difficulties. This is another way of saying that you need to understand the marketplace, the changes emerging in the political, economic, social and technological milieu. Are your accumulated ideals and perspectives obsolete? The current economic climate is undergoing a once-in-five-centuries transformation. This presents a unique set of challenges.

Two forces which drive the marketplace are fear and hope. Fear is associated with defending your transaction while hope is associated with growing your transaction. The first stage in mastering the market lies in defending the transaction.

Box 7:1 - The Chinese Harley Davidson

While I was travelling through Pakistan, visiting family, in 2003, I came across a street with a series of motorcycle shops. I was astounded to see Harley Davidson copies being sold at ridiculously low prices. Brand new bikes still wrapped in cellophane were being sold at £400 (at this time the pound was still backed by the British government and was strong). I looked at all the different models of bikes and couldn't believe how cheap they were.

I asked the owner of one shop why he bought the Chinese bikes, why he has switched from Honda, Kawasaki and Suzuki. His answer was simple: 'I can sell a lot more of these bikes. More people visit my shop; more people are browsing around. All of these that couldn't afford a bike before are coming here now to buy these Chinese bikes because they can. Before, when I used to sell the original Japanese brands, I was competing with other bike sellers and our margins were quite low. Our margins now are terrific because, not only can we sell a lot more bikes, we also can make a lot more on each one we sell.'

'How the hell are the Chinese doing this?' I thought. I asked one of the Chinese suppliers who was making one of his regular visits to the bike shops, 'How do make such cheap bikes?' At first he wouldn't talk to me. He must have thought, 'Who the hell is this guy?' Then he answered, 'Well, our costs are very low to begin with. We hardly pay anything for the land because we have a communist backdrop to our capitalist face, so we can control land prices thereby reducing rent significantly allowing us to cut costs. So we don't pay any real rent and our energy costs are subsidized by the government.

Every time industry piles up in one area, the government spreads it out to make sure that we're not treading on each other's toes. The only things we really have to pay for are the materials and the labour needed to put the bikes together.'

I decided to take a ride on one and mounted the most expensive bike, a huge road hog with the largest engine. It cost £400. It sounded just like the real thing. I felt good on that bike. I'm no bike enthusiast, but I did like it. I was told it could do up to 100 mph, quite fast enough for me. 'In fact I don't even want to go that fast,' I said,' I just want to get from A to B and show the girls what a man I am!' The shopkeeper laughed and so did the Chinese bike supplier. We had some tea and then I left for home.

Chinese copies of everyday motorcycles, which people bought just to get around, were £150 brand new. The Chinese manufacturers had a strategy. Their aim was to offload these bikes in order to replace a Honda transaction with one of their own. They knew what they were doing. They wanted to replace Honda, Suzuki, Kawasaki and Harley Davidson as competitors. In order to suffocate the competitor, you have to take orders away from them. The process starts with one order. If you can take away one order, you can take away four orders, and eventually 40,000 orders.

The effect this has on the competitor is disastrous. If they are operating in an economy where prices and operating costs are too high, they will be adding those costs on to each transaction. This will make them uncompetitive. The Chinese know this. They know that the Achilles heel of Western economies is their economic system. The competitor is vulnerable. If the competitor is vulnerable, you don't really have to fight it that hard because the costs of operation will have made its organization very brittle. If Chinese manufacturers can sell enough bikes, they will shut down the competitor and kill the brand.

Chinese bikes are still very cheap. Anyone considering buying one just needs to go to Alibaba.com. Have a look at all the different sorts – there are hundreds, in all shapes and sizes.

To understand where we are in the marketplace, we have to establish what our after-market services look like and what our competitor's after-market services look like. An example of this analysis is shown over the page:

Competitor	Our services	How do we attack the competition?
Does our competitor offer better prices? What does he offer and how does he offer it? What is his position?	Are our prices competitive? What do we offer and how do we offer it? Can our costs be cut?	Can we launch a price-based attack and defeat him on price? Can we lower costs and increase prices at the same time?
Does our competitor offer better delivery services?	What do we offer in delivery and what are we missing?	Can we launch a delivery-based attack and defeat him by offering a faster delivery?
Does our competitor offer better quality?	How many returns do we get from customers, for whatever reason?	Can we launch a quality-based attack and defeat him on the cost of poor quality?
Does the competitor have more customers?	How can we grow our customer base?	Can we approach his customers (if we know who they are) and offer them more?
Is he making a profit or loss leading?	How can we make a profit and stay in business?	Can we attack him with a better yield performance or overtake him in this market?
Are his employees suffering under pressure?	Can we recruit his most productive employees by offering them better terms, and use them to attack their former employer?	Can we seize his talent, taking the value added knowledge from his power players?

Li Shufu

Geely production By Siyuwj - Own work, CC BY-SA 3.0,

Box 7:2 Geely: The Coming of Age of the Chinese Auto Industry

Li Shufu is regarded as China's Henry Ford. Born on a rural farm in 1963, he used to take pictures of villagers for a fee while the cultural revolution was taking place. When he finished school at 17, he used his graduation gift of 100 Yuan to buy a camera. At this point his entrepreneurial skills were born. After years of taking pictures, he had saved enough money to go into a new line of business, stripping precious metals from fridges. Eventually this led him to start selling refrigerator parts. In June 1989 the Chinese military cracked down on rioters in Tiananmen Square. 'We felt very insecure,' says Li Shufu, 'so, for the sake of safety, I gave up everything.' It wasn't clear whether the government would continue market-friendly policies so he hedged his bets and stayed quiet for a time. Then, in the 1990s, he decided that his real ambition was to build cars. He began by opening a motorcycle plant (at that time China wasn't distributing licences for the auto industry), but at the same time he was studying the auto business. In 2000 (when licences were granted) his company Geely came into being.

They began by taking American cars apart, then building their own models powered by Toyota engines. These first models were crudely assembled and production did not exceed 5,000 units in the early days. Today Geely produces 1,500,828 cars a year in 2018 and is growing rapidly, along with other Chinese car companies. Geely has a market cap of $22 Billion in 2022 and is exporting cars to the Middle East, South Asia, South America and other hard-to-reach places around the globe. It also supplies black cabs to London under a joint venture programme, produces electric cars and owns Lotus and Volvo. 'How to make cars is no longer a big secret,' says Li Shufu, Chairman of Geely. 'The technologies are widely used and shared.' The Chinese have entered the market in a highly professional and successful manner. It is likely that they will come to dominate car sales through price alone. If they can somehow attain and remain in the centre of the electrification revolution, they will be supplying cars to the world for centuries to come. Can the USA stop them? Highly unlikely.

> The Geely 7Tao is a very powerful construct indeed. The interesting thing is that the very companies that sell parts to Ford, VW, Mercedes and other Western car manufacturers also supply the same parts to Geely and other Chinese manufacturers. They are essentially using the same supply chain to create competitive products for different markets, then attacking Western manufacturers who have used Chinese supply companies to cut costs.
>
> From very humble beginnings, Geely has grown into a business that is successfully taking on the best in the world. This success illustrates the art of industrial warfare at its best. Shut down your competitors as fast as you can through order suffocation! Amazing.

After Market Begins with the Sale of a Good Quality Product

The key to achieving sustained business is implementing a growth strategy. Some firms are still wedded to the strategies they learnt from the likes of Six Sigma, Lean or 20 Keys, which think defensively. 7Tao incorporates defensive methods but it goes a step further and focuses on attack.

7Tao encourage competition that reflects the ways in which the business world operates today. We teach the most effective and ferocious economic fighting methods. Students take part in ruthless forms of economic combat and use methods that go beyond those developed in the 1960s, taking us into the 2020s. There is no hiding place for those who engage in the 7Tao method: it forces firms to confront the difficulties of the globalised world and motivate their workers. The art of management is leading your workers. Your employees need to understand the firm's problems: they must be allowed to see the pressures and to participate in the identification of solutions. It may be difficult, but you must make the worker believe in what he is doing. A manager that fails to fire up his workforce will miss the opportunities presented by changing market conditions.

7Tao encourages workers to fight for their livelihoods, to take part in successful projects that will help sustain the business. In a 7Tao class no employee is bored to death with statistics or having to learn endless foreign terms. The number of internal changes and external strategies in the marketplaces will increase dramatically as workers fight to improve their business. Their emotional involvement in their work will keep customers coming back for more.

Source Pictures: Wikipedia

Box 7:3 The Story of the Hummer: Industrial Warfare in Action

Industrial warfare is graphically illustrated in the story of the Hummer, also known as the Humvee by the US Army. We all knew that the Chinese were producing a cheap copy of the Hummer H1 called the Eastwind, as you can see above. But this is not the issue here... The issue here is industrial warfare.

General Motors, the stricken American giant, tried to offload the Hummer brand on the Chinese, but after long negotiations the Chinese declined to buy the brand and its associated vehicles. *The Guardian* reported on 24 February 2010 that 'the hummer brand would be wound down'. When the deal with Sichuan Tengzhong Heavy Industrial Machinery fell through, the brand was discontinued.

Even the US Army had decided that it would make no new purchases of the vehicle. Everyone involved in producing Hummer vehicles was out of a job. A standard tactic in industrial warfare is to watch carefully as a stricken opponent falls to its knees and then offer a very small sum for the brand, the machines, the parts and anything else you can grab hold of in the fire sale. You offer to buy it for next to nothing and watch the seller cave into the pressure. Delay, delay, delay the deal until the seller is unable to continue trading. You learn from the theories of industrial warfare that the most important thing is to bide your time until the opponent yields to your demands. You force them into a compromising position where they will be forced to accept a pittance for their asset.

Their only alternative would be to die what they may perceive to be an 'honourable' death. Nobody needed the Hummer anymore. The vehicle had no value in today's world of high fuel prices and onerous tax systems. It was way too expensive, too big, too brash. It only served the super-rich and there are few of them left in the world as the economy changes to suit the Chinese. Anyway, why buy an expensive American Hummer when you can buy a perfectly viable Chinese copy. It's a cheaper way to make the same bold, brash, silly statement.

Case Study 4

John Bradley of The National Skills Academy for Manufacturing

The National Skills Academy for Manufacturing is a government agency that has called 7Tao in to various companies to upgrade their performance to world-class levels.

John Bradley, Consultant for NSAM (UK), explains why the results of the systems implementation were such a revelation.

The National Skills Academy for Manufacturing (NSAM) are a training, education and consulting company specifically designed to up-skill the nation's manufacturing industry, enabling them to compete globally through learning and skills. NSAM work under the Sector Skills Council for Science, Engineering and Manufacturing Technologies, and they work with all the UK global manufacturers and supply chain in the metals, mechanical and electrical, electronics, aerospace, automotive, marine and bioscience industries.

I met Amar while he was employed by a college working in continuous improvement systems in the local engineering industry. We witnessed a presentation he was giving about the 7Tao system and instantly recognised its potential in the marketplace. What he had invented was a balanced economic manufacturing business learning system which was potentially a mixture of Asian and Western offensive and defensive management systems and engineering competencies. Once our organization analysed the system in the ways of operation, we realized its application to our needs at NSAM immediately. There is a reason why customers return to 7Tao repeatedly: it is because of the transactional bias of the system. It really focuses down and pushes into the value of each process as it travels through the whole manufacturing process. The system is ferocious in its implementation, with a set of pressures built into the attack and defence processes which force the employees of the organization into competitive combat. This is highly reflective of the modern world which we live in today, especially with the rise of China being one of the most important factors in the running of any manufacturing business.

Compared to the Six Sigma and Lean programmes the West were running, 7Tao was powerful, controversial and developed to learn the skills needed for economic battle. This was not an average system. 7Tao had both attack and defensive strategies which could unsettle a competitor when being used against them. We decided to test part of the system within the education framework of a company we found named Centurion Electronics PLC. The first stage of implementation was defensive. Amar taught them the principles and techniques of 7Tao within a simulation. How people change when they are put into a competitive environment was amazing. The teams we observed were placed into three sets of five people. They were then given a task of building a racing car in a controlled environment where they were allowed to attack and defend against each other.

The environment of the task was built in from the beginning with a view to attacking and defending against their competition head on. One team would be attacking the second while the other team was attacking the third. Each one of the teams was trying to secure market position over the next and win transactions against each other.

The system was an enormous success, with huge gains to the business being achieved throughout its implementation – huge gains from the point of view of saving money, looking at the market and the competitors in a new light, and ensuring the profit margins of the company were being applied in the correct way.

This has been further implemented successfully with Johnson Matthey, and again with major business benefits. The 7Tao system was designed to engage corporations that wanted to compete in harsh economic environments where survival is the key. 7Tao seeks out environments where economic combat is taking place – aggressive environments with high competition, companies which need help to grow and to survive, companies that are not afraid of going into the marketplace and fighting their competitors in their home markets.

7Tao would be an unbelievable system in a global economic downturn, a completely balanced offensive and defensive toolkit for businesses enabling them not just to survive but actually to grow in a severely competitive global market.

This is what 7Tao does: it teaches you the most fundamental and obvious economic fighting techniques in an environment that requests them. This is what makes it stand out from the rest of the systems out there. We had been using Six Sigma and Lean Manufacturing, but clearly nothing like this had really come across in industry. It was something which was unique, built upon the principles of Chinese industrial and economic battle methods which were light years ahead of the competitors.

The beauty of 7Tao is that it looks at winning the game, not winning the rules. This is what makes the Chinese competitor far more capable than the ones who are resident in the West. Their ability to out-manoeuvre, out-think and out-play the competition is what makes them powerful beyond our wildest expectations. This environment, which has developed recently in the last three or four years, is not about a change in competitor, it is about a permanent change in business environment. The world is in a completely different economic place from where it was a decade ago, with more changes occurring in a year than have occurred in the last one hundred put together.

The 2008 worldwide economic recession: Amar had told us several times throughout the years that we were heading for a depression, one of the most serious we will ever witness in the history of economics. At the time, none of us at NSAM believed him. Amar informed us of the importance of the cyclical patterns of this economy and how the depression would bring profound changes to the world in its geopolitical, economic and social contexts. At that time this seemed distant to us. Most of us ignored him as someone who was whacky, of left field, as someone who had difficulty understanding economic ideas.

He knew from Fred Harrison that these economic crises would take place, but the 7Tao system is ideally placed as a counter to the depression. Although the system is well built and advantageous to manufacturing businesses who use it in periods of economic growth, I believe it is also the only system which deals with the challenges which we face in the recent depression which announced itself in 2008. Amar and Fred were correct, and nobody really believed them. This difficult economic environment was developing and building strength through 2009 and 2010 and would continue for at least a generation into the future. Another even deeper recession is being forecast by Amar in 2026. This could be devastating for the world economy as a whole, not just the West because all our global economy is now intertwined together. We all go up and down in one go because of the alignment of the cycles.

7Tao is now sitting in the sole position, not pole position, of having the only economic offensive and defensive business system which is built to commandeer difficult times and depletion climates. It is amazing how forecasting ability, combined with creativity, capability and understanding, came to create this system of paramount importance. Everybody can talk about an event after it has happened, a few can see an event before it happens, but only in very rare circumstances does someone somewhere actually prepare for the event with a viable answer.

Predicting the US China trade war ahead of time is certainly an amazing achievement. People still do not believe that this happened, that Amar could have predicted it so accurately. And in the way he expected, along with his system being staggeringly relevant to the subject matter turning up in 2018. As the year progressed, Amar's 7Tao became even more relevant as each and every element embedded itself in the unfolding process as the US and China negotiated their respective positions.

I believe 7Tao is the only organization that has invested time, money and effort into preparing a vehicle for navigating this depression. That is truly amazing and a work of genius. I also believe 7Tao is one of the essential tools which could save a manufacturing economy from total devastation in this depression which the world is facing." By John Bradley. National Skills Academy for Manufacturing. Partner in 2010.

Box 7:4 Washing Clothes

The washing machine made in the West (left) costs $650; the one made in China and delivered to your door by the internet-based retailers (right) costs $100. The difference is $550… Worth a gamble by a hard-pressed family in the present financial crisis?

The home is the centre of human life, the backbone of the family; it is the place where children have their best memories of childhood. Dominating purchases for the home is key to building a customer base. Because families live in clusters, and pass information from one to another, persuading one family to purchase your product is the key to breaking a competitor's hold over a marketplace. It is a matter of 'entry point'. How do you enter into a household's process of purchasing and push away a competitor from a loyal family? Most of us expect the current depression to last at least ten years into the future.

This will give China a big window through which to enter into our marketplace. As the economic pressures on families increase, their budgets will decrease and their disposable income will be stretched. When an economy is depressed, the main aim will be to buy products of the best possible quality but at the cheapest price. Manufacturers need to target retail chains like Walmart which offer goods at the lowest prices. Any rising power will fight on price when it enters a market, just as Japan, Korea, Malaysia, India and Hong Kong did when they started… China is doing the same now. The Chinese are entering the price game, but they have to fight every single competitor in the marketplace. They have to take on Western manufacturers as well as the above-mentioned countries' brands. To be able to sell their washing machines cheaper than all the others already crowding the marketplace will require an all-out attack strategy both within a developing China and externally, in the world they export to. You must always start with a cheap product, and enter a market when it is depressed by the 18-year cycle. Once you have entered the marketplace, the aim is to put the other players out of business. When one transaction replaces another factories transaction, it will be because of demand relevance alone. Nothing else!

> The ones who are most vulnerable in a depressed marketplace are those offering luxury brands at excessively high prices. The ability of these high-value manufacturers to shift their products will fall dramatically. To steal every possible transaction, you need to access every place where there may be a demand for your goods: websites, distribution chains, retail stores, sales venues of every sort in a targeted area.
>
> The children will see your trademark and associate your brand with their mother. It will become embedded in their minds. So how do you make sure that the children in this family grow up with your washing machine, and not someone else's, as part of their lives? How do you make holes in your competitor's production line? If you can take one sale off your rival you can take 100,000 sales off them. The first blow is the most important.
>
> There are over 11,500 different washing machines on offer on Alibaba.com. The choice is almost endless, from every third-world design to every first-world design. The number of manufacturers is mind-boggling. So many all looking for the first blow...
>
> The difference in price between the Western-manufactured washing machine at $650 and the Chinese washing machine at $100 is $550... Would a family struggling under the weight of the financial crisis take the risk?
>
> I think so. They may not even have a choice. And if that washing machine turns out to be of good quality, if it lasts a reasonable time, it will be bought by other family members and recommended to friends.

Aftermarket: The Belt and Road Initiative. Getting there first.

The Belt and Road initiative (BRI) is a global infrastructure development strategy adopted by the Chinese government in 2013 to invest in 74 countries and numerous international organizations. It is considered to be the centre piece of Chinese leader Xi Jinping's foreign policy. The Belt and Road Initiative will include investments such as infrastructure buildings, ports, skyscrapers, railroads, roads, bridges, dams, coal fired power stations, airports, railway stations, tunnels, and motorways. BRI will cement China as the primary exporter in every one of the 74+ countries that it touches. The silk route of old has just been given a modern makeover allowing China to take supply of the world's Island of Eurasia. In a 2019 study conducted by Global Economic Consultants, they found that BRI was likely to boost world GDP by $7.1 Trillion.

Belt and Road Initiative is about one thing, getting Chinese goods into 74 countries stores on a daily basis. Every train, plane and automobile that carries products made in Chinese factories will be delivering seamlessly to every corner store, departments store and online warehouse throughout Eurasia cementing the weight of the global transaction firmly in Chinese hands. The reason why the Chinese have invested so much in BRI is because of return customers. They want them to keep coming back. This is classic aftermarket strategy, deliver the goods directly to the customer and supply them for the rest of the generations to come. They must come back because they built the roads inwards into their countries.

It will lock out the transatlantic cycle from even competing with the Eurasian economic drive and will break the hold that the Western governments currently have over the third world countries of central Asia, Africa, and South America. In industrial war language, this will starve the transatlantic competitors into the shadows of their former selves. When the BRI reaches 65% of the global population and 40% of world GNP according to World Pensions Council, the Chinese will be commandeering the policies of more than half of the world's leadership.

Trading back and forth, goods will be exchanged from those 74 countries back to China, with raw materials and manufactured goods being traded with the 1.4 billion Chinese people. In all cases, there will be a complete dedication to the transaction. 7Tao will be the basis of trade as these people exchange with each other to gain wealth, material goods, dignity, and respect. Central geographies to the BRI will be the Islamic countries and central Asian Islamic states as primary arteries of goods and movement across the super continent.

The sheer amount of tonnage being shifted throughout Eurasia will be in the millions of tonnes of goods per day. This will power Chinese factories for decades to come as they fill the shelves of every retail outlet in the Middle East, Africa, Asia, Europe, Southeast Asia, and the Indian subcontinent. The sheer turnover of goods and services being consumed by these countries will be more than all the total value of the Transatlantic cycle as the direction of trade and balance of the transaction centres between Europe and Asia. The Middle East will be the resource station where large amounts of oil and gas are supplied to the BRI fuelling its growth and maturity over the next three decades to come.

Belt and Road Initiative will have a direct effect on the transaction. Every one of the 7 parts of the transaction will allow the Chinese exchange to become more attractive and much more focused on the needs of the customer. Once this has been achieved, the customer will always come back because they will come to depend on the product. The Belt and Road Initiative is being designed to support the 7Tao of the transaction. As the flow of goods and services increases, so does the unity of the people and the need to practise diplomacy. Within these 74+ countries, it will become difficult to have a conflict. All the other countries involved will intervene because any conflict between the members of the Belt and Road Initiative is a threat to all members, like what NATO say in their security alliance. This will make unity levels very strong and legal systems will have to adapt and grow to reflect the needs of each country and all the countries involved in the Belt and Road Initiative. This is the biggest development in the last 3 centuries since the silk route was established of old.

This means that there is a new Rules based order coming and how it will be developed will be influenced by those who are a part of the community of nations within Belt and Road Initiative. The total population involved in Belt and Road Initiative involved 66% of the world's population consuming manufactured goods on a daily basis. These are massive numbers, the competition will be huge and industrial warfare will be rife in all peoples, businesses, and countries. Solving these problems which industrial warfare brings to the world stage will require intelligence, diplomacy, and creativity. It is inevitable that legal systems will need to grow to contain these battles.

The map opposite displays the belt and road initiative as it grows to eclipse the Transatlantic cycle. This development will be a watershed event greater than anything the world has witnessed in the last 250 years. This will lead to greater numbers of trade movements across multitudes of vast landscape. The Transatlantic has tried to stop this using military means, but the combined intelligence services of the belt and road countries has managed to ensemble a huge resource of manpower and fact based intelligence to protect the rise of Eurasia. All 74 countries have enormous capabilities and increasing financial clout adding value through the BRI development schedule. The increasing number of security issues will allow greater and more diplomatic embrace between countries as they resolve around China to house the new silk route.   Source www.merics.org

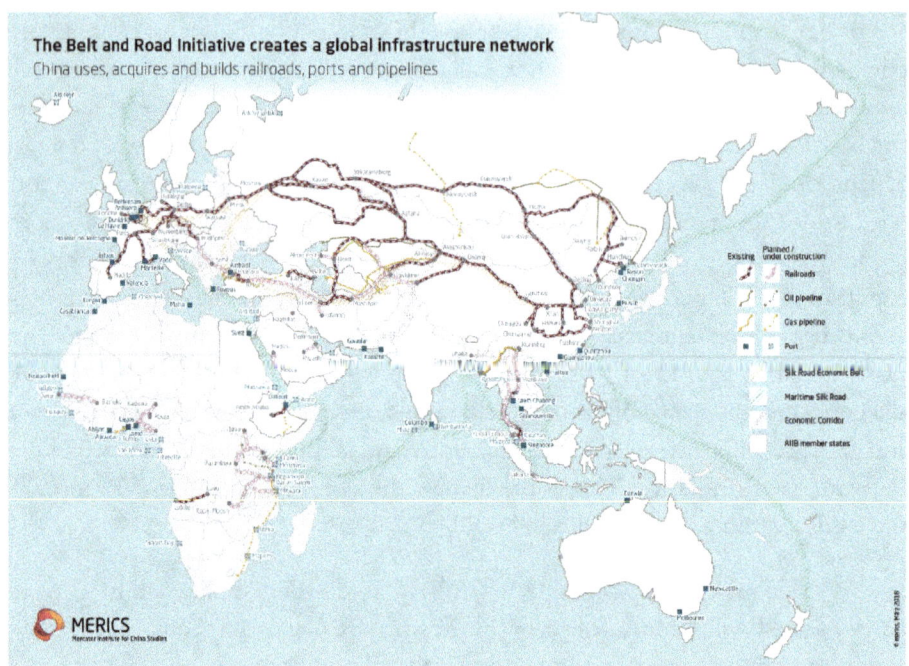

Source: Merics, Marz, 2018

Aftermarket support requires some deep thinking

So what does good aftermarket support systems look like within the core of the transaction?

Businesses are finding that offering solutions in total care, instead of just products was key to profitability and influence over manufacturers of original equipment. Selling spare parts, upgrading, repairing, reconditioning, carrying out inspection service, maintenance of goods and products, observing guiding and nurturing sales processes, providing technical support, consulting and training was a very profitable way of creating relationships with the customer and the supplier.

Aftermarket services represent 8% of gross national product in the United States of America. Over the years, companies have sold so many goods and services in automobiles, white goods, electronics, computers, and software that the maintenance and sustainability of these goods will be required for years to come. This means that American business will spend $1 Trillion annually on products which they already own. Supply chains in the United States currently earn 29% to 50% of revenues on products they have already supplied in the marketplace. The Belt and Road Initiative will require approximately 10% of total throughput revenue in maintenance care.

An Accenture study revealed that General Motors earned relatively more profits from $9 billion in after sales revenues in 2001 than it did from $150 billion of income in car sales. Large corporations around the world have won their customer loyalty and built a base of support in after sales support services. Wall street even tracts companies after sale support prowess by linking stock process directly to how diversified and ingrained the companies after sales support strategy is with that process linking to customer. In short, after market support is how you sustain your customer base and innovate to deeper, wider and better products services through feedback mechanisms.

Most OEM's such as car companies will partner and supply to warehouses such as Euro Car Parts who supply all of the garages in a geographic area. These trends allow online delivery systems in aftermarket support franchises to take place. A business will strike deals with as many OEM's as possible and then use a wall of supply services to gain a foothold in a geographic area. Third party vendors such as Halfords and Ron Skinner and Sons have become so price competitive that OEMs lose most of the aftermarket the moment the initial warranty time comes to an end.

Companies that operate in the field of aftermarket have one main problem at hand. Stock levels are too high and too much cash is tied up in inventory. Turnover and stock turns can be difficult to predict because how do you know when something is going to break down? And here lies the problem, lead times are too high because of the inability to predict demand, and if lead times are too high in repair and overhaul because of waiting for parts and components, then customers become unhappy because they don't get to use the product. If the product then sits on the repair bay for too long it is losing the company value because it is a liability and not a useful asset. This product is also costing the customer in lost earnings and the repair station in storage costs. Taking too long to repair a product can lead to obsolescence and damage the relationship with the customer. Aircraft manufacturers such as Textron Lycoming can reap benefits from an initial sale 30 years after the product has been sold to the customer. They must service and resupply the aircraft component for three decades leading to a lucrative relationship between customer chains and the company. The longer the life of the product, the more opportunities the OEM will have to keep producing parts. If a company can have an excellent aftermarket support facility in every area of operation, they can cross sell and up sell in all the associated markets as well.

A company that can manage a strong aftermarket facility will have enormous potential in the OEM sector of its business because its continuous improvement cycles will be directly in tune with customer demand. This allows product development to massively increase innovation cycles competing better against rivals. Once you have a strong aftermarket support facility, you will also have a very strong product development facility because the source of the next generation of product will lie within the shop floor of the aftermarket support facility as they learn about which components lasted the longest and which break down most often over time. The biggest problem with aftermarket support facility is predictability, predicting 'when' the most difficult issue is in the aftermarket support process.

'What can go wrong will go wrong' is the saying. In the aftermarket facility, managers 'what will go wrong, when will it go wrong and where will it go wrong?' They try to answer this question by doing what every knee jerk manager does in the world. Stock up with parts that they think will go wrong… and there is the biggest mistake. You can stock your products to 10 times the value that you currently stock, but you will still not be able to completely predict the demand for product repair. One could approach the aftermarket predictability problem by analysing usage rates and only stocking to usage of the particular component. But these are notoriously fickle to product and in 8 cases out of 10, the actual usage rate is either higher or lower than what is expected. So how do you solve the aftermarket problem?

When aftermarket theory is applied to the Belt and Road Initiative, we can begin to set up ideas of how hundreds of thousands of aftermarket companies will be operating within every country to service the massive infrastructure that supports the trading superhighway. And also, the sheer amount of large vehicles such a trains, trucks, ships, airliners and containers that will be building this massive development.

Companies that operate within the After Sales environment of Belt and Road Initiative might want to consider the Six Step approach to manage their support services:

1: Identify which products to cover. The older the product gets, the more it will need replacement parts, the more you will find it visiting the repair station. Support all, some, or competing products. The belt and road initiative will involve railways, roads ports and airports. All these logistics hubs use massive infrastructure to support the peoples of Eurasia and they need to be maintained after the BRI has been built.

2: Create a portfolio of products and services. For example, for an existing or supported product, list down all the support services you will be covering in that range. For each support mechanism write down the turnaround time for that support service with prices attached. You must support the aftermarket logistics hubs and the machines that use those hubs from all over the world.

3: Select business models to support product ranges. For example, companies may rent a product by the hour instead of buy it and pay for repairs. You may choose to have 50% ready to go products in the workplace and 50% already in the field products ready for breakdown allowing you to reduce lead times, turnaround times and inventory rates. You might want to store trains, planes and trucks for the repair process and just give the customer another one to use to get their jobs done.

4: Create teams to service stations. Your organization structure must have lists of who will be managing which part of the support process and contact details. This operation is all about customer service and reach. Provide as much visibility, focus and incentives to customers as is possible. This means each section of the Belt and Road Initiative will have huge responsibilities and accountabilities in the aftermarket support process.

5: Know your supply chain. Find out where all your parts suppliers will be, what your greatest weaknesses are. What parts are runners, repeaters and stranger's according to your usage rates and make sure that you have excellent stock sharing capabilities with them. In the Belt and Road Initiative, Air Sea and Land vehicles must be sustained and maintained in every way possible so that they do not become a blockage for the economic drive to unite 100 or so countries in the long run.

6: Check those speed dials. Evaluate against, competitors, history, improvement rates, benchmarks, and customer feedback rates. Make sure that aftermarket service is measured and carefully planned in planned and unplanned maintenance. Supporting the Belt and Road Initiative will consume entire countries industries as the 74+ countries band together and provide a network of support systems. Each nation must uphold the massive after support process that will be required to maintain and sustain the economic ecosystems which the Belt and Road Initiative will create across the nations of Eurasia. This will be a mammoth task which needs to be taken on by each individual country as they maintain their part of the new silk road.

Not only must the roads be maintained, railroads, tracks, airports, bridges, canals, rivers, water supply, drainage, forestry, grasslands, wildlife, emissions, climate change, sustainability, taxation, toll booths, control mechanisms, diplomacy and medical support systems need to be provided for all that will be working to sustain the Belt and Road Initiative after it has been built.

The same above listed six principles of aftermarket support systems will be applied to the trains, locomotives, trucks, planes, airliners, freight, cars, vans, waste removal vehicles, garbage removal trucks, fuel stations, gas pipelines, oil pipelines and water transportation systems. There is much more to the Belt and Road Initiative after market than meets the eye.

Xi Jinping Signs with Polish Prime Minister.

By Andrzej Hrechorowicz – Kancelaria Prezydenta RP, commons.wikimedia

A Chinese super port: Picture By Alex Needham.

Yangshan Deep Water Harbour Zone. Commons. Wikimedia.

CHAPTER 8

Tao 5: Customers: Do You Have Enough of Them?

The global population may be eight billion, but for the corporation the only people who matter are those with money to spend. Attracting customers is central to success. The competition is cut-throat. China is determined to wrest from Western manufacturers the loyalties of people who used to buy their favourite brands of goods made in Milan, Munich and Milwaukee. And when it comes to branding their goods for recognition by potential customers, the Chinese are not slow in learning the art of salesmanship. That's the brutal lesson of what Hollywood calls 'product placement'.

Routinely, Western manufacturers have insinuated their products into scenes in Hollywood movies, hoping that this will have a subliminal effect and pull in customers. Watch out for the Volvos that feature in so many car chases. There used to be a gentleman's agreement that limited the number of products being slipped into people's minds as they followed the twists and turns of a story on the big screen. The Chinese, however, have no respect for that tradition – witness *Transformers 3: Dark of the Moon*. You will recognise household brand names coming as thick and as fast as the action by alien robots. As the *Financial Times* reported on 20 July 2011: 'The Chinese branding campaign is the largest so far in any single Hollywood movie, highlighting Chinese companies' determination to go global and also use international marketing techniques to raise their domestic profiles.'

Forty years ago, a car manufacturer had to compete with two or three main rivals for a customer geography. Today that number exceeds fifty, and many of the products have a more valued reputation than the one you want to sell.

Customers' priorities vary from price considerations to delivery, quality or after-sales support. The pressures placed on the corporation by customers come on top of those imposed by shareholders. They have altered the working environment, reducing job security. One consequence is a reduction in the scale of operations as firms retrench into smaller units of production.

This causes immense problems to the health of the family unit and affects every transactional process in countries around the world. In these times of financial austerity, customers are opting for cheaper-end goods, emphasising the practical needs of 'now'. These price considerations impose huge pressures on a business to cut costs, which is conventionally translated into the need to cut the labour force. Managers are being short-sighted: they are cutting value-adding workers and processes so that they can survive to their next pay cheque. This creates the same self-fulfilling prophecy that is infecting governments. Politicians think that, for a nation to recover from the global recession that began in 2008, they need to cut spending. This is the trap set by the rise of China in the world economy. Deflation – the downward pressure on prices – was caused by China. As its goods, made with the aid of cheap labour, flooded the markets, Western corporations fell for the idea that, for them to survive, they also had to downsize and cut costs.

Western consumers demanded cheap prices. China fed that need as it transformed itself from a communist state playing second fiddle to the Soviet Union to the most powerful factory floor the world has ever seen. China could supply everyone in the world and still have a huge reserve of cheap labour ready to tap when the time came to expand its industrial base. Customers love China, and China loves its customers. Now desperate businesses around the world are asking, 'What can I do to stay in business?'

To retain the loyalty of a customer, you must design the right transaction, something to which the customer will return repeatedly to satisfy his needs. The real question is, 'How do I defend against a competitor who recognises no rules of engagement?'

Further to this, it is vital that the competitor understands exactly what the opponent is fighting for. Can loyalty cost as much as the competitor is charging the customer? Can brand loyalty be broken in times of distress? Can the customer simply choose another cheaper brand over the competition?

All of these factors come into play during times of recession and depression which is why I have emphasised the utmost importance of these periods in this book. It is during testing times and hard economic environments that innovation and adaptation begins to rear its head. The population begins to adapt. It is during these times that the governments also rob the population for more taxes. This drives innovation lower and ends up being the real reason why economies fail. The lower the taxes, the more business is attracted, the higher the taxes, the more business goes elsewhere for better pastures.

Here in the UK, Boris Johnson and Rishi Sunak have absolutely no regards for the hardship of people, for the rule of law or for the state of the economy. Instead of helping the nation, they have increased taxes to breaking point where living is becoming increasingly difficult. It is almost as if they planned the destruction of the nation as they deliberately squander the incomes of people on taxes which they don't even need. The question arises 'why are they doing this?'

The reason is hidden and devastating. They are getting ready for the 2026 crash because they have absolutely no way out of it. They have to rob the nations employees first so that they have something to give back when the crisis arrives. Interest rates will be racing to the moon and people will be going through exceptional hardships as they struggle to meet the monthly living expenses. It is quite obvious what they are doing. Boris Johnson and Rishi Sunak know what is coming, and they are getting prepared to face these impossible odds while they still can. Nothing can stop the 2026 depression and economic collapse. It is on its way.

Defending Customer Strengths

As competition rises exponentially and prices come down, firms need to ask: 'What are my transactional defences? How do I ensure that customers don't defect?' Remember that the pressures you are facing are matched by similar pressures on Western consumers. So the objective is to do more for less – a frightening prospect for companies facing the fiercest of competition.

To defend the customer, we must analyse competitors' strategies and compare our strengths. If we break our product or service down into its component parts for comparison with our competitor's, we may detect where the value lies.

It's just a matter of time before the smart customer also sees where the value lies in the products he buys. If your product has the least value, this will soon be reflected in lost orders, to the point where your business disappears. The customer will go elsewhere in search of value.

Pictures from Wikipedia

Box 8:1: The Currency War

It's all over the news. It's the only thing Ben Bernanke talks about. George Bush complained about it. Barack Obama keeps mentioning it. It gets so much press coverage that it has branded the Chinese 'currency manipulators', but that is unfair. On 1 April 1994 the Chinese said that they would tie the Yuan to the Dollar and the Americans were very happy about it.

Nowadays, as the currency war heats up day after day, the Americans are not happy. The Chinese are threatening to dump the dollar and the Americans are calling them currency manipulators. The truth of the matter is very simple. As the American industrial empire collapses, a new competitor is advancing and the dragon is breathing fire! The big difference is this: the Chinese have a history of sound money; the Americans are just printing dollars to stay economically viable.

Other differences are easy to see as well. The Chinese export a lot; the Americans have a lot of imports. The Americans export dollars in return for goods from around the world: the world exports value and commodities and the Americans return the favour by exporting dollars – not even actual currency, just figures on a computer. The world produces and America adds zeros on a keyboard. The world pays for the enormous empire America bases in their countries. That is its primary export – militarism.

It should be noted that due to the development of Donald Trump and the US China trade war, the weight of the transaction in 2022 has shifted almost completely towards Eurasia. Yes, USA is trying its best to disrupt in Kazakhstan, Afghanistan, Pakistan, Uzbekistan, Georgia, Russia, Ukraine and the South China sea, but these efforts will bring little fruition. Labelling the Chinese currency manipulators isn't going to work when the only thing you have in common with them is the Dollar. They are allowing the USA to lead until the West makes its own mistakes that they can't stop. Namely, the constant inflation combined with the 18-year land cycle which punishes the west - on time - every time.

Attacking Customer Weaknesses

If your customer is a firm that is struggling, it makes sense to reach out and help it. That customer needs to be protected from the pressures of the marketplace. You can help it to achieve its full potential. This may mean offering to place a person inside the customer's business, to develop standardization and strengths that are to everyone's mutual benefit. This will create unity and strength in the long term. Trust is developed through the tackling of issues of concern to both partners.

Your competitors will also be dealing with their customers. Can you reach these customers by using any of the 7Tao procedures covering price, delivery, quality, after market, customers, shareholders and employees? After all, it is in their interests to switch their loyalty to you if you are the stronger business. The key issue is 'reach'. Most companies know their competitors' customers. One way to entice them away is to offer free samples. These can be targeted at customers who may be open to a better deal than they have been getting from their existing suppliers. A simple brochure will not be effective in a saturated marketplace. Potential customers are more likely to be impressed by a unique sample which they can try out before deciding whether to change their buying habits. But a sample can be a two-edged weapon. A shrewd customer may use it to get his current supplier to offer better terms (such as a cheaper price), taking advantage of the personal relationship he has with them.

Customer Starts with the Order

Opportunity comes only every so often. Confidence can easily be shaken if you go into business thinking only about profits. Establishing customer relationships early in the life of the business is of paramount importance. A set of standards needs to be established. It is fundamental that you set yourself apart from your competitors from the start, by being not just different but more exciting. Setting yourself apart starts with the first order. To achieve this, disciplines, sometimes unlikely disciplines, can come from anywhere to contribute to a set of targets which have to be achieved. Car companies like to start in the design office. They come up with ideas about shapes, sizes, colours and technologies, all aimed at creating a new breed of product.

Box 8:2

The Renault Saga – an example of industrial warfare

Picture: Wikipedia commons 2012: Public domain.

On 7 January 2011 Reuters reported from Paris that French intelligence services were investigating a possible Chinese connection in an industrial espionage scandal at car-maker Renault. Three Renault executives, including one member of a management committee, were suspended. The industry minister Eric Besson said, 'I am not authorised to say anything on the subject.' Nicholas Sarkozy ordered the country's intelligence services to establish whether China was involved.

I laughed when I read this. Have they only just figured it out? What's all the fuss about? This has been normal practice for generations, ever since industry began! In the 1950s the Soviets were known for pioneering the 'glue shoe' technique. They would send their spies into a plant building an aircraft and they would walk right next to the machines which were producing various parts. They had glue on their shoes, so all the different types of alloys being used would be picked up. They would get samples all the metals needed to make a copy of the aircraft.

Nowadays, they don't even need to get the samples. They can just source a comparative machine from your competitor. Some collusion would allow for up and coming challengers to kill your business. Rules schmules. This is how industrial warfare is waged! It's not supposed to be fair; it's supposed to break the rules! It's supposed to steal your technologies and cut you in half! When I attend exhibitions in various industries around the world, I often get offered bribes to favour some contract.

> This is common practice in the executive world. You are offered money, or women, wine and song. Executives with shaky personal lives are exploited. Contracts or materials are taken straight out of your plant into a competitor's. It doesn't even stop there; it may be stolen from them as well! The thief will know that he can also be targeted. All these people have user groups which share technology and fight for profits. There are no rules, there is no copyright. Get used to it. The world is different now. Don't complain, you'll only look stupid whining about things you cannot change. Industrial warfare is a game of take it while you can, the rules are broken daily and there is not a lot we can do about it, taking the perpetrator to court will not work because they don't turn up.
>
> The USA is at pains to find the right solution to these problems which they face against the world. Why not consider 7Tao battling each of the opposition manufacturers instead of simply trying to resolve the issue with legal means. Perhaps if we looked at the problem in a different way, we might get more credibility and closer to a possible solution?
>
> If you show your opponent the stick of 7Tao as well as the carrot of negotiation, you might become more successful not just with the Chinese, but the whole world. Everyone is engaging in Industrial Warfare from all culture's regions and countries. As computing, AI and 3D capability increases, so will the ability to break the rules. The question comes how are you going to police this increasing industrial warfare scenario? Are you going to put the whole world in jail or blow them up? You might just be tempted to blow them up, but the damage that's done will unite the Eurasian opposition even further. A better solution would be to train up the Western manufacturing houses to protect themselves and allow them to develop their own ways of survival. The whole world is moving towards independence from order grip. Why not allow the manufacturer to protect themselves using 7Tao as their primary industrial martial art?

They will then test whether the idea will work by displaying it in the marketplace. Some ideas are radical, some conform to current market practices. The aim is to offer a range of ideas which take the trends of today forward into the future. This process has a complex set of objectives behind it: to appeal to customers, to establish the reputation of the company for the future and to attract investors' money. If your product speaks the language of the times, it can dominate the whole industry and displace competitors who are locked into obsolescence. When a customer places the first order, the most important thing for you to do is to correct any mistakes. You *will* make mistakes, but as you correct them your brand will make headway in the market. Mistakes come in two inter-related forms:

process mistakes and product mistakes. The 7Tao strategy is to deploy well over 256 tools specifically designed to eliminate mistakes in a product or process. Each of these tools predicts the environment in which mistakes are made and provides an immediate remedy. Your going to have to protect yourself with a better product which fits price delivery and quality objectives, otherwise you will not be able to attack your competition if you do not have a perfect defensive structure which your enemy cannot break.

Box 8:3
Sample Tools Used to Correct Mistakes

Human resource development and measurement – Production development and measurement   Materials management measurement and supply chain measurement – Customer satisfaction development and measurement – Benchmarking systems development and measurement – Design process development and measurement – Financial systems development and measurement – Information systems development and measurement – Operational level savings – Tactical level savings – Strategic level savings – Cost of defence team – Total savings made in the plant – Production technique and manufacturing technique – Preventative tactics – Team development 1-4 – Improving inspection – Non-stock production – Over-production – Waste arising from time on hand – Waste from transporting – Processing waste – Unnecessary stock on hand – Unnecessary motion – Defective goods – The Nagara system – Target costing – Kaizan costing – Territory System based Engineering – Flatter organization structure – Shorter lead times – Zero watch manufacturing – Tied processes – Scheduling and control – Supply chain development – Output schedule – The four-relationship model – The four goals of improvement – Don't drown in computer hardware – The availability and use of Poke Yoke systems – The creation and hiring of a Poke Yoke team – Directing the operational master – Measuring return on investment – Measuring return on assets – Measuring return on sales – Cash flow improvement analysis – Number of improvements per employee – Operating costs reduction – Customer loss and retention rates – Supplier-to-business ratio – Economic value added – Number of inventory turns per annum – Escapes process – Employee training hours – Materials fill rates and days of supply calculation – Order fill rates – Reduction in time to production – Defects per unit versus defects per million.

Pictures by Dan Smith and Alberto G Rovi: Wikipedia

The Toyota-Ferrari Formula One Scandal

On 17 January 2006 Andrew Walker reported to *Autoworld* that former Toyota F1 principal Ove Andersson had been charged in the Toyota-Ferrari spy scandal. The aerodynamics expert and the chief designer no longer work for Toyota. The case centred on allegations that Toyota stole software from the Maranello team and used it to test aerodynamic data for the 2003 and 2004 Toyota single-seaters.

Such cases are common in Formula One according to Alex Hawkridge, head of the Toleman Group who began the company's foray onto the F1 circuit. He recruited Ayrton Senna and was instrumental in setting up many of the engineering personalities famous in F1 today.

He explained that industrial espionage is common in the motor racing industry in general: 'People are always trying to steal from one another. This is one of the primary reasons that I have encouraged selected secret F1 teams to learn 7Tao and industrial warfare because it would help them to protect themselves in this ferocious climate of competition.'

He would not name the people involved in learning the 7Tao system in case it should compromise them but he made it clear that he believed that it was of fundamental importance to anyone working in a high competition environment such as F1. '7Tao is like a martial art for corporations and business teams,' he explained. 'The only time a competitor knows that you know it is when you actually use it in a corporate fight situation. You don't go around showing this off in an open environment. The only time someone will understand that you know something different is when you use it to protect yourself in a difficult situation. The results are simply mind-blowing.' He explained his case as follows. 'I have been working within the Formula One industry for generations now. I knew Enzo Ferrari and we used to discuss with many other personalities within the field what difficulties Formula One would go through as we all competed for intelligence on each others' products. This situation was steadily getting worse as the more competitors came into the field, the more ferocious the fight would be. It was undoubted that rules would be broken, lines would be crossed, and losses to one company would affect the rise of another.

> Once I realised what the 7Tao system was offering, I spread the word and explained to selected personalities that it was fundamental that they learned 7Tao because it would help to protect them in the world to come. Essentially, they knew I was telling the truth and we took it on in a big way. However, there was one condition which we gave to the teacher and the students, that word wouldn't get out that the Formula One industry was doing this until the courses had been completed and the information had been passed over. In this way, a few years of practising the techniques of industrial warfare would give such an advantage to the competitors that the rest would be left reeling, thinking how did they do it? It is for this primary reason that we have kept the users of the system secret for so long.'
>
> Alex Hawkridge has used the 7Tao system to practise industrial warfare to his maximum advantage. Even in retirement he is holding meetings, designing seminars and giving lectures on the importance of economic and industrial fighting methods to Formula One.

One of the most exciting industries we are involved with is Formula One. Cutting-edge processes and materials, state of the art combustion technology and fire-breathing performances fit well with the radical stance of 7Tao. Alex Hawkridge explains his journey with 7Tao and guides us through his experiences with the technique as it travels through his industry. 'I have worked in high level motor sport for over 45 years and in 1984, as boss of the Toleman F1 Team, I signed the legendary Ayrton Senna as my lead driver during his first season in Formula 1.'

www.Evenflow.co.uk, 17 February 2009

Case Study 5

The Formula One Industry

Formula One industrialist Alex Hawkridge called 7Tao in to assess the industry and provide a road map showing how it could negotiate a time of financial crisis. One of our first 7Tao customers, he influences all aspects of motor sport and has been at the cutting edge of Formula One theory since its glory days in the 1970s. He has a close relationship with the Ferrari design teams. Many of his team members from his days as Chief Executive Officer of the Toleman Group went on to become CEOs of well-known multinationals, including Virgin. Here Alex explains his involvement with 7Tao and its implementation in all areas of his industrial world.

Alex Hawkridge was Chief Executive Officer of the Toleman group from 1968 to 1992, when it was sold to Tibbett & Britten PLC. The group was originally a car delivery company working principally for Ford. Alex transformed the business and by 1976 it was the largest company of its type delivering over a third of all new cars in the United Kingdom. At the time Alex joined the Toleman Group, the largest transporters carried five cars per truck. By the time Alex left the industry, each transporter was able to carry twelve large executive cars.

Pictures from Wikipedia commons

To promote this business, Alex formed Toleman Motorsport, which won the Formula Two championship sponsored by BP, with tyres supplied free of charge exclusively to Toleman cars by Pirelli. 1981 was the year Toleman Motorsports entered Formula One with British drivers Brian Henton and Derrick Warwick. In 1984 Alex persuaded the legendary Ayrton Senna, who had just won the British Formula Three Championship, to drive for Toleman.

The team was sponsored by Magirus trucks, owned by the FIAT group who also owned Ferrari. To pull off a sponsorship deal like this was unique in the sport. Alex had a close friendship with Enzo Ferrari and it was through this that the Pirelli deal had been brokered, and led to sponsorships with Candy, Diavia, Sergio Tacchini.

Alex Hawkridge writes:

As an independent consultant specialising in business turnaround situations, I have worked very closely with Amar Manzoor and his excellent team at 7 Tao and have received first class support in implementing what is clearly the most productive transactional improvement system ever devised.

The proven track record of Amar working in this field for over fifteen years enables him to go into any situation and in seven days and seven ways bring immediate and self-sustaining improvement with typical savings being at least ten times cost, and in cases I have experienced several hundred times cost.

7Tao has very fast implementation as it can be simultaneously introduced on a top-down and bottom-up basis as the customer chooses. The system is so powerful that benefits are immediate and keep improving fast.

I have recommended to the United Nations that they engage with 7Tao for a one-week trial in any area or discipline so that the full and immediate impact of 7Tao can be objectively measured. Once convinced of the huge benefits available, your people can be trained and accredited in the UK and be supported perpetually wherever you are in the world. It is a technique which can be applied to any business with a transaction. This means any business can quite easily be supported in the 7Tao tools and techniques from the beginning to the end of their business process.

The System is based on equal Defence and Attack manuals, which lead individuals to widen their horizons, see the big pictures and work laterally on transactions. This leads to fewer tiers and fewer columns in an organisation with major headcount savings, but greatly improves teamwork across the board.

The system fights internal weakness by highlighting every occasion when a threat may arise and provides appropriate actions to deal with the threat. It encourages everyone to work towards a level playing field internationally. It also seeks out the competitor's external weaknesses and overcomes them through competitive means within the legal framework. It really is a very powerful system designed for the challenges of the 21st century."

The Regional Comprehensive Economic Partnership: RCEP

"The Regional Comprehensive Economic Partnership is a free trade agreement among the Asia Pacific Nations of Australia, Brunei, Cambodia, China, Indonesia, Japan, South Korea, Laos, Malaysia, Myanmar, New Zealand, the Philippines, Singapore, Thailand and Vietnam. The 15 members account for 30% of the world's population (2.5 billion people) and 30% of the worlds GDP $30 Trillion, making it the biggest trading bloc in history. It is the first free trade agreement to involve among the largest economies of Asia including China, Indonesia, Japan and South Korea." Wikipedia. 17th Feb 2022

"For the first ten ratifying countries, the trade pact took effect from January 1st, 2022. It is expected to eliminate about 90% of the tariffs on imports between its signatories within 20 years of coming into force, and establish common rules for e-commerce, trade and intellectual property. RCEP will offer significant economic gains for signatory nations, boost Covid-19 recovery and pull the economic centre of gravity back towards Asia leaving the United States behind in economic and political affairs." Wikipedia 17th Feb 2022.

2.5 billion people is a lot of customers. In any business, the first step of a relationship comes from customer demand. When you have a capability to supply 2.5 billion people in large container ships, you will have a very strong basis in which to supply your factories. Factories are what makes up China's power. When you add up the supply chain, the sheer number of factories on the Chinese mainland will be filled with orders just on the RCEP alone. If we add in the Belt and Road Initiative and the fact that 65% of the world's population is covered by the Belt and Road Initiative movement, we have just reached 95% of the world's customers. In industrial war language, this is total domination of the transaction with natural cost delivery advantages for centuries to come.

The question is how do you compete with this level of penetration into the world economies? Quite simply, you also have to begin by creating trading blocs along geographical lines. This is done by having friendly relations among the peoples of the world and not by invading their countries and forcing them to buy your goods. Afghanistan still bought Chinese made goods right along with American soldiers in the same bazaars as they were fighting each other in the Afghan war from September 11, 2001, to September 11 2021. The winners were traders who would buy from China and supply to the local businesspeople. Indeed, for everyone western Tractor sold in Afghanistan, China was selling 50 tractors. They were dominating the market in Original Equipment Manufacturing and the resulting aftermarket sales process that resulted in the penetration to Afghan farmers. When the Americans left in 9/11 2021, the first action for the Taliban was to go and sign a trade deal with China and start becoming part of the Belt and Road Initiative. The Taliban jumped at the chance to trade with the rising superpower and have good neighbourly relations with them. In fact, they even signed multiple infrastructure and mining deals to help them to pay for the economic development of Afghanistan. The Taliban have to find a way to pay for the Islamic welfare state they intend to build in their country. The number of deals are all based around mining and infrastructure development of roads, highways, rail and tunnel based technologies. The Taliban know that they need goods, and they need them fast. They are actively supporting their universities as they try to man these projects with their own people and create a talent pool of engineers and workers to support the needs of the infrastructure maintenance in the country.

What this means for the RCEP is that more customers have arrived, and they have a lot more needs. The Taliban will provide access for risk taking Asian businesses if they can sign into the RCEP and grant them investment opportunity into their lands. This will equal 2 decades of development for the people of Afghanistan and will generate large amounts of throughputs into the warm water's strategy of China. Indeed, the links with Pakistan are strong as they lead directly to the export port of Gwadar in Karachi Pakistan.

How RCEP and Belt and Road Initiative engage Afghanistan after 40 years of conflict will a uphill test for the nations of the world. The Taliban are currently busy engaging all the different countries who are guiding them into the economic development of their country. They are mostly being guided by Pakistan, with whom they have cultural, territorial and blood relations in two provinces and have excellent consulting capability in these areas. Deals are being done and development is being planned. It's only been 4 months of the Taliban in power, but the plans being fomented will ensure that Afghanistan becomes a part of the international community of BRI and RCEP with trading and supply of goods and services. RCEP or the Regional Comprehensive Economic Partnership against the CPTPP or the Comprehensive and Progressive Agreement for Transpacific Partnership. So, which one do you join? Both features East Asian members and are the only multi-lateral free trade agreements signed in the Trump era.

The United States of America needs to compete on a macro level, and not just on an international legal level. The basis of transactions should be the 7Tao, there should not be a captive marketplace unless you want to have military leverage

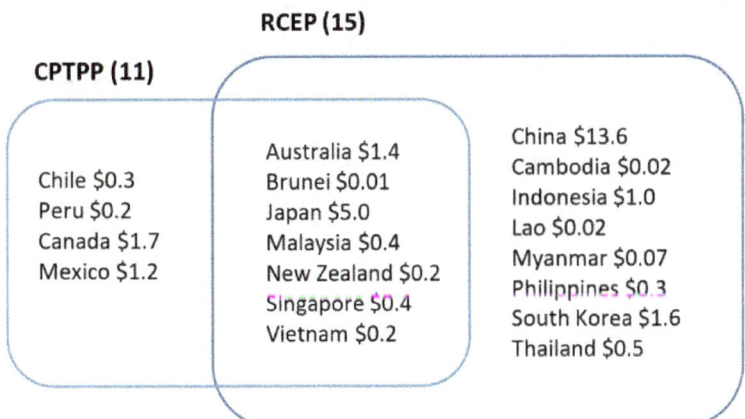

over the countries you want to trade with. If this is the case, and the approach s security and military based, USA may not get any trade deals thus bringing harder economic downturns in the North American geography. It is very important that America signs with the RCEP, the BRI, the CPTPP, and as many free trade agreements (FTA) around the world as possible. This will allow American made manufactured goods to flow freely around the planet thus reducing tariffs which are holding back the movement of goods and services.

Free trade agreements are designed primarily to reduce tariffs and increase trade allowing competition to reduce prices. In this way demand can easily find supply and the best transaction can be engaged to get the best economy of scale between buyer and seller.

For the United States of America to compete on a global scale, they need more free trade agreements like the USMCA, a free trade agreement with Europe reducing tariffs, and free trade agreement with Asia to allow American exports to be a choice for Asian firms. The freer trade agreements they can sign, the more likely we are to find American made products purchased and shipped to those countries. Further to this, American factories must be able to offer their goods to all 8 billion people around the world in all spheres of influence. If American factories can supply there, they will also have a presence in those countries from an aftermarket viewpoint, eventually leading to an Original Equipment Manufacturing presence. If there is a Chinese factory present, there should also be a challenging American factory to balance the market out. Yes, this is more complex equation than this description of a simplistic nature, but at the end of the day it comes down to just one question. How easy is it for the consumer to buy an American made product? If it is sitting in the showroom or on the shelf, it will be an option. If it is not sitting on a shelf, it will not be an option and will result in a missed sale. The more Free-Trade Agreements America can sign and take part in, the more potential outlets for American made products, this will undoubtedly result in sustained factories and a manufacturing industry which will permanently build a presence in foreign lands using franchises, partnerships, and export agreements.

Military Warfare VS Industrial Warfare

The war on terror didn't yield any real benefit to the Western nations. Sure, it filled the arms companies' pockets with cash for a while, but generally – it didn't really benefit the common man on the street in the USA or in the UK. What we have found is that the old model of 'make war to make money' is becoming increasingly obsolete as time goes on and much more dangerous to employ because of the sheer amount of technological growth which has being completed around the planet. Kinetic wars don't make much sense anymore. This is not the 19th or the 20th century where these colonial models of invasion yielded booty for many generations or decades to come. The nature of the challenge is on the shop floor and within the retail shelf now. As competition has shifted into the financial and supply chain arena, the nature of conflict has also taken on this direction too. The industrial war has arrived with Donald Trump, the 45th President of the USA being the first person to recognise this fact. Now it's a question of fighting it while playing by the rules.

What China considers rules may not be accepted by America and vice versa what America considers rules may not be accepted by China. Either way, we have to get an agreement of some kind in place between these two giant superpowers who respectively control, 20% of world trade each, leaving the rest of the world to distribute 60% of world trade among themselves. For a customer to decide is where the rules should apply. And this means setting standards. The standards that need to be followed need to come from the European Union, China and America. We already have the International Standards Organization, which designates standards such as ISO 9000, which is a quality standard ensuring that corporations meet Quality and Stakeholder needs. Many standards companies exist to help customers reach into countries for export, the more these standards companies are employed to help guide international trade deals, the easier it will be to sign into a trade deal.

Trade deals should be easy to sign if more standards companies can be employed into the signing process. If a country can sign into standards organizations, it should be relatively easy to complete trade deals with that country.

Standards organizations include:
- ISO - International standards organization.
- ANSI – American National Standards Institute.
- BSI – British Standards Institute.
- NIST – National Institute of Standards and Technology.
- IEC – International Electro-technical Commission.
- IEEE – Institute of Electrical and Electronics Engineers.
- FDA – Food and Drug Administration.
- ASTM – American Society for Testing and Materials.

If these standards institutes can be a part of the trade deal process to inspire confidence in quality, reliability and build process which is safe for use across the world, then trade deals will be done quite easily because the space area for blame is reduced leading to a more productive relationship.

Kite marks help a company and a consumer exchange goods and services by increasing confidence and helping the purchase process gain new products. These are western kite marks which we find in many of our hardware stores and our retail outlets.

These kite marks allow standards organizations to guide through trade deals for products. Many of these standard's organizations have offices in every country of the world. They help to smooth the exchange of goods and services across multiple countries. This is an excellent way of ensuring trade deals remain relevant to customer confidence across the nations of the world. If we can get many of these types of standards to guide our trade deals processes, we will end up increasing access to each other countries customer bases allowing us to trade better with a wider appeal of products and services across the globe.

These will also help to repeal and drive down tariffs which make the exchange of goods and services harder. Rather than increasing tariffs which can cause trade wars, it is better that we remove tariffs and make progress on finding the causes of our disagreements using up to date investigation and solutions development techniques.

Trade wars do not benefit anyone, however, 7Tao can provide a solution to the next generation of problems. Most of these problems do not lie in defects, however, they lie in corruption of processes and of products. If we can remove corruption at all levels of industrial society, we can easily overcome the challenges which plague the development of factories and relationships between supplier, competitor and customer. If this confidence can be increased leading to customer in roads, we will have much greater and smoother trading relationships housed by good strong legal systems.

Universities will become obsolete, unless they join the Eurasian landmass.

Universities were well respected during the sixties, seventies, eighties, and even nineties. People who graduated from university often had a career in front of them, they were trusted to be the drivers of industry, given leadership positions, and empowered with a voice that was heard. Universities were the harbinger of intelligence and purveyors of nations that were respected. Classic red brick institutions such as Oxford, Cambridge, Harvard, and Yale were not just places where you graduated in established subjects such as engineering, medicine, and law. They were badges of honour that were used to get into the best positions and best jobs in the country. Not anymore.

Nowadays innovation doesn't require thinking in a library, being taught how to think, and then coming out with theories about how to develop a certain field. The new industries are made by dropouts and nonstarters. People who lost faith in the education system and decided to just make it on their own. Many famous names come to mind when thinking about this modern phenomenon. Steve Jobs, Mark Zuckerberg, and Bill Gates are just some famous ones. They paved the way into knowing that education can be restrictive. In today's day and age, it can become a noose round your neck in the form of a repetitive mundane job that is unforgiving as it marches you towards your grave. So, while the universities struggle to sustain a system that is becoming increasingly obsolete, these dropouts indicate that there is something missing with the way in which thinking is done. They don't want to think like that, and as they become successful and begin showing results, people are listening to them.

Inventors in Universities

Universities are still excellent places where you go to discipline yourself to learn how to think in a structured and coordinated manner. But they are not the innovation hubs that they used to be. In decades past, to invent something, you needed a laboratory, investment, guidance, previous knowledge that you could develop and take forward, skills to build that knowledge, and a team to help turn those theories into practice. But the more people that got involved, the less the objective was achieved, and the more diluted the aims became.

The environment that is to come is very similar to the environment of the past. If we go back multiple decades, we see that Isaac Newton, Nicola Tesla, Albert Einstein, Isambard Kingdom Brunel, Michael Faraday, Frank Whittle, and many others like them had one thing in mind. These individuals move humanity forward.

Most of these inventors didn't even finish their education and hated being boxed in at school. Many of them that had exposure to university didn't go there to get a piece of paper. They went to university to use its resources to find out who they were and what they wanted to do in life. The university was simply there to help them to find out about themselves, and the ideas they were thinking about.

People like to call these individuals geniuses, labelling them and not understanding their passion for what they believed in.

These so-called geniuses were driven people, laughed at, mocked, discarded, belittled, and pushed to the side in such a cavalier way in most cases by the educational institutions that they attended and by the cultures that infest those institutions all over the world.

This attitude of disregarding and belittling is now on the back foot. Universities don't have the attraction that they once used to. Today, you can go on the internet and download knowledge to help you do what you want to do. 3D printing can overtake manufacturers and help you realize your vision and creation. Communications can allow you to find your team across the world, and the curtains have been removed on culture and ethnicity allowing you to accept that there are other people in the world who can think along the same lines as you do.

The Future of Universities

I recently visited Farnborough Air Show in the UK, which is a biannual event attracting thousands of aerospace enthusiasts from across the world. It was revealing indeed. The price of aircraft has been reduced dramatically. People were downloading documents from the internet and making aircraft in their back gardens. You could buy a Spitfire at 80 percent size manufactured by an aircraft enthusiast that was fully functional for less than £100k. There were many others who were manufacturing aircraft within their own sheds, garages, and local industrial units. With regards to the big manufacturers, they were struggling to make a dent in the marketplace because of massive overheads and crippling costs. Military aircraft used to be made by multitudes of companies just two decades ago. Today there are only a few remaining big manufacturers.

Farnborough for me was all about two big aircraft companies: Airbus & Boeing. The industrial battle for transactions was happening as the two giant competitors from Europe and America wrestled for sales of aircraft. The only difference between these giants of industry and the small back garden boys was big money. These giants had access to finance and the small back garden boys had access to passion for doing what they love. I can see clearly now. The future of industry is in the hands of the small, financially embattled, visionary inventors who work to see their idea through with tears, worry, no help, and no support. This is where the future lies. I could go further; it is a reflection of the past where inventors were the first to see the future and prepare for times that they saw coming and no one else did.

Nicola Tesla, Albert Einstein, Michael Faraday, and Isambard Kingdom Brunel all had their 'who's laughing now' moments as they rose to prominence. In these uncertain times, these types of people are rearing their heads again, but this time, let's not laugh at them and listen to what they have to say. In these uncertain times, these are the people that will lead us out of the climate of uncertainty and into certainty, they are people of passion, immense drive, and incalculable bravery. These are the true warriors now. We must know who they are, and we must pay attention to them. Just like in the past, the future lies in their hands.

Universities were relevant during the industrial revolutions of the Trans-Atlantic cycle in the 1700's onwards. They must now join the Eurasian cycle to remain relevant because the cycle of learning and innovation has moved into these areas. The demand for universities is huge, but the students from China, India and Eurasia are coming over here to learn. Universities must think about how to get involved in the new Silk Road that is forming in Europe and Asia. For the University system in general, relationships with the transaction begin with training the new generation of employees. This requires thoughtful rebalancing and redesign of logistics of the university system. The University must go to the customer now because they will stop coming to transatlantic cycle to learn.

CHAPTER 9

Tao 6: Shareholders: Do You Make Enough Profit?

The Argument of Shareholders

Dividends are the be all and end all of corporate business. Once shares become locked into a growth pattern, it's almost as if new business ideas and pent-up creativity unleashes itself through all the corporation's offerings to the marketplace. This is the truest of all statements: if the share price of your company continues to grow, it is accumulating value, it is storing value, it is attracting value and it is investing in further value.

However, what drives the share price is not price, it is the perception of value. 7Tao is remarkably successful in increasing share value by ferociously attacking any non-value-added process. It measures the return on investment of every project we monitor and the success of each is recorded at the end of the session with the issuing of a receipt. This receipt is the final document to be handed to the student who has learned how to practise transactional excellence in the workplace.

The beauty of the system is the fact that work is looked upon as a transaction and not just as work. The value of the transaction is spread throughout the workflow of the whole organization as the product travels to the point of completion. It is the constant extraction of non-value-added work from a job holder's processes, and the implementation of powerful transactional work methods, that shows every worker where he belongs in the business and what part he is expected to play. The accumulation of value is added up at the end and is reflected in the balance sheet of the business. We can immediately see how a particular product, process or employee relates to the money the organization makes.

Defending your share and attacking your competitor's share is of the utmost importance in the 7Tao of business. To perpetuate growth, you must constantly be adding value to the shares and taking away any corrosive non-value-added process to increase dividends. So, what is 'non-value-added' and how do we quantify what value added is?

Defending Shareholder Strengths

You need to eliminate every action or condition which does not contribute to profits. True, there is necessary waste in every action within a process, just as the human body is made up of bones, which are necessary, as well as flesh, which achieves performance. Getting lean is one thing but learning how to propel yourself in the international field of industrial warfare is quite another. Being fit is a good option; being fighting fit is perfect for the practitioners of the 7Tao. To achieve shareholder returns, we must engage students with trust and allow them to work in their own areas on processes they feel are important to them. Trust is the key.

Workers will already know what is good and what is bad within their work environment, they just need to be given the key to doing their job better. Arming them with the skills required involves teaching them to understand the international environment. They must see the difficulty that is approaching them in the form of global competition led by the Chinese. Only then will they care about the work they do and understand that they have to learn how to secure their workplace.

In the 7Tao assessment each worker completes a job and is judged in relation to a set of specific targets. Some targets relate to job measurement and fulfilment, others to the achievement of profit. The most important aspect of any job is the profit that job makes for the company. The company is measured by the profit each job makes. However, it is not wise to overload a worker to keep the profits flowing. That will not actually increase the profit, it will just increase the workload and lower other parts of the transaction which are as important as the return on investment per job.

For example, if you load too much on a worker, you sacrifice quality; if you sacrifice quality, you end up delaying delivery. If delivery is delayed, you will lose money on price, and the share price will be affected by that individual transaction or batch of transactions. Unbalanced processes lead to a haemorrhaging of money, which will make the business unprofitable. If the business starts making losses, you will lose shareholder value. If you lose shareholder value, you lose capital to reinvest into the business. If you lose capital to reinvest, you end up having to compete with players in the marketplace who have more money than you. Things can turn bad quite quickly. The question to ask is, 'How many times have I seen this happen before?'

This happened throughout the UK. The Thatcher years of Conservative government saw the dismantling of manufacturing industry. Manufacturing was thrown out and service industries were bought in new ideas, new computers, new rules – out with the old and in with the new. This was a fatal mistake, as this financial crisis has proven. There was nothing left of value when the recession hit. Competitors such as Japan and Germany had been derided for sustaining their sluggish manufacturing industries, but their tortoise positions were right; it was the UK and the USA that were wrong. Japan and Germany still have world-class manufacturing industries; the UK and USA have depleted theirs to the point of no return.

One of the main reasons this happened was the misguided perception that service industries are superior to manufacturing. They are not. Hairdressing is not a real industry; manufacturing cars is an industry. Service industries do not export products which earn value. You earn value by selling something you can see and touch. China is rich entirely because its industrial revolution is based on exports. Germany is successful because of its exports; its manufacturing industry is its primary ambassador to other countries.

Japan, Germany, and China have one thing in common: they take the competitor head on as they seek to establish the transaction. China makes price its primary strength, Japan concentrates on delivery and quality, Germany primarily on quality. These strengths add value to sales, which raises the share price and revitalises the company as it develops the next generation of products which will be in tune with the next generation of global challenges. Is it so hard to see the importance of shareholder value?

Attacking Shareholders Weaknesses

As shareholders are constantly seeking a return on investment, they are a fickle breed. If a share price starts to fall dramatically, they will jump ship. Their primary interest is in making money. CEOs are hired and fired on the wishes of the board, whose eyes are on the share price. When a company's share price starts going down, the major shareholders may well transfer to a competitor, setting off a collapse in the value of the company.

But just as they can run from you, they can also run from your competitor. If you can sense that your competitor is losing shareholder value, why not make them an offer early on, before they collapse, to save shareholders money? Shareholders need to be constantly reassured that you are doing well. To defend their interests, they need to be able to spot value. The 7Tao system is unsurpassed at defending shareholders' interests. It constantly reinforces the movement of value to the top of the organizational structure. The constant removal of non-value-added weaknesses sustains the share price and ensures good value in every single job within the business. The more workers engaged in the competitiveness of the transaction (their doing the job is a transaction), the leaner and meaner that transaction becomes. Every job within the workplace is a transaction because you are paying for that work to be done. In your workplace, there is a constant interaction between transactions as money changes hands and value is transferred from one process to another. To sustain this movement of money internally, you have to weed out any weakness that a transaction may hold and expel it from the organization, leaving only the value-added in place. This is achieved by thorough training and a constant movement from non-value-added to value-added processes as workers complete their jobs.

Shareholder Value Starts with Sustainability and Ends with Growth

Sustenance to a worker means having enough work to keep him in his job, which is his livelihood. Sustenance to a shareholder means maintaining share value. Sustenance to the business means keeping its customers. How do you keep the work coming in, provide excellent value to the owners of the business and at the same time increase value for the customer of a product or service? It's quite a challenge, isn't it? The 7Tao transactional dominance method constantly challenges every job within the organization to balance every transaction. The more that people undertake projects within their job role, the greater the movement away from non-value-added towards value-added processes.

The results show immediately because anything not connected to price, delivery, quality, after market, customer, shareholder, or employee growth is discarded. Every project is judged in terms of the transaction, and as a result each transaction becomes not leaner but stronger. The aim is not to get the company lean; the aim is to make it strong. This is the aim of the 7Tao system: to get the company strong enough to tackle any challenge it may face in the longer term.

Every time shareholder growth analysed, it should be from two viewpoints. Internal and external. Internal shareholder growth means looking at all processes in the company and getting appropriate yield from each element of work being conducted. This means that each process of work must yield profit and work as efficiently as possible. These processes must be revised all of the time in transactional terms to keep the company adapting and relevant in the marketplace. Externally, it means one measurement – Sales of the product in the marketplace.

Case Study 6

Sample Return-on-Investment Receipts

The following scans of receipts show the way in which transactions are converted into processes with the help of the 7Tao methodology. The main aim of the Eastern way of thinking is not to think of work as work, but to think of work as money. We don't go into work to be good at what we do, we go into work to be good at business. Business is about making profits, gathering yield, and running a successful enterprise which makes money for all of those people involved.

Note: These *names* have been changed to protect the identities of the student, however, the results are real results in real companies.

Receipt 1: John Spooner.

Receipt 2: Michael Eisner.

Receipt 3: Terrence Boeing.

Receipt 4: Mamasimou Dangli.

Receipt 5: Michael Stone.

Receipt 1: Time-reduction project. **John Spooner** decided that he was taking too long to produce parts, so he applied 22 tools to achieve time reduction. Saving time affected the whole transaction, producing excellent results all around. The ROI is measured against the money the company paid for his training.

7Tao Receipt: Defence: John Spooner.

Before Description	7Tao	After Description
Cost: £6250 lost per annum	1: Price	**Saving** £6,250 per annum
Delay: 250 Hours per annum waiting time	2: Delivery	**Time saved:** 250 hours per annum waiting time
Problems: Waiting on dies. Quality of dies.	3: Quality	**Solutions:** Eliminate waiting time and improve die quality
Support problems: Bottleneck at operations	4: After Market	**Support solutions:** Removal of bottlenecks
Customer requirements: On time Delivery of orders	5: Customers	**Customer satisfaction:** Orders delivered on time
Non Value added Waiting time for dies. Machines idle	6 Shareholders	**Value added** Payback ratio ROI = 2.5 : 1
Employee disadvantages Frustration, Lack of knowledge of tools, Lack of improvement	7 Employees	**Employee Advantages** Gained knowledge of tools, Feeling of empowerment ownership of workplace.

Receipt 2: Michael Eisner is an engineering student who wanted to apply his knowledge to the materials-handling section of his cellular workplace. He already knew that improvements could be made. He applied 26 tools to look at ways of making his cell better and used 13 tools to look at attacking all the areas which the supply chain was using to extract unjustified profits. The results were tremendous: a return on investment of 9.5 to 1 was seen as he launched an attack on the weak processes within his cell and defended against waste in work practices.

7Tao Receipt: Defence: Michael Eisner.

Before Description	7Tao	After Description
Cost: £23,734 of non value added costs	1: Price	**Saving:** £23,734.62 of non value added costs
Delay: Time taken to heat and cool material	2: Delivery	**Time saved:** Cooling saving 178.5 mins, Heating saving 40 – 70 mins.
Problems: Bottleneck at annealing	3: Quality	**Solutions:** Reducing heating and / or cooling times.
Support problems: Show delivery to next process	4: After Market	**Support solutions:** Fast delivery to next process
Customer requirements: Slow cycle time	5: Customers	**Customer satisfaction:** Fast cycle time and better on time delivery
Non Value added: Cooling non value added time. Heating added value time	6: Shareholders	**Value added:** Payback ratio: ROI = 9.5: 1
Employee disadvantages: Lack of problem solving skills	7: Employees	**Employee Advantages:** Skill and confidence to tackle problems

Receipt 3: Materials waste-reduction, a beautiful project by **Terrence Boeing**, who produced flooring. The student realised that a certain process within the factory was not making money simply because it was not being given any attention. He applied eight materials theory techniques and, by attacking weaknesses and defending strengths, transformed the process so that it yielded a profit and was not just a necessary waste. This resulted in a ROI yield of 1:54.8 across a team of three people on the process map.

7Tao Receipt: Defence: Terrence Boeing.

Before Description	7Tao	After Description
Cost: £137,000	1: Price	**Saving:** Obsolete parts and equipment £137,000
Delay : Unknown parameter	2: Delivery	**Time saved:** Estimated one hour per person per week
Problems: Lost parts. Loss of space. Clutter. Excess inventory.	3: Quality	**Solutions:** 5S and 5C, Visual Control, more work required.
Support problems: Unknown. Need training.	4: After Market	**Support solutions:** Need training and ownership
Customer requirements: More organization	5: Customers	**Customer satisfaction:** Happier customers
Non Value added: Difficult to measure	6: Shareholders	**Value added:** Payback Ratio: ROI = 1: 54.8
Employee disadvantages Health and safety problems. Lack of space	7: Employees	**Employee Advantages** Improved education Improved performance

Receipt 4: Mamasimou Dangli saw that he was running a process which was unsafe and unprofitable, yet ignored by everyone going about their daily business in the factory. A packaging system was damaging rolls of carpet being sent out to customers. Mamasimou tackled the problem and created a new system of packaging which did not damage the product. The results of the implementation yielded an ROI of 1:7.5

7Tao Receipt: Defence: Mamasimou Dangli.

Before Description	7Tao	After Description
Cost: Costs of annual manufacture £99,985.60	1: Price	**Saving:** Actual saving: £18,747
Delay: Total process time 800 min	2: Delivery	**Time saved:** 150 min: 18.75%
Problems: Waiting time. Untidy area.	3: Quality	**Solutions:** Removed waiting time. 5S and 5C in the area.
Support problems: Never had any complaints	4: After Market	**Support solutions:** Sustained
Customer requirements: Maintain quality with faster delivery	5: Customers	**Customer satisfaction:** Quality sustained with faster delivery. Customer happy.
Non Value added: Some inspection time removed	6: Shareholders	**Value added:** Payback ratio 1:7.5
Employee disadvantages: Limited knowledge. Unknown improvement targets.	7: Employees	**Employee Advantages:** New skills. Confidence. Understanding.

Receipt 5: Michael Stone worked for a large international conglomerate which supplied all sorts of high-value components to international industry. He began the 40 hours/40 tools training course offered by 7Tao. He fought hard in the economic combat scenarios, defending and attacking opposing teams coming from all directions. The results were excellent. Right across the organization, his project affected every process and product that passed through it. A return-on-investment ratio of 1:14 was achieved through a little study and an objective view of how his section of the business should operate.

7Tao Receipt: Defence: Michael Stone.

Before Description	7Tao	After Description
Cost: Total waste £34,770	1: Price	**Saving:** Total savings £34.770
Delay: Finding tools and parts. 60 hours / 6 jobs = 10 hours per job	2: Delivery	**Time saved:** 54 hours
Problems: Rework. Repeat orders. Long delivery cycles.	3: Quality	**Solutions:** No rework. No repeat cycles. Shorter delivery cycles.
Support problems: Not happy with late delivery	4: After Market	**Support solutions:** No more late deliveries
Customer requirements: Rework, reorder	5: Customers	**Customer satisfaction:** Improved satisfaction
Non Value added: Rework. Re-order.	6: Shareholders	**Value added:** Payback ratio ROI: 14: 1
Employee disadvantages: Unable to meet customer targets. Low morale of team. Confusion.	7: Employees	**Employee Advantages:** Aware of waste costs. Apply to their areas.

A sample company yield report:

A large corporation in the South of England worth well over $10 billion decided to try 7Tao. They had tried everything else over the years but failed to implement even the simplest of theories. The reasons for the failure were evident as soon as you started speaking to the shop floor personnel: 'Lost in the implementation process …', 'Got too complicated … Couldn't understand a word they were saying …', 'Too mathematical and statistical, it just put us all right off – it became so tedious we just couldn't go on …'. 'We used to just turn up to get out of work and have a sit down …', 'Great place to have coffee and biscuits and listen to some bloke telling everyone what to do and how to do it …'. 'These things are great to just waste some time and even have work pay for it just to tick some boxes.'

I told the corporation that 7Tao would be completely different, far more exciting and much more professional because it would be run by them and not by a teacher. They didn't buy any of it. Too many people before me had tried and failed. Why should this be any different? The latest fad is just a fad, something to be discussed on the golf course as they tried to work out what to do to improve their business. This was going to be a really hard sell.

Eventually they decided to give me a chance. The results were simply amazing after a short forty-hour course: a return-on-investment average in the class of £343,000 on an investment of just £25,000.

Because of the financial details disclosed, and the fact that the corporation is worth $10 billion, we give only the first names of the students and I have deleted details about the company, its nature, and its work. Stunned at the results, the corporation eventually became a regular customer, completing many of the 7Tao waves and cycles. In all cases, these students studied the internal process changes. They were constantly attacking each process to remove weaknesses and introduce or defend strengths ensuring relevance in the marketplace.

Yield = estimated cost of programme/total number of estimated savings = ratio of return

Total cost of programme: £25,000* (2009 – 7Tao testing stage)

<u>**Total *estimated* yield**</u>**: £343,395.6/£25,000 = 1:13.7**

* Excluding any cost of equipment in set-up operations, e.g. new tools required in testing and implementation.

Name	Yield	Saving	Comment
Jones	1:4.58	£11,479.33	Actual savings in inventory tooling. Identified excessive stock built up over a number of years, maybe even decades. Cut down space utilization, removed excessive waste, had a clean-up and clear-out. Clearly a successful project by Jones and team but sustaining the gains will be very difficult because of the lack of education, motivation and buy-in from maintenance team members.
Duncan	1:4.58	£11,854.61	Savings in inventory tooling. As above, yield has been split between three cooperating members. Sustainability problems will be continuing for the short term at least. Quick wins in visual control and inventory control with low-hanging fruit immediately tackled. Successful project parameters by Duncan. Next set of problems revealed.
John	1:4.58	£11,386.21	Savings in inventory tooling and stock control. Identified multiple wastes. Clean-up and 5s operation has gone through two cyclical sweeps. Room needs to be swept at least 5-6 times to achieve world-class standards. As predicted, 5s and visual control have revealed the true source of problems.

Simone	1:2.25	£5,645	Saved two square meters of space within the room where he operates. One square meter of space is worth £2,500. Good return for computerizing an outdated 1980s process. Well done.
Anthony	1:5.7	£14,145.60	Excellent returns on project. Well executed, planned and thought out. A very good attempt at first pass improvement. A clinical and clean application of knowledge. Good application of materials learned within his own working area. Very well done.
Raquel	1:7.1	£17,750	Working with a high-variety, low-volume operation, Raquel has managed to tie down a very difficult process. Working with indefinite demand, variable costs and erratic figures, Raquel has bought about stability in an unstable process. The project needs further work.
Francis	1:84.26	£210,668.19	Francis has a potentially powerful project. If the 'in-line' measurement system is successful, customers will be retained and successfully won in the future. The figures are real in relation to past history and future achievement. These figures will attain reality after calibration and testing of new equipment takes place, and with immediate effects on the customer. This is an important project. Francis must be given support and a chance to learn to apply techniques to his workplace.
Tony	1:3 (1:19.2)	£48,601.40	A very good visual-control project targeting immediate returns. The process showed high-impact gains which were immediate. This is a world-class project with very high performance parameters. Tony understands his

			environment and has applied knowledge to his work area, producing significant results immediately. Estimated savings for the returns throughout the year will be in the 50k region. Tony understands the process well and owns the problem.
Mansing	1: 0.5	£1,306	Although this is the beginning of the project, it is likely that the yield will grow further as processes 2, 3, and 4 of 4 are given sweeps. This will result in further improvements which will give the factory some important results. This has resulted in immediate savings. It is very likely that these will span out to create even higher savings once the improvement has matured through processes 2, 3, and 4. The results of this project will be in the tens of thousands, possibly into hundreds of thousands if the process is sustained to level 3 and 4 in the 7Tao completion stages.
Michael	1:4.22	£10,559.32	An immediate-impact project which has attained very quick results. Excellent work, Michael – a very good project with excellent returns. A quick well planned and clean implementation with high quality returns with good results which see immediate effects.

Talking about a revolution… It's easy to see the benefit of investing in project-based corporate stimulation. You only must analyse the receipts and immediately the benefits come to life. The most important element to any company in the world is the return on investment. Employers want the people who work for them to make money for them. You are not in business for the sake of doing the job, much as workers may love what they do. But how do you get a better performance out of the same people? By doing things differently. Not by working harder, just by being a little more intelligent.

Motivation is key. When a Grand Master goes into a business, he has to ask some fundamental questions. Motivation needs to come alive within the workforce. A standard set of questions needs to be asked if performance levels keep returning to the mean. It is not methodology that matters, but the people who want to make that methodology work. Some of these questions are listed below, with the reasons why they are important.

1: Have you used continuous improvement strategies before?

It is important to know what previous experiences employers have had. Most will have tried other techniques, and they may have been burnt. If they were unhappy with the results delivered, it is time to try a new avenue, a new way of upgrading the business.

2: Have the strategies failed to give you what you want?

Business managers who have been scarred by philosophies which preach excellence but do not deliver results need to be handled carefully. It is important that the right strategy for improvement is used to reflect global changes. As competitors rise, previous models of operation will become obsolete.

3: Are your people sceptical about development techniques?

If your strategy is to bombard your employees with statistics which are of little interest to them, they will fail to implement your changes because they will not feel involved. It is vital to make involvement and motivation the key drivers of a strategy for improvement because only then will a workforce want to do well.

4: Are you afraid of global challengers such as China and India?

The Chinese have completely different ways of thinking and different rules of engagement with the competition. They are in active pursuit mode when it comes to catching up with the global leaders, and with so much financial clout and so many people to employ they will soon succeed. The model has changed from a third generation to a fourth-generation system. If you have a third-generation mindset (assuming that conditions are like they were in 1980 to 2000) you will struggle to compete. You will not be able to absorb the pressures of the new marketplace.

5: Are you downsizing?
If you are cutting bodies and processes, this will reduce the competitiveness of your business. It is in your interests to sustain as large a workforce as you can. It is your economic fighting unit. Preserve your workforce and project it into your target markets. Downsizing reflects a lack of orders and transactions. If you are downsizing, you are losing business and the road to eventual closure will become more apparent as time passes.

6: How much is the financial crisis 2008 and the deeper one in 2026 affecting your business?
This is not a normal financial crisis in 2008; in particular, yhe 2026 financial crisis is a 'depletion' – rather like oil depletion once the reserves run out. In an economic depletion business dries up because of process obsolescence. There is business in the world, but those who cannot change into a new uniform of competition will suffer the greatest losses. They will be left behind as trade moves elsewhere on the planet.

7: Would you like to achieve an ROI of 1/10 and above?
To transform your business for the modern world, you need to distribute the current and future business pressures equally among your employees. Every job holder within the business has to be trained in systems which produce excellent results. They must understand the pressures involved in competing in the global village. Competitive thinking is required. Everybody needs to understand the culture, creativity, and ferocity of the competitive marketplace.

8: Do your employees crave excitement in the workplace?
If your employees are bored, over-cautions, hard to motivate and resigned to their fate, then you have problems. Development of the culture of excellence in employees requires constant nurturing and investment. It is not wise to rely on processes used in third-generation models of improvement – they will not achieve a different set of results. Employees need to be given the chance to excel at what they do. More importantly, they crave recognition of their achievements in their job. This is not easy to satisfy. You need to understand the workforce. Listen to suggestions and complaints, and to the whispers of small groups struggling to get noticed by the management. Hopelessness settles in when work becomes a dreary operation. Mundane activities, which may not even add value, will affect the

motivation levels of a workforce. It may go unnoticed for decades as workers slowly become numb to an outside world which they are not in touch with. They only notice that it has reached them when their jobs become obsolete or a plant has to shut down. It is essential for Western managers to allow their workers to experience change. They need to set up project teams and expose them to the problems the company faces as it competes in the outside world. Only this way can we begin the process of repair in the West.

9: Are you looking to innovate in process and product?
Both product and process, require constant change. The aim of companies like Toyota Motors is to instil a culture of change which spreads among the workforce and is not restricted to their design departments. These offices are just a reflection of the intellectual quality and disciplined approach of all their employees. The employees did not join the company thinking in this way, they had to be trained. Because the pressure of Chinese growth has forced companies to think differently, some larger competitors are finding new ways to work, opening their minds to different points of view, and looking for every angle that will help them compete globally and stay ahead of the competition in both process and product.

10: Is profiting from job and process your primary goal?
Good profit margins are a company's main goal. Profit accumulates through each job holder playing his particular role. As global competition increases, they must be able to sustain a fourth-generation mode of thinking. Keeping profits up is an exceptional challenge today because of the number of competitors fighting for a slice of the market, and the financial crisis is only going to get worse as the number of competitors keeps growing. It is essential that the processes of each job holder should yield profits in the way work is done, the world is perceived, and new everyday challenges are tackled.

The 7Tao system begins by defining 7Tao as the starting point. Then comes the transformation process, built around the excitement of defending and attacking, which leads to an understanding of the Chinese way of thinking about business, the financial crisis, the increased amount of competition across the world and the dangers involved in doing business. The 7Tao system ends with defining the improved 7Tao as the end point.

This cycle is repeated again and again until the optimum level of results is achieved. Each cycle is the same. Power, reach, efficiency, and excellence are related to every job across the organization. The more people that do 7Tao, the more powerful the organization becomes in every area where the transaction is defined, consolidated, and improved. Waste is discarded, motivation is improved, understanding is achieved and, most importantly of all, the return on investment shoots up as the experience of 7Tao propels the workforce to greater heights. This is the art of industrial warfare!

Asian Infrastructure Investment Bank

The Asian Infrastructure Investment Bank (AIIB) is an international development bank which has been created to level up economic and social wellbeing of the peoples of Asia. The AIIB has 105 members and 16 prospective members from around the world. The bank started on Christmas day 2015 after ratifications were sent by 10 member states holding the initial capital stock.

The United Nations has addressed the launch of AIIB as a growth mechanism for improving sustainable development and increasing accountability in global governance. The starting capital for the bank was $100 Billion.

The bank was proposed by China in 2013 and the initiative launched at a ceremony in Beijing in October 2014. The AIIB is a natural competitor to the World Bank, Asian Development Bank, and the International Monetary Fund.

The power of the International Monetary Fund and the World bank may have been neutralized with the creation of the AIIB. The ability for these international financial institutions to extract wealth from the countries they lend to with various financial tools involving compound interest rates has been fizzled. If countries have a better option, or a more reasonable and fairer option to escape the slavery of compound interest rates, they will take that option every time.

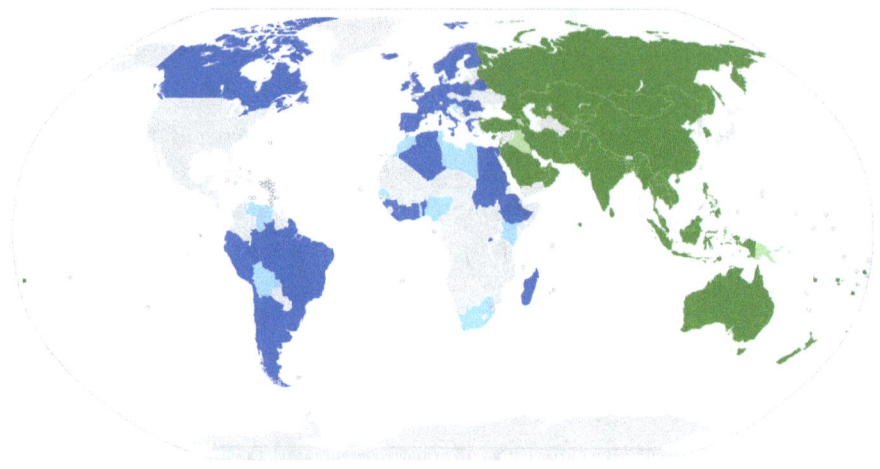

AIIB Shareholder map
Regional Members : Non Regional Members: Prospective Members
Illustration by L. Tak

The Asian Infrastructure Investment Bank (AIIB)

In March 2015, the United Kingdom Chancellor of the Exchequer, George Osborne announced that the UK had decided to apply to join the bank, becoming the third western country to do so after Luxembourg and New Zealand.

Much to the chagrin and criticism of the United States of America, a representative of the Obama administration told the financial times "We are wary about a trend toward constant accommodation of China, which is not the best way to engage a rising power." The official further stated that the British decision was taken after "no consultation with the US". In response, the UK declared that the subject was discussed unofficially multiple times with the then US Treasury secretary Jack Lew for quite a few months before the decision."

Following the criticism, the White House National Security Council in a statement to the Guardian, declared:

"Our position on the AIIB remains clear and consistent. The United States and many major global economies all agree there is a pressing need to enhance infrastructure investment around the world. We believe any new multilateral institution should incorporate the high standards of the World Bank and the regional development banks. Based on many discussions, we have concerns about whether the AIIB will meet those high standards, particularly related to **good governance and environmental and social safeguards.** The international community has a stake in seeing the AIIB complement the existing architecture, and to work alongside the World Bank and the Asian Development Bank."

Once Britain joined the AIIB, all of the other countries attained the confidence to join the bank too. Suddenly, that hesitance to upset the USA had disappeared. Then the whole world applied to join the bank and take part in the financial element that is required to develop the infrastructure of the Belt and Road Initiative and the Regional Comprehensive Economic Partnership. The pieces had fallen into place for China and the stratospheric rise of the middle kingdom had begun wherever the Belt and Road Initiative could reach. Germany, France, Italy and Spain all followed the UK's decision to join. Eventually, most of Western Europe had joined the bank.

The three of the four members of the Quad, as it is known today, are all members of the bank. India, Japan, South Korea have all joined. Even Australia, Saudi Arabia and Israel who are staunch US allies have joined the AIIB. So much for the security partnership longevity. The world is a different place to what it used to be. The financial, political and security reach of China has grown to such a level, that we have developed a momentum internationally which reaches across multiple geographies of the 5 continents.

The power of these three massive intercontinental institutions, AIIB, RCEP and BRI touches nearly 80% of the world's population and is financed by the AIIB with literally no constraints whatsoever to hold them back. A move of this magnitude will envelope and draw in 90% of the world's corporations through bidding and development strategy. Any large conglomerate will be looking for ways in which they can be a part of this initiative to grow their company in this part of the world, and then stay a part of it sustaining themselves well into the future centuries to come. Eurasia was about to enter the first world and these coming four decades from 2020 to 2060 would be the most important part of any fortune 500 corporations' growth plans.

AIIB vs World Bank, International Monetary Fund and Asian Development Bank.

It's going to be a battle between these international institutions. The ways and methods of the WB, IMF and ADB mirror each other because all of these institutions were designed in the USA during the last 250 years of transatlantic reign.

This is to be no more. According to the international economic hit man, John Perkins on Al Jazeera. 'We economic hit men have been the ones who been responsible for creating this first truly global empire and we work many ways. But perhaps the most common is that we will identify a country which has the most resources a corporation will covet and then arrange a huge loan to that country from the **World Bank** or one of its sister organizations (such as **IMF** or **ADB**) but the money never actually goes to the country, instead it goes to our big corporations to build infrastructure projects in that country, power plants, industrial parks and ports. Bribes, that benefit a few rich people in that country in addition to our corporations, but really don't help a majority of the people in that country at all. However, it is those people that country who are left holding a huge debt. It is such a big debt that they cannot repay it and that is part of the plan. They can't repay it and so at some point, we economic hit men go back to them and say "listen, you owe us a lot of money, you can't pay your debts, so sell your oil real cheap to our oil companies, allow us to build a military base in your country, or send troops in support of us to some other part of the world like Iraq. Vote with us on the next UN vote." To have their electric utility company privatised, and then water and sewage system privatised, then sold to US Corporations or other multinational corporations. This is a huge mushrooming thing, and it is so typical of the way the International Monetary Fund and the World Bank work. They put a country in debt. It is such a big debt they can't pay it and they offer to refinance that debt and pay even more interest. And then, you demand this quid pro quo which you call conditionality or ***good governance which*** means basically that they have to sell off their resources. They sell literally everything, including many of their social services, their utility companies, their school systems, sometimes their penal systems, their insurance systems to foreign corporations. So, it is double, triple, quadruple whammy'.

So this is the 'good governance, environmental and social safeguards' which the White House National Security Council was talking about. Looks like the most important subject in the world is now Anti-Corruption, against the very people who are suggesting that the third world complete anti-corruption drives to serve the deals that have been originated by the economic hit men such as John Perkins.

7Tao - Attacking corruption

The 7Tao attack methodology is designed to fight corruption. Specifically, the kind of banking, corporate, conglomerate, national governmental, institutional, departmental, process-based corruption that infests these kinds of international deals. The attack process looks for DNA traces of corruption in the transaction flows of the company, these show up during efficiency and effectiveness testing.

The best part of 7Tao attack system is that it directly focuses on the anti-corruption element which infects every transaction within the financial deal being suggested and undertaken. Economic hit men like John Perkins are easily found out and exposed thus avoiding signing into deals which exploit the poor populations of the world. Any part of the seven parts of the transaction will glow red when corruption is detected in a process flow.

The power of the 7Tao anti-corruption attack method is brutally designed to counter the devastating effects of corruption before compound interest rates can strangle and suffocate the entire people of a country. The 7Tao attack method focuses not on just the corporation but the actual linkage between the financial, corporate, and subcontracting interests within each deal. Nothing escapes its grip as 7Tao reaches and suppresses all transactions to remove all cancerous content before it can enter the people's livelihoods.

The implementation of the 7Tao Attack method is to train people to use it for themselves. The 7Tao system is designed specifically to allow third world workers and officers to train in the methodology. 7Tao has strategic, tactical, and operational techniques which are specifically designed to beat the challenge of corruption at every step of the deal being done. No matter what the process is, whether manufacturing, financial, infrastructure, farming and agriculture or even retail – 7Tao removes the potential and the actual measured capacity for corruption. 7Tao can get to the core of the process and root out corruption from the process core consistently searching for origins. 7Tao does not look for governance as its procedure. It is a process-based engineering method and is very mathematical in nature, when applied with modern financial constructs, the engineering application comes to life breaking the back of corrupt procedures and processes from inception not allowing them to gain a foothold in a country, company or transactional process of any kind.

The power of the 7Tao attack technique comes from its lethality from the outset. The corrupt practises are provided to the student, so they understand exactly what an offender is looking to do inside the deal to implement a corrupt deal. The 7Tao system already has people in place in the department who are familiar with the technique, this creates a natural barrier for the targeted entity to defend themselves. As explained numerous times in this book, 7Tao is at its most effective when the officers of the department, business, country, and corporation are capable of implementing the technique and using it's to defend their own interests whether in the buying or the selling process.

7Tao challenges the oppressor.

Being able to stand up to an oppressor is one of the most gallant actions any person can take. History is littered with man and women who risked life and limb to do what is right against forces which tower over them. They died in the face of danger but left a spirit of defiance behind which infected the remaining people who stood up to carry the flag and eventually overcome daunting and inescapable odds.

The 7Tao attack method is made up of 12 strategies to attack corruption and defeat it before it becomes cancerous and endemic within a measurement system. 7Tao contains 48 attack tactics to defeat corruption when it is already embedded within a middle management setting inside a country, department, corporation, or a business. 7Tao contains 192 operations to help remove corruption from daily processes inducing ethics throughout every process it encounters inside a plant, manufacturing facility, government department or public service of any kind. The threat from 7Tao is so potent that even bribery is caught at an early stage.

However, the only way to implement 7Tao in a company or government department is to train its workers and officers. When 7Tao is learned by the officer in charge as a complement to Six Sigma, 20 keys and continuous Kaizen improvement, it becomes capable. The role of an officer changes from whistle blower to improvement engineer. He is now helping to drive out corruption from the processes which they are analysing as an improvement activity rather than a criminal detector. Anti-corruption systems are built into the processes of the company creating systems of operation on a daily basis. 7Tao is built to take things a step further from process and product improvement into actual environmental improvement across the board and is applicable to every company in the world. Over the page we have listed some of the attack techniques 7tao will use to remove corruption from the company processes.

The new world has yet to establish rules and regulations which need to be followed. As we can see in the recent uprisings in Pakistan. Imran Khan completed a magnificent job running the country for four years. However, due to the interference of outside powers, he was removed and replaced with extremely corrupt, uneducated, village idiots who are now fighting with each other to steal the little money he has saved from running the country properly. Pakistan is now ripe for economic hitmen to arrive into the country and do dirty deals with the devil possessed politicians who are rubbing their hands to line their own pockets with IMF, World Bank and ADB loans which they will take back to their foreign bank accounts and leave Pakistani nation nursing the compound interest rates that will be strapped around the Pakistani peoples necks in the decades to come. The techniques that are being used on the Pakistani people by the economic hitmen arriving are listed in the box over the page.

This list however, is not exhaustive. There are many more structures and applications where economic and industrial hitmen can use multitudes of techniques, systems, methodologies, technologies, finances and philosophies to supress a nation, competitor, corporation or business against the wishes of the people. It is important that they are studied by everyone.

> **Box 4:4: Some of the Attack Techniques Studied: (Repeated again)**
>
> Here are some of the attack techniques studied by 7Tao students as they figure out how the modern-day industrial world operates.
>
> Attacking customers – Attacking shareholders – Attacking employees – Attacking the ideals and culture of the company – Attacking suppliers – Attacking logistics – Attacking management – Attacking finance – Attacking information – Attacking ideas and concepts.
>
> Using deception – Employing spies – Manipulation of information – Sabotage: orthodox and unorthodox techniques – Trickery and deceit – Delay tactics – Creating fear in organizations – Removing motivation – Destroying unity – Using laws against a competitor – Exploiting arrogance – Exploiting business environments – Removing strictness – Attacking the plans of a competitor – Ranking and isolating terrain – Attacking the manufacturing process by using over-production – Attacking the company using waste arising from time in hand – Inducing transportation waste in an enemy's business – Increasing processing waste – Installing extra stock on hand to increase waste materials – Creating unnecessary motion and extra movement – Increasing defective goods throughout the plant chains – Attacking leadership systems – Weakening long-term strategic planning through constant destruction – Attacking customer and market focus – Attacking information – Attacking human resources – Attacking the management of processes – Attacking business results – Attacking workers – Attacking materials – Attacking machines – Attacking manufacturing methods – Attacking the measurement system – Attacking places – Attacking procedures – Attacking policies – Attacking agility – Attacking partners – Attacking innovation – Attacking legitimacy – Attacking the culture of an organization – Pre-emptive attacks – Attacking brands and brand identity – Attacking protocols and standards – Attacking the 7Tao consumption criteria.

Russia and the alternative to the SWIFT banking system.

Originally started in 1977, SWIFT was designed to help American and European banks to perform correspondent banking services. Today, this non-profit co-operative facilitates $1.5 trillion payments per day. It does this not by moving actual money, but by allowing banks to debit and credit their accounts as payments are moving trade around the world.

But its competitors are appearing everywhere, even within the SWIFT system. The swift is called the 'Fintech' system. As it was designed back in 1977, it has carried the design characteristics of the era with it into 2022. This makes it ripe for attack by competitors. New Fintech start-ups such as Ripple and Facebooks 'Diem' system are beginning to bite at SWIFTs wings with their plans to challenge the existing dominant competitor through distributed ledger technology.

Internal challengers who have been hamstrung working within an uncompetitive transactional system have also begun to challenge the SWIFT system. JPMorgan have been using a blockchain based system called Onyx with a messaging system called Liink. This is moving billions each day.

Russia and China have not yet developed a system which has rivalled the SWIFT system, but they are currently developing one right now. It will take a major conflict in the lands of Eurasia or a change in circumstances to force the market to use this new system. This will render the SWIFT system powerless as people are forced to buy oil and other commodities through a new system of payment.

This will be taken on by large corporations as well as they adapt to the circumstances. It will not be a case of lets leave SWIFT and join the new block chain or Chinese system… rather, it will be a whole menu of systems which large corporations will have on their books as the risk is spread across the world and not held through one choke point where one country has the dominant control over the transaction process. Massive changes are currently taking place as risk is measured in with geopolitics as a primary architecture.

The shareholders have realised that the new system will be vital to their survival. This is exactly how shareholders think, in terms of risks and returns. They will always calculate according to their losses and gain and use the most important strategies to limit their losses and maximise their gains.

Beijing is racing ahead with its digital currency and creating increasing optional choices in its product coupled with speed as it unveils innovation after innovation in its features. This digital currency is designed to overtake and defeat

SWIFT as it grabs the trophy of world trade from the United States of America. The Chinese competitor will not be the only competitor. Many different competitors both private and national public will arise which offer to dismantle the control of the transactional system in one particular area of the world. Corporations will have to design entire jobs and employment systems around the movement of money. New departments dealing with international trade will spring up inside the change plans of corporations as they handle the multitudes of competitors who will be non-profit in moving transactions across multiple geographies. Anti-corruption process will need to be applied to stop criminal organizations taking over portions of the new systems as security will be a primary content within the usability functions of these new SWIFT systems. The best ways for this are national banks such as the Bank of China, the Bank of Russia, the Bank of England and the Bank of America to house these new SWIFT systems. In this way, all the national banks can group around the international bank system to use the new SWIFT networks.

As many different competitors to SWIFT emerge, threatening countries such as Russia for geopolitical manoeuvres in Europe will be reduced to very little in leverage. Countries such as Russia will be planning their moves with all risks, gains, losses, challenges, and threats to their national security by taking these factors into account in any military move they make. Military and industrial warfare both have a shareholder policy which is interconnected in geopolitical and economic movements. SWIFT will not be gone; it will just be another consideration in the many international systems which are springing up to disrupt the existing order.

CHAPTER 10

Tao 7: Employees: Are Your Workers the Best They Can Be?

China, Napoleon once warned, is a sleeping giant. 'Let her sleep, for when she wakes, she will shake the world.' The politburo in Beijing has woken up; it has emancipated the people's energies. The giant now stalks the world markets.

The result in the West is a challenge for employees. Sustaining employment in the middle of a recession is difficult enough, obtaining employment is even harder. The worst part is the insecurity and mistrust of the employer. No job is safe. Even public service jobs may be cut to 'eliminate waste'. Job security is now linked to performance. Low performers are discarded so that the company can move forward. This insecurity is going to grow more intense in the years to come. The depression will become entrenched as China outperforms its competitors. Pressures will be heaped on business leaders and shareholders. Growth will be difficult to achieve and sustain.

The jobs-for-life days are over. Self-employment will be the new reality, with people taking on work when it is available. Companies in Asia are developing an entrepreneurial model built around family units. Mothers, fathers, sons and brothers work together to sustain an existence. If you do not have that family unit around you to provide support when times are bad, your life will be turned upside down when you lose your job. You risk losing your home if you are unable to pay your mortgage. You may end up with no place to stay, and unable to support your children. This threat brings massive psychological pressures into the workplace. Fear will be constantly hanging over your head. Ask for a pay rise and you risk being fired. With little self-respect, you feel there is no dignity in work. This is a mind-numbing existence, living from one contract to the next, one day to the next, knowing that the tap on the shoulder could come at any moment. These are the pressures which face increasing numbers of workers.

There has been an enormous growth of small businesses operating from home. Some are successful, most never get off the ground. The environment tends to be undisciplined, and usually you have to travel to places you don't want to be. The work is a lonely treadmill which is a preparation for your first heart attack.

These are conditions that contribute to the undermining of the family structure, the culture of the country and religious life.

Work has almost become the enemy of life itself. Do you work to live, or do you live to work? From the 1960s to the beginning of the new millennium, my father used to work to live. I spent many a day with him, discussing the issues of the world. He had time to give me his attention. He went to work at a certain time, and he came back at a certain time. I knew when to ask him something, when he was feeling sleepy and when he needed to go shopping. This run-of-the-mill existence was pure utopia when we look back now. There was so much to look forward to because we knew where we were going. It's just not the same anymore. The world has changed. The nature of work has changed. The nature of people who go to work has changed. The social systems which surround their lives have changed. Everything has metamorphosed into something unrecognisable to those of us who embarked on careers at a time when you could go to work at nine, come back at five, and go to bed at nine again.

Defending Employee Strengths

Developing a skilled workforce is fundamental to managing your business. To achieve a skilled workforce, you have to make sure that an employee is trained to think like an accountant, a quality engineer, a delivery driver, as if they own the business, and as if the customer is ever present, watching over them.

How do you spread the pressures on the business evenly over the workforce in a way that actively nourishes the corporate strength? You must develop the attitude, drive and sincerity that unites the business owner with the workforce. As change is constant, adapting to change is also constant. Different times will require different strategies to sustain the competitiveness of the workforce and the business. This adaptation is the remedy for reducing uncertainty and maintaining a strong team-based ethic. Every worker needs to be seen as a transaction, as a link which helps to sustain the company and allows it to make a profit. The stronger each link, the more effective the company will be. If all the links are strong, the company will be in a position to attack the marketplace and overtake competitors. Any employee can be a weak link in the chain, rendering the company vulnerable in the marketplace. The competitor's transactions will start to eat into those areas of the marketplace where your business is weak. It is fundamental that your workers understand how important it is for them to do their jobs well. Defending the business translates for each worker into defending his job. If every worker defends his job by ensuring that every task is completed to the best of his ability, your business will be well on its way to success.

When a third world country wants to compete in the global marketplace. They will want to harness the power of their peoples. To do this, they have to possess a supportive leadership which has their best interests at heart. In the case of Pakistan in 2022. The leadership is the most corrupt in history of that country. It is al most as if it has been designed and put in place to destroy the nation by the Americans and the Europeans. However, so many changes are taking place in Eurasia that the environment that these corrupt leaders were used to has collapsed. They are the ones who now stick out like a sore thumb and it is them that are in danger. People are rising up all over the world and sticking pitchforks in the face of these corrupt politicians whether in America in 2021 January 6th or in Pakistan in April 2022. They simply don't accept corruption anymore. You want your country back – you have to fight for it. You have to defend competitiveness and attack corruption – as above.

Criteria	Questions you need to ask yourself
Price	Am I as successful as my counterpart in my competitor's business? What can I do to work more efficiently and effectively than him?
Delivery	Do I deliver on time or am I a persistent late deliverer? Are my late deliveries causing problems to people who are waiting for my work to be completed? How do I improve my performance?
Quality	Is the quality of my work acceptable? How do I reduce the number of mistakes I make? How can I isolate and remove any problems in the work I produce?
After market	How can I support the worker who comes after me and works on the product I produce? Can I contribute to a support programme to make the job easier as work is passed down the value stream?

Customers	Are customers happy with my work? How do I account for any difficulties customers face when they buy the product? How do I ensure that the work I do is traceable to the point of sale? How do I ensure that the work is completely accountable and sustainable? How can the customer interface team contact me when it needs to solve problems? Do I have a system of problem-solving which I can use to help them to maintain customer accounts?
Shareholders	How do I make my work profitable? What do I need to do to ensure that my input is a value-added contribution to the company? Can I reduce waste in my process and increase value-added input by working with other teams in the plant?
Employees	What skills do I need to do my job properly? How do I acquire the necessary tools and techniques to sustain my job in the marketplace and help grow the company? What projects do I need to undertake to gain more knowledge and skills so that I can perfect the process I am responsible for?

Attacking Employee Weaknesses

Weaknesses exist in all organisations. That is not necessarily the fault of the management. Changes in the marketplace, particularly in a fast-moving environment, quickly alter the status of your finances, processes, people, machines, materials, output and procedures. In a learning environment, these weaknesses will usually reveal themselves, but if the rate of change increases too rapidly, weaknesses will accumulate to the point of uncompetitive processes. These weaknesses will, of course, also affect your competitors. The challenge is to remove your weaknesses at a faster rate than your competitor.

Weaknesses flow from all levels of personnel, from the shop floor to management and boardroom. If you attack your own weaknesses by learning to recognise them, you will also be able to identify weaknesses in your competitors. And that is the source of victory. Once you identify your competitors' weaknesses, you can steer your organization to the point where it will win the race for contracts.

Box10:1

3D Food Printing

A 3D food printer sounds like something out of *Star Trek,* but it's not out of this world. It's up and running at the French Culinary Institute in Manhattan – and in five years, it could be in your home. As part of a project at Cornell University, a group of scientists and students built a 3D printer and began testing it out with food. The device attaches to a computer, which works as the 'brain' behind the technology. It doesn't look like a traditional printer; it's more like an industrial fabrication machine. Users load up the printer's syringes with raw food – anything with a liquid consistency, like soft chocolate, will work. The ingredient-filled syringes will then 'print' icing on a cupcake. Or it'll print something more novel (i.e. terrifying) – like domes of turkey on a cutting board. 'You hand [the computer] three bits of info: a shape that you want, a description of how that shape can be made, and a description of how that material that you want to print with works,' says Jeff Lipton, a Cornell grad student working on the project. Lipton is pursuing a PhD in mechanical engineering.

Laurie Segall, CNNMoney, New York, 24 January 24 2011

3D printing is crossing boundaries into segments never seen before in the food industry. Now cake manufacturers find it relatively easy to design a Cake and print it out. The prices in China begin from just £299. Recently, just investigating the food printing growth market, hundreds of ranges of printers are coming out with prices that begin from just £150 in China to £25,000 machines being used in large food manufacturing plants in the Mid West of America. Food printing is now even becoming a reality to solving the climate crisis as nations look for ways to feed their people.

Weaknesses originate from the point of the order all the way through to the delivery process. To isolate and remove them, you need to start with the right people in the right places. These people are usually on the front line, at the organisation's cutting edge. They need to be trained to recognise weakness, to exploit any chinks in the competitor's armour, and to have the will to penetrate any marketplace at any time.

You need to search for signs of weakness in your competitors constantly. This requires tact, intelligence and an acute eye. If you spot a weakness, you can intercede with your strengths. Not all of your competitors will act ethically. Some will look for every opportunity to cut you down by any means. You need to be forewarned and prepared for difficulties in the global marketplace.

If you want to achieve excellence, this aim has to be at the core of the transaction as you prepare for battle. The questions in the box below are designed to guide the direction of your actions to ensure the defeat of your competitors. There are over 256 strategies calculated to ensure, not just a level playing field, but awareness of when to engage a competitor in industrial battle and when to remain disengaged. The questions can in fact be endless, but these examples may be helpful.

Criteria	Questions
Price	Are our prices lower than our competitor's? Is the competitor acting unethically in order to achieve the transaction? Is the competitor winning contracts through deals we do not understand? Is this a fair bidding process or is there an inner circle we are not part of? Can we provide more value than the competitor and, if we can, do we still have a chance of winning? If we did not win, what influenced the outcome?
Delivery	Can the competitor deliver on time? What is their record on delivery and how does this compare with ours? What can we do (that is ethical) to ensure that our delivery rates are better than the competitor's in a bid? How can we explain the

	strengths of our business and show that we are the best in the marketplace? Can we point to a comparative analysis by a trusted third party which confirms our position?
Quality	How does our reputation for quality compare with that of our competitors? How do we identify and secure a position on quality which demonstrates our commitment to reliability of product or service and delivery? How do we use our strengths against our competitors' weaknesses without the competitor realising what we are doing? Can we prove our reputation for quality by pointing to statistics, accolades, awards and achievements? How can we demonstrate our diversity, and the reach and quality of our workforce, in order to present a global view of our organization? How can we ensure that our entire workforce is better than our competitors' in training, achievement and the ability to deliver the product or service?
After market	How can we impress the customer by demonstrating our current performance? Can we quote other customers, whether smaller, equal or bigger in size than the one we are dealing with? How do we ensure that the after-market support we offer the customer is right for them? How do we find out what the customer's future demands will be? How do we connect to their needs in the current environment? How does ours compare with our competitor's after-market strategy? What are we missing that he is doing? Is he doing anything better than us? How do we ensure that we are at least as good as our competitor in all areas, and better in some?
Customers	Does the customer recognise our position? Does he think we are better than our competitor? How do we get feedback and develop a relationship him? How can we move into his environment so that we can monitor what he needs and when he needs it? Can we send in a company ambassador to help him through any day-to-day difficulties? How do we find out whether a competitor is in a stronger or weaker position than us in the marketplace on an order-by-order basis? How do we

	know what kind of relationship the competitor has with the customer? How do we project a better image of our company than our competitor? Are there weaknesses in our competitor's relationship with the customer and if so can we exploit them? How do we find out what these weaknesses are? What are our strengths in dealing with the customer? What are our weaknesses?
Shareholders	Do our shares provide a better dividend than our competitor's? Is our share strategy wide enough to encompass all our activities? Are our shares divided into different types with different strategies, to reflect the various parts of our business? Are we getting enough press coverage to demonstrate our growth and deflect pressure? What strategies do we have to sustain share value and increase our share of the market? How can we encourage our competitor's shareholders to move into our stocks instead? Is our excellence strategy really increasing the value of the corporation? Are we demonstrating our seven strengths of the transaction in order to win confidence and encourage investment? Is our growth strategy providing solid baseline growth? Are the seven transactional elements reflected in a rise in share price?
Employees	Are our employees better trained than our competitor's in the seven elements of the transaction? Are they able to fight harder in the marketplace? Are we capable of taking on competitors in culturally diverse and challenging marketplaces? Is our workforce trained in transactional dominance methods so that we can overtake established competitors in foreign marketplaces? Do our workers understand the threat from the East, and that we will have to face competitors whose trading styles are brutal, unrestrained and sometimes unethical? Do we have enough trained masters in the workforce to take on new competitors?

Box 10:2 Three-Dimensional Printers

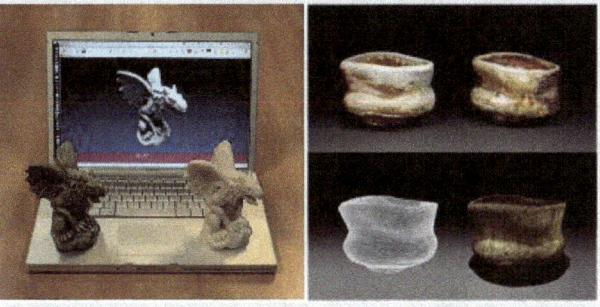

Images: Wikipedia: Aloopingicon and John Balistreri

Three-dimensional printing makes it as cheap to create single items as it is to produce thousands and thus undermines economies of scale. It may have as profound an impact on the world as the coming of the factory did ... Just as nobody could have predicted the impact of the steam engine in 1750 – or the printing press in 1450, or the transistor in 1950 – it is impossible to foresee the long-term impact of 3D printing. But the technology is coming, and it is likely to disrupt every field it touches.

Quoted from *The Economist*, 10 February 2011 leader

Modern technology has advanced in leaps and bounds. It has already transformed printing, the spoken word, the media and film, and it is now advancing into manufacturing industry. Numerous products have been developed by 3D printers. In fact, the sheer number of 3D printers now being developed have allowed the miniaturization process to accelerate from a slow start to rapid speeds which are disrupting manufacturing industry across the world. This has affected the transaction for everyone as the spread of technology and capability to produce more technology has brought down prices, increased product delivery speeds and managed to remove previously taught skills out of the manufacturing process. It is likely that this AI drive will soon spread into every corner of the planet in everything we do, eat and breathe. Soon you won't have to buy things from shops any more. If you'd like to have something, you can make it right away at home! The technology is already spreading across the world as people use 3D printers to produce whatever goods they want.

What will happen to established manufacturing industries once the materials used in these printers diversify from just plastic to all types of steel and other metals?

You'll be able to replace parts and make actual products at home for next to nothing! Already massive changes are occurring in manufacturing industries as 3D printing takes over the mould and production processes. In this democratic and far-reaching revolution new products are being created which have no copyright loyalties whatsoever! I won't need to buy a spare part any more, I can make it right here at home. No need for a factory, no need to order a thousand pieces ... no need even to make expensive phone calls in an attempt to track down a supplier. What if ... I never have to buy the things I need ever again? What if all I have to do is to buy the materials which the 3D printer will use to make the product? I won't ever need to order from the original manufacturer ever again ... These are scary times indeed. The Chinese are now producing the cheapest 3D printers on the market and proliferating the technology everywhere you look. The pace of change is incredible. Overnight 80% of the world's production processes will be affected. According to a recent article from sculpteo, a company of BASF: 2022'

4D printing is the process through which a 3D printed object transforms itself into another structure over the influence of external energy input as temperature, light or other environmental stimuli. The technology is part of the MIT Self assembly lab. The purpose of this project is to combine technology and design to invent self assembly and programmable material technologies aiming at reimagining construction, manufacturing, product assembly and performance.'

This will spell the end of the assembly line as AI eats into small suppliers manufacturing processes. Maybe even the end of the factory as we know it. This will have devastating implications for work as we know it. This begs the question. Will 4D printing make subassembly work and the small factory go obsolete through transactional attack process?

Employees are Valued by Knowledge

We live in a knowledge economy. A knowledge economy is based on mathematical, logical and engineering excellence beyond our expectations. To excel, adaptation is the key. If we do not train our workers to adapt, like still water we will stagnate while competitors flow onwards.

Businesses have to adapt all the time to a deluge of changes imposed by the imperatives of technology, legislation, financial conditions and, above all, the pressure from Eurasian competitors. In the old days you could hire a few rare PhDs and put them in a room to argue out a strategy for the future. Not these days. Now you need to train your workforce in techniques that will enable them to navigate the business through enormous pressures relentlessly pounding the defences of the sector you are in, not just of your firm. It's as if trades are being attacked directly as the number of competitors grows day by day. The Asians have their way of thinking, Europeans compete using their styles and the Americans have their own ways; however, the sheer number of competitors is so large, and the pool of markets is so limited that it is impossible to move into a marketplace without having to fight competitors, or without falling foul of a culture and its legal systems. And Mr Corruption will no doubt be there to meet you as soon as you enter. To run a successful business in this complicated world, you need employees who are the most aware, the most knowledgeable and the bravest, who possess a capability and motivation forged of steel.

The Chinese have sent many traders into a change resistant Africa, armed with basic economic fighting methods. Millions of Chinese arrive on merchant ships every year, unloading manufactured goods on to the African quayside, displacing indigenous workers and foreign competitors. They rely entirely on the seven principles of the transaction. They talk to the buyer about price; they get him to experience the goods; they extol the quality of the goods; they provide after-market assurances such as, 'If you don't like it, you can bring it back,' a gesture calculated to win trust. They gauge the customer by reading his facial expressions and measuring the time he remains at their stall. Simultaneously they calculate the profits they are about to make. When they sell the goods, they re-order the best lines, avoiding products that did not sell so well. They have a trading tradition that stretches back five millennia. China is the most powerful and hardest-working trading nation the Africans have seen in the last century. Africa is actively embracing China. No bullets, no bombs, no threats, no arm-twisting – a little palm-greasing is bound to take place, but the Africans are getting more than they ever received from the West. The key to Chinese success is in the way in which they conduct transactions!

The US China Trade War: Defending competitiveness and attacking corruption.

The US China trade war is the early stages of the conflict between an incumbent superpower and a rising superpower as they engage each other in the process of Thucydides trap. It is inevitable that these two powers will collide as they grow to dominate the globe in industrial policy and strategy.

12 of the 16 engagements in the past 5000 years in Thucydides trap has resulted in war. If a war is generated between the US and China, this will result in a thermonuclear conflict which will wipe out the world. No form of life will survive as nuclear winter descends upon the planet. Only cockroaches will survive, the rest of the planet will burn for eternity.

The US China trade war is a disagreement which the US has foisted upon China. The allegations are many including unfair trading practises, forced technology transfer to Beijing and intellectual property theft. The Trump administration indicated that these practises may be a primary contributor to the US China trade deficit. The Trump administration began raising billions of dollars in tariffs to buy time to consider the direction of the US China trade war. In response and counterattack, the Chinese government accused the USA of nationalist protectionism and took measures to launch actions against the Trump administration.

The relationship between the two is very simple. China buys very little from the US and sells them a lot. This is leading to a massive trade deficit every year for the USA as China is making around $375 Billion dollars in export success in 2017. Not only is it putting Chinese products on every shelf in the United States, it is also suffocating competitors within the manufacturing industry of the USA and holding down inflation. This is especially prevalent in the voters of the Rust belt, who were instrumental in the election of Donald Trump for the 45th President. These were the primary states where the swing voting took place and Trump was elected to office.

China banned Soya beans, and various products which were being shipped from the USA and began seeking alternative suppliers of agricultural goods to the USA such as Brazil. The conflict escalated throughout 2019 and 2020 and is still taking place today as the US and China exchange economic blows into who needs to export more to whom. In January 2020 the two sides reached a difficult phase one deal. This expired in December 2021 with China failing by a wide margin to purchase American goods and services as agreed. By the end of the Trump presidency, the US China trade war was widely characterised as a failure.

Back in the 1980's, Donald Trump had a different enemy, Japan. He blamed them for everything including their trade practises and how they ripped off the US manufacturers through poorly designed trade deals. He whined constantly about how poorly designed trade deals were making it uncompetitive for the American manufacturer. Same thing here with Middle Kingdom, imposing tariffs became a major steppingstone to engaging China in his presidential campaign. However, most economists do not believe trade deficits pose a real threat to the American economy. Nearly all economists interviewed and surveyed proclaimed the tariffs would do more harm than good to the American economy and some advocated alternative means to address the trade deficits and the accusations of unfair trading practises with China.

No one wins a fight.

It is often said in Martial Arts that 'no one wins a fight'. In the case of the US China trade war, both countries have suffered along with the rest of the world as the world economy adapted to the growing reality of the US China Trade War. In the United States, it has resulted in much higher costs for manufacturers as they must pay for raw materials purchases thus taking away any real benefit of not doing business with China. On the other side of the world, in China, it resulted in a slowdown in the rate of industrial output growth as old customers disappeared and new customers were sought for the manufactured goods which China was seeking to export. This resulted in even more trade deals and extra capacity into the Belt and Road Initiative, as well as the RCEP deals to incorporate further countries and industrial capacity into the current process of Eurasian growth.

Exports had already been declining due to the recession and competition from elsewhere in Asia, but the new trade war had accelerated the decline into a more vertical drop as manufacturers struggled to adapt to new political and economic conditions.

On both sides of the US China trade conflict, supply chains started to shift to other parts of Asia and the Americas. This led to fears that a decoupling was taking place shifting these two superpowers apart as they began to onshore manufacturing capability and sought to bring back entire supply chains.

Just when trade relations were about to get better, it got much worse. The trade war coupled with Covid-19 pandemic led to the astronomical rise of inflation across the western world which could only be dampened by interest rates. It was not just manufacturing industry that suffered as a result of the trade war. Bonds would also be affected as the purchases of financial instruments declined. The Pandemic also brought the supply chains of the world to a halt as they completely stopped producing and moving very large amounts of goods. Airports, travel, ships, aircraft industry, airlines, trains, and motorways all suffered as the Covid-19 virus made its way through the world economy leading to shut down after shutting down anywhere where two or more people would sit down.

When the economy got back to normal in 2022, inflation was rife and the ability to arrest inflation had been significantly reduced. The only way bonds could be purchased again, and inflation reduced was to go back to China to begin the supply chain delivery system again, and to raise interest rates to bring some much-needed life back into the currencies as they were dwindling in value. Governments around the world were taking similar steps to address the many difficult issues which the two problems were causing to the world economy. The US China Trade War and the Covid-19 virus had bought to the world stage a near vertical decline in the stock markets losing 30% of the stock market value on Dow Jones from 30,000 down to 18,000 on April 4th, 2020. This is also called the Inverted Yield curve to mask over the fact that this is the mid cycle recession. These problems are in built into the taxation systems and cannot be removed.

To defeat these two problems, it was vital that reactionary motions stop between the two superpowers. It was time to go back to the drawing board and try to resolve these issues in a structured way.

American complaints

Donald Trump first got the idea of tariffs in his head back in the eighties when America had a little competition from Japan using the infamous Toyota Production System as a primary set of tools against the might of the US Economy. Toyota, Nissan, and Honda knew the pressures that were facing the daily American consumer and designed their cars to fit those pressures by cutting costs for the consumer, increasing reliability and performing extraordinary aftermarket support services for their cars. This allowed the Japanese to have excellent inroads into the American market especially after the 1973 oil crisis. Once they had a good foothold, they grew their market share into a dominant part of the American purchasing landscape. Eventually, they would end up building plants in America because Honda, Toyota and Nissan were now an integral part of the American economy.

Tariffs didn't work against the Japanese; they won't work against the Chinese either. Domestic manufacturing practises in the Japanese competition relied on third generation techniques such as Toyota Production System, Total Quality Management and 20 Keys of Manufacturing success. Donald Trump played the same card against the Chinese in the 2016 elections, and this became a major part of his success in winning the 2016 election.

The complaints Donald Trump made were as follows:

- The Chinese were major currency manipulators. This made it impossible for our companies to compete with Chinese companies.
- They stole US technology.
- Forced technology transfer through economic partnerships.

- Forced economic conditions and partnership protocols.
- Breaking promises.
- Not honouring agreements.
- Not completing targets and cheating on targets.
- Intellectual property theft.
- Cyber intrusions into US Commercial networks.
- Reverse engineering of established US Goods and services.
- Forced joint ventures.

Jim Schultz, Former white house council said that "Though multiple presidential administrations – Clinton, Bush and Obama – "The United States has naively looked the other way while China cheated its way to an unfair advantage in the international trade market."

Over half of the members of American chamber of commerce in the Peoples Republic of China thought that leakage of intellectual property was an important concern when doing business there. It was a matter of time before the Americans responded. The actions of the Chinese trading practises did not fit in with the American models and Western legal models of doing business in general. However, these models did not fit into anywhere in the Eurasian continent. They only worked where the Western legal system could be enforced. If the Western legal system did not exist in the areas where the West was trying to export to, the American administration would cry unfair! It was anything goes, loose economic practises from third world countries generally ruled the economic airwaves. None of the 5 billion people of Eurasia followed western rules of trade. That's just how they work. It is we in the West that must get used to it. We must learn the new ways of the world. Just as we learned Lean Manufacturing, Six Sigma, Taguchi Methods, Total Quality Management back in eighties off the Japanese who learned it from us back in the 1950s, here in the West from scholars such as W Edwards Deming and Joseph Juran – whom we in the West ignored and mocked. So these eminent scholars went and took their trade to Japan. Toyota, Nissan, Honda, Isuzu and Mitsubishi listened carefully to what they were saying.

We will have to do the same thing here when competing against China, we have to listen and try new methods so that we can have a chance to compete again on a level playing field which is much shallower than the one we faced against Japan in the 1980's.

The Eastern fight is one of elbows, knees, punches, kicks, grappling, trapping, and pushing. We in the West are still going on about Queensberry rules. Perhaps it is the Queensbury Rules that is holding us back? Has anyone ever bothered to ask that question?

In March 2018, Donald Trump said that 'Trade Wars are good and easy to win'. CNN.

During August 2019, Donald Trump said that 'I never said that China was going to be easy'. CNN.

Chinese complaints:

The Chinese government has a bone to pick with America as the problems between the two increased across the board. The Chinese made the following allegations.

- The USA was stifling China's growth.
- The USA was the centre of corruption and was accusing China of corrupt practises.
- The US actions were making negotiations difficult.
- The US had no evidence of wrongdoing against China.
- The US Trade representatives were operating with a presumption of guilt on the Chinese.
- The US was making claims without evidence and based on speculation.
- The US was a colonialist empire that was using the World Bank, the IMF and The ADB to oppress third world countries. They would not let the Chinese in to free the people of the third world.
- The US was holding Africa and South America back from economic development.

The Chinese government denied that forced transfer of Intellectual Property is mandatory practise and displayed the power of domestic R&D performed in China. Larry summers, former US secretary, even admitted that Chinese leadership in some technological fields was the result of 'Huge government investment in basic science' and not theft of US properties.

In March 2019, the national people's congress endorsed a new foreign investment bill, to take effect in 2020 which prohibits the forced transfer of IP from foreign companies and grants stronger protection to foreign intellectual property and trade secrets. China had also planned to lift investment restrictions into the automotive industry in 2022.

The Inauguration of Joe Biden

Economist Paul Krugman said in September 2020 that if Democratic candidate Joe Biden won the U.S. presidential election, he should maintain a tough stance against China, but focus more on ***industrial policy*** than trade tariffs. Paul Krugman knew that the conflict was about to turn industrial and away from the Trade War. Stopping the Chinese selling to us and getting blocked from selling to China was not going to get us results. We had to complete the job by competing with the Chinese. The first stage was to understand the new game.

Joe Biden declared that America would declare 'extreme competition' with China in the realms of industrial policy, instead choosing to take China on in the very same way they took on the Japanese during the trade disputes with Japanese during the 1980's.

They would complete this analysis of 'extreme competition' by learning about the opponent and adapting to the style of fighting which the Chinese were currently practising.

This would mean training the entire American workforce in new techniques of operating in a world where the old rules would no longer apply. This would also engage the European workforce and also the broader third world workforce in general along with the Chinese workforce.

The aim of the new extreme competition would be to find a new set of rules that all players could be happy with, the practises of corruption would end, and we could look forward to a new world where trading would be completed methodically and with good faith among nations. This could be done using the 7Tao industrial warfare technique.

Instead of fighting in the international marketplace and doing untold trillions of dollars in damage in the US China trade war, we could instead fight in the classroom and find solutions to the trade war issues within the confines of the research area and a simulation-based fighting ring. This could have major benefits for both economies as they and many other countries, as they train to resolve the issues which are plaguing the world economy.

What the world says about the trade war with China:

- Minxin Pei, a scholar of Chinese politics at California's Claremont college, declared that 'Xi Jinping's ambition for China's revival as a world power had been revealed as hollow through the continuing trade dispute.

- Joe Biden commented: 'While Trump is pursuing a damaging and erratic trade war, without any real strategy, China is positioning itself to lead the world in renewable energy'.

- A Harvard poll in 2019 (Caps Harris) found that 67% of the registered voters wanted the US to confront Beijing over its trade policies despite the fact that 74% of consumers were shouldering the tariffs.

- Mark Penn said that 'They [American public] realise that the tariffs may have negative impacts on jobs and prices, but they believe that the fight here is the right one.'

- Since China was the leading source of key medical supplies, this raised concerns that US tariffs on imports from China threaten imports of medical supplies into the United States exacerbating the need for goods from China during the Covid-19 pandemic.

- In the 2018 G20 Summit. The trade war was on the agenda for discussion.

- Jorge Guajardo, the former Mexican ambassador to China said that 'One thing the Chinese have to acknowledge is that it wasn't a Trump issue; it was a world issue. Everybody is tired of the way China games the trading system and makes promises that never amount to anything.'

- A March 2019 Reuters article said that the European Union shared many of the Trump administrations same complaints with regards to China's technology transfer policies and market access constraints. Many European diplomats agreed with Trumps goals, even if they disagreed with his tactics.

- Singaporean Prime Minister Lee Hsien Loong said that the trade war was negatively affecting Singapore and described it as "very worrying". He urged the US and Chinese governments to change their approaches.

- Prime minister Boris Johnson said, "We don't like tariffs on the whole".

- European Council President Donald Tusk said, "The trade war risked causing a global recession".

- The Chilean vice minister for trade, Rodrigo Yanez, told CNBC that "It's very important for Chile that a trade deal between the U.S. and China is signed soon".

- Most countries in the world want to trade with the Chinese, the Trade War is getting in their way. They will abandon the West if these actions are kept up. A better way must be found to resolve this disagreement between the US and China without blocking each other's purchases. This was partly to blame for today's inflation problems in 2022.

The recession of 2019 to 2021 arrived on time as predicted in an Epoch Times article featuring Amar Manzoor and Fred Harrison in March of 2016. We correctly predicted the recession to turn up on time for these two years. 2019 to 2021. We call it the mid cycle recession. The fact that the US China Trade War and Covid-19 pandemic was used to cover up the fact that this recession always happens in the middle of an 18-year real estate cycle has been omitted. For some reason, there is always a massive disruption that takes place to cover up the inverted yield curve and the mid cycle recession. The last time it was a combination of distractions, featuring Y2K, the terror attacks of 2001 September 11th, and finally Enron, Worldcom, Tyco and all of the others involved in stock and investment frauds.

Made in China: 2025

Empowering the Chinese workforce is the main aim of Made in China 2025. The Chinese want to be able to export every product ever in existence on the planet. Made in China 2025 is designed for one purpose only: The Chinese Employee.

They want to compete with all manufacturing industry in the world, in all products, in all classes, in all quality levels, in all marketplaces of all five continents. This is why they are signing trade deals with every country. They want total industrial domination.

Made in China 2025 is a national strategic plan and an industrial policy of the National People's republic of China to further develop the countries national manufacturing policies.

They intend to transform the manufacturing sector from a low-tech factory of the world into a national manufacturing powerhouse featuring high tech manufacturing capabilities. This will be on top of the low-tech factories featured across China. The Made in China 2025 plan was to transform the manufacturing sector from a low-tech labour-intensive workshop into a more technology sensitive powerhouse.

The goals are also to increase core materials usage in domestic terms from 40% by 2020 to 70% by 2025. The initiative encourages independence from foreign suppliers by increasing production in high tech products and services. Central to this plan is Chinese Semiconductor manufacturing which is also be on shored by American manufacturing industry as well. The industrial war has begun with two countries on shoring as much manufacturing onto their shores as is possible as they realise that the more manufacturing plants populate their country, the more powerful the country will become and the more chance they have of winning the US China industrial war.

As Paul Krugman has said, focus **more on industrial policy rather than tariffs.** Bring the plants home, understand the international architecture, and then beat China at their own game. The trade war has morphed into an industrial war between the two superpowers as they position themselves to challenge each other in relations with the outside world. Whoever can have better relations with the rest of the world will win this US China 'intense competition'. The Biden administration has realised that they will have to fight China in an industrial war like the way in which they adapted to the Japanese ways of thinking back in the 1980's. Slowly but surely, both the Chinese and the Americans are adapting to the realities that this confrontation is bringing to the fore. It is inevitable that they will both get together eventually to come to a resolution designing solutions that accommodate them both.

The main aim of Made in China 2025 is to support the Chinese workforce by using this drive to power the Belt and Road Initiative, the Regional Comprehensive Economic Partnership, and the numerous Free Trade Agreements which China has with many countries of the world. If all these Free Trade Agreements operate according to the way in which the Chinese have designed, it is likely that this will power the Chinese manufacturing economy for the next five centuries to come. If this is the case and it becomes true, the Chinese manufacturing worker will be busy for a very long time and the Chinese factory will be humming along for centuries to come. It is likely that this industrial war will be the core of conflict in the coming 21st century and well into the 22nd century.

All the Free Trade Agreements combined with infrastructure development, supported by the AIIB shareholders, and populated with RCEP will ensure the free trade of goods and services between Eurasian countries, thereby cementing China as an international giant which it has now become. China will now have export markets across the whole world as they engage on a growth path which doubles China's GDP every decade. Will this ever stop and are we even able or committed to stop them? Why would we want to stop them after all, what have they done wrong? The legal systems of China are growing, and they are defeating every competitor under the marketplace in the ensuing industrial war. Made in 2025 is already here, and it is now a reality powered by Free Trade Agreements. China has already won… It is the rest of the world that has to catch up.

The following is a list of free trade agreements in the Chinese network. The create orders for the Chinese factory. More Free Trade Agreements means more orders. More orders mean's more growth. More growth means stronger bonds between China and the free trade countries signatories.

Regional Comprehensive Economic Partnership (RCEP)
China-Cambodia FTA
China-Mauritius FTA
China-Maldives FTA
China-Georgia FTA
China-Australia FTA
China-Korea FTA
China-Switzerland FTA
China-Iceland FTA
China-Costa Rica FTA
China-Peru FTA
China-Singapore FTA
China-New Zealand FTA (including upgrade)
China-Chile FTA
China-Pakistan FTA
China-ASEAN FTA
Mainland and Hong Kong Closer Economic and Partnership Agreement.
Mainland and Macao Closer Economic and Partnership Arrangement

Free Trade Agreements Currently under review and developing further

China-ASEAN FTA Upgrade
China-Chile FTA Upgrade
China-Singapore FTA Upgrade
China-Pakistan FTA second phase
China-GCC(Gulf Cooperation Council) FTA
China-Japan-Korea FTA
China-Sri Lanka FTA
China-Israel FTA
China-Norway FTA

China-Moldova FTA
China-Panama FTA
China-Korea FTA second phase
China-Palestine FTA
China-Peru FTA Upgrade
China-Nepal FTA Joint Feasibility Study
China-Papua New Guinea FTA Joint Feasibility Study
China-Canada FTA Joint Feasibility Study
China-Bangladesh FTA Joint Feasibility Study
China-Mongolia FTA Joint Feasibility Study
China-Switzerland FTA Upgrade Joint Feasibility Study
China Fiji FTA Joint Feasibility study.

The rise of expendable jobs and their impact.

The culture of zero hours contracts is causing much distress in the United Kingdom. Employers will hire people with no guarantee of work. This can be translated as "we will call you when we need you."

This attitude of employer-to-employee contract is forcing the people to choose multiple jobs with different employers in the hope of picking up work to pay their living costs month to month. Not only is this occurring in the UK, but in other countries as well. It is detrimental to everything the UK economy has been built upon over the last 50 years since the war. A question arises from two angles of inquiry, employee, and employer. The first being employee uncertainty and what this can do to the social fabric of the country.

Imagine, a worker goes from one day to the next answering calls. "Can you do two hours here? Maybe three hours the next day? No hours the third day, and work all day on the fourth day?" As the person accrues working hours during the week, they can total only enough just to pay the room rent.

This is giving rise to larger growth in illegal activities just to make ends meet, which puts more pressure on the authorities to keep control of difficult situations. Not only that, it puts great pressure on the police forces of the UK as they discover that zero hours contracts have a great part to play in the statistical measurement of crime.

So, what do the police do? They record all the data and just pass it on as feedback systems explaining that most of the low-level crimes are associated with poverty. The same goes for hospitals, social services, employment agencies, and other support services as they heave under the burden of society which is in decay because of the uncertainty of the employment environment.

The loss of good manufacturing jobs is at the heart of this issue. The plants which sustained the ecosystems of towns have now vanished, leaving a public which is scavenging hours for survival. This is the primary reason why the political atmosphere has become so charged in the geographies of Europe and America. This does not just reflect in the voting patterns of people with Brexit, the U.S. Elections, the Italian elections, and in the German elections; it also reflects quite clearly in law and order, healthcare, narcotic usage, and in the breakup and no formation of families. Combine these forces with the fact that upon each family are massive rises in house prices, affordability problems of daily living costs, and that the inability to provide a stable environment for children leaves society vulnerable. When all these factors combine, that's when the backlashes begin on the systems which exist to sustain a country, resulting in breaking point pressures as people turn against the status quo.

On the flip side, employers have no choice but to offer zero-hours contracts, because they are simply treading water with their balance sheets. Combine this with the fact that onerous tax regimes are pushing the extraction process from every business at breakneck pressures, the business will end up cannibalizing whatever it can to stay afloat.

So, are rents too high? Or is the rent-free competition of online retailers killing the competitors? Or are online markets reducing the need for rent in the first place, thereby driving rents down and changing the face of the high street or the mall?

Online corporations such as Amazon attack every piece of retail by seeking out the retailer and killing his ability to pay his rent, this is suffocating them of transactions. Once you lose transactions, your store becomes empty; if your store becomes empty, you can't pay the rent; if you can't pay the rent, you close down.

The key to survival is having a rent-free business. Once you don't have to pay rent, or you can just deliver from an online shop, you spread the demand for goods from a clustered business park or mall into a small well diffused operating system which can be effectively run from your back garden. A lot of people are doing these types of business in the UK as they transform themselves from having a service business based on foot flow to having a service business based upon click flow. The services sector has truly changed the way in which we live and consume products.

This self-consuming cannibalistic cycle is not just affecting the employee and the employer. It is rapidly eating into the tax systems as well, leaving the taxman to seek out punishing regimes of enforcement as they seek out sources of value. The employee simply cannot keep being taxed even more to a breaking point, they will buckle under the pressure, thus creating even more strain on the public services.

Where is the most value kept in the UK? You guessed it: house prices and rent. They are about to go after the property owners and the residue systems which kill the businesses. Many large property holders rent out houses and businesses as they squeeze the public along with the tax man. By the time the business has paid the taxes, been fleeced by the landlord, and oppressed their employees to the point of self-destruction, there is nothing left for the business. So, we can drive the battle down to one conflict, in the UK at least, which is the tax man against the large property holders.

This is the crux of the next 10 years as the tax man begins the preparation process for taxing the landlord. Here in the UK, they have already begun to implement data gathering processes, finding out who is paying rent and where this rent goes, how it is spent, whose name the properties are under and how the wealth is being distributed. The key question to the tax man is the rent process itself, if someone is paying rent, and do you tax the property or tax the rent?

CHAPTER 11

The Asian Age – Or a New Partnership between Co-operating Cultures?

Geopolitics of the Eastern Shift

The shift eastwards started in the 1960s, when Japan made a bid for her share of the markets of the world. With the arrival of China, the competition has become as fierce as it can get. Nations are now using all available assets to dominate other nations in the global marketplace and win transactions with consumers.

You can see where military confrontations are taking place. If you examine the world map and locate the hot spots you will see that China is being confronted with military weapons to counter her preferred method of attack – industrial war. The military conflicts are an extension of the economic conflict between America and China. In areas where China is increasingly assertive economically, you can discern the onset of a war. China is seeking control of the world's diminishing natural resources to feed her industry through Belt and Road Initiative, RCEP, CPEC, Free Trade Agreements. This is bringing the Eurasian cycle into conflict with the Transatlantic cycle. The motives of the two opposing forces are easy to identify.

It is clear that the USA is militarily defending its economic markets while the Chinese are on the offensive. One is forced into the position of *violent preservation* while the other is pursuing *powerful economic expansion*. The Chinese are trading ferociously with their targeted markets while the Americans are battling to keep their markets flowing. The Chinese are winning. They have huge financial surpluses; the Americans have gigantic debts. The Chinese have a 'good guy' image – their expansion seems benign; the Americans are seen as the 'bad guys' with their military interventions and oppression of the Islamic world.

The American administration is at a loss to explain why Eurasia is exploding economically while the Transatlantic world is being depleted of transactions. The Americans, of course, have an excellent understanding of military warfare; but Asians have an excellent understanding of industrial warfare. China is gaining rapid economic traction and the USA is slipping into irrelevance in the global marketplace.

Can the rapid decline of the West be reversed? What do we need to do to preserve peace as Eurasia increases its dominance over the planet's transactions under the leadership of China? The answer lies not in violent preservation but in ferocious economic competition on terms completely different from those of the past two hundred years.

The rules of economic warfare have been transformed: it is now the 'lowest common denominator' of the transaction that is fundamental.
Either you sell your product and buy what you want, or your competitors sell their product and buy what they want. Success depends on industrial fighting style and the ability of the manufacturer to capture the imagination of the purchaser.

The Chinese ace cards are geography. The Middle Kingdom is in the middle of Eurasia. Their advantage is that the Belt and Road Initiative reaches into every corner of the Central Asia, Russia, Europe, Middle East, Southeast Asia, India and touches the warm waters of the coast of the Indian Ocean. China can reach every part of the Eurasian continent with many ports on the South China sea leading to export around the world. China can import all the resources it needs from the Middle East and the Central Asian states. This allows China to absorb the natural resources of the continent and manufacture all of the goods that it is capable of, delivering them to every corner of the globe through land, air and sea. As Europe realises that the rise of China is going to be inevitable and the country is impossible to invade because it is too big, too diverse and very well armed, they will begin to explore other options to accommodate Chinese existence. Historically, China is not an invading power, they don't like to be in other people's countries with uniforms.

The Chinese tend to grow their way out of problem relationships through developing partnerships and economic expansion plans. The Chinese have a very strong tradition of trade in these countries and the revitalised new silk route will be a valuable part for growth for all 74 nations which the Belt and Road Initiative touches. The bigger challenges for China will be the language, cultural and racial barriers as they trade their way through Eurasia. They will have to spend enormous amounts of time and capital training their people and educating them to operate in Eurasia. It will take the Chinese at least one century to fix trading routes, develop relationships, create solid ports, train stations, and allow people free movement of goods and services so that they can enhance their lives. To be able to challenge the Eurasian continent, we must do the same and allow our people to grow through training and education so that they can be a part of this process. The next 1000 years will be trade based relations throughout the Eurasian heartlands.

Education is the Key, Practice is a Fundamental Factor

Supply		Demand
Price: We want to supply a product at a price you can afford.	There are 7 components of **supply and demand.** The customer represents demand and the supplier represents the product.	**Price:** We want to pay as little as possible for the best possible product.
Delivery: We want to get the product to you on time.		**Delivery:** We want it on time.
Quality: We want perfect quality to meet your requirements.		**Quality:** We don't want a poor quality product.
After market: We want to preserve our relationship with you.		**After market:** We want after-sales service.
Customers: We want as many customers as we can handle.		**Customers:** We are going to pay you good money.
Shareholders: We would like to make a profit on our investment.		**Shareholders:** We will pay an affordable investment for the product or service business.

Employees: We want our employees to be the best we can source for the markets we are competing for.		**Employees:** We want our goods to be made by the best people in the marketplace.

The Eurasian development curve has its roots in Japanese post-war expansion. The rest of Eurasia learned from the Japanese and is applying their theories while adding their own cultural wisdom to the transaction.

The West has an excellent understanding of some of the components of industrial warfare – defence tools and methodologies such as Six Sigma, Lean, MVT and Total Quality do point businesses in the right direction. However, what is required is a total re-education in the theory of industrial warfare. The third generation set us off in the right direction, but the fourth generation will ask much more of us as the sheer amount of competition has heated up in every country of the world. We must learn the competitive practices of business across the world today. Western governments must be unrelenting in their drive to remain relevant in the global business arena.

The key lies in preparing the workforce for global competition. We must train our workers to compete in a Eurasian-driven world dominated by China. To succeed in this new world, the first thing to understand is that the old world is finished. We must not seek solutions from the past because none of them will reflect the new realities. Preparing the workforce will require significant investment but they must learn to adapt to a new business culture informed by the historical apparatus of the East. The British government is preparing for this new dawn, gathering the resources required to face a world it last saw in the fifteenth century. As the West declines and the East increasingly drives trade and investment around the world, new modes of thinking will arise as the centre of trade shifts.

It is essential that governments support commercial enterprises and the education process. Every employee needs the right qualifications to compete in the global village. There are important decisions for governments to make:

1: How do we ensure that our industries are supported in their drive to sell to others?

2: How do we secure stability in the marketplaces where we want to trade?

3: How do we prepare our working population with up-to-date qualifications in an entirely knowledge-driven global economy?

4: What do we need to do to build alliances between our businesses and the countries they seek to trade in?

5: What current competitive strategies are there which represent the future and not the past?

6: How do we instil a competitive fighting spirit in our workforce so that they will fight as ferociously in an industrial war as they would against an invading army?

None of this will be easy. Western corporations are still relying on the practices of the 1960s, 1970s and 1980s while the East accelerates into the future. China is determined that next-generation business excellence will be their only consideration over the next three to five decades at least! Nothing is going to deter them. The question is whether Western corporations will be able to learn the difference between third- and fourth-generation business excellence (as outlined in Chapter 2).

China is Back

In the 1500s, who would have thought that the feudal and internally broken culture of the West would come to dominate other nations for the next five centuries? Britain, Spain, Portugal, Belgium, France, Germany, and other would-be imperialists were constantly fighting chaotically among themselves, never agreeing on the best way forward, and not unified in any way. That internal eruption of chaos, however, was the driving force behind the growth of several Western empires.

A desperate fight for survival and drive to push trade, by whatever means, to all parts of the planet resulted in companies like the British East India Trading Company taking control of lands far beyond the old world they had known. Christopher Columbus had set sail for India and when, inadvertently, he reached South America instead, where he called the natives Indians. At that time the Chinese empire was one of the richest in the world. They had ships that could dwarf the *Mary Rose* by a factor of 14 to 1, such was their display of might. But the mantle of the East contracted, and the West ascended in the competitive global cycle, establishing a growth path that would encompass many industrial revolutions. The resemblance today is uncanny if you look at this the other way around. The USA is circling the globe with aircraft carriers that dwarf other vessels. Some are the size of 5 football fields back to back.

The Chinese are generating fierce competition at levels not seen in the last five hundred years. They are starting to replicate the rise of the Western empires, driving in the same direction. As the USA displays its military might, the Chinese are sending out small but dynamic trading parties to circumnavigate the globe and look for opportunities to sell their goods. Hundreds of thousands of Chinese leave the mainland every year to settle in other countries and set up businesses which import goods made in China. The third world has never had it so good. So many affordably priced goods are arriving on their shores that the way in which they live is being transformed. Every consumable item imaginable is being sold to people who are reaching out to the modern world. They want clothes, televisions, cars, computers, kitchens, and machinery to enhance their own lives and develop their countries.

The Chinese have a successful strategy. Rather than deal with the despots in government, they sign deals and transact directly with the public. There is corruption, but less among the people who access the demand directly, so more products reach the people in the street. The Chinese are looking for one thing only: *the transaction*! They want to move as many goods as they can into the land they wish to conquer by using the arts of industrial warfare. They don't need to blow things up, they don't need to wear uniforms, they don't need a massive show of force, they don't need to make the natives kneel.

My teacher Sifu Yang Por informed me, 'Son, we want factories internally in China and shops externally in other countries of the globe.' The goods that China makes need outlets in the rest of the world. The more demand for their factories, the more profit for China. The more they make, the more they sell of the next generation of product.

Development is so rapid that there are problems with inflation and the ability to control the pace of economic growth. China is facing the standard problems of classes in the mainland combined with shortages of space in the workshops of the world. Despite these difficulties, China continues to manufacture goods at a rate unseen in the last five hundred years. Their industrial warfare ruthlessness is annoying Western entrepreneurs like Sir James Dyson.

> Sir James Dyson, one of Britain's leading engineers, has complained to David Cameron after the emergence from China of at least 100 copycat versions of one of his products left his business nursing costs of £10m.
>
> Sir James has called on the Prime Minister to raise the issue when he meets the Chinese premier, Wen Jiabao, tomorrow.
>
> Sir James, the company's founder, said that Dyson's Air Multiplier bladeless fan has been the subject of at least 100 patent infringements across 20 countries, all originating from copies produced in China.
>
> James Hurley, *The Sunday Telegraph*, 26 June 2011.

I don't understand why Sir James Dyson is complaining. This is the normal style of business in the East! They have been operating like this for thousands of years because they do not recognise copyright. It's not part of their culture, it's part of the western culture to endorse and enforce copyright. As long as they can make it themselves, why should they direct business through James Dyson's company? What is the most you can do to them, James? Are you going to send armed forces to invade China to stop them from copying your products? Are you going to complain and slap the table? Are you going to ask the government to change the law?

The only option available to James Dyson is to learn the arts of industrial warfare himself. He needs to understand what the new world looks like, so he can start the journey into a planet where there are no **Queensberry Rules!** The strongest, fastest, brightest, and most appealing wins. The loser goes out of business.

You simply cannot use traditional styles of boxing against these people. You have to develop new methods and learn to understand the new ways of fighting for the transaction. The Chinese don't wear boxing gloves, it's bare-knuckle trading. They don't agree that punches below the belt are illegal; they will punch, kick, knee, and elbow where it hurts most. Using knife hand, finger jabs, leopard fist, snake fist, hammer punch and heel kicks are part of their fighting culture. You are not in a position to tell them that their martial arts style is inferior to boxing, it simply does not register with them. They don't wear gloves to protect the fists, they don't have any rules, and their arsenal of industrial weapons is far superior because of the number of tools they have in their arsenal. They won't wait till you are ready for honourable combat, they'll hit you as hard as they can when you're not looking. The best part is they don't think there is anything wrong with the way they trade. They don't understand why you complain so much. When a Chinese trader's foot connects with a Western competitor's face, *that's what it's supposed to do! The aim is to defeat you, to sell their product, to make the customer come to them and not to you! This is 7Tao: the art of industrial warfare.*

It's simple for the third world in general and not just China: focus entirely on the transaction. If you see a competitor company trading on your patch, attack it directly and steal its customers. Start with entrapped customers who may not be able to afford to but are forced to buy, then bring the market down to the lower level of buyers. This will see off the higher sellers of goods as the market drops in price, creating more competition. Under-capitalised monopolies are cracked, and more ferocious and desperate traders take over.

The massive tidal wave of affordability is affecting all the major brands. It's not just Toyota, Nissan, General Motors, and Renault that are suffering. Every established brand is taking kicks on the chin as customers who used to walk through the door don't come any more. The pressure that new Chinese sellers are exerting on established brands keeps intensifying. Within China, too, manufacturers who have priced their products too high are finding themselves in difficulties. The competition is so intense that even recently established Chinese brands must fight like tigers to retain their market share. As the dust settles in the global marketplace, we will see that we have awoken to a new world in which the arts of economic warfare are the be all and end all of survival. The older third generation thinking, and methods just don't reach the levels of intensity required in the new world.

Throw away the Queensberry Rules

Competing in the modern global economy requires a complete rewiring of systems the West established in the last century. We grew too civilized economically and depended on the past to sustain us. We were complacent, thinking the competitor would never come, and too tied up with red tape.

Sun Tzu says, *'Do not depend upon the competitor not coming, depend on being prepared.'*

It is not too late. We still have an infrastructure which, if invested in properly, could stand up to the Eastern goliath. People can be re-skilled to take on the new challenges. But we must stop thinking in terms of Queensberry Rules. We must get down to the fundamentals of economic battle and teach our people the principles of the transaction. Waging a physical war against people who want to do business with the Chinese won't help us, it will only make us hated. Forcing others to 'stay with us or die' is simply stupid. China followed that path when it began to turn inwards in the 1400s: invading and oppressing, they forced other nations into the emerging Western economic net. Eventually the warring kingdoms within China brought about a slide towards complete annihilation. If we are to avoid that fate, the way in which we think about trade has to change. We will have to educate our new generation in the subject of economic and industrial warfare. This will demand diligence and motivation from both governments and employers. A brave new world has developed virtually overnight, so suddenly that most of us are yet to understand that previous methods of trading and of industrial warfare are obsolete. Previous ways of thinking will have to change if we are not to lose everything. Changing the way we think starts with education and ends with results.

Education and training

Workforces in the West must be trained to tackle the challenge which the rise of the East will bring to our shores. Currently, we are woefully underprepared and not in control of our countries as we face the daunting climb of a 3000 year economically dominant civilization on not just on the British doorstep but on everyone's doorstep. How do we protect against a world that does not respect the rule of law in trading as we understand it?

Internal and external Law Enforcement

We cannot control what is outside of our borders in the UK, but we can be aware of it and be prepared for it. The legal system won't help us and will bog us down in a load of paperwork that gets us nowhere. This legal system of Britain is adapted to administering the UK, it cannot deal with the third world. They don't understand or respect the British legal system. We must deal with the difficulties of Britain with a very harsh stick and put our foot down now that Brexit has been achieved.

Externally, we must face down our competitors and our enemies with a strong understanding of what the world has become. We cannot afford to play catch up when the rules are not respected any more. Viewpoints from angles never before considered must be considered and current strategy which does not adhere to the reality of a future which lies in front of us must be discarded. At the same time, we must respect the talent that peoples of the world bring to our shores, this means retaining the good and throwing out the bad. To achieve this, we must have a legal system and laws which support our law enforcement services. An efficient practise of expulsion of bad, criminals and corrupt individuals must be practised. Anyone that brings corruption and criminality to our shores must be dispatched.

We have to attract the most talented individuals and bring value to our shores. This means creating an environment which is conducive to economic growth. If our streets are clean, our people are safe and content with security inside the state. Then, businesses will naturally develop, and captains of industry will start to arrive, and our country will rise. Our shores will once again be teaming with industrial giants looking to get a foothold in Eurasia.

We will have to prepare our workforces with training methodologies such as 7Tao that prepare our workforces to receive the challenges which the new economic landscape will present to us. If we don't prepare, and we are not ready when the competitor comes… then our fate is sealed. Failure will be set in stone for our people. The first, second, third and fourth generations of business covered in Chapter 2 must be studied, because it is within analysing the changes that we can find out what the future looks like.

Eurasia has formed overnight. An environment of business is being nurtured that we are not accustomed. If we are to succeed in this new world of Eurasian dominance, we must train, educate, and prepare to meet our challengers, because they are many and we are few.

A world map of military bases around the world.

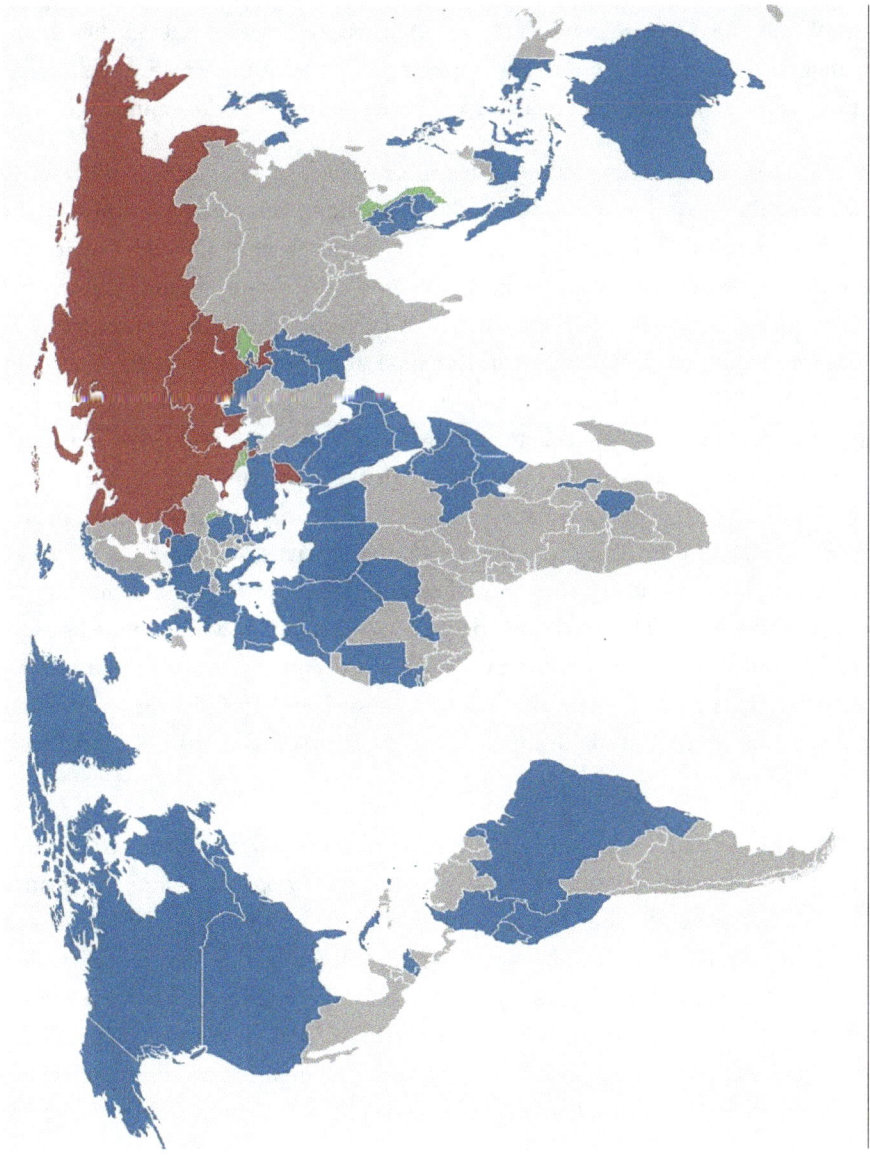

Blue = USA   Red = Russia   Green = USA and Russia overlap.
Source: Bigthink.com, Swiss Institute for Peace and Energy Research (SIPER)

The US military footprint is huge and quite frankly put, a useless costly enterprise which is effectively a weight around its waist and ball & chain to the US foot. While the Chinese have built an industrial empire; the USA has built, maintained and expanded a military empire to all parts of the world. It just keeps getting bigger with more military bases with each pentagon budget announcement.

The military industrial complex which Eisenhower warned us about is now eating the Taxpayer of the USA and this is resulting in massive pushback right into Washington DC. This is what resulted in the election of Donald Trump and the rejection of the status quo. Quite simply, the US Empire cannot be described as in-decline, completely the opposite, it is in even more expansive and spreading thinner and thinner around the world as time goes on! It is the USA that is in decline internally and it is the us Empire that is killing the USA externally. The bigger the Empire gets, the quicker the USA dies with each 18-year cycle. The more that the great recessions grow and overwhelm the US economy, the further the empire reaches to compensate it and balance the need for territorial expansion and resource consumption. The more this stretching happens, the more the US must invade, the more colonialist they must become, the more oppressive they are to the rest of the world. The need for expansion to survive is now testing the borders of China and Russia in military terms. They will eventually feel the need to take over India. This land is where the riches, resources and wealth overwhelm even the Americans and will feed the empire for a few more decades. Just like it did with the British empire.

The cost and survival of the US Empire is driving its expansion. The key word is COST. The Chinese expansion is based entirely upon economics, logistics and industrial prowess. The US is now in the same position the Soviet Union was in 1988, at the cusp of a fall which will be brought about by the 18-year cycle which arrives in 2026. The Soviet Union dissolved on 26 December 1991, after ten years of fighting the Afghan war. The US Military Empire will be in deep trouble in 2028, in the depths of the 18-year land cycle downturn. The financial organisations which have been fuelling the latest housing balloon will be at the brunt of the downturn, with inflation running rampant, Treasury Bonds being abandoned, confidence in currencies of the West being lost, Crypto currencies having more clout than that which the central banks give out for free. With a possibility of Weimar republic just around the corner, may lead to a dollar which loses 90% of this value in 2025 to 2028. The Pound and the Euro will also be affected as they are grouped into the basket of deplorable currencies. The knee jerk reaction to raise interest rates will come out of the blue as governments race to beat their competitor in interest rate rises. And ban all crypto currencies. The people of the US and Europe will revolt and gain confidence as they rebel and form into powerful militias rising up against the states.

The US will abandon the military bases, just as it did in Afghanistan, the planes and tanks will be turned back into ploughshares, pots and pans. The United States of America will not have time to maintain the empire it has built around the world. It will be too busy fighting the insurgency at home as its own people rise up to challenge the government in the increasingly difficult situation, with a polarising population dividing up in the ideological divide of Republican and Democrat. This time however, they will not be uniformed soldiers fighting for the establishment of the United States of America. The sheer number of forces competing for a piece of land will be enormous ranging from South Americans, Republicans, Democrats, African Americans, Native Americans, Canadians, Chinese, Japanese and the British will want a say in the coming difficulties which divide up the USA as well. The Civil war in the USA is forming right in front of our eyes.

This is exactly how the Americans beat the Soviets in 1991. The economic system defeated the USSR, they just simply outperformed them in production and manufacturing. The Americans knew how to fight an industrial war back then in 1991. They had mighty corporations such as General Motors, Ford and Chrysler dominating the planet in their respective fields. However, instead of expanding the industrial footprint and partnering with the planet, they instead had the first gulf war. This one war led to an ever-increasing amount of expeditions for the military industrial complex. One Islamic country after another was engaged and invaded repeatedly. If it was not directly invaded, they invaded by proxy using economic hit men and the threat of war against the Muslim states. This led to a massive guerrilla war by people all over the world who began rebellions and fought back against the invading US troops and proxies. The people fought back any way they could, guerrilla, military, proxy, financial, industrial, boycotts, media, secretly and openly in plain sight.

The US Empire was fighting everyone everywhere. But the biggest threat was yet to come, and it came from within. The 18-year cycle hit the US so hard in 2008, that the global banking system almost collapsed. This time, in 2026, the US empire will be tested again, and its faulty economic system will be hit again by the very same cycle as 2008, the United States has this enshrined into its economic constitution by the founding fathers themselves.

The cancer was already inside the USA, as it is in most of the West. The 18-year cycle is what killed the Soviet Union, it nearly killed the USA in 2008. The 18-year real estate cycle will annihilate the USA in 2026 with its effects being felt in all parts of the world.

The last time in 2008, the global financial crisis penetrated the heart and the brain of the world economy. This crisis resulted in the collapse of Lehman Brothers, downfall of America's automotive sector, and complete shattering of American employment with people losing everything they had to the crisis. The Troubled Asset Relief Program (TARP) covered every large corporation in America that was in trouble by purchasing company assets and stock. Basically, it was a massive 'quantitative easing' based cover up. A big network of financial band aids and patches which tried to boost investor confidence that everything was normal and covered by the government. This time however, the blue areas of the map on page 283 will be abandoned completely outside of the United States as the transactions dry up and the economic world looks completely different to the one, we are used to today. It may be that Donald Trump is back in power in 2026 as the American voter tries to vote the inflationary pressures away by wishing for a bygone era when the economy did really well during Trump time. They will be hoping that he delivers the growth parts of the 18-year cycle. Donald Trump, if elected again, will not deliver anything. He will be facing the brunt of the 18-year cycle collapse and the blame will be put on him. Or any other president who is in charge when the cycle comes to an end, will face the same calamity.

This time in 2026 however, the crisis will be global and will hit all of the world's economies at the same time. As China covers up the Evergrande crisis, more property crises will be brewing under the massive swathes of buildings being scattered in the Megacities of China. For now, in 2022, Evergrande is the country's biggest bankruptcy case. But with 2026 depression-based depletion coming, Evergrande will seem like a small leaf in the midst of a financial tornado. A minor consideration compared to the gigantic crisis which will spread across the world like an eclipse of the Sun by the Moon. This one will hit all the economies of the world at the same time pummelling every source of value in all parts of the world.

The primary target for the 2026 depletion will be the bonds and currencies of the world. The only way to save these will be the race to raise interest rates by the central banks of the world.

The 2026 crisis will spread everywhere around the world, infect everything of value, collapse any property-based transaction and take away incomes from the richest to the poorest on earth. To get ready for this moment when the whole world looks completely different, we must begin now in preparation for that time.

China is in good shape to take over.

By 2025, the Chinese Infrastructure projects will be in use and still being further developed around the Eurasian continent. This will prepare it for the collapse of 2026 very well, although the house prices of the world will be dropping like stones in deep water, even in China. The actual infrastructure will be in good use to move Chinese goods around the world. The Chinese must rush to build these so as to pick up the baton of Western leadership when it passed in total to the East. China will be taking a leadership position and reaching into the heart of the 74 countries of the belt and road initiative. Western Europe will be coming in to negotiate with the Chinese and see how they can serve the ancient silk road by becoming a part of it. The hundreds of big deals being done with countries of the RCEP will interweave with the Asian Infrastructure Investment Bank, The Regional Comprehensive Economic Partnership, the Free Trade Agreements, the China Pakistan Economic Corridor, the China Iran deal and the many other groupings which are being developed with China throughout the world will help the middle kingdom survive the oncoming depletion which heads our way.

China is already the greatest exporter to America and her exports grew in 2021 while the pandemic was slowly coming to an end.

According to Shen Weiduo and Chu Daye of Global times.

Foot note: Global Times Article: Published: Jan 14, 2022 10:02 AM Updated: Jan 14, 2022 09:28 PM : US' trade with China surges 28.7% in 2021, but widening deficit proves tariffs 'a failure'

China has grown in every part of their economy in all exports, in all factors, in all regions and in all parts of the nations they deal with. Their industrial warfare strategy has managed to penetrate all parts of the global economy. Shen Weiduo and Chu Daye write:

'Trade between China and the US soared by 28.7 percent and amounted to $755.6 billion in 2021'

'According to Chinese Customs data released on Friday (Jan 14th 2022), China's exports to the US increased by 27.5 percent in 2021, while imports grew by 32.7 percent, reaching $179.53 billion.'

'China's yuan-denominated trade with the ASEAN, its largest trade partner, increased 19.7 percent in 2021.'

'Chinese trade with the EU and the US, its second and third largest trade partners, rose by 19.1 percent and 20.2 percent, respectively in 2021.'

'Its trade with economies involved in the Belt and Road Initiative (BRI) grew by 23.6 percent, 2.2 percentage points higher than the overall growth rate, Customs statistics showed in 2021.'

'In 2021, China's trade in Yuan terms to the 14-member countries of the Regional Comprehensive Economic Partnership (RCEP) was also up 18.1 percent year-on-year, accounting for 30.9 percent of the country's total foreign trade.'

In every Free Trade Agreement that China has signed in all countries of the world, it has resulted in growth of epic proportion for both parties of each signatory. The results have been phenomenal in all areas involved. China is now taking part in every segment of the global economy and its growth is increasing even further as each development stage pulls in even more manufacturing industry, further demands for its services and even further use of personnel in both Chinese and counter signatory circles. These relationships will grow even further into the future as the demands increase to envelope agricultural, manufacturing and services frontlines.

On the counterpart empire, the US is still trying to bring back Transpacific Pact and other trade deals with other groups, but these are weak and built on the military industrial complex-based industries. Even when the Russia Ukraine crisis happened in 2022. The US Defence secretary was balking the sale of M1 Abrams Tanks and F35 Jet fighters trying to do deals with Ukraine. As the US Targets the leadership of Ukraine, the Chinese target the corner shop and make sure that the stocks are shelved with Chinese made goods for distribution into the streets of Ukraine. If the restocking process involves Chinese made goods daily, the Chinese will be winning the industrial war. This is exactly what the Chinese are looking for; restocking Chinese goods daily and making sure that the supply chain can use CPEC, RCEP and Belt and Road Initiative to make sure that shelves of goods are never down or empty in Ukraine or anywhere else in the Eurasia. The Chinese will even sell to the US Bases in the military empire.

To make this happen, the Chinese regularly visit 7Tao and ensure that it reflects the realities of currency, economics, inflation, costs, logistics and affordability of the consumer. China's power will keep growing so long as they have a direct relationship with the consumer on the streets. China will keep growing as they can make a connection with the wallets of 8 billion people of the Earth. China will keep growing if their 7Tao is much stronger than their competitors to keep them away from taking shelf space in the corner shops and retail outlets. Chinese production will keep humming if they can provide access to the skilled manufacturers of the Middle Kingdom. They will be creating training stations, language centres, student exchanges, friendly ties programs and helping to build the nations all over the five continents they trade with. The friendships will increase, and China will be the centre of influence in cultural and information terms. They will not however, tell people how to believe in their God, punish them for their culture, and they will not interfere in their national affairs. China has just one simple aim, Chinese made goods in the worlds retail stores and friendly relations with their people. As Calvin Coolidge, 30th President of the USA, said of America "After all, the chief business of the American people is business. They are profoundly concerned with producing, buying, selling, investing and prospering in the world." This role is now seated by the mainland.

Middle East and Iran:

The Chinese are now increasing the global reach of their industrial empire in Iran. The recent Iranian ministerial visits have steadily shifted away from the West and straight into the arms of China. They have signed a trade agreement and expect to supply raw materials and oil to China in return for the manufacturing capability and reach of the Chinese supply chains. Even through the sanctions imposed by the United States, the Chinese feel they can defy the sanctions and have enough financial and industrial clout to ignore the effects of the penalties, as it has in the tariffs imposed by President Trump during the trade conflict in 2018.

The Draft agreement has an openly belligerent statement in an 18-page agreement obtained by the New York Times. The $400 Billion agreement would give rise to oil, telecommunications, manufacturing, logistics, ports, railways banking and hundreds of other trade avenues within Iran. Iran will then supply China heavily discounted oil for the next quarter century.

"Two ancient Asian cultures, two partners in the sectors of trade, economy, politics, culture and security with a similar outlook and many mutual bilateral and multilateral interests will consider one another strategic partners," the 18-page document says in its opening sentence.

This 18-page draft was an open arms engagement with the rest of the world. The Chinese are quite obviously saying, we will work with anyone, please just give us a call. We will sign a deal with you too, no matter who you are, no matter which part of the world you are from and no matter what your politics currently entails. We want to trade with you. If we can do business with Iran, we can do business with anybody! They are quite openly defying the existing position of the American empire without any military engagements, just like the United States did back in the late eighties against the Soviet Union. The Soviet economic model had no answer to the American democratic model of politics backed by a very powerful industrial empire built out of the ashes of World War Two. Back then, the United States didn't have any competition because the rest of the world was in ashes, so it inherited the rebuilding of the world after WW2 and the remains of the British Empire.

The Chinese were embracing communism to survive the next 50 years, effectively putting them out of business and the Soviet Union was not a competitor with its command-and-control economy. This time however, it is different. The Chinese have created a no holds barred economy which is does not play by the obsolete rules of the 20th century. While the West reinforces its military posture with an economic mechanism essentially belonging 350 years in the past, backed up by a military which is essentially built around an infrastructure and engagement model of World War 2 and the cold war, things have moved on and industrial warfare has now gained relevance, leaving military warfare as an artefact of history.

True, you cannot have an industrial empire without a military defence system which protects your industrial base and your manufacturing industry. So, the Chinese built nuclear weapons first, settled down to communism for 30 years, and then stabilised the country, gently industrialising while staying out of sight and out of mind. They denied leadership position and refused to build an empire. Intelligent.

As indicated in the military base map of this chapter 11. China has literally no bases in the world except for Djibouti, right next to the Americans and the Russians in the same plains. However, their industrial empire touches every soul on the planet.

The Chinese have enormous firepower though throughout the South China Sea, Hypersonic Nuclear Missiles and ever better land, sea and air weapons systems being developed with processing and computing speeds on par with the United States of America. The faster and better software and hardware advances in computer systems, the faster the development of weapons systems to protect their economic empire. This will be the defensive side of the Chinese strategy, militarily present the opponent with so much danger… that they limit the manoeuvres and threats to minimal and incapable levels.

On the attack side, they have engaged industrial warfare with every industry and are beating every competitor with ferocious success on every level. Factories in the world ask what is the Chinese secret? The answer to that lies in their understanding of the Transaction. They have understood 7Tao and they use it against every competitor factory with devastating results. The result is measured on the retail shelf – whoever buys the Chinese product wins the fight. This transactional understanding is what will keep China on top of the world economy for centuries to come, if not millennia.

China – Defend Militarily, Attack Industrially – a winning formula… the only Achilles heel in this equation? The 2026 depletion-based depression driven by the 18-year land cycle. How badly will the 18-year property land cycle affect the Chinese industrial giant?

United States of America – Defend Militarily, Attack Militarily, sell military weapons across the world… the only Achilles heel in this equation? The 2026 depletion-based depression driven by the 18-year land cycle. How badly will the 18-year property and land cycle affect the incumbent empire, the United States of America?

Both will be affected in the negative, we will have to wait and see what the devastating effect of the land and property collapse will bring. The one who hits the ground last will be the winner. Both of them will fall in economic terms and one will hit the ground faster and harder than the other one depending on what actions they take to lessen the speed of the fall into the ground. This will be at least 100 times bigger than the 2008 recession and 100 times faster. My instincts tell me the one who has the most dependable currency will be the one who survives the fall. The other one might become the next Weimar republic. Game over.

CHAPTER 12:

Concluding Industrial Warfare

Conclusion 1: President Trump fights back in Industrial Warfare

As soon as Donald Trump won the presidency, he engaged in Industrial Warfare. The aluminium industry, the steel industry, the car industry, and the aircraft industry were all receiving protective tariffs. Donald Trump is engaging all countries at all levels after decades of the United States being abused through obsolete trade deals. It was always going to be the case. The loss of industry after industry has left entire communities desolated by factories leaving the United States to go elsewhere to produce their products and send them right back into the United States to earn currency. Shareholders earned huge dividends and customers were delighted at the lower prices of goods and faster delivery of products through "pile them high and sell them cheap" strategies that benefited the companies that sold these products.

(Picture by Michael Vadon: Wikipedia public commons use)

Most countries in the world took advantage of the liberal economic policies of the United States, which encouraged outsourcing to a degree never seen or done before in the history of the U.S. economy. Trump has single-handedly taken the globalists head-on and outsmarted them all in ways that we cannot even fathom.

Not only did he do this throughout the election process by citing the concept of industrial warfare, he used the concept of industrial warfare to win the hearts and minds of the American people.

It is fair to say that he has been talking about this problem since 1987 when he first saw the siphoning of American manufacturing industry to Mexico, India, Bangladesh, Vietnam, Japan, and every other rising industrial nation on Earth. People who went to work in the morning at 9 a.m. and came back at 5 p.m. building great American brands suddenly found themselves flipping burgers and doing security work. It was an employment sadness that afflicted many families in the United States – the sheer lack of opportunity for upwards growth was boxing many American workers into a corner.

This was in the heart of many American workers voting motivation. The loss of the factory in a town or city resulted in the depletion of industry and buying power, which in turn increased poverty levels throughout the economic region. In the supply chain orders dried up and entire communities were left desolated from the industrial depletion of the plant. This not only affected every family in the town, it gave rise to poor motivation, unaffordable basic goods and services and a rising Opioid crisis that replaced the industrious nature of the American people.

The shock of the 2016 election was not just predictable, it was expected. The entire rust belt states, centering around Michigan, made their voice absolutely clear. We want our jobs back, we want our factories back. We want people to represent us who will represent our hearts and minds.

Industrial Warfare

Peter Navarro, co-author of "Death by China," has been talking about industrial warfare for nearly two decades and realized early on that there was a possibility that Trump was going to win. He quickly rose to prominence within the Trump circles as a man who could be counted on to help Trump to fight back on all forms of industrial warfare in its many forms, styles and systems all over the world and plan to win back America's manufacturing industry.

This strategy would begin in the form of tariffs against products that were shifted during bad trade deals signed in previous administrations, these trade deals had become obsolete in the new Eurasian World Order. Tariffs are a good place to start when fighting industrial wars, primarily because you want to give yourself room to breathe as you begin to map out a strategy of how to protect your product against competitors, who want to push you out of the transaction process and finally out of the marketplace itself.

This same process is happening all over the world as nations begin to adopt Trump-think and start to protect their nation-state against competitors who want to steal the marketplace. This is especially prevalent in the British Brexit process as industries are being courted to stay or come to Britain through a liberal engagement policy. This is very beneficial for the working population as Britain itself prepares to globalize and create an industrial infrastructure that returns to what it had during the 1960s before the EU project came to life in 1972. As the different British Prime Minister's negotiated to make the Brexit process as smooth as possible, they have just one thing on their mind: Where are we going to get manufacturing plants from?

This is the primary goal that the British are considering as they look into a future where artificial intelligence and ferocious competition are corrosively attacking workers in Britain with suppression of wages, inflation of the currency, and a waning of incomes. The Prime Minister is correct in thinking that the European Union should be allowed to have free trade agreements with Britain, but Britain should also have free trade agreements with the entire world as well. That's all 200 countries, equal opportunity to set up our industries to serve all of those 200 countries without any form of restrictions whatsoever.

Every country is thinking of the same thing: We want to be first. Just as Trump says, "America first," Britain says "Britain first." We British are doing our absolute utmost to ensure that there will be a place for our people when the economic atomization process runs its course. The financial crisis of 2008, which is still continuing under the radar, has forced entire economic blocks to lose faith in the very capitalist process that drives them.

Attack and Defence

Much of Trump's campaign discussion on the economy was pointing to unfair trade practices and he was specifically pointing at China. However, it's not just China that does this. Every country, company, organisation, individual and person with greed will do these types of practises – however, China was without doubt the most capable and ferocious. They were good at winning transactions, and that is the essence of Industrial Warfare. Winning transactions through attack and defence manoeuvres are what makes industrial warfare so powerful. But you have to know when, how, why, where, and who to attack and what to defend. This can be the "be all and the end all" of battle.

Every plant in the world is considering the transactional process as they try to figure out their place in the world economy. For them to survive, it is very important that they consider the power of industrial warfare that Trump has used so effectively to win the hearts and minds of the American people.

Yes … Trump is doing it. Anybody can see that Trump is practicing industrial warfare. He is actively engaging plants and fighting from the front lines. He is leading the charge to take American industry back. The discipline has become so important, and the talk has become viral across the world.

Manufacturing plants in every area of the world are studying the problems, the talk, and the combat taking place and watching very closely as country after country declares battle, calling it trade war. As governments around the world step up to tariff the doors to global trade, the plants that they serve are asking some very serious and difficult questions.

Trump fought for the American people. Theresa May fought for the British people while she was Prime Minister. Prime Minister Shinzo Abe fought for the Japanese people. Prime Minister Modi fought for the Indian people. Imran Khan fought for the Pakistani people. Xi Jingping fought for the Chinese people. Every Prime minister and President have to fight for their people. The era of industrial warfare has arrived, and populism is fuelling its relevance on the global marketplace.

Conclusion 2: Unfair trade practices and their origin.

Unfair trade practices are in everything we do. They have been around since the beginning of the hand clubs being made by cavemen, which then morphed into spears and then arrows. Unfair trade practices are driven by hope and fear, jealousy, and greed. These are basic emotions which drive the human race which cannot be removed from mankind because they are placed inside of us all. We have a natural tendency to want something and will do anything to get it, mostly through legal means and hard work by hook, in some cases through illegal means by crook.

Everyone in the world calls American trade practices unfair. Everyone in the world calls Chinese practices unfair. It's a question of standing and angle of sight. If China wins, America will shout unfair. If America wins, China will shout unfair. Therefore, there are two ecosystems being forged here over the coming two decades. There will be the American sphere of influence and the Chinese sphere of influence. Both ecosystems will be against each other, and both will have advantages and disadvantages attached to them. America and China both have their work in front of them because if a smaller nation such as India is not happy with one, they can always go to the other. It is like two shops right next door to each other selling the same goods. Both will have to practice their prices, delivery, quality, aftermarket support, treat their customers nice, talk to their shareholders nicely and treat their employees with reverence if they are going to succeed. The rest is all industrial warfare.

Everybody on earth copies something from one another. We have all done it, we have all plagiarized in small amounts, taken ideas from one stage, and transferred it over to another area of application. This is how locomotive trains turned from steam to diesel, from diesel to electric. This is how product development is born, applying one technology in a particular field, and then applying it to a different field. We are now trying to create an electrification revolution to rid the world of fossil fuel consumption, fight climate change and change the way in which we move. China only did what Japan did during the 1970's onwards. Every country that engages in an industrial revolution will embrace this type of behavior. It has happened repeatedly in the past and will happen again in the future. Every industrial revolution contained nations who wanted to emulate what the leader was doing. The British have been watching emulators like the United States of America copy them ever since they started the first industrial revolution back in the late 1700's. The USA was stealing workers, resources, entrepreneurs and land back in the 1700's. It did what it could to survive as a nation, including passing the Chinese Exclusion Act of 1882 banning Chinese women from emigrating to the United States of America. Currently, China was undergoing its century of humiliation with two boxer rebellions marking its historical landscape and the Opium Wars darkening the history of one of the world's great civilizations.

The real reason why the USA is worried about China is because they are afraid of losing transactions to the Chinese in terms of manufacturing industry. They are worried about losing control of the world's Island, Eurasia.

That's Europe and Asia combined together as an economic entity with power and reach across the entire world. Eurasia, the world's Island, is angling to control every transaction in the global economy.

To achieve this, China, Russia, Iran, Europe, and Asia must tear away from the old rules of trade and legal wrangling. This means operating on principles that do not follow the rules set up by the World Trade Organization. The sheer scale of growth cannot be hindered by disagreements and hand wringing based upon the Western control methods established at a time of heavy colonialism (see chapter 2).

This leaves little room for diplomacy. Trade wars lead to industrial wars which have historically led into full scale military conflict. The Chinese are already building artificial Islands in the South China Sea which cannot be sunk because they don't float. If these Islands cannot be sunk, then they can be used in replenishment duties to help with sinking American battle ships and aircraft carriers. The only way China has been invaded in the past centuries has been through the South China Sea.

The Chinese and the Russians have enormous military firepower. Any escalation or push into the Asian area, whether through North Korea, South China Sea, Middle Eastern battles, Eastern European pushes by NATO or African intervention, or sanction-based warfare will result in direct escalation of a kinetic conflict which will include possible use of weapons of mass destruction. The Chinese and the Russians have mastered RYAN: Range, Yield, Accuracy and Number which allows them capabilities to strike anywhere on the earth with limitless strikes, arrays of warheads tipped with deadly destructive nuclear capabilities combined with landing on pinpoint accuracy. These weapons are now so capable and so deadly, that even their limited use can have clean up repercussions across the planet lasting more than a millennium. **Ray Dalio's** graph on the next page paints a realistic picture of the meteoric rise of China as it becomes relevant to the world economy. It is not difficult to see where the world is heading as China rushes to the top of every country's decision making process.

Source: https://www.gurufocus.com/news/1145110/ray-dalio-says-chinas-economy-will-soon-surpass-the-us

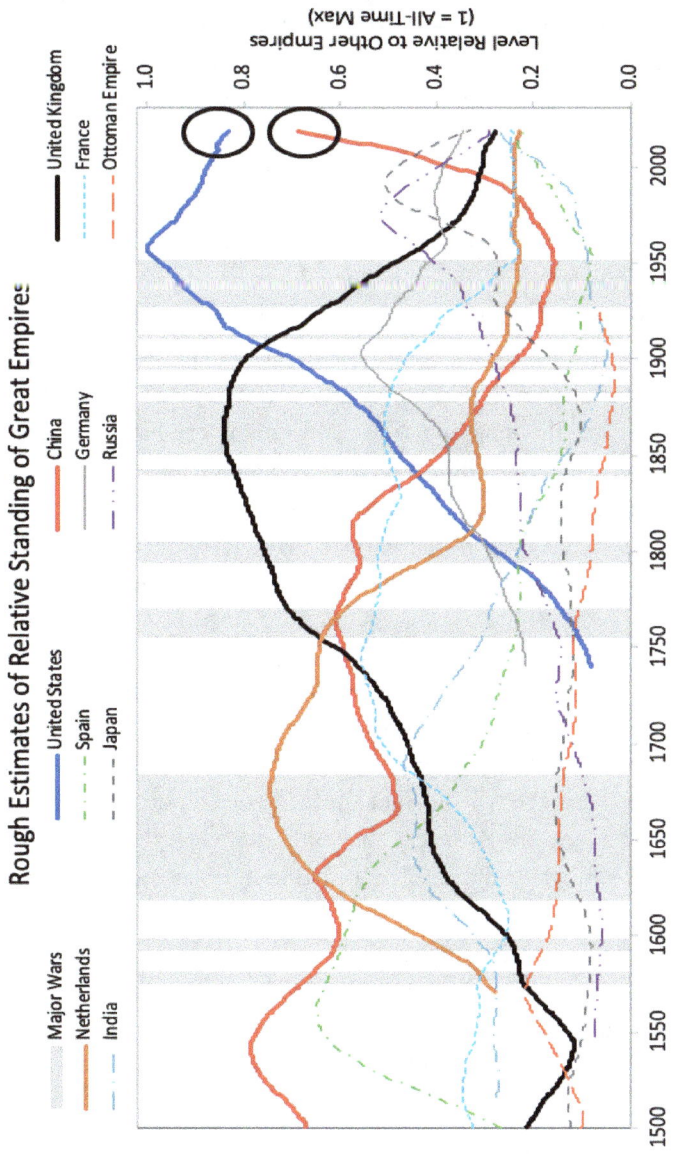

Conclusion 3: Trade war or Tirade war?

China exports $510 billion a year into the USA. Most of these products are consumables going directly into main street. America exports $160 billion to China every year. The difference is $350 Billion surplus going into China's pocket. When China does this with America for 40 years, she ends up with a lot of money. When China does 7Tao trade combat with every country in the world, China ends up with too much money. China now has a problem on what to spend all this money on.

China chooses infrastructure through initiatives such as the 'Belt and Road', CPEC, Gwadar, Islamic Countries Initiative, RCEP, Free Trade Agreements and many others she is planning. They are developing the markets of Africa, South America, Middle East, Southeast Asia, Central Asia, and Europe. These are just the main arteries of geography. They are also reaching into and developing every 'third world' country. Every transaction that takes place, contains the 7Tao. Therefore, the shipping lanes and containers have become so busy leaving Chinese ports. These ships are now becoming expensive to maintain and run. China is building even more ships, even more ports, and even more containers to get the shipping lanes even busier with so many different initiatives across the world. Nearly every container has 'China shipping' painted on the side.

Chinese goods sell everywhere and compete with everyone. The Chinese would much prefer to work with Japan, South Korea and Malaysia than compete against them militarily. But some are becoming wary of long-term intentions of such a giant economy which has only recently reared its head again after 200 years of sleep. Understanding the rise of China means understanding all of the factors at play in the rise of a new Superpower. They only rise when the other one recedes, just like the USA did when the USSR receded in 1991 at the end of the 18 year cycle. China began its accelerated rise in 2008 financial crisis with the Birds Nest stadium hosting the Olympics showing the Americans who will be ruling the world after the end of the last 18-year cycle. The 2026 end of 18-year cycle will place China on top of the world map. The main aim of China is to build an economic ecosystem which locates the Middle Kingdom as the center of Asian gravity throughout the world.

Once momentum has been gained in this drive throughout the Eurasian heartlands, they can easily absorb the talents of the Eurasian continent in all of the industries that will power the transactional relationships between the regions of the

Middle East, Central Asia, Southeast Asia, Australasia, Africa, South America, Europe, Russia and most importantly, China.

Picture: Public Wikipedia domain.

This is not just an enormous development for trading interlink; entire continents are actively being interwoven in a trading relationship within their borders. Basically, it's the whole world absorbed into the central hub of China.

It is understandable that the US tirade against China in the trade war has such massive news headlines. The challenge of China is real, and the economic leapfrogging process is at speeds never witnessed. There is no doubt that the US-China trade war will affect every transaction in the world as it morphs into a full industrial war. All governments are involved. The leaderships of every national legislative committee will consider the US-China trade conflict. Even the smallest governments on Earth must consider the US China Trade War. This industrial competition between the USA and China will last for the next 100 years, unless the

USA is defeated and sinks into irrelevance in the next few decades through another economic crisis coming its way in 2026.

The key in this process is finding out the bearings of the conflict and where countries stand with regards to their decision making. Every country, company, corporation, investor, buyer, seller, and owner will take this into account when considering what moves to make when choosing between these two giant industrialized nations as they tussle, struggle and wrestle for the control of the world economy. This US-China trade war will be the dominant industrial conflict of the 21st century. The Huawei battle is just an example of the many different battles to come as the trade war transforms into a full-on industrial war. Every industry in all parts of the world will be involved as the ripples and waves of industrial warfare come to their shores.

While Joe Biden gathers 'the Quad' of India, Japan, Australia, and the USA, they will struggle to define how they will engage the massive challenge of a rising China. The meeting will be no more than a meeting because they don't understand the power of 7Tao which lies in the heart of every buyer and seller on Earth whom China appeals to. The meetings will continue, and the quad will shout, wring hands, throw out opinions, air their frustrations, bellow blame, try to come out with useless ideas of the how they will try to break the partnerships which China has established in their quest for world trade. In the end, the answer will always end up as… "But they have an unknown number of Nuclear Weapons, and they are prepared to use them in combination with Hypersonic delivery systems". The Quad will stand dazed and confused. The shortages of ideas present in their bland faces as they see the virus of obsolescence eat their shops, factories and high streets. Anyone can see the economic depletion passing through the streets of London and other capital cities of the world as buying power transfers to the internet transaction process and the factories of China. Is it too hard to see that the future of warfare will be industry based or will you still deny it? Go ahead, bellow, yell and shout your opinion. It won't change a thing. The future of warfare is industrial, and everyone knows that transparent fact.

South Korea, India and Japan will be asking one question. Why should we fight our nuclear armed neighbor China when we can join in with RCEP, Belt and Road Initiative, Islamic Countries Initiative, CPEC, Free Trade Agreements and other initiatives to trade with the world?

Conclusion 4: Diffusion of the world economy.

During the 19th and 20th centuries, decisions were easy. You bought a plane, train, car, scooter, bicycle, and hair dryer from the Western nations of Europe and America. The only issues to argue about were prices. They were very high because the stranglehold over the economies of the third world were so tight that the Western nations could easily extract whatever mineral resources that they needed into their sphere of influence in exchange for manufactured goods. The Universities of the West housed all the leaders of Eastern countries thereby influencing the decision-making processes of those particular countries at presidential level. Trade deals made easy, don't even allow the competitor to come into a market area which the West controlled. The Western economy was so innovative that competitors simply could not catch up.

The key to breaking away from any process is not to believe in it. The relevant words are obsolete, irrelevant, waste, unnecessary, outdated, archaic, superseded, and immaterial. These words are dynamic change processes which will render your company, country, institution, or government incapable of handling the new pressures which change will throw at you. When change happens, people go into fight or flight mode. This can be seen in the Brexit process or the third-party process of politics which is sweeping the entire world. Brexit is not just a flag or indicator of populism; it is the change which the British have indicated will be sweeping the Earth as people reject what they have been told in the press. There are many forces which are contributing to this breakaway process, but the main one is industrial. People want their stability back, they want their jobs back, they want their factories back and this process is causing riots in the streets of the world from 'yellow vests' protests in France to economic migration from Africa. If there is one process which Donald Trump administration has started very successfully, it is the 'first' principle. Like America puts America first, every country is following saying, 'we – us - first' including the European Union.

The diffusion process is leading to mass atomization of culture, families, economies, governments, and institutions on an international basis. With change and atomization reaching these extraordinary levels, it is practically impossible to forecast exact trends on what will happen in the future. 7Tao transactional analysis provides a chance to learn about where you are in the process of change, how to handle unforeseen circumstances and to accept that adaptation is the key to discovering the effects of dynamic change. The new world is not a vision of glory or utopia provided by some obsolete government of the past shouting equity. The new world is what you define as your world and how you want to conduct your transactions in an environment of brutal competition with no-holds barred contests into winning the marketplace.

Technology is just a factor for enabling that process. To be a part of the East, we must think like the East. It is an absolute fact that this is something which got Donald Trump elected. The Eurasians do not think like we do. And they have no intention of changing. If we want to do business in that world, we must think like they do. This is what 7Tao attempts to achieve, how do we think like they do and what is their fighting style when considering this fact? There are no Queensberry rules here. This is all out industrial warfare which requires leaders of all types to decide on whether to stay thinking like we do here in the West or think like they do in the East. If you want to think like they do in the East, then its industrial warfare. If you still want to think like the West, powerful methodologies like Six Sigma will guide you just as well as they used to do in the past, but the past is no more. The challenges of the future are different. They will require new visions of thinking and application of new knowledge to an emerging future.

Conclusion 5: What lies ahead ... the recessions to come in 2019 to 2021 and from 2026 to 2035.

The last time the 'mid cycle recession' came was in 2000 to 2002 (explained in chapter 1). It resulted in the death or near death of companies such as Enron, Worldcom, Tyco and others which littered the headlines. There was a simulated crisis called Y2K which caused panic to the internet-based companies resulting in the dot.com crash which rendered the collapse of companies like Amazon, Ebay, Bookings and Myspace. Further to this 9/11 happened which led to the greatest invasion of the third world in history, specifically oil rich countries of the Middle East – an oil and arms bonanza resulted as a result of this 20 year military endeavor in protracted guerrilla warfare throughout the Middle East. I like to call this 'the earnings recession'.

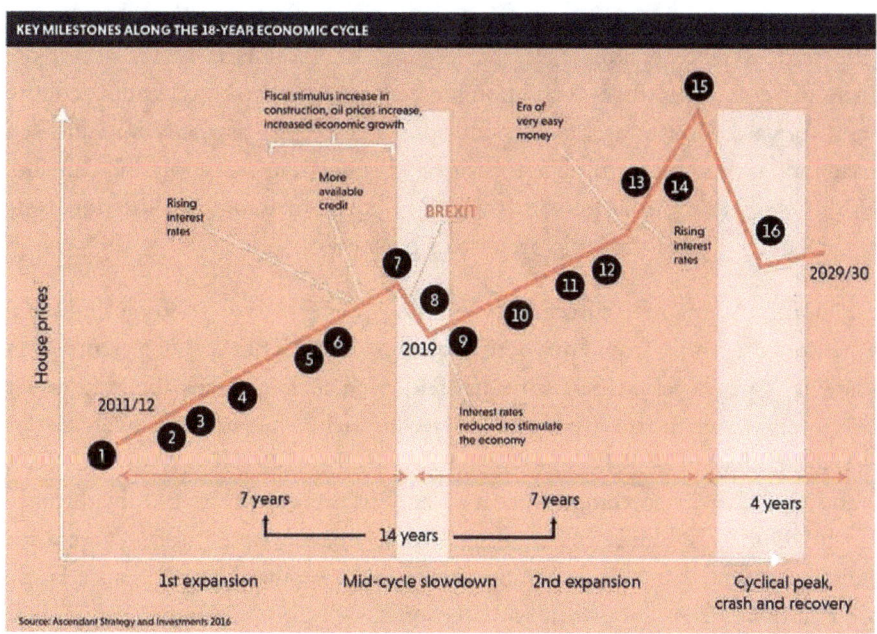

Source: Ascendant Strategy and Investments 2016.

The other recession, the bigger one, is called 'the savings recession', but the savings recession is about to rear its ugly head in 2026, exactly 18 years after the 2008 crisis. It will be 100 times worse than the 2008 recession, because you can't print your way out of this one. The bond cycle has turned, and interest rates are in a rising cycle for the next 30 years. It is the biggest recession that will ever occur for the West, and it will spread across the world like wildfire. The mid cycle 'earnings' recession always occurs 7 years (2019 – 2021) before the savings recession which will occur in 2026. The race to rise interest rates is now on as the three main torch bearers of the world economy – The US, the EU and China central banks all compete to raise interest rates to curb inflation before it ravages their economy. They must choose – House Prices or the Money in your pocket. Roof over your head or food in your belly. 2026 will indeed be catastrophic.

So what happens in the 2019 - 2021 recession?

The 2019 earnings recession. (And I have written about this in Epoch Times 26th March 2016 – "Economists explain why our economy crashes every 18 years") All of the engines of earning, like the corporations which are currently driving the stock market to ever higher performance are subjected to the pressures of the mid cycle recession. This means Amazon, Walmart, Ebay, Facebook, Google and countless others built upon the new age internet-based trading culture driving forward a business model built upon completing as many buy and sell transactions as possible to fulfill that basic need of economics, supply and demand. You want something, you see something, you buy something, and the other guy sells something. That's the basic premise of business.

First point: With the current competition being so astronomically high, competitors can come from anywhere and in any form. They are all around us, in basements, garages, libraries, bedrooms and even in businesses thinking about undercutting, independence, growth and getting rich. They are effectively out to steal transactions and they are in existence all over the world. They want more, not less and they will do anything to get it – the global competitors call this process 'Growth'. During the mid-cycle recession, these smaller competitors, also known as innovators who watch their competition grow big, lethargic, and unsustainable will come out of the woodwork and feed on the flesh of the huge corporation. These competitors are already within the corporation itself and all around it. The 2019 / 2021 recession is just a trigger point for them to come out. So much trade will be conducted online that the high street will lose tens of thousands of stores in the UK. Leading to massive unemployment and a supply chain crisis because everything is now trucked to its destination.

Second point: The 2008 great recession has not actually gone away; it is still there under the façade of current economic performance driven by house price and land price growth. The debt being accumulated is even larger now than it was in 2008, the foundations of the economy are even weaker than they were in 2008. During 2019, it just doesn't appear to be the case because of the massive rise in the stock market and street-based economy due to confusingly low interest rates, tax cuts which were invested back into the stock market leading to an inflated stock market bubble, this has also raised house prices to unaffordable levels. If the bubble bursts in the stock market, the housing market will then be stocked even further leading to an extortionate property market financed by loose lending from the banks. This is exactly what happened in 2003 to 2008.

Therefore, the Fed is so busy raising rates because they will need ammunition later on to lower rates. If they don't have enough room to cut interest rates, they may end up having no bullets to fire. Best to prepare by raising rates so that you can at least take them back down later. If they can't lower interest rates to low enough levels, they will end up going into negative interest rates, and people will have to pay just to keep their bank accounts. If the 2019 / 2021 recession ends up retriggering the pressures already pent up in the western economy from the 2008 recession, we could see a combination of the two recession forces wreaking havoc upon the stock market, housing market, banking system, currencies, weakening bond markets, the financial instruments market and finally pension systems as well. The 2019 to 2021 recession will be the biggest downturn in many centuries knocking the UK and the world out with possibly vertical down drops in the stock markets. The fact that the Coronavirus pandemic added to these pressures makes the situation even more devastating. The can is about to be kicked down the road again as we approach the 2026 recession. In expectation of the 2026 depletion, it is possible that inflation may lead to hyperinflation. Either way, there are few options for the world economy other than a possible interest rate hike which eclipses the 1990 interest rate hikes. It is likely that a late cycle interest rate surge is on the cards as this book is printed leading to massive downturns in the property market. Governments have no way out, if they print too much, hyperinflation will kill their economies bringing about a global Weimar republic, and if they raise rates as violently as possible to curb hyperinflation, they will collapse the property market. This will be further accelerated by 2026 land price collapse leading to catastrophic property downturn leaving house prices 25% of their 2025 value.

Third point: During 2001, many corporations suffered as the confidence in the stock market was thrown into the trash pile by innovators such as Ken Lay of Enron and Bernie Ebbers of World Com. Values disappeared overnight and thousands were made redundant, lost their jobs, or were kicked out of work with nothing but the shirt on their back. True, they controlled the effects of the recession by kicking the can down the road and pushing the property market instead. They put a couple of people in jail and made it look like the situation was managed, by sweeping the mess under the carpet.

So an accumulation of events were used to blanket the mid cycle recession ranging from internal distractions such as Y2K. Criminal investigations such as Enron, Worldcom, Tyco, Arthur Anderson, Global Crossing, Xerox, Martha Stewart and Adelphia dominated the headlines but did not cause massive stock market rupture in 2001. Further to this, to cover it up, 9/11 attacks dominated the headlines resulting in the invasions of Afghanistan and Iraq. These were all used to cover up the mid cycle recession, the earnings recession which always occurs 7 years after a major financial crisis.

The 'powers that be' moved the investment interest from the stock market into the housing economy which was now beginning to become very bubble like from 2004 onwards. This time in 2021 is much worse because we live in an environment of heavy quantitative easing, or printing money and a recession classified as the worst in 300 years in the UK at least. The COVID 19 Pandemic has been the mother of all cover ups as the recession hit the streets of every country in the world. The worst recession in 300 years killed the supply chain over an 24 month period, covering up the recession to the point of perfection. As soon as the recession ended, so suddenly the pandemic began receding and people returned to the streets to a changed world of supply chain shortages, labour shortages and goods shortages. From 2022 onwards, the bull market in property prices begins leading to massive house price rises and destructive escalation of liar loans all over again. Inflation will run rampant and bond prices will collapse as currency and economies combine to become unattractive investments. This will lead to a massive rise over and above the required interest rates to bring inflation to heel. It is possible that interest rates go higher and higher as they struggle to keep prices under control and keep inflation under control. It is also possible that the world's central banks take part in a 'race to the top' as an interest rate war is declared. The country with the highest interest rates rises has the confidence of the bond buyers. If inflation begins to go above 7.5%, we could see central banks begin competing to raise interest rates across the world. He who has the highest interest rates sells their treasury bonds.

Then 2026 comes, the recession declares itself and suddenly, the whole thing comes to halt. This bubble will burst, just as other bubbles have burst in the past. If the recession of 2019 to 2021 led to the deepest fall in 300 years in Bank of England history… then what will the big one look like in 2026? In short, it will be catastrophic. This will be the final recession, a depression so deep that it brings the entire world economy to a close. The financial systems will come crashing down as no answer is found to a plummeting stock market, land market, currency market, bond market and job market. Everything will be worth nothing unless they keep pushing interest rates up. Anything less than 25% interest rate will not arrest hyperinflation as it picks up pace during 2021 onwards. The 2026 recession will be a combination of forces placing massive pressure on the property and land markets. All economic indicator indices will be thrown to the dogs as value is wiped out from under the investors feet. This time however, printing money will not be an option because of runaway inflation and very difficult circumstances. The property market will take the hit as house prices plummet.

The best part of this is that no one is going to believe it. They will simply scoff at it and just keep on going pumping borrowed money into massively inflated property prices. They will keep pushing the house prices up until the bottom drops off. Better than this, entire businesses will be using their profits to buy up property, forcing rents and land prices even higher thinking they are making a quick buck. Stock market will be placing bets on inflating house prices and then …. BOOM and bust.

The impact of the 2026 on social circles will be devastating. Repossessions and court orders. House evictions and fights in the streets. Pressure being placed on Police, Medical and Emergency services in general. Cutbacks in those very services just like in 2011. Tax hikes killing the economy. Tax rates being reduced. House prices plummeting leading to mass sales and get out of the door while you can strategies. Landlords trying to compete for sales as fast as they can. Increased pressure on families to stay together in three generations, Grandparents, Parents and Children. Governments fighting inflation because they simply cannot control food prices. Tax rates bearing down on peoples shoulders.

This doesn't lead us to any answers at all, the only thing this does is ask some very wide questions that this economic environment scenario is painting. These are painful questions that the leaders of the world need to ask in every country on the planet except those who are so backward, so barter based, that they don't understand what the fuss is about. When the ship sinks, it's the ones who are in the water who have learned how to swim. A daunting hill to climb is in front of us as we scale the 2019 to 2021 recession and consider all of the theories that have been used to cover it up. The problem is that there will no cover ups and no excuses in the next recession of 2026 because the pressures which surround this recession will not allow respite. Inflation will be high, bonds weak, interest rates constantly raised, taxes up, food prices rising, repossessions and foreclosures everywhere, and internal social problems will plague the nations of the world.

"What was that sound? ... That, my friend, was the sound of a bursting more like exploding bubble."

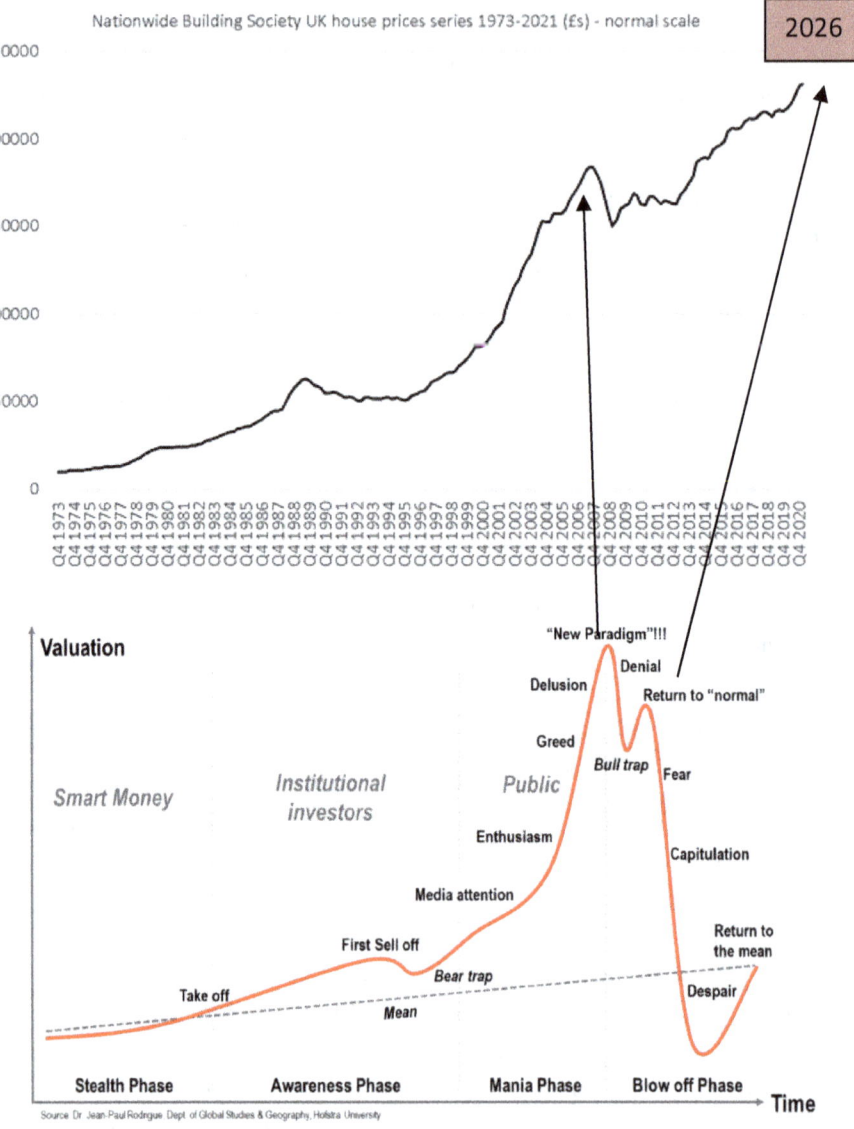

Source: Dr Jean Paul Rodrigue. Stages in a bubble. Department of geography. Hofstra University.
Source: Nationwide Building society. UK House Prices Series: 1973 - 2021

If all of this printed money is looking for a way to settle, what if it settles in the property market through loosened lending practices like Lehman Brothers bank and 5% mortgages? What if the housing bubble has grown to such massive proportions that it is just too hard to reach for the common man except through loans of millions of dollars? What if printing money and QE leads to hyperinflation? What if the stock market collapse cannot be contained and it gains a downward momentum which leads to downswings in all investments? What if the stock market goes down 50% or more? What if the central banks cannot save the banks second time around with Quantitative Easing? What if the coming financial crisis is immune to previous actions of QE, non-existent interest rates and government bailouts? I could go on, but I don't think there will be any benefit because the audience in all its forms can come up with a thousand more questions concerning how they see things from their position.

Late cycle interest rate rises look on the horizon. If central bankers do not respond quickly to the specter of runaway inflation, it will become more difficult to control later on. Any more than 7.5% inflation will require interest rates of 15% to bring it back under control. Any less will lead to massive uncontrollable inflation rises which will grow every month. These will weaken bonds as investors ask for more returns on their investment to confidently purchase bonds in a country. If bond prices lose confidence, the country in general will lose confidence. It is vital we raise interest rates to reflect this fact and control inflation early on in its growth cycle.

What I am contemplating is that this has happened before on a smaller scale back in 2008 and the recession hasn't shown any signs of losing strength. It will happen again in 2026 so we need to start changing our thinking to preserve our countries. Our countries are made up of people and we need to start listening to the people – if we don't listen to our people, populism will morph into civil wars and maybe spill over into the streets as people begin to invade the parliament houses of the world.

The most challenging recession arrives in 2026 and it may be one hundred times the size of the 2008 great recession because it will be striking much deeper into the heart of the global economy. It may strike right into weakening bonds, banking, currencies and into government's taxation systems. This will annihilate the future of the West and in many ways the East simply because the global economic DNA is designed to fall down at very specific times in 18-year cycle periods. To find the cure for these timed recession cycles we need a remedy which requires the world's economies taking some bitter and sour taxation medicine. Changing the taxation policy to balance all three taxation entities requires that we Tax Profits, Wages and Land as capital. Currently we only Tax the Profits and Wages, we may need to Tax the land as well through a Land Value Taxation system of some sorts proposed by Henry George.

Conclusion 6: Avoiding a WW3 kinetic confrontation with Russia, China and everyone else.

Modern missiles are becoming smart, and all warfare is moving towards missiles, drones or rocket based kinetic structures.

All over the world, missiles are becoming smarter and better quality. Guided by RYAN, (Range, Yield, Accuracy and Number) they are becoming more capable in lethality thus rendering the previous equipment and war models increasingly obsolete. It is worth us looking at these developments to see where we have come from, where we are now and where we are going.

Picture: Wikipedia Commons Use. A MIRV vehicle carrying 10 Thermonuclear warheads.

In the past, missiles were expensive, cumbersome, big, bulky, easily breakable, poor quality, with hit rates which were negligible at best. The first ones such as the SA2 were labeled 'lucky strikes'. They were so difficult to launch, required much maintenance, many crew to operate and were ineffective that it was difficult to use them at all. However, countries still bought them just to say – 'we have some SA2 ground to air systems which we can use to shoot your incoming airplanes down'.

The planes were just as bad. In most cases the fighter pilot didn't know of heat seeking missiles until they exploded in the general area. They had radar jamming and some inadequate form of warning that there was a missile coming in. Evasive maneuvers were taken so long as the pilot was incredibly intelligent and responsive. If the pilot knew that one was coming in for a kill, a few evasive aircraft maneuvers would be enough to get the missile off the airplanes tail. The chances of shooting a plane down were so small, most of the time that the missile was considered as just another disruption on the way to a mission.

In the present day, missiles have come a long way. The Russian R73 Missile can see targets 40 degrees off its centerline and has a 30-mile range. Hit rates are dramatically improving as target capability and warhead diversity allows for greater direct and partial impacts, leading to immediate elimination method or partial wounding methods disabling the aircraft to such a point whereby the remaining flight becomes a danger in itself.

American AMRAAMS are just as good if not better at seeking and eliminating their targets. The shoulder fired Stinger missile, since its introduction in the 1980's has its hit rate creeping up as the seeker heads grow increasingly more sophisticated.

These missiles have become smaller, more capable, and much easier to manufacture all across the world. Many countries can now produce a MANPAD (Man Portable Air Defense System) missile system. These MANPAD factories can be found in every country, and they are called 'aerial denial management systems'. They are easy to make, easy to carry, easy to fire and they are increasingly effective in targeting and acquisition process with the breakneck speed of digital electronics systems development. Best of all, they are becoming very cheap to produce.

The same can be applied to the larger missiles carried on the back of pickup trucks, on the back of mobile road launchers and in silo's everywhere around the world. The world of missiles is becoming a stark reality that we must understand because the very nature of our military structure depends on them.

In the future, missiles will only get better. Now that Artificial Intelligence is seeking a faster path to commercial relevance, it is likely that the products which governments require will be delivered even faster than ever before. Missile systems development will lead to even more effective missile systems being employed thus creating massive hurdles to military expedition. This will lead to obsolescence in the ways in which the military is organized and executed. The current military will become obsolete as change forces its way through the transactional structure of military systems. Air force jets will give way to drones. Army soldiers will give way to Robots. Navy vessels will become smaller, and more drone based in both surface and undersea vehicles. It's a complex world and technological developments coupled with vast arrays of innovative cycles are making it increasingly difficult to control, both internally within the countries of the world and externally in terms of foreign policy; the way in which military techniques combined with technological prowess are used to impose power over other nations. The world just does not respond to power projection the way it used to. Resistance has become a diverse set of strategies, tactics and operational techniques.

This leads us to the question of fighter jets. Are they still the romantic defenders of our countries they used to be, or have they also become obsolete? Increasingly, the use of drones, arrays of pilot sense complexity, a variety of options, smarter missiles with clearer vision and more visual warfare scenarios are making the jet fighter obsolete.

The advent of drones was the first change which rendered the pilot obsolete. This transformation is now heading down various other roads embedding itself into commercial airlines and artificial intelligence-based flight systems as commercial airlines begin considering remote based flight systems around the world. This development almost always begins in the military, just like the satellite phone and the Willy's Jeep from WW2. Nowadays, everyone has a mobile phone and a Jeep or SUV.

The changes that the military is bringing to remote based flight aircraft are justified with many different roads leading to multiple arrays of innovative technologies to adapt to the new and discard old. Museums will need more space as the number of old technologies reaching obsolescence open floodgates. Vintage is not just a word in current times, it is a reality which every tech company is grappling with in every sphere of operation in all parts of the world. As soon as a technology appears in the marketplace, it is immediately rendered obsolete in part as a competitor takes that technology, upgrades to achieve more for less and that technology is then copied further as the manufacturing crowd fight over the price of the new technology – the price is bought down, and mass produced and distributed. This is what is destroying orders for the next generation of jet fighters. It is their rapid obsolescence in a world where these types of air warfare platforms are becoming increasingly ineffective against modern missile systems and in most cases counterproductive to the aims and objectives of a nation seeking to stabilize itself in an environment of economic uncertainty.

My point here is simple. If the old mechanisms of economic dominance are not working, as the old infrastructure of empire glory ends, if the associated management and production methods have become increasingly obsolete, not just for jet fighters and the aerospace industry in general but for every industry everywhere... then what is required of the new environment of war?

This leads us to the ultimate Kinetic Weapon system - nuclear weapons. And this is not a place where humanity needs to tread, because it will be the final footprint for all living creatures on this planet. Nuclear weapons are useless, and everyone knows it. Why? Because of the clean up afterwards, It would take, 4 million years of half life to be exact, to clean the mess that they make on Earth. But they are the ultimate deterrent.

So, what happens when you launch a nuclear weapon at your enemy? Well, let's describe it and take you through a step-by-step description of the catastrophic effects a nuclear exchange can have.

The first stage is the photon blast which releases 70% to 80% of the bomb's energy. This usually results in burns of temperatures in Megakelvin which disintegrates anything which stands in the blasts way through the immense heat being produced by the flash, around 10 million degrees Celsius or more. The next stage is the supersonic blast front which knocks down everything in its path. The third phase is the overpressure phase which has the same effect as being a mile underwater. The fourth phase is the negative over pressure phase, has the effect of being at very high altitudes without being able to breathe in thin air. At this stage, the fires ignited by the electrical firestorm sets everything alight creating fires which burn with increasing ferocity across everything in their path. A 20-megaton bomb causes fatal third degree burns at 40 km range. In the megaton warhead range, the fireball rises so high that it enters the stratosphere range where there are no discernable weather patterns. This makes the fall out last months and years as the radiation is distributed across the continent, thus creating what is known as the nuclear winter which blocks out the sunlight for years or even decades to come.

Multiply this effect thousands of times over in an ongoing nuclear exchange and you have a nightmare scenario which ends the human race and every living creature which ever walked, crawled, or swam. I cannot believe that they are actually considering the use of these weapons in the corridors of power as they sit making decisions in the ways of cancelling the 1987 INF Treaty. This is Armageddon in the most realistic form, these weapons ensure the destruction of humanity. As we hurtle towards global nuclear war, we must come to know and design as many cut off mechanisms and back door peace channels as possible to avoid a rapidly forming conflict scenario which can escalate to levels which do not allow any return to normal for the next thousand years.

The British are a very stable and thoughtful people. They knew that when the British Empire officially came to an end in 1950, they handed the baton of leadership over to the Americans in such a secure manner with a well-oiled bureaucratic machine that it looked like the British Empire never existed in the first place. The Americans simply took over and expanded their economic operations across the planet. The rise of Russia and China are a different set of challenge parameters and the risk of fighting them grows increasingly destructive for the planet. They will inevitably result in a clash of some kind and all players know this as they gather positions and allies.

Conflict must be avoided at all costs as the time taken from the first bullet to fire from a soldier's gun against the USA, China, or Russia, to the time the first nuclear weapon arrives on an enemy city will be short. The de-escalation systems need to be thick, fast and extremely effective from the beginning of hostilities as the first bullet being fired from a soldier's gun to the possibility of a Sarmat-28 with 16 thermonuclear warheads landing upon a country with a delivery time of just 30 minutes from launch.

Hypersonic nuclear weapons and glide vehicles.

Russian hypersonic nuclear weapons travel at Mach 25. Nothing can stop them, only Vladimir Putin himself with a self-destruct button. America can have a missile defense shield and an anti-missile defense system... but they are pretty useless. All Russia or China have to do is fire three or more at once and control the way in which they're enter the Earth's atmosphere at Mach 25 or more.

Its game over if these types of delivery systems come into play in the coming years. These kinds of weapons ensure that there will not be nuclear war. Even thinking of fighting an enemy who has these hypersonic weapons leads to disaster. No wonder the Biden and the Trump administrations are saying that there will be extreme competition with China and not conflict.

Artists impression by David Neyland: Hypersonic Glide Vehicle.

Conclusion 7: US-China Trade War can be resolved but it needs to be understood through a transactional eyeglass.

Trumps Trade Wars vs Biden's Extreme Competition:

So how do you define extreme competition? It is basically, fighting with no rules to stop or restrict you. It is unfair competition. The very thing we are complaining about to the Chinese and getting them to stop.

It is likely that unfair competition will consider that two economic ecosystems are about to be formed with America and the Western centric economic, technological, and transactional domain, and on the other side the Chinese economic, technological and transactional domain.

The winners are the customers of both superpowers as they choose what is best for their 7Tao in the country that they reside. This will be a dynamic competition which pits the best companies from America against the best companies from China. It will result in battles for market share and market dominance with innovation battles dominating the landscape as each superpower struggles for relevance among the other countries and marketplaces of the world.

The trade war was ineffective because it stepped backward and built a tariff wall against China. This just made the American consumer angry because they couldn't purchase cheap goods. The best way to move forward is to repatriate the supply chains back into the country of origin and build an export-based business model which retains manufacturing industry and supply chains within the home country and targets other countries for exports through trade deals. This is the best model for challenging China. This is also China's selected model for challenging the USA and the European Union in the battle for the world's global marketplaces.

7Tao may become a component for any battle with China because it will drive the purchase of Chinese or American product. It may even begin to consider a new set of rules for the 21st century as the old 20th century rules fade into obsolescence. As the competition between the two superpower heats up, it is very likely that they will be constantly sitting down to discuss the next generation of rules of engagement as they try to avoid war and bring stability to their countries and the global marketplace. **Pictures: Dan Scavino / US dept of State.**

It is better to talk to the Chinese, engage them, meet and discuss the terms and conditions of the next phase of industrial competition. There are two directions forming here: The first is a lasting economic agreement which is not based on the previous set of WTO rules that are too old to handle the population, cultural, historical, structural changes which have already transformed the global economy. There are indexes which summon to measure as much as they can about the damage which tariffs are doing to the stock market but at the end of the day, the true measure comes down to just two measurements. How many factories and how many jobs are leaving the Chinese mainland to avoid the tariffs? Where are they going? It looks like the American factories will not be returning to the USA, they are finding other cheap manufacturing places to settle in such as Vietnam, Malaysia, and Cambodia.

That said, the supply chains which China has ingrained into their economy run so deep, the ports and infrastructure which she uses to run that supply chain so vast, that factories have no choice but to stay in China as a matter of convenience. The tariffs are disrupting a well-oiled Chinese industrial master plan which is traversing Eurasia.

Belt and Road will simply grow even further as it becomes more entrenched throughout Europe and Asia. Five billion Eurasian people need to have market access, economies need physical roads, and roads lead to economic development. The belt and road initiative is recreating the old silk route and building a newer one which crosses areas never before ventured in Eurasia.

The second choice is to fix the economic challenges which China is being accused of perpetrating by the USA. This requires an acute analysis of Industrial Warfare which involves analysis at continental, international, national, regional, and local levels – and specifically at plant level. The real problem comes from analyzing human psychology and industrial competition at factory level operations.

This is not going to be an easy task; corporations, factories, supply chains, workers and politicians need to find a better solution than heading into a full-on economic war which can lead to a catastrophic and escalatory kinetic exchange.

The aims must be simple: Every factory, every worker and every policy maker must look to solve this issue. This requires reading, learning, practice, and implementation of small incremental projects which can lead to sustainable viable solutions designed to work at the plant level. Industrial warfare simulation creates an environment where these solutions can be thought through with intricate planning and design of new processes which reflect the new sets of rules that need to be created to succeed in the new world. These rules must reflect of climate change, environmental sustainability, and energy consumption for them to succeed where the others have failed. If not deterred, the US-China trade war will lead to a massive confrontation beginning in the South China sea which escalates and expands into a shooting war which when begun, will be impossible to stop because of the alliances which Eurasia is forming as it transforms into an industrialized version of the world's Island.

The US-China trade war will morph into industrial warfare.

The Trump administration paid close attention to Chinese economic development when he was campaigning for the 2016 elections. They used the arguments and threats of China throughout the elections while they contemplated the origins of industrial warfare. However, the intentions of this book were to discover new rules and new ways of adapting into the world economy. 7Tao's intention was to contain the battle to the classroom and find solutions to this problem before a trade war can ensue. 7Tao does this by fighting it out in the classroom rather than the marketplace. The only element that leaves the classroom is a solution.

According to Jack Ma, the founder of Ali baba, the US-China trade war can drag on for more than 20 years. Henry Paulson of the Paulson Institute warns of the dangerous long-term impact from the US-China trade war. Many other commentators are providing warnings both for and against both the US and China about the impact of the trade war.

The US-China trade war will stretch well into the 21st century and will be the dominant feature of the next generation's decision-making process. One thing is for certain, the US-China trade war will affect every single transaction on the planet. The next 100 years of transactions being conducted in any part of the world will involve the touch of the US-China trade war. The likelihood of reaching an agreement between USA and China on the trade issues is very high, sooner or later they will come to a resolution of some kind designed for public consumption.

However, even if they do announce the resolution of the trade war, the conflict will continue as industrial warfare under the waterline. The dorsal fin of trade war going under the water does not mean that the industrial warfare entity does not exist anymore. Trade war just went into attack mode and became industrial warfare. When the predators operating in industrial warfare mode are not visible, they are hunting and dangerous.

For this US China conflict to be resolved, we will require an ongoing process of early adaptation and study. This means that the following people will need to be involved in the 7Tao process from every country of the world. National leaders, presidents, prime ministers, policy makers, chief executive officers, factory managers, supply chains, middle management, and factory workers. 7Tao is an attempt to understand and resolve the greatest challenge of the 21st century between the two superpowers of China and the USA. It is paramount that everyone concerned with a transaction be involved in the study of the solution process which can be initiated to bring this confrontation to a close peacefully democratically speaking, a solution is one which is owned by everyone. It will take time, negotiation in every factory, every office, and every university; one transaction at a time and one project at a time.

Applying 7Tao to China.

Tao 1: Price: The Yuan has been tied to the dollar since 1994 for 30 years at 8.28 Yuan to 1 Dollar. They make cheap products shipped to your door.

Tao 2: Delivery: Ali Baba, e-commerce, Regional Comprehensive Economic Cooperation, Free Trade Deals with multiple countries in all 5 continents help to deliver Chinese goods.

Tao 3: Quality: Improvement of quality using education systems, technology enhancements, artificial intelligence and precision engineering will make their quality products and performance better.

Tao 4: Aftermarket: Belt and Road Initiative will sustain delivery to 74 countries.

Tao 5: Customers: Belt and Road combined with RCEP, and 5 continent's Free Trade Agreements will deliver to 80% of the world's customers.

Tao 6: Shareholders: Asian Infrastructure Investment Bank and corporate shareholders will enjoy the profits of the above 5 Tao elements to deliver massive financial growth.

Tao 7: Employees: One billion Chinese will be employed in factories, farms and offices across China for centuries to come.

7Tao is all around us.

The computer you use every day has 7Tao inside it. The curtains you draw daily. The toothbrush you use. The shower you take. The coffee you drink. The chair you sit on. The car you drive. The clothes you wear. The restaurant meal you eat. The gasoline you put into your car. The tires you replace to your car. The service your give to your car. The presents you buy your kids on Christmas day. The medical insurance you purchase for you and your loved ones. The airline ticket you buy. The price comparison websites you use to guide you. The Taxi you take to the airport. **Everything that involves a purchase requires 7Tao.** The only time 7Tao doesn't come into action is when someone gives you something for free. When does that ever happen in this day and age? They only way to stop 7Tao is to stop capitalism itself. If you are buying and selling anything, it is inevitable that you will be using 7Tao without even knowing it. As soon as you get your wallet out of your back pocket, you will be getting 7Tao out of your back pocket.

7Tao defines the transaction. We conduct transactions every day from our birth to our death. We use 7Tao every day without even knowing it from birth to the day we die. It is vital that we understand 7Tao, because 7Tao is what drives our world. It is an integral part of the world economy.

7Tao begins when a currency unit is applied to purchase a product, where there is any form of currency, there is 7Tao. As soon as a Dollar or a Pound is applied into the core of a transaction, the seven elements of 7Tao will come to life as that currency turns into a transaction which then fuses supply and demand. Demand will pull in supply for product and service, the means of driving that product or service is currency and the measurement are the seven elements which make up the transaction. If any one of these 7Tao or 7ways are not present, the transaction will not take place. No price, not delivered, poor quality, no support, no customers, no profit or no workers means that product or service will not be consumed. The Chinese understand 7Tao clearly, and therefore they are winning.

In the final chapter 13, I provide a 'Sun Tzu based blueprint' which I use to characterize the Industrial War between the US and China. Throughout this document, the structure is based on the Art of War by Sun Tzu, however, the actual flesh and operating structure is based on the modern corporation.

The final chapter is intended to be a useful document that the reader turns to each time they are in trouble in the marketplace to which they operate and understand the combat arena's and in the economic environment to come in the next decade. My aim is simple; to help the reader understand where they are and to use this book as a resource to navigate hostile business territory and a constantly evolving economic landscape which is increasingly dominated by the global trader.

I have been using Chapter 13 now for nearly 20 years since 1999, sometimes on a daily basis and it has been instrumental in guiding me in difficult combat situations when teaching large corporations how to fight. This chapter has even served me personally and has not allowed me to be attacked in any way and in any form. I hope that this document is also useful for the reader as they discover their strengths and their weaknesses with regards to their job, business, market, region and country. This will be a completely different world which beckons us in the decades to come. The challenges we had during the 20th century have morphed into more diverse set of amalgamated problems which need to be studied differently. Corruption has now worked its way into our personal lives and has worn down rule of law to the point whereby the law itself has become obsolete.

I hope Chapter 13 serves you as much as it served me for the last two decades. Good luck to everyone who is an avid reader of Sun Tzu's Art of War.

My version is 'The art of industrial warfare' a pocket guide to the 21st century of industrial combat.

CHAPTER 13:

The Art of Industrial Warfare

© All rights reserved, 7Tao Engineering Ltd

1: Initial Estimations.

We must acknowledge the fact that industrial warfare is a necessary priority for any corporation operating in the global marketplace today. Industrial warfare is the basis for growth or decline, the way to profit or loss and the key to economic growth. The implications need to be analyzed and thought through carefully.

...

To begin with, we must structure our organization along the following lines, evaluating how each relates to the other and honestly examining the best way to apply them:

1. the 'strategy' of the business.
2. the 'market' of the business.
3. the 'organization' of the business.
4. the 'leadership profiles' of the business.
5. the 'laws of business engagement'.

Strategy is about aligning the workforce with the direction of the leadership.

Market is about assessing whether it is expanding or contracting and what its constraints are.

Organization looks at the ease or difficulty with which the company can meet the market's requirements. The organization has to be in tune with the needs of the market or it will die through irrelevance.

Leadership expresses vision, understanding, discipline, benevolence and reward.

Laws of business engagement have two aspects: the internal development of the business which needs to be well organized, systemic and flexible, and the external development which focuses on the management of the competitor, destroying their expectations and creating conditions where they cannot succeed.

There are no business leaders who have not heard of these five factors, and those business leaders who do not understand them will not be victorious.

...

When estimating the comparative value of various options to find the best way to stay ahead of your competitor, ask the following:

Which business has the best strategy?
Which business leader has the greatest ability?
Which leadership structure has gained the advantages of business agility?
Which business has more money and shareholder power?
Whose workers and personnel are more knowledgeable?
Whose business methods and paradigm shifts are more in tune with reality?
Whose metrics, missions, visions and targets are clearer?

From these we will learn of the chances of victory or defeat in the market place.

These rules are universal in business, if they are ignored, the business will collapse. If a business leader follows these questions and breaks them down to their core, he will begin to progress to market dominance. If any leader dismisses these seven questions for their organization, dismiss that leader.

After estimating the profits to be made in the market, put the 7Tao (Tao = way) plan into effect using the top down model of implementation. These models must be supplemented by operational plans that reflect the changes in the market. As for strategic management and development, it is about steering the tactical levels of the organization to achieve the main goals of the company. This is to preserve ourselves and grow, while simultaneously attacking, weakening and destroying the competitor through our 7Tao attack methodology.

Within this lie the fruits of market dominance.

...

Industrial competition is the way of deception, thus, though you are capable, display incapability to your competitor.

When creating new products for the market, display a different direction to where you are actually going. When retreating from a business target, remain in close proximity to the competitor's aims and keep the competitor in sight, do not allow your competitor to master timing when retreating to the safety of your core business. The competitor will almost certainly fail when they move forward to penetrate your core market.

…

Send the competitor in the wrong direction, create waste in their company and attack their market presence. Do not allow them to form relationships with their shareholders, customers and employees.

If they are a large corporation, focus on product weaknesses as they will be lethargic in response. If they are wily, adapt to them and corner them by forcing them to make mistakes. This will suck out their cash flow.

If they are forceful, tempt their arrogance and force them to make mistakes in the market.

Increase the number of 'steps back' they should take, and correspondingly 'steps forward' in the wrong direction.

Implant regret into their company and remove 'right first time' from any action which they undertake, in this way they will be directionless and entrapped between confusing decisions constantly assigning internal blame within their business.

If the company is united, separate them by attacking their direction, motivation and unity.

Always attack where the competitor is unprepared.

Tariffs are used as fire attacks to buy time for a temporary stretch of time, they are not to be overused or the enemy will think that you have no other option. Tariffs when used incorrectly can have a double-edged effect on both the competitor and the home company. They may end up damaging everything and burning the entire economy down in a scorched earth policy and approach. They are to be used sparingly and with care.

Widen the conflict using history, fear and daily life. Involve all of their 7Tao in the equation.

These are the industrial warfare strategies, tactics and techniques of the modern business conflict which cannot be predicted in advance. Each has its own application, and each business situation will have its own pressures which request the use of a strategy, tactic or operational technique.

Before any business conflict, the attacker who is confident of victory against his opponent will have many factors supporting his endeavor to attack.

Before any business conflict, the attacker who realizes he faces certain defeat against his opponent will have many factors supporting his decision not to attack.

From these perspectives, it is possible to calculate victory or defeat in the market place. Therefore we must plan with many equations before we indulge in the art of industrial war.

2: The 7Tao of Industrial Conflict.

In general, the strategy of attacking the industrial competitor is this: when considering an attack on a competitor we must look at the 7Tao of success. Attacking these 7Tao is the most important characteristic in dismembering the competitor's business.

The first is Price.
The second is Delivery.
The third is Quality.
The fourth is the After Market.
The fifth is the Shareholder.
The sixth is the Customer.
The seventh is the Employee.

It is important to attack the opposition's 7Tao by organizing forces to remove the competitor's effectiveness.

To achieve this, ensure you recognize limits of action. Know where there is victory and where there is a trap. Only the wily attacker knows how to do this without entrapment in the enemy's business terrain.

We must organize our company to understand the monetary value in the industries in which we practice conflict. To achieve this we must break down the core of the competitor's aims and objectives. These are the 7Tao of market success, industrial dominance, and profit from a business environment – breaking these core elements of a transaction is the primary aim of an attacker and defending them is the primary objective of the defender.

These must be the most important objectives when considering an attack on the competitor. One who is excelled in attack does not think about why the focus must be on these 7Tao. He will attack and destroy the competitor's 7Tao value while focusing on winning market share by defending the strength of his transaction.

...

When employing your workforce in competition - your currency, policy, and education system must be supportive of a long and protracted battle. Unless the foundation systems are supportive and adaptive to the conflict environment business marketplace, the competitiveness of your company will collapse as your transactions foundation weakens. Your business will be exposed to added attacks on your livelihood. Value will seek a better home if it is not taken care of in your business transaction.

One who excels at employing attack strategies does not oppress the roots of operational employees who work on the shop floor, he does not force the operational employees to work hard and then fleece profits for themselves at the top of the organization structure. If this 'self cannibalization' is being done in an organization, it is a sign that dark days are coming ahead. The company will be disbanded, Strategic, Tactical and Operational employees will flee.

The remaining employees will be at middle management levels employing tactics of employment preservation by attacking the internal balance of the corporation. It is important that corporation finds these employees and removes them before they do irreparable damage to the working, value added and operational levels of the organization.

If strategic, tactical and operational employees are running away from the organization, then there are signs that decline is coming.

Collapse of the competitor will ensue. These are the results of an ineffective defense.

3: The 7Tao of Industrial Strategy.

In the industrial war context, it is better to take over a company intact, and then to break it down into component pieces, sell the unprofitable components while keeping the profitable.

Do not betray the competitor's troops during takeover; make them your own, promote them, give them opportunity and hope, so that they may buy into your strategy supporting growth.

To destroy your competitor using brute 7Tao 'face to face' combat is not the pinnacle of excellence. The best business leader breaks the competitor's spirit to compete and then drives him to give up before a corporate battle can ensue.

Ensure that the battle is psychological at first. Do not allow the competitor to see that you have weakness. Overwhelm them with excellence by way of the following five factors.

1: Company history: If you are young, show a good future. If old, show a good history.

2: Company strategy: If you have a good strategy to compete, force the competitor into compromising positions.

3: Company excellence: Show professionalism and superior conduct in all operations, tactics and strategies, whether in defense or attack.

4: Company dominance: Show dominance in the market, in the field or in skill. Metrics will be the keys in the astute measurement of who is large and who is small. Appeal to the intermediary, make him yours.

5: Company size and weight: If small, show lightning maneuverability. If large show power and control over the market

In corporate and industrial war, we must move by way of logistics. This means using the logistical prowess by way of the six forces of logistical excellence.

1: Thought logistics: We must out think the competitor and be able to see the strategy of his attack against us.

2: Personal logistics: Movement inside a company. Ensure that your personal position is well protected inside your home company to contribute to the 7Tao, thus making your transaction strong and guarded.

3: Internal logistics: Ensure that the internal competitors are not able to fathom the movements of the person, teams or groups internally within the company. Rise above them internally by showing excellence to the 7Tao. Protect the transaction of the company by process, from the order taking place to the time payment is made.

4: External logistics: (Local) Ensure that the local competitors are not able to fathom the company's movements in dominating a local market.

5: Physical logistics: Do not allow the corporation's competitors to realize the movements of your company. Deceive them at every stage. Do not allow them to see your strategy or know your movements.

6: Corporate strategic logistics: Out think your competitor by sending him in difficult directions at strategic level. Use tariffs to block on equal levels at international, national regional and local levels. When the competitor imposes tariffs in return, increase the tariff rates thus creating blockage and bringing market transactions to a halt until the game can be changed to suit your purpose. Do not lay siege to his product or his institution. Any well built surroundings of product development will be extremely hard to dominate. Always attack by innovation, this is what enables the leap frog of established brands. The enemy's establishment must be worn down by way of protracted assaults rendering the enemy products obsolete to the marketplace.

If tariffs are counterproductive, then allow for reasonable negotiation with quick results, otherwise, the marketplace will suffer as a result of the 1 to 1 force of battle. Allies, competitors, customers, marketplaces, supply chains and governments will be damaged as a result.

It is the rule in industrial war:

If our forces are 10 - 1 surround the competitor and devour him.
If five to one attack his 7Tao.
If twice as numerous, divide his market attacking forces in two.
If equally matched, offer battle by way of 7Tao.
If we are inferior, we can avoid him.

In industrial war, size can become an advantage and disadvantage, it is a matter of structure and command.

The leader is the corner stone of the corporation; if the leader is complete at all points, the corporation will be strong; if the leader is defective, the corporation will be weak.

There are three ways in which a leader can bring misfortune upon his workforce.

1: By forcing the workforce to complete tasks that they are incapable of completing, being ignorant of the fact that they are incapable of completing the task. This is called hobbling the workforce. If the leader pushes the workforce and middle management joins in the pushing of the workforce, then the workforce will flee leading to increased staff turnover.

2: By attempting to govern the workforce in the same way that he runs his household, being ignorant of the conditions which are required to run a workforce. This causes restlessness in the workers mind and will fuel professional rebellion. A battle will ensure between middle management and the workforce.

3: By employing middle management subordinates without any reviewing policy or analyzing adaptation to the positions which require filling. He will quickly lose the respect of his workforce which will divide into two – management and workers. 'Them and us' will ensue. This will result in increased conflicting scenarios where the corporation will suffer as a result.

Now the workforce becomes restless and distrustful, trouble is coming for the leadership in terms of rebellion. Anarchy and a lack of control will consume the workforce, and so problems will arise.

Attack by way of deception, encourage poor leadership in the competitors ranks. Engage in hiring for them, spring forth people who will be used to damage the direction of the competitor.

Attack the competitor 7Tao using leadership which is bought. Make the 7Tao the enemy of the competitor and the ranks within the competitors will be scurrying for places to hide from the truth. The good middle management officers will flee and the bad ones will remain securing 'silo' based the long term employment within the business.

Thus we may say that there are five essentials for victory:

1: He who knows when to engage and when not to engage the competitor will know when victory is achievable.

2: He who knows how to handle both superior workforces and inferior workforces, both inside his workforce and inside the competitor's workforce. Thus he may vision victory with clarity.

3: He will win whose workforce is driven by strong motivation and discipline of the 7Tao.

4: He will win who while being prepared himself in every direction he chooses, awaits for attacks by the competitor who is unprepared.

5: He will win who has industrial and corporate capacity and is not interfered with by shareholders or the owners of the business.

Hence the saying: If you know the enemy and know yourself, you need not fear the result of one hundred corporate battles. If you know yourself but you do not know the competitor, for every victory gained by yourself, you will also suffer a defeat. If you know neither the competitor nor yourself, then you will lose in every business battle

4: Industrial Tactical Movements.

When moving the organization, place your company into a position of movement where defeat is unthinkable. Then attack the competitor. Here we have to think of the 7Tao of the marketplace indicating our transactional position and the competitor's transactional position. Ensure that it is the competitor that is trying to avoid the challenges of risking their 7Tao, make his transaction in danger by risking attack against you.

The attacker must be the one throwing the challenges at the defensive competitor from a position of unattainable reach.

To secure ourselves against defeat remains within our own hands, but the opportunity of defeating the competitor lies with the competitor himself.

The powerful corporation dominates the market through defense and then presents challenges against the competitor in the form of attacks to defeat him.

Security against defeat requires defensive tactics hence the use of Strategic Defense Masters, Tactical Defense Masters, and Operational Defense Masters who will protect our 7Tao. This implies that we must implement all available strategies of defense in order to keep our organization balanced.

Ability to defeat the competitor requires taking the offensive. This means that we must have a superabundance of strength. To engage this strength we must attack the competitors 7Tao. To achieve this requires the implementation of attack strategies by Strategic Attack Masters, Tactical Attack Masters and Operational Attack Masters who are constantly applying offensive pressure against the competitor internally and externally to legal systems of the world.

The defensive structure must defend us from our own complacency and our own weaknesses. The offensive structure must increase the competitor's complacency and insecurity, thereby increasing the chances of success in destroying the 7Tao transactional power of the competitor's organization.

Standing on the defensive indicates insufficient strength, as we are constantly defending our own 7Tao from numerous attacks from our competitor, this means we are constantly trying to save ourselves from both attacks from the competitor and market obsolescence.

Attacking requires superabundant strength as any extra power in our organization is used to attack the competitor. This will engage saved resources or borrowed resources from institutions such as banks and lenders.

Any profits must be used not just to show development, but to remove the competitor from the market place or reduce him to manageable levels by taking over him or making him small enough to handle.

The company who is skilled in defense buries themselves in the depths of 7Tao transactional excellence. They are unreachable from the attacks of the competitor.

The one who attacks encompasses the sudden and the powerful. They attack from a great height and are unfathomable in their attack methods. No one can see them coming, and they are under estimated when they are attacking by way of concealment of strengths.

Achieving victory over the enemy is not an easy task. It requires diligence and sacrifice. To see victory within a common frame is not excellence. It is not excellence to fight all competitors and defeat them all.

To lift an autumn hair is no sign of great strength, to see the sun and the moon is no sign of sharp sight. To hear the noise of thunder is no sign of a quick ear.

In order to create excellence, you have to create from anew. You must do what no one else can do. See what no one else can see. Achieve what no one else has achieved. Complete what no one else has completed. Attack in ways where no one else has attacked. Defend in ways no one else has defended. You must hit the competitor so hard and in such silence that he does not know that he has been hit until years later. He must not understand what his defeat looks like. It is even better to make the competitor help the defeat without him knowing that he is helping his own defeat.

This is done by innovation in product, process, people, procedure, placement and power.

Innovate in material, method, management, money movement and metrics, in this way, no one can touch you whether attacking or defending. They will never fathom your movements in business development. They will be at a loss to know the next move.

History has judged the clever competitor as not only the one who wins, but one who wins with ease. The clever competitor will use the energy of the competitor to win and not his own.

Battles are won by making no mistakes in Strategic, Tactical, and Operational levels of defense.

All the way through battle, mistakes cannot be made when observing the requirements of the 7Tao. All of the 7Tao transactional demands must be met.

The attacker is well aware of the detailed requirements for defeating the competitor. He does not miss the chance to defeat the competitor by studying the transactional strengths and weaknesses of the competitor internally within the competitors business and externally within the marketplace.

The 7Tao Grandmaster of attack and defense cultivates moral law in his own organization. He reinforces method and discipline in the art of industrial war - in this is the power to control excesses. This lies in creating simplicity in processes and removing complexity which can clog the arteries of the business information, finances, materials and innovative growth.

In terms of industrial and business methods in controlling excess by removing waste:

Firstly, we have measurement and metrics.

Secondly, estimation of resources required.

Thirdly, calculation of investment and prospective gains.

Fourthly, balancing of risks with respect to gains and prospective gains.

Fifthly, the chances of victory over the competitor.

It is not good enough that you win, the competitor must lose, be taken over and their presence be eradicated from the market while sustaining the moral law of business. Ensure that takeover remains your first line mission, closure must be the second mission.

A victorious 'market dominant' organization cannot be challenged in this dominance except through the vassals of time, the challenging organization cannot remove the defending organization except through protracted market attacks.

The organizations market geography is product domination with a brand linkage. To dominate the brand and product is to dominate the market and control the consumer's decision. This is the pinnacle of power, to control the decision making power of the customer. The defending organization must not allow the attacker to enter the marketplace.

The onrush of a conquering organization is like a bursting of waters into a chasm 'a thousand fathoms deep'.

5: 7Tao Energy in the Organization.

Controlling the organization is a matter of dividing up numbers.

When controlling a large number, spread them into controlled subdivisions. When controlling a small number, spread them into controlled divisions.

Fuse the 7Tao into the workers process, job and product from the top levels of the organization to the shop floor and throughout the supply chain. In this way competing with a large force is like competing with a small force, the chief question is 'can the workforce keep in mind the 7Tao from the start of the job in the company to the end process of collecting the cash?'

To remain confident that your workforce is intact, make sure that they can stand the brunt of an attacking enemy and remain glued to the 7Tao transaction of your corporation.

To achieve excellence, our defense must be direct and our attack must be indirect.

Victory comes from innovation in every detail of attack and from innovation in every detail of defense.

The impact of your workforce must be like water against boulders, smashing them against each other and moving them with the power of the commercial tidal wave which you have become.

You must be all inspiring in becoming water, unfathomable, and unstoppable – while totally destroying, surrounding, suffocating and drowning the competitor.

In industrial and corporate war, direct methods may be used against the attacker to enjoin battle, but indirect methods must be used to gain victory. These are the way of symmetric and asymmetric attack, also known as disruption, distraction and devastation.

Indirect tactics, or asymmetrical engagement in business, is as inexhaustible as heaven and earth, as unending as the flow of rivers and streams, like the sun and the moon, they only end but to begin anew, like the four seasons they pass away to return once more.

There are not more than 7Tao in business, yet the combinations of these 7Tao can produce global strategies of great effect, damaging attacks, as well as defenses which are unable to be scaled.

There are not more than five musical notes, yet their combinations can rise to more melodies than can ever be heard.

There are not more than five primary colors, yet in combination they produce more hues than can ever be seen.

There are not more than five cardinal tastes, sour, acrid, sweet, salt, and bitter, yet their combinations can yield more tastes than can ever be tasted.

There are 256 techniques, tactics and strategies of defense and 256 techniques, tactics and strategies of attack within the current 7Tao construct, yet the combinations of these systems exceed infinity. The combinations are endless and can only be managed by those who are intelligent in the practice of industrial warfare. The more practice the Grand Masters of Industrial Warfare encourage, the better prepared the troops are in industrial battle.

In corporate battle, there are not more than two methods of fighting. Attack and defense using the ways of orthodox (Symmetrical) and unorthodox (Asymmetrical), yet those factors can give rise to endless series of maneuvers.

Attack and defense inside and outside of the corporation lead unto each other in turn. It is like a moving circle, you will never come to an end as each strike and parry leads to ever increasing opportunities to develop and enhance. Such is the importance of direct and indirect conflict in business. It is conflict that is the mother of all creation, it is conflict that ends the obsolete, it is conflict that is the precursor to death, it is conflict that creates life. The study of conflict is the Grand Masters most important aim in any corporation, because within this lies the fruits of victory or the roots of defeat.

The 'quality of the decision' is like the well timed swoop of a falcon which enables it to strike and destroy its victim.

Therefore the good corporate attacker will be patient in his coming, measured in his approaching footsteps, and prompt in his decision.

Energy in the workforce is like the bending of a bow, the decision like the release of a trigger.

Amid the turmoil and difficulty of business there may seem disorder and yet no real disorder at all. Amid the confusion and chaos, your structure may be without head or tail, yet it will be fool proof against defeat. If the competitor cannot visualize the structure of an attack method, he will not be able to guard against it.

If an attacker makes it seem uncertain where he is going, the defender will not know what to defend against. Feigning direction is fundamental to winning in the long term. You may have to suffer defeats in battle in order to win the war at a later date.

Appear in disorder but postulate perfect discipline. Simulated fear postulates courage, simulated weakness postulates strength.

A corporate leader who is skillful at keeping his competitor on the move maintains deceitful appearances according to which the competitor will react. He will sacrifice something from the company, so that the enemy corporation may snatch at it. He will then entrap the competitor, thus encircling for the kill.

By holding out baits to the competitor, he keeps the competitor on the march, with a body of picked men he lies in wait for the competitor.

The clever corporate manager or director looks to combine energy to achieve multiple effects. He does not require too much from individuals. Hence his ability to pick out the right men and utilize combined energy. He is excellent at recognizing synergy, he converts it into creative and innovative energies used in defending our organization and used in attacking the competitor.

The business team (Strategic, Tactical and Operational) then becomes the frontal force of the organization, like a boulder forcing down a mountain to take away anything which is in its way.

6: Attack and Defense using Weakness and Strength.

Whoever releases their products first and awaits the competitors to catch up will be fresh for the fight. Whoever arrives second in the market place and has to hasten to the competition may be exhausted in the battle for market dominance because of branding disadvantage.

Therefore, the clever leader imposes his will on the competitor but does not allow the competitor to impose his will upon him.

By holding out advantages to him, the business leader can cause the competitor to approach on his own accord, or, by inflicting damage, he can cause the competitor to stay away.

If the competitor is undisturbed you can harass him and threaten him, if well supplied with stocks, he can be starved out of cash. If the competitor's order books are full, they can still be attacked, through time.

The workforce may be able to dominate markets with little resistance if the battle develops into areas where there is little or no presence from the competitor.

You can be sure of succeeding in your attacks if you only attack those places where the competitor is undefended or weak in defense structure. You can only ensure safety of your market defense if you hold positions which cannot be attacked.

The techniques of defense encompass disciplines which are dedicated to the support of the 7Tao. The combinations in using these disciplines allow the defense to make endless patterns.

...

To defend the organization we must support the business transaction by way of waging constant industrial warfare. 7Tao uses the following defense disciplines:

Awareness revolution – so that all of our workforce understand the importance of what we do.

Total productive maintenance – to keep the organization's wheels oiled and ready for business conflict.

Value engineering – to encourage in our workforce the importance of process innovation.

Design – constant movement in our management of the customer's individual needs.

Information engineering – knowing how to develop information to use to adapt to customer terrain.

5'S systems – keep our people well aware. All of our systems are clean and healthy.

Worker creativity – Make the manufacturing system comfortable to the needs of the customer stance in the market.

Industrial engineering – clean the blood and arteries which the organization uses to defend itself.

Forecasting – to keep the vision of the corporation's needs adaptive concerning short term objectives.

Quality assurance – to keep decay away from the value of our 7Tao.

Leveled Production – to support the heartbeat of the company, thus improving endurance capability.

Flow manufacture – to remove any jerk reactions from our organization. Peaks and troughs have no effect when flow is implanted into the 7Tao.

Standard Operations – practice in the operational arts allows the workforce internal stability in the defense of the company.

Kanban – does not allow over eating of resources making the workforce sloppy and lazy. Feed the manufacturing and production system the right amount of inventory to remain fit, lean and maneuverable to difficult business situations.

Multi process handling – to help the workforce to stay adaptive and constantly able to embrace changes in the environment.

Scheduling and time control – the workforce can know when the 7Tao are at their most manageable, the pace of the organization movements is well controlled.

Changeover reduction – changing from one set of manufacturing direction to another without falling into delay, confusion and decay.

Cell layouts – the workforce constantly uses flexibility in the developments of the cell to adapt to the customer and market environments.

Visual control – the workforce must know the state of the manufacturing system and must be able to tell when the manufacturing system is becoming non productive.

Kaizan – the workforce must be able to see the future and adapt appropriately, thus protecting 7Tao.

Business management methodology – the workforce must be able to make quick, well informed decisions about how to preserve 7Tao.

Human systems training – the mind of the organization must be well trained in the arts of patience and stability in the management of the 7Tao vision.

Inventory management – the corporation must not rely on having too much inventory weight as this sacrifices stability, speed and adaptability in the market.

Project management – the corporation must learn to implement one bite at a time with each bite, 7Tao must be fused into the project.

…

Hence that leader is skilful in defense where his opponent finds it very difficult to attack the leaders 7Tao transaction.

Hence the leader is skilful whose opponent does not know what to attack. The **forms of attack** are *completely different* to the **forms of defense**.

To be successful, the attack must break down the rules of engagement between the defender and the attacker.

When attacking; use the divine art of *subtlety and secrecy*; learn the *invisible*, the *inaudible*, the *discrete*, the *work of the shadows* and the *movement of the wind*. It is through these that attacks can be successful.

You may advance and be absolutely invincible if you make for the competitor's weak points. You may retire and be safe from pursuit if your movements are more aggressive which will break the competitor's standards of competition.

If your pace is more rapid than your competitors, then the pace of battle will produce increasingly ferocious levels of attack across multiple target areas in the competitors body.

If we do not wish to fight, we use deception to stop him from engaging us. All we need to do is throw something odd and unaccountable in his way, to distract his attention and remove his focus from our 7Tao and defend the wrong areas of his 7Tao transaction.

We must form a logical, united and highly respected body while the competitor is split up into factions. Hence there will be a whole united body piled up against many factions. This means we will be many while the enemy is only an underpowered few.

And if we are able to attack an inferior force with our superior force, our opponents will be in dire straits. If they are in dire straits, their actions will be increasingly weak while they stretch to reach unattainable goals.

We must use all combinations possible to attack both legal and illegal, both orthodox and unorthodox, both circuitous and direct, both symmetric and asymmetric. Traverse inside and outside the competitor to divide him, to make him look everywhere, to make the competitor complete actions which make no sense to him or to us in terms of the 7Tao of Industrial combat.

Dismay him to make him tremble with fear at the uncertainty he is facing. Make him understand areas where he should not be, force him to undertake unachievable strategy, make him understand weak leaders. Allow him to receive confused instructions internally and externally. Such is the power of Industrial Warfare when it is applied in its most ferocious form. Industrial warfare can penetrate any environment and any situation to influence the results of any competition where transactional relevance is taking place.

The spot where we intend to attack must not be made known, the competitor will have to prepare against a possible attack at numerous points. Thus, his forces are distributed in many different directions. The number we will have to face at any give time, point, and place of attack will be few and under resourced.

Should the competitor strengthen his front then his rear will be weak, should he strengthen his rear his front will be weak, should he strengthen his left his right will be weak, should he strengthen his right his left will be weak, should he strengthen every where, everywhere will be weak.

Numerical weakness comes from preparing against possible attacks. Numerical strength comes from compelling our adversaries to make preparations against these attacks whether they appear or do not appear.

Knowing the time and place of the coming battles, we may concentrate from the greatest distance in order to fight. Adaptability requires speed of response, readiness and counterattack.

Though the competitor may be greater in size we may prevent him from competition in the market place, we must scheme, simulate and spy in all manners and in all ways, so as to discover his plans and the likelihood of their success. Unless we know what the competitor's attack objectives are, we cannot defend against them.

Rouse him, penetrate the ranks of his employees and learn the principles of his activity or inactivity.

Force him to reveal himself or entrap him using our spies, so we know in advance his vulnerable spots.

Carefully, oppose strengths and weaknesses with your own, so that you may know where the competitor's strengths and weaknesses become apparent when pressure is applied.

In making tactical movements in your workforce, the highest pitch you can make is to practice concealment and deception. Conceal your dispositions and your movement and you will be safe from the most subtle of spies and the machinations of the wisest brains from your competitor. Do not allow the competitor to know your directions, give him false information and make the competitor chase ghosts so that they expend energy and pursue resources travelling in the wrong direction, targeting the wrong areas.

His frustration in defeat will force him to spend even more resources to recover from defeat which has been discovered on his doorstep.

How victory may be produced comes from the competitor's own tactics – that is what the multitude cannot comprehend. The competitor must be provoked to make moves which can then be used to position him for defeat.

All men can see the tactics whereby we conquer the competitor's 7Tao, but none can see the strategy that is used to bring victory. This comes afterwards once all moves have been made. A strategy can be used to sell victory to conquer even more marketplaces, however, the victory cannot be repeated. Each victory is a creation of the actions of environment.

Do not repeat the tactics which have gained you in one victory, but let your methods be regulated by the infinite variety of circumstances.

Corporate tactics are the forces of the 7Tao, they are like water, the cheapest, the fastest, the most reliable routes are chosen to feed the requirements of the shareholders, customers and employees using purposeful solutions to their problems.

Like water they will hasten demands until the appropriate price can be achieved.

So in business conflict, avoid what is strong and strive at what is weak.

When approaching a defeated enemy, look to salvage value from the assets of the defeated competitor. Entice value away from them and towards our boundary.

Flexibility is the key to the fourth generation business conflict. You must think carefully allowing competitors to produce intelligence which is actionable and which can carry your aims and objectives under the costs and resources of the competitor.

Like water shapes itself according to the ground area which it flows, the business leader works out his victory in relation to the competitor type that he is facing.

Therefore, just as water retains no constant shape, so in business war there are no constant conditions.

To attain the power of water like movements, we must use the disciplines of attack. In order to fathom and defeat the competitor, we must wax and wane – carefully.

Although these conditions are direct, their application is indirect and the combination of their movements may be used with the force of any choosing.

To become successful in victory we must traverse between circuitous and direct, legal and illegal, light and heavy, orthodox and unorthodox.

When attacking, we borrow from the divine arts of subtlety and secrecy. Through it we apply the elements of invisibility and the attacking disciplines which bring weakness and loss to the competitors 7Tao, while preservation and gain to our own 7Tao.

...

The composition of the following elements, bring about excellence of **Attack** in all of its forms.

Orthodox and unorthodox – use these methods to realize secrecy and protracted pressure on the competitor.

Deception – confuse the competitor.

Exploiting arrogance – use the arrogance of the competitor's organization to break his structure.

Attacking stock – to tear feeds into the competitors manufacturing system.

The five types of spy – use the different spies to extract from the competitor.

Attacking processes – do not allow his processes to function.

Sabotage – sabotage mind, method, spirit, medium and body.

Attacking plans – do not allow the competitors plans to succeed.

Using spies and intelligence gathering – gain information from the competitor.

Creating fear – do not allow clear thinking in the competitor's camp.

Attacking processing – ensure that what comes out is not what the market required.

Destroying unity – break down the ties that bind the competitor's organization together.

Attacking production – slow the production systems of the company.

Causing delay – increase the number of delays inside the competitors flow streams.

Increasing motions – cause the competitor to increase effort and motion incrementally to maintain markets.

Attacking quality – remove the competitor's ability to be on target.

Increasing laziness – remove the ability of the competitor to be prompt and energetic.

Trickery and deceit – use trickery to send the competitor in different directions.

Attacking internal logistics – dismember the infrastructure of the company and break down their internal organs.

Using lawsuits against the competitor – use legal issues to entrap the competitor.

Exploitation – exploit opportunities in attacking the competitor both internally and externally.

Bribery – bribe individuals, teams, friends, partnerships, and leadership to break down their motivation to survive in the marketplace.

...

Using corporate attack methods is a matter of mixing and matching. From the prescribed methods, one can create any variation from which to breakdown and eliminate the competitor.

If we can modify attack and defense tactics in relation to our opponent and thereby succeed in winning, we may have a natural born leader.

The five elements of water, fire, wood, metal and earth are not always equally predominant. The four seasons make way for each other in turn. They are short days and long. The moon has its periods of waxing and waning. It can therefore be understood that all of the 7Tao are not all important at the same time, one may be more important than the other in relation to the market they are attacking and defending against.

We must understand from this that there is no one application to all techniques. Each one is alive and has choosing of its own time and application. Let the technique lead, do not force situations unless there is an attacking or defending reason behind it.

Use the 7Tao with respect and wisdom. There is no way that subtlety, invisibility and silence can be defended against if the competitor is the one who is making the opportunity for us to strike.

...

7: Maneuvering the Organization.

In business and industrial war, the Grand Master receives his commands from the CEO and the feedback systems of the business. These feedback systems are manned by the strategic, tactical and operational masters in both internal defense and external attack.

Having collected monetary investment for battle and intelligent strategy, he blends and harmonizes all of the elements of his attack and defense policy at Strategic level.

After that comes the tactical maneuvering. Tactical movements are the most difficult to achieve. The difficulty of tactical maneuvering consists in turning the circuitous into the direct, turning adversity into advantage, loss into gain, and misfortune into fortune.

Thus to take a longer route, after enticing the competitor out of the way though starting after him, to reach the goal before him…shows art in controlling deviation.

Maneuvering with a disciplined workforce is advantageous, but with an undisciplined workforce is dangerous. When a workforce is hobbled, they will balk at the middle management officers who in turn will attack the workforce, breaking the company naturally.

If you set a fully equipped workforce to snatch an advantage, the chances are that you will be too late. On the other hand, to detach a flying column for the purpose involves the sacrifice of heavy investments in innovation to test the marketplace. A balance must be sought for the attention to detail that is required when moving forward.

Do not force your workers to over work, as then, the leaders of your production line may fall into the over production trap set by the competitor.

In this way the stronger workforce will be in front, the weaker ones will fall behind and on this plan, only one tenth of your output will be clear, the rest will be stuck in movement of goods, storage, work in progress and rework based errors. The seven wastes will strike the heart of your organization reducing your cash flow position and effecting shareholder value.

If you work long hours to reach the goal and outplay the competitor, you will lose the leader of your first team and only half of your workforce will reach the goal, as the slower workers will not catch up. Don't work too fast, work to the rhythm of the marketplace.

If you work half of the production orders, only two thirds of your workforce will reach the goal, the rest will produce weak performance in quality and your reputation will be damaged. Poor quality will lead to rework or outsourcing options.

A workforce without its material supply is lost, without its direction it is lost, and without supreme logistics it is also lost.

Do not enter into partnerships until you are acquainted with the designs of your partners.

Do not enter into an economic environment until you are familiar with the hardships involved in the economy, its strengths and its weaknesses, its pitfalls and its precipices, and its advantages and disadvantages.

You cannot turn natural advantage into account unless you make use of the people who live in the target economy.

In business, practice dissimulation and you will succeed. Always simulate industrial battle because this is where we can gather expectation of the competitor and ourselves.

Whether to concentrate or to divide your workforce must be decided by your circumstances.

Let your speed and rapidity over take the highest benchmark. Have waste levels non-existent in terms of wasted actions, but keep some waste in order to have room to breathe.

In taking the competitor's market, plunder their customer list and provide benefit to those customers so that none can displace you. This is called establishing your position.

…

Let your management divide the spoils of growth among the employees and shareholders of the organization when you capture a new market. Let it be divided up among the conquerors for the benefit of the workers, issue stock to them and create a sense of ownership of the company. You have now created loyalty among your best troops.

Always question vigorously before you move in the market. Under stand in detail the art of 'cause and effect'.

The logistics of the competitor is captured by the arts of deception and deviation.

Good communication is the power of a speedy organization. But do not communicate overly excessively or you will lose the direction inside your organization.

Form a single united body in the management of your employees. This is the art of handling large corporations with large masses of employees. Split them and control them as valuable entities. All metrics internally must be related to the 7Tao or they will lose their way in the marketplace.

Always convey to your workforce the correct information, in the correct ways of communication, so that your people may be motivated throughout their operations.

Remember that without proper communication, a whole workforce may be robbed of its will to succeed, and the leader may be robbed of his presence of mind.
Too much communication, too many presentations, too many opinions, too many initiatives, too many ideas and too many chefs in the leadership team will

lead to battles in direction. This will in turn lead to the same officers creating their own ships and sailing away from the main fleet.

Once this behavior is realized, it will infect all officers who will have their own aims and objectives thus disuniting the organization. Ensure that all elements of control are retained in clear metrics and targets within the business.

An employee's spirit is keenest in the morning, by midday it has begun to flag, and in the evening his mind is bent on returning to his family life. Ensure that you support the last part of his day, so that he returns in the morning fresh and ready to love the work.

A clever business leader therefore avoids a competitor whose workforce is keen for competition, but attacks a corporation whose workforce is sluggish and unmotivated. This is the art of studying the competitor's mood. A sluggish workforce will show signs of fatigue and will have high staff turnover. Thus we can attack the competitor through the 7th Tao of the employee.

Be disciplined and calm, await the fear and indecision of your competitor, this is the art of retaining self possession.

To be near the goal while the competitor is still far from it, to wait at ease while the competitor is toiling and struggling, to have customer orders while the competitor struggles for customers, this is the way of preserving company strength.

Refrain from attacking a competitor who is leaving the market, and do not attack a competitor who is calm and confident in his forward and backward movements, this is the art of studying circumstance.

Do not challenge a dominant competitor unless you have clear advantages of innovation which he does not have.

Do not disturb him when he is making a mistake.

Do not swallow the bait offered by a competitor.

Do not stop a competitor from exiting a market and returning to his home or his core business.

When you surround a competitor, leave an outlet and a direction so that he may go back to his home market without any real competitive friction, offer him 'join us, fight or go'.

Such is the art of economic, business, industrial and manufacturing war.

8: Variations in Industrial Tactics.

The Chief Executive Officer receives the call from his shareholders, assembles his employees and concentrates his development on building the marketplace by winning customers.

When in a difficult business environment, do not encamp and sit still, keep your product line and your workforce moving so that they can never find your position in the market. Obsolescence is the eternal enemy in any marketplace position.

Do not linger in isolationist economies. When cornered in the market, plan your way out of adversity. When you have no choice but to engage in industrial warfare, use the industrial defense and industrial attack methods to defend your corporation.

There are the paths which must not be followed, competitors who must not be challenged, leading positions in the market that must not be contested, and demands of the owners / shareholders which must not be obeyed.

The leader who knows how to balance the variations involved in industrial attack and industrial defense will know how to handle the creativity of his workforce.

The business leader who does not understand these variations in his industrial defense and attack formations, may well be acquainted with the environment of business in general, yet he will not be able to turn his knowledge into practical success.

The student of industrial war who is not versed in the 7Tao will be varying his plans even though he is acquainted with many advantages. He will fail to make the best use of his workforce.

Hence, in the wise business leader's plans; considerations of the 7Tao in business advantage and business disadvantage will be blended together. He will know what to avoid and which is the clearest path to follow.

If our expectation of advantage is tempered in this way, we may succeed in accomplishing the essential parts of our business plans.

If we are in the midst of difficulty we are always ready to seize on advantage, we may extricate ourselves from misfortune. The more your workforce is in tune to the 7Tao demands of the market, to the competitor strategies, and to our strategies; the more able we will be to communicate with the needs of the 7Tao.

Reduce any regional business players by inflicting damage on them. Make trouble for them. Keep them constantly engaged. Hold out advantages for them to keep them away from your targets, aims and objectives…This will keep distance between you and your real goals.

Do not rely on a business not entering your dominated market, rely on your readiness to slow the competitor down, break him, and deceive him. Do not rely on his not attacking your market presence, but rather increase the potential for your industrial defense. Do not rely on a competitor not attacking, depend on being prepared.

There are five dangerous traits which may affect a leader.

1: Recklessness – this leads to destruction.

2: Cowardice – which leads to market capture by the competitor.

3: Hasty tempers – which provokes poor decision making and emotional exuberance.

4: Self Adoration – A delicacy of honor which is sensitive to shame.

5: An over caring of his workforce – this will ruin his chances in industrial conflict because of the erosion of discipline, speed, and order execution.

These are the five traits of a inadequate business leader. Anyone of these will ruin his chances of success in industrial conflict.

When a business is taken over, or the old business leader has been pushed out, the cause of his demise will surely be found among these five dangerous faults. Let them be a subject of study among the industrial leaders of the world.

Therefore, if a leader suffers from any weaknesses where narcissistic personality disorder can be exploited, encourage that leader and place him in the position of extreme power. By that, the institution will be damaged beyond repair and will spiral downward rapidly, unable to return to its once great heights, fear and respect.

If uncountable allegations are plaguing a leader, make those allegations bigger so that further resources can be spent upon achieving a set of goals which have no merit, value or truth.

If the enemy is chasing a lie, encourage them, ensure that they are boxed in by aims and objectives of their own creation.

...

9: The Workforce on the Move.

Level down peaks and level up troughs in business as much as possible, in this way stability and a constant flow will constantly surround your strategic, tactical and operational attack and defense moves to dominate the market.

Only stop to make the next rest when you are looking for directions, but ensure that production and delivery to the marketplace never stops, the only rest taken by a business leader should be for pausing to think while still moving your business forward.

When instigating large changes in an organization, it is like crossing a river. Move quickly and ensure that any new systems which are addressing paradigm shifts are quick in their achievement of results. Cross change pattern terrain quickly and beware of complex implementations. Do not allow targeted employees enough time and resources to create machinations against the organization, this can do enormous damage to the objectives of a company on their way out of the corporations control area.

When a competitor is upgrading himself in his onward march to become dominant in the market place, it will be best to let the implementation begin and then deliver lightning attacks on the competitor corporation to make it fail. This will make the leadership scared to upgrade any visions of business improvement.

Attack them with multi disciplined variations of the industrial defense and industrial attack methods.

In passing through recessions, get over them quickly without any delay. If forced to compete in a recession, you should have good cash flow standing by you.

Find cover in low cost manufacturing areas and provide space for your cash to move, in order to fulfill the needs of the owners and shareholders.

In a level, well forecasted environment ensure that you have safety plans in place so that traversing becomes easy. In this way when you are attacked by a competitor, you will have a direction in which to turn. Always stay prepared for them at every turn and give yourself room to maneuver.

All workforces prefer a full order book to an empty order book, but there is never a full order book. So how does a leader ensure that he has a near full order book and keeps to that target?

If you are careful for your work force, stick to your dominant position in your core business, in this way attacks by the competitor will not be easy to mount. This will spell victory for you because attack is expensive.

Don't approach or attack companies who are unrivalled in their business, unless you have ways of overcoming their core strength.

Avoid pitfalls of high research and development, unless you can keep your aims in the discovery.

Avoid difficulties of rescuing dead products, unless you can sustain revitalization and create yesteryear in fashion.

Do not invest in cornered downward spiral companies, unless you can provide a way out for them.

Do not buy stock from a company which is losing its presence in the country of settlement, unless you can resettle them elsewhere in a fertile economic environment.

While we keep away from such places, we should get the competitor to go and invest in these areas, to weaken them while we grow stronger.

We must use all the variations of attack and defense to ensure that the competitor is stuck in areas which we wish to avoid.

If in the neighborhood of your internal business, you have high movements, lots of interaction, open door policies, multi community environments and a supply chain which is constantly open to development. Be careful because, in this mix a competitors spy, ambush and attack planner could be waiting.

When a competitor is close at hand, he is relying on his natural strength of position. It is not advantageous to attack him except through innovation.

When he keeps away but tries to provoke you using industrial attack operations, tactics and strategies, he is anxious for you to make a move.

If he is open and accessible, he is awaiting you and will try to surround you by learning as much as he can about your designs.

Movement upwards in the market shares shows that the competitor is advancing, the appearance of adverts on screen means that the competitor wants to make us suspicious, and push us into action to counter him through competition. He wants to expand the marketplace and create a revolution to attack and existing technology. This is when technological change turns into a movement. Upon the creation of a movement of change, the market will see entire technology chains change their transactional structure. Economies will shift and transactions will change in every way possible.

When a paradigm shift takes place in the way in which economies work, it is best to have money ready for adapting to change. It is wise to expect that 9 out of every 10 people will be affected by that change.

If stocks and shares start to move in heavy downwards or upwards movement, then the startled short stock investors players will know that an attack is taking place in the market. The weaker, more undisciplined shareholders will quickly move away from the company by selling the stocks and switch to other companies. This is what the weaker and less loyal investors will do. Look for droves of leaving and joining shareholders to read changes in products or strategies.

When there is money being raised in the stock market, it is the sign of products advancing and gaining presence. When stocks are growing slowly, it indicates that a wider and deeper approach to business is being made.

Activity to and from in the businesses core market operation means that the business intends to make the market its core over the long term. The business is now reinforcing its peripheries to ensure appropriate defenses against attacks from outside competitors. This is also known as the barricade strategy.

Humble and hidden words with increased preparations are signs that the competitor is about to advance. Violent language and driving forward as if to surge are signs that they will retreat.

When smaller, compact or easier to build products are entering the market, it is a sign that the competitor is forming for battle.

Merger offers without rules for consummation indicate a plot for usage of the business competitor or alliances over the short or long term.

When activity in business is erratic and then suddenly uniformed, it means that a critical moment has come.

When some products are leaving the market and some are entering the market, be careful because it could be that an economic recession is coming to the marketplace. It is therefore wise to begin heavy innovation to defend an old market and to innovate to enter a new market in order to retain customers.

When workers stand around idly, talking in small groups, this means de-motivation and strong back biting is taking place against different parties in the organization.

If those who are sent to collect finances line their own pockets first, it means the workforce is suffering from cash problems as well as the combinations of too much expense.

If the workforce sees advantage in the market but it is unable to harvest it, it means that the ideas, plans, and supporting entities are incompetent and exhausted. The problem lies in the tactical officers who are unable to secure the marketplace from the position of middle management.

If there are large disturbances in the organization structure, it means the leader's authority is weak and there is a cost problem inside the organization.

If there are problems in communication and back biting without limit, it means that sedition is a foot. If the middle management is angry and disturbed, it means they are weary and oppressed. They will begin to damage the aims of the corporation within the reach of their position.

When a workforce is lean, with no real intention of settling in an area but moving on to greater dominance of the market, with no structure nearby, with no real bricks and mortar investment in the market under which they will operate, then they are coming simply to attack the market area and to degrade the existing players in the market. Watch out for their powers because they will be ready to fight to the death.

The sight of workers whispering together in small groups, backbiting, hind talking, and reminiscing with regret and destructive vision means they are disappointed in their organization and differ with the leadership of the company.

Too many rewards signify that the enemy is at the end of his resources, too many punishments means that the organization is extremely distressed and fearful.

To begin with great visions and then to suddenly retract, running from your own aims and objectives shows a complete lack of intelligence or realistic creativity.

When consultants are sent with compliments, it may be a sign that the competitor wants a truce. When consultants are hired to takeover strategy, it means they will be taking blame, covering up, making sure, auditing or coming in to allow for greater room for failure.

When engineers are hired to develop a company, it means that the corporation is about to create new products and change for the better.

If the competitor's workforce develops plans to create products but does not enter the market because their eyes are concentrated on the company, then this situation requires great vigilance and circumspection, it means that they are searching for correct timing to attack. Your defenses must be ready.

When two organizations of the same size are symmetrically opposed to each other, this means that there is a market stalemate. What we can do is simply concentrate our workforces, and keep a close watch on the competitor until the market has run its course.

He who underestimates his opponent and uses no planning before moving into a market will simply be overtaken by his competitor.

If employees are punished before they have grown attached to you, they will not prove submissive and will be rebellious, so they are useless to the aims of the organization.

When employees have become attached to you and punishments are not enforced, they will still be useless, as they will be resistant to change.

Treat your employee's with humanity and care in the first instance to garner respect and trust, then later enforce iron discipline in their ranks coupled with simplicity in aims and objectives. This is a certain road to success in the market place.

When in development, employees achievement orders are habitually enforced, the workforce will be well disciplined, if not, discipline will be poor and hard to enforce.

If a leader shows confidence in his men but insists on his orders being met, the gain will be mutual.

If you are situated from a great distance from your competitor and the strength of the two plants is equal, it is not easy to provoke a battle unless you are competing in some market. If the markets are completely different, do not attack where you have had no experience. You will be disadvantaged immediately unless the competitor is also a novice.

There are six positions connected to the ground reality in the market. The leader who has a responsible approach must be careful to study them.

A workforce is exposed to six calamities which lead to defeat:

1: Flight

2: Insubordination

3: Collapse

4: Ruin

5: Disorganization

6: Rout

If market conditions are equal, if one company is hurled against another ten times its size, the result will be the *flight* of the former.

When the common employee is too strong in knowledge and professionalism and their management too weak, the result is *insubordination.*

If the management is too strong and the workers are too weak, the result will be poor 7Tao and *collapse*. You will go out of business with the latter and be in dire financial straits with the former.

When management are empty in thought, creativity, insubordinate, and upon meeting the competitor, they begin to implement their own plans from a feeling of resentment, before a business leader can tell whether he is in a position to fight or not to fight the competitor. The result will be uncoordinated movements and ultimately *ruin.*

When the business leader is weak and without authority, when his orders are not clear and distinct, when there are no fixed duties assigned to officers and men, and ranks are formed with no real value added contribution to the goals of the organization, the result will be utter *disorganization.*

When a leader who follows the 7Tao, is unable to estimate the competitors strength, allows his organization while inferior to engage a superior one, or hurls a weak directive against a powerfully defended one, he will be faced with *rout* of the business and the gradual disappearance of the industrial presence in the market he operates.

These are six ways of courting defeat, these must be carefully noted by a business leader who has attained a responsible post.

...

The natural formation of demand is the workers best ally, However, the following conditions will apply in industrial combat situations across any business environment and economic geographical terrain.

The power of *estimating* the adversary, of *controlling* the forces of victory, of shrewdly *calculating* difficulties using the tools of industrial warfare, the *danger* involved in industrial conflict, the *distances* involved in realizing the aims and objectives of the 7Tao…this is what constitutes the test of a great business leader.

The business leader who knows these things, in industrial conflict puts his knowledge into practice, will win his battles. He who does not know these forces which worship the 7Tao, will surely be defeated.

If industrial conflict is sure to result in victory, then you must engage, even though the owners and shareholders forbid it. If industrial conflict will not result in victory, then you must not engage the market even though the owners and shareholders cry out for industrial conflict to be engaged.

The business leader who moves forward with great humility and severe intelligence without fearing disgrace and humiliation, is the pinnacle of the organization and the pride of the business owners.

Regard your employees as your children with the same dignity and enforcements, they will follow you into the deepest of business engagements and will stand by you even during the end of the organization.

If you are indulgent, but unable to make your presence felt, kindhearted but unable to enforce your commands… you are incapable of quelling disorder. Now your employees are likened to spoilt children, they are useless for any practical purpose.

If we know our own people are in a condition to attack, but unaware that the competitor is not open to any attack, we have gained only one half of our market aims.

If we know that the competitor is open to attack but are unaware that we are not in a condition to attack, we are only halfway to our market aims.

If we know that the competitor is open to attack, and also know that our workforce is ready to attack but are unaware that the nature of the business environment makes conflict impractical, we are still only halfway to our market aims.

Hence the experienced employee, once in motion, is never bewildered, once he has started on his direction he is never at a loss.

Thus is the saying:

If you know yourself and know the enemy, your victory will not stand in doubt.

If you know highs and lows, you may make your victory complete over your competitor.

10: The Six Business Environments.

We may distinguish six types of business environments.

1: Accessible.

2: Entangling.

3: Temporizing.

4: Narrow.

5: Precipitous heights.

6: Positions at a great distance from the competitor

Ground markets which can be freely accessed by both us and the competitor are called *accessible* markets. With business environments such as this, enter and dominate the market first using a low cost and productive quality spot in the market. Carefully protect the delivery of products and reduce your time to market. Now you will be able to engage the customer ahead of your competitor in a level playing field.

Business environments which are abandoned but very hard to reoccupy are called *entangling*. From a position of this sort, if the competitor is unprepared, you will capture the market that he holds and defeat him. But if the competitor is prepared for your launch, you will fail to capture any ground in the market. Return to the original position will be impossible, disaster will now ensue. Entangling environments usually contain the remnants of depletion forces which have passed through the previously industrially dominant estate. Once depletion has settled into an estate, it is very difficult to remove the powerful tentacles of the depletion process.

When the position is such that neither side will gain by making the first move, this is called *temporizing* ground. In a position of this type, even though the competitor should offer us attractive bait, it should be advisable not to stir forth, but rather to retreat, thus enticing the competitor in his turn. Then, when the workforce has made a set of directions into the market, we may now attack his fragility in movement, and deliver our attack on his business with our advantages. Temporizing ground indicates that forces are equal and markets are ready for one to one combat based on transactional dominance. In this environment, both forces will be fighting for each customer one transaction at a time.

...

When we have managed to secure a *narrow* market which is high variety and low volume, high R & D, and high cost products will presume the norm. Occupy these areas first and increase the barriers to entry. Now we wait for the competitor to arrive and try to come into the market. Do not attack the competitor's narrow (low variety, high volume) market.

Do not try to go after him until barriers to entry are only weakly defended. In this environment, the competitor will be seeking to establish foothold in a very highly competitive market where customers are used to supply from one or two dominant players. In this narrow environment, it is best to revalue the 7Tao to suit the lower rungs of the customers and then work upwards through continuous improvement and market combat with the competitors.

With regard to *precipitous heights*, if you are arriving before your competitor, you should occupy low cost, high quality and quick delivery positions. Now wait for him to enter the competition arena so that you may compete. If he has occupied this position before you, either try to go higher and beat him on the value of 7Tao or try to entice him away from this market through purchase of the entity, corporation, designs or business. Limit the number of entry points into the marketplace and ensure that he abides by your laws when using this type of industrial attack.

Positions of a great distance from the competitor require the defender and the attacker to think about logistics. It may be required that shipping great distances becomes a key in operating in a foreign market. You must consider the operating characteristics of supplying to distant markets. A distant market may kill the competitor if he is facing a powerful opponent who is skilled in controlling his 7Tao.

Be weary of supplying great distances unless you have a superior product which responds to international demand on its own merit and demands from the marketplace. Be wary of asymmetric re-engineering methods because they follow this type of product and market situation relentlessly. The best method of blocking a position from a great distance is to apply defensive measures such as tariffs to create space for industrial combat at a later date.

...

11: The Nine Situations of Business.

The art of industrial war recognizes nine varieties of business situation:

1: Dispersed business situation

2: Facile business situation

3: Contentious business situation

4: Open business situation

5: Intersecting business situation

6: Serious and testing business situation

7: Hemmed in business situation

8: Difficult business situation

9: Desperate business situation

When a business leader is defending his own business environment, this is called a *dispersed* business situation.

When he is penetrating a new market where his competitors are stable and are hostile to his forward penetrating movements, this is called *facile* business situation.

When we hold a business environment which has great advantages to us as well as to our competitor, this is called a *contentious* business situation.

A business environment where there is space to strategize and grow is called an *open* business situation. It must be dominated with diverse market fulfillment strategy.

A business environment which forms the key to many other business situations is called an *intersecting* business situation. He who occupies this business situation will sustain phenomenal growth and unpredictable levels of success in any venture they undertake.

When a business has penetrated into the heart of a *hostile* business environment, meeting a set of well dug in competitors who have fortified business positions, it is called a ***serious*** business situation.

Legal barriers, trade barriers, protectionism, lower prices, more capable workforces, a united front against your market penetration, or any other business environment which is hard to traverse, this is called a ***difficult*** business situation.

Business environments which call for the company to traverse through narrow and defined business opportunities with high variety and low volume, through difficult break through points, through tortuous set up procedures, through high investment and initially low output; This is called a ***hemmed in*** or *saturated* business situation.

A business environment upon which we can only be saved from destruction by direct conflict with the competitor, this is called a ***desperate*** business situation.

...

In a ***dispersed*** business situation, therefore, do not engage your competitor directly.

In a ***facile*** business situation, do not stop moving towards your objective.

In a ***contentious*** business situation, do not attack the competitor.

In an ***open*** business situation, do not try to block your competitor's direction.

In the business situation of ***intersecting*** opportunities and cross roads, join hands with allies and gain partnerships. This will enable you to have the size required to complete the attack strategy.

On *serious* business situation, extract as much value as possible.

In *difficult* business situation, keep moving as fast as possible. Bring many different products onto the market, extract value and move on.

In *hemmed in* and *saturated* business situation, use the strategy of industrial war wisely... to pull yourself out of a difficult situation and gain domination of the market through variations of constant attack.

In *desperate* business situation, fight your way using the art of industrial war attack and defense methodologies.

Those business leaders who are skilful know how to drive a wedge between the competitor's front and rear. They know how to drive conflict between his large and small divisions. They know how to stop the high performance worker in the workforce from rescuing the low performance worker. They know how to stop the management rallying the workforce of the competitor. They know how to force management to sell out the workforce for the cheapest possible price. The competitor cannot win unless they are aided and abetted by the leadership and management of the competitor.

When the competitor's work force is united, they must apply attacking force to keep you in disorder.

When it is to the competitor's advantage, they will move forward, when otherwise, they will stand still and look for a way in which to move forward.

When looking at your competitor, in order to control him, begin by seizing something he holds dear, then he will be amenable to your will. He will then do as you command by sustaining his position while enforcing yours at the same time.

Speed is the essence of industrial warfare. Always take advantage of your competitor's un-readiness. Force your way using unexpected strategies and routes. Attack not just the business environment of the competitor. Attack the competitor directly. Attack his alliances. Attack his supply chain. Attack his transaction by attacking his 7Tao.

The following are the principles to be observed by an invading business into a market. The further you penetrate into a market, the more your workforce will come to depend on you. Thus the competitor's defenses against you will not stand. You must feed from the competitors supply chains when entering a market to secure long term market presence.

Make as many production order capabilities in fertile business environments as is possible in order to supply your factories with demand. Sprinkle the important essence of the 7Tao into the heart, mind, and motivation of every employee in the business. Innovation will then be directed by the 7Tao transaction as demand changes.

Carefully study the well being of your workforce. Do not over tax them. Concentrate your energies and hoard your strength. Keep your business continually on the move by testing new products and services through market measurement.

When you strategize do what no one else has done before and go where no one else has gone before. Be innovative, the leading creative edge will be forged in your name in both product and process which both have integral yin and yang relations with each other.

...

Throw your workforce into positions of direct combat with the pinnacle of the competitor's standing and they will prefer corporate death to flight. If they face redundancy or no job, they will place their uttermost strength into battle and achieve the impossible. This is best done through sending teams of attackers ahead of time to coax and provoke your competitor.

Workers, when in desperate situations will lose their sense of fear, but do not destroy their health through want of greed in extracting yields from them. You will end up destroying their motivation and their drive to fight for their company.

If there is no place of refuge and the workforce know that they are being supported by the management…then they will stand firm.

If they are in a hostile business situation, they will show a stubborn will to succeed. If there is no other way but to fight, they will compete hard to survive in any difficult business situation.

In business and industrial war, do not try to preserve your own position by creating invisible work. An employee must recognize that he has no choice but to fight the competitor, once he realizes this, he will contribute to the 7Tao of the organization.

Value added must be seen by looking at what the skills of the worker are, rather than telling him to do what does not come naturally to the worker.

If workers do not have excessive wealth, it is not because they detest material goods and market purchases. If they do not have long careers, it is not because they dislike job security. However, once you place them into a situation where they have to fight the competitor, they will muster the strength to see themselves out of difficult and testing situations.

Once the workers are cornered into a situation where they must protect the company, the workers will be forced to place themselves in the way of challenge in order to overcome the market position of the competitor.

The skilful organization may be likened to a snake, when the competitor attacks the back, the front strikes to defend itself. When the competitor strikes at the front, the back will strike to defend itself. If the competitor strikes at the middle, the back and the front will strike to defend themselves.

In this way, the skillful Grand Master of Industrial Warfare will know how to use Strategic, Tactical and Operational defenses against multiple competitors. The skillful Grand Master of Industrial Warfare will know how to use Strategic, Tactical and Operational attacks against multiple competitors. The Grand Master will be able to dominate battle in any environment, terrain and business situation.

Can corporate enemies become friends? If the task of unifying is going to be beneficial to us both, they will challenge the task and overcome it together, this will happen just as the left hand helps the right and the right hand helps the left even though they are opposites. This is called alliance development for a short period of time. In most cases such as this, they competitors will learn together and then attack other smaller or disunited players in the marketplace just to keep the market to themselves.

Hence it is not enough to put one's trust in technology alone. The defense of a business must not be conducted by putting up barriers of trade, economic, and distasteful strategies. The customer will see through the charade and choose to go with whoever has the best 7Tao.

The principle on which to manage a workforce is to set up a standard of excellence which all must reach, this is called high quality performance without measurement. It is assumed that the quality of a product and service will be perceived as high quality.

How to make use of high performance workers and low performance workers? This is a question involving proper use of skill and application of talent in the right areas.

Thus the skill of a business leader is as though he is leading a single employee slowly by hand.

It is the business of an organizational leader to be quiet and ensure that secrecy is upright and just, while he is maintaining order.

The business leader must be able to mystify his managers and workers by motivating speeches and appearances without being subjected to dishonesty and fraud. He must be able to keep them in total ignorance except for instructions which add value to the organization. When dishonesty and fraud is found in a leadership position, incarcerate that leader and make them an example for the whole marketplace to see. Prevent any damage to the business culture or to the reputation of a manufacturing company, product range and nation. Be lethal in punishment at any strategic levels of operation.

By altering business arrangements and changing plans he keeps the competitor without definite knowledge. By shifting his camp and taking circuitous routes, he prevents the competitor from anticipating his purpose.

At the critical moment, the business leader pulls away the rug from under the worker's feet, and forces them to confront the challenges which encompass business conflict. They must now fight the competitor on multiple levels in varied environments.

...

Information is presented, but no one knows as to the true direction of the company. What you make your competitor see and what your true direction is must remain within your closest circles.

The different measures suited to the nine varieties of the business situations, the expediency of aggressive or defensive tactics, and the fundamental laws of human nature, these elements must certainly be studied.

When invading a new market, the general principle is that penetrating deeply brings cohesion, penetrating a short way brings dispersion. This is an approach to a dispersive business situation.

When you leave the business headquarters behind, take your workforce with the help of alliances, this is an approach to a critical business situation.

When you penetrate deeply into a market, it is a serious business situation. This will require long term investment and deep market presence with long term planning before entering a market position in a target territory.

When you penetrate a market by going shallow, this is a probing approach to measuring a business situation. Here you are measuring counter strikes and seeing how many competitors will come to attack you when you decide to enter into the situation in a serious way.

When you have a competitor's dominance to your rear, and very difficult challenges in front, this is a hemmed in business situation. Articulate the best way in which to steer out of this situation using backward and forward strikes without leaving too many footprints while making your way out.

When you have no refuge at all it is called a desperate economic situation. You must fight to bring on line the appropriate way out of this debacle.

Therefore in a dispersed business situation, inspire your workforce with unity of purpose.

In a facile business situation, the business leader would see that there is close connection between all parts of his organization structure.

In a contentious business situation, the business leader should speed up the operational levels of the workforce and flatten the organizational structure so that orders are smoothly translated to the bottom of the company.

In an open business situation, the business leader should keep a vigilant eye on all of his defensive protocols.

In a business situation of crossroads and intersecting highways of many different competitors, the business leader should consolidate his alliances.

In a serious business situation, the business leader should try to ensure a continuous stream of orders and keep his order book filled.

In a difficult business situation, the business leader should keep pushing on the path to profitability.

In a hemmed in business situation, the business leader should block any way of going back to a projects beginnings.

In a desperate business situation, the business leader should proclaim to the workforce the hopelessness of saving their roles in the company other than to fight to the death for their jobs.

It must be the employee's disposition to offer a motivated role when surrounded by problems, to work hard when he cannot help himself, and to obey orders when he is at risk of losing his job.

We cannot enter into alliances with neighboring competitors until we are acquainted with their designs. We are not fit to lead a workforce into a direction until we are familiar with the market we intend to dominate, its peaks and troughs, its life and its death, its capacity for growth, and its technological strengths and weaknesses. We shall be unable to turn advantages into monetary account unless we make use of consultants who are familiar with the market, conflict standards, number of competitors, business environment and the situations that it will produce with regards to ferocity of industrial and economic combat

...

A newly formed business leader does not ignore any of the following five business principles by way of consulting the Grand Master of Industrial Warfare.

When a newly formed business leader attacks a powerful competitor, his leadership shows itself in preventing the concentration of the competitor's forces. He will over awe his opponents, and so their shareholders are prevented from joining against him.

The great business leader does not rally himself with fame and fortune alone, nor does he foster the power of other leaders and corporations. The business leader will carry out his own secret designs, he will always keep his competitors in awe. He is thus able to capture markets and over throw the current competitor's dominance.

When providing rewards to employee's, do so without prejudice. Issue orders and business designs without regard to previous arrangements. You will be able to move the whole workforce as though moving only one employee.

Confront your employees with the order itself, never let the employee know your design. When the outlook is bright, bring it to the shareholders, customers and employees eyes. Motivate the employee with the dangers of failure when the situation is gloomy.

Place your workforce in deadly challenges and it will survive according to conditions, plunge the workforce into deep challenges and it will creatively work itself out of gloom and come into safety.

It is precisely when a workforce has fallen into harm's way that it is capable of achieving victory. It must see the visual challenge in front of it to achieve victory.

Success in industrial warfare is gained by carefully accommodating and adapting ourselves to the competitor's purpose and exploiting their weaknesses and guiding the competitor's strength in the direction of our choosing.

By persistently hanging onto competitor's weaknesses, we shall succeed in the long run in killing the competitor's leading financial objectives. If any one of his 7Tao are weak, attack that particular Tao until the competitor begins bleeding in all of the rest of his 7Tao thereby reaching economic death and inducing depletion in the lands of the competitor geography. This is called the cunning and powerful way to achieve victory over the competitor.

During the times taken in confrontation with the competitor, block his directions using the defensive methods. Destroy any official statements and representations by removing authority and truth from the statements.

Stop the passage of any consultants and remove any spies by rooting them out. Be stern and commanding in business meetings, so that you may control the situation.

If the competitor does not cover the whole market, rush in and take his place and dominate the market through multiple arrays of products, strategies and services spanning the entire business environment.

Forestall the competitor by seizing what the competitor holds dear, then wait for his arrival in the market, as soon as he arrives fresh, attack him immediately.

Once you have gained momentum using orthodox movement and have the competitor following orthodox engagement, attack him using unorthodox strategies, tactics and operations so that victory becomes nearer. Ensure that he delivers the victory and then hands his plants over to you – intact and preserved with operational output.

At first, when a competitor is sizing you up to find out the best ways of attacking either your dominated marketplace or your ability to enter his marketplace, exhibit the notion of dullness, vagueness, and ambiguity.

When a competitor gives you an opening, strike with speed uniformly until the competitor is broken. It will be too late for the competitor to oppose. He may then follow your lead in asymmetric business methods, if he has the remaining strength to do so, but by that time you will be able to put yourself in a position where you can buy the smaller competition and use them to attack the existing larger competitors in the marketplace.

It is wise to use the experience of the smaller competitor's culture, proximity to the population, ease of movement among the locals to attack the marketplace. They form a better alliance in movement back to the territory we intend to target.

12: Physical Attacks on a corporation, market and country.

There are five ways of attacking with physical strength.

The first is to stop workers from functioning properly.

The second is to stop inventory.

The third is to stop logistics.

The fourth is to stop supply chains.

The fifth is to create problems inside the competitor's production line.

In order to carry out an attack, we must have all the means available. The material for raising a physical attack must always be available to our employees in the competitor's organization.

It is very difficult to carry out physical attacks unless you are aided internally from within the competitor's organization. These opportunities will come from identifying and exploiting weaknesses in all of their forms among the competitor's assets.

There is an appropriate time for completing physical attacks, and special days for starting a conflagration.

The proper season is when customer orders are high, the proper days are when the competitor's business is moving at a quickened pace, awaiting to move at a quickened pace, stockpiling to capture the market, and increasing maintenance to prepare for the market.

When the competitor is successfully growing, he will pay scant attention to the fact that he may be attacked as his entire concentration will be on selling the results of the balance sheet.

...

In physical attacks, one should be prepared to meet five possible developments.

The first is: When a physical attack is effective in the competitor's environment, respond at once to take the customer's off the competitor accounts. We can do this by applying tariffs to stop particular products from entering our destined geography, these are physical barriers to stop products from coming into our country. However, these will damage many elements of the 7Tao and must be used with care and within limited time use.

The second is: If the physical attack is not successful, but the competitors remain quiet, bide your time and do not attack the customer order. Compete naturally with each 7Tao transaction.

The third is: When the physical attack has reached its peak effectiveness, follow it up with an attack to take the customer, gauge carefully because if this is not possible, stay where you are.

The fourth is: If it is possible to make physical attacks, ensure you deliver your attack at a favorable moment. Attack through the cyber, real estate and direct sales drive.

The fifth is: When you complete a physical attack, do not stand in front of the competitor, ensure that you are hidden when taking the competitor's value. This is called stealing a competitor's value chain without him knowing. We can then make the competitor work for us.

Resorting to physical attack too quickly is a sign of desperation, non physical attack and complete starvation of the competitors business is the most powerful way to subdue competition and win the entire market.

A market demand force for a product that is new will last long, but a receding and declining market soon vanishes for older obsolete products. Always stand by the growing and powerful market forces and product life cycles. Slowly abandon that which is becoming obsolete and stay ahead of innovation to show relevance to supply and demand in the marketplace.

In every workforce, the five developments connected with physical attacks must be known, the movements of the customer demand calculated and sight based close watch kept for the proper time for attack strategy.

...

By means of unorthodox engagement, a competitor may be stopped, but not squeezed of his markets.

Unhappy is the business leader who tries to win his battles without cultivating the spirit of enterprise on his gains in the market, by sharing the booty of the marketplace with his shareholders and employees, the result is a general waste of time and stagnation.

Root out corruption and immediately fire any business leader who holds all the gains for himself and his team of collaborators in corruption. These are the ways that a corporation can be devastated and poor reputation bought into the entire marketplace. It is vital that any form of corruption which reaches to the top of a business is killed immediately because this will damage the transactional reputation of that business permanently.

Hence the saying, the enlightened business leader lays his plans well ahead. The board of directors cultivate their resources in all areas and ensure that correct accountability is sustained throughout the corporation by creating vital examples of excellence from the top down to the bottom rungs of the corporation.

Move not unless you see an advantage, use not your workforce unless there is something to be gained, compete not until the position is critical.

No business leader should put his organization into a market simply to gratify his own achievements and pride. No Grand Master of Industrial Warfare should engage a competitor simply out of temper, anger, annoyance, or pique.

If it is to your advantage, then move forward. If not then stay put, otherwise the competitor will take the value of your 7Tao and your organization will disappear.

Anger may in time change to gladness, vexation may be succeeded by content, frustration can still be contained, a smaller organization is still in existence, and a weaker organization can still be made strong.

But an organization that has once been destroyed can never come again into being, nor can lost products ever enter into the market again.

Hence the enlightened business ruler is heedful and the proficient Grand Masters are full of caution. This is the way to keep a market in peaceful demand and a workforce in tact with supplying that demand.

13: The Use of Spies in industrial warfare.

Raising a large workforce and implanting them in a hostile environment with impossible challenges curtails heavy losses on the corporation in terms of motivation, manpower, and resources. It causes a drain on the state of the corporation's balance sheet. The daily expenditure will amount to 25% of the budget of a corporation. There will be commotion in the ranks of the shareholders and the supporting employees of the corporation. The supply chain will suffer and this will then infect the other customers of the supply chain in the marketplace. Half of the employees, the customers, and the shareholders will abandon the organization.

Hostile corporations may be facing each other for years, engaging themselves with orthodox defense and orthodox offences, striving for a victory which is decided in a single product, in a single time, with a single introduction strategy.

This being so, to remain in ignorance of the competitor's condition simply because one is 'tight fisted' and 'greedy' is sheer stupidity. A business leader who cannot afford a small amount of money to find about the competitor is the biggest loser of all business people. He is at the height of folly and at the pinnacle of the measures of irresponsibility. He will break down and destroy the nature of his own organization because of his inability to spot danger in the competitors attack strategy. This type of business leader who does not reward employees, who actively transfers the product into the competitors hands, who holds partnerships with the enemy in the name of peaceful market coexistence, who does not heed to a history of attacks by the competitor, is the worst type of business leader. He should be terminated immediately.

One who does not invest in espionage and spying activity is no leader of the business, no help to the shareholders, has little responsibility to the employees, and has no commitment to customers. He is no master of 7Tao and does not know the meaning of true market dominance. He is unskilled in the Art of Industrial Warfare and will be annihilated at the first signs of combat against a powerful adversary.

Thus, what enables the wise and good business leader and directors to strike and conquer, to achieve aims beyond the reach of ordinary men…is foreknowledge.

Now, this foreknowledge does not come from guesses, forecasting, estimation, assumptions, prayers, hopes, or dreams. It cannot be inducted by experience, nor by any deductive calculations.

Knowledge of the competitors can only be obtained from other men and through accessing information. We must actively make use of spies and intelligence gathering in the competitor's ranks and in the marketplace itself.

We must make use of the five types of spy with their associated spying opportunities. Each of these will present their own advantages when achieving the aims of extraction from the competitor's business.

There are five types of spy:

The first is the *local* spy.

The second is the *internal* spy.

The third is the *double* agent.

The fourth is the *expendable* agent.

The fifth is the *living* spy.

When all of these five types of spy are at work, none can discover the secret system. This is called the divine manipulation of threads. This is the business leaders most divine and precious faculty in reference to industrial warfare.

It is vital that these five types of spy are handed all of the tools and techniques of industrial warfare to allow them to succeed in any transactional environment. Cyber, physical spies, collaboration, purchasing and hundreds of other spying techniques can be combined together to form pictures of strategies, tactics and operations in the establishment of the best position under which to fight an industrial war against a nation or against myriads of corporations within a business environment.

Having *local* spies means employing the services of the employees of the competitor.

Converting spies, getting hold of the competitor's spies, and then using them for our own corporate advantages, provides us with inexhaustible advantages.

Having doomed and *expendable* spies means making them do things openly for the business of deception. Allowing our spies to know of them and report them to the competitor.

Surviving spies are those who bring back news from the competitor's corporation.

It is very important to keep intimate relations with spies by covering the relationship with them by friendship. None should be more liberally rewarded. In no other business should greater secrecy be observed.

Spies cannot be usefully employed without a certain intuitive sagacity.

They cannot be properly managed without benevolence and straight forwardness. Without subtle ingenuity of mind, one cannot make certain of the truth of their reports.

Be subtle, be subtle again and then use your spies for every kind of engagement in the competitor's business plans.

The most dangerous spy is one that completes his tasks for no money, simply because he wants to dominate the marketplace and help the nation he serves. Placing one of these in jail will produce one hundred more to take his place. We have to be careful in understanding his aims and objectives in industrial warfare.

If a secret piece of news is divulged by a spy before the time is ripe, the spy must be fired together with the man to whom the secret was told.

Whether the object be to crush a corporations marketing drive, to storm a market, or to remove a key engineer, it is always necessary to begin by finding out the names of the attendants of any meetings among which the spy was present, the aids in the organization, and the security personnel in the camp. Our spies must be commissioned to the find these people and manipulate them into coercion with our aims and objectives.

The competitor's spies who have come to spy on our corporation must be rooted out, and tempted with bribes, led away and comfortably housed. Thus they will become converted spies and available for our service to extract from our competitor's.

It is information gathered from the converted spy, that we are able to acquire and employee local and internal spies for the purposes of extraction for our company. It's also owing to the competitor's spy that we can cause the expendable spy to carry false information to the competitor.

Lastly, it is upon these presumptions and information that the living spy and surviving spy can be used upon appointed occasions.

The end aim of spying in all its five articles of variety is 'knowledge from the competitor'. Knowledge can be gained from the converted spy. Hence it is very important that the converted spy be treated with the utmost liberality.

Of old, the rise of the powerful corporation was due to the competitor's spies who had provided information to their company.

Hence it is only the enlightened business leader and the wise Grand Masters who will use the highest intelligence of the workforce for the purposes of spying and thereby achieve great results.

Spies are the most important element in many ways for the corporations. It is on the spies that a corporation's ability to move will stem from.

THE END

Index

Academy 19, 147, 186
Accenture 195
Adaptation 41, 54, 200, 248, 256
Affordability 157, 271, 280, 289
Afghanistan 15, 39, 49, 136
Africa 111, 158, 192, 257, 300
Aftermarket 195, 184
Age 183
Agriculture 13, 60, 76, 241
AIIB 238, 237
Air Road 174
AirBnb 76
Aircraft 14, 94, 99, 277
Airplanes 51, 175, 312
Ali Baba 87, 145, 191
Altro 128
Amazon 149, 306
America 46, 119, 202, 205
AMRAAM 313
Ancient 13, 18, 24, 55, 290
Apple 96
Army 15, 38, 112, 185
Art of War 119, 140, 184
Artists impression 317
ASEAN 71, 269, 288
Asian 62, 238, 240
Astronomical 28, 100, 260, 306
Attacking 120, 142, 158, 203, 222,
Austerity 28, 83, 200
Australia 111, 172, 239, 269
Autoworld 207

Bangladesh 270, 294
Bank 28, 32, 41, 42, 238, 240, 244
Bank World 32, 38, 68, 76, 237, 240
Barnfield 18, 19
Bases Military 283, 27, 291
Battle 73, 24, 93
Begin 29, 49, 54, 57, 184
Beijing 41, 50, 237, 245, 258, 265
Belt and Road 191
Benchmarking 92, 206
Best 62, 69, 149, 247,

Betray 331
Bide 385
Biden Joe 54, 98, 264, 302
Big Diesel God 119
BIT NVQ 4, 145, 169
BITCOIN 149
BMW 83, 93
Boeing 96, 99, 110
Bonds 136, 137, 260, 269, 237
Boom and Bust 68, 309
Bradley John 19, 147, 186, 189
Brexit 49
British 19, 31, 44, 64, 77, 143
Bruce Lee 49
Bubble 109, 310
Burning 144, 328
Bursting Bubbles 166, 310, 338
Business 17, 43, 67, 271
Bush George 202

Camaro 97
Capitalism 13, 23, 38
Cars 38, 88, 97, 106, 117, 171, 175
Case study 99, 128, 145, 169, 186
CEO 18, 28, 43, 63, 74
Changing 21, 63, 171
China 125, 140, 159, 164, 183, 190
Chinese 41, 159, 164, 180, 183
Chosen one 23
Clothes 190, 141
Coke 96
Cold War 51
Collapse 13, 15, 28, 37, 39
College 18, 186, 265
Colonialism 38, 42, 47, 298
COMAC 94, 96, 108
Communism 13, 34, 38, 42, 50
Companies 26, 32, 65, 74, 95
Comparing 51, 53
Comparison 13, 31, 201, 322
Competition 116, 21, 23, 25
Conflict 13, 67, 273, 328
Confrontation 24, 52, 142, 268, 273

Constant 26, 49, 75, 154, 161
Corn Flakes 97
Corporation 27, 33, 38, 41, 67
Corruption 54, 241, 358
Counter 94, 108, 111
CPEC 24, 273, 289
CPTPP 213
Cruise 167
Currency 62, 78, 85, 137, 245
Customers 199, 201, 203
Cycle 31, 33, 36, 61

Dalio Ray 299
Damaging 92, 228, 265, 328
Danger 52, 105, 138, 236, 242
Davidson Harley 91, 180,
Death by China 294
Decline 31, 53, 63, 65, 260, 274
Defeat 38, 86, 112, 182, 242
Defending Aftermarket 184
Defending Competitiveness 258
Defending Customer Strengths 201
Defending Delivery Strengths 139
Defending Employee Strengths 248
Defending Price Strengths 117
Defending Quality Strengths 157
Defending Shareholders 221
Defense 18, 335, 337
Diesel 119, 297
Delivery 138, 144, 149, 158
Dependence 41, 77
Desolation 45, 81,
Destroy 70, 89, 121, 249, 314
Destroying 42, 44, 62, 110, 314, 325
Detroit 45, 70, 73, 75, 113
Development 29, 65, 191, 240
Diffusion 303
Dimensional 16, 132, 255
Display 47, 86, 149, 205, 277
Disruption 27, 74, 76, 152, 266
Dollar 55, 120, 137, 258
Dominance 26, 27, 38, 41, 74, 223
Donald Trump 22, 24, 54, 91, 293

Dragon 40, 49, 53, 74, 83, 122
Drury's Engineering 169
Dunn Richard 169
Dynamics 83

Eagle 51, 97, 98
Earn 79, 130, 179, 195
East Asian 32, 31, 33, 40, 212
East Middle 14, 15, 38, 55, 81, 137
Eastern 16, 17, 23, 24
Eastwind 185
Ebay 304, 306
Economic Power 60, 39, 86
Education 20, 31, 66, 275, 281,
Effective 23, 27, 81, 120, 133, 184
Eisner 224
Electrical 66, 186, 215, 315
Electronics 33, 75, 186, 194
Eliminate 56, 75, 88, 121
Emissions 198
Emotional 76, 184, 359
Empires 15, 38, 277, 299
Employee 248, 250, 256, 267
Energy 55, 56, 70, 117, 339
Engage 71, 89, 92, 93, 95, 98, 114
Engineering 16, 20, 64, 108, 169
England 19, 38, 42, 147, 230
Enron 14, 266, 304, 307
Environment 43, 63, 72, 74, 88, 123
Enzo Ferrari 207, 209
Essential 13, 59, 64, 76, 117, 189
Estate 37, 36, 52, 133, 286
Eurasian 32, 50, 69, 73, 86
Euro 319
Eurofighter 60
Europe 32, 37, 38, 42, 43, 47
Evaluation 218
Even Flow 208
Expendable 270
Externally 121, 224, 278, 281

F16 Falcon 39, 162
Face 63
Factor 17, 34, 35, 42, 275
Factories 15, 23, 32, 38, 49, 66, 291
Factors 34, 35, 42
Fall 34, 59, 135, 222, 284
Fate 70, 177, 235, 282
Faunce 48
Fear 28, 47, 78, 120, 179
Ferrari 96, 207, 208, 209
FIAT 209
Fierce 78, 81, 122, 273
Fighting 49, 78, 89, 90, 98, 112
Fiji 270
Financial 15, 17, 48, 53, 84, 193
Fintech 245
Fleet 162, 356
Flooded 44, 200, 314
Flowing 33, 221, 273
Flying Cars 174, 175
Focus 34, 51, 67, 103, 105, 114
Food Printing 251
Force 15, 40, 59, 60
Ford Motor Company 33, 46, 65, 96
Foreign 59, 65, 94, 113, 123, 172
Forging 91, 144
Formation 24, 30, 62, 152, 271, 358
Formula one 208, 209, 207, 169
Four Season 36, 61, 340, 352
Fourth Generation 63, 67, 69
Frame 336
Freight 198
Future 19, 26, 31, 47, 58, 62, 63

Gains 338, 386
Gamble 207
Garnering 139
GDP 211, 268, 192
Geely 183, 184
General Electric 43, 44, 47, 97,
General Motors 31, 33, 47, 96, 117
Generation 63, 64, 65, 66, 67, 69
Geniuses 218

Geographical 56, 69, 114, 158
Geography 81, 199, 213, 274, 300
Geopolitics 202
George Bush 202
Georgia 202, 269
Germany 16, 38, 46, 83
Getting 116
Giving 116
Giants 27, 32, 98, 218
Global 13, 17, 21, 26, 68, 113
Globalisation 44, 72
Goals 266, 267, 326, 346, 359
Good Quality Product 184
Goods 31, 33, 38
Governments 28, 29, 45, 69
Grad Student 279
Grand Master 337
Graph 48, 109, 110
Graph bubble 310
Graveyard of empires 15
Greece 42
Green 283
Greig Sneddon 145
Grip 28, 98, 106, 139, 241
Group 21, 28, 209, 235, 246
Growth 17, 29, 41, 45
Gulf War 285

Hainan 14
Harley Davidson 91, 180, 181
Harrison Fred 43, 45, 189, 266
Hawkridge 208, 209, 210
Henton Brian 209
Historical 27, 47, 57, 64, 154
Honeywell 43, 97
Hostages 27
House 62, 310
Huawei 96, 302
Hub 31, 197, 217, 301
Hugo Boss 83
Hummer 185
Humvee 202
Hurdles 19, 21, 313

Iceland 269
Idealised 37
Identity 126, 244
Ideological 39, 50, 57, 58, 59, 285
Implementing 147, 184, 210, 242
Importance 60, 61, 67, 203, 207
Imports 75, 92, 211, 265, 288
Inconceivable 27, 297, 300
Incumbent 13, 258, 292
India 71, 81, 86, 133, 192
Individual 64, 68, 120, 170
Industrial 60, 61, 111, 147, 208,
Industry 65, 66, 112, 147, 208, 264
Inflation 72, 136, 260, 266, 284
Infrastructure 60, 65, 75, 191, 196
Initial 94, 116, 195, 325
Initiative 76, 191, 192, 196, 211
Institute 215, 283, 320
Intellectual 92, 11, 211, 236, 258, 262
Intentional 14
International 61, 64, 65, 221, 246
Investment 76, 78, 120, 134, 165
Iran 86, 287, 289, 290, 298
Iraq 86, 240, 308
Islamic 192, 212, 273, 285, 300
Israel 86, 122, 239, 269
ITEC 26

J10 53, 122
J20 97, 140, 164
J31 53
J8 Finback 14
JF17 Thunder 162
Jack Welch 43, 44
Japanese 66, 75, 83, 116
Japan 16, 21, 32, 33, 38, 46, 47, 55
Johnson Matthey 145
Jobs 28, 41, 43, 164, 270
John Bradley 19, 147, 186, 189
Joshua Philipp 21
Juran 21, 33, 147, 262
Just in time 43, 71, 138, 158

Kawasaki 180, 181, 197
Kinetic 51, 112, 135, 214, 298, 312
Kingdom United 209, 238, 270
Knowing 18, 20, 23, 89, 109, 217
Knudssen 46
Kondriatiff 34, 35, 53, 61, 62, 65
Korea 190

Labelled 98, 134
Labor 18
Laugh 19, 41, 155, 159, 218, 219
Leadbeater 46
Leadership 47, 50, 52, 63, 69, 74, 81
Lee 49, 266
Legal 24, 30, 49, 70, 95
Legislation 65, 257
Lehman Brothers 28, 54, 137, 286
Levers 45
Liberal 15, 293, 295, 390
Life 27, 41, 56, 65, 70, 89
Lives 43, 44, 70, 166, 170
Liz Faunce 48
Lucy Colbeck 48

Madame Li 141
Made in China 16, 53, 267
Magnetism 42
Mainland 16, 211, 269, 278, 289
Managerial 29, 90
Manoeuvring 353
Manufacturing 13, 15, 46, 186
Market 13, 21, 23, 26, 28, 33
Martial Artist 19, 73, 79
Mass production 65
Matthey Johnson 144, 145, 188
Mercedes 83, 92, 93, 184
Metals 141, 145, 204, 256
Mexican 265
Middle Class 44
Middle East 289
Military 14, 15, 18, 24, 27, 38, 283
Millenia 276
Millennium 27, 29, 47, 50, 57, 62
Miniature

Missiles 87, 167, 291, 312, 313
Mobility 175
Models 73, 85, 154, 197, 214, 234
Monetary 68, 76, 155, 174, 237
Multinational 31, 209, 240

Napoleon 247
Nations 73, 76, 89, 98, 112, 135
Nationwide 310
Nepal 270
NESCOM 167
Nissan 117, 171, 261, 262, 280
North America 28, 134, 213
Norway 32, 269
NSAM 186
Nuclear 82, 130, 238, 291, 298

Obama 23, 26, 54, 79, 202, 238
Obsolete 73, 82, 101, 121, 153
Order 66, 69, 78, 102, 106, 113
Organization 69, 77, 81, 88, 116
Orthodox 89, 340, 349, 350

Pakistani 146, 162, 243, 296
Pat Patel 128, 132
Peking 164
Pentagon 26, 284
Philosophies 81, 103, 147, 234
Pirelli 164
Price 64, 66, 67, 72, 74, 78, 87
Prices House 44, 53, 147, 169
Prices Land 180, 306, 307
Prices Share 75, 100, 107, 129
Printing Money 84, 137, 155,
Quality 64, 66, 71, 85, 100, 102
Quality poor 158, 161, 174, 182
Quantitative easing 44, 156, 286
Queensberry rules 82, 88, 97, 111

Railways 197, 290
Ray Dalio 298, 299
Recessions 34, 151, 152, 156, 289, 304, 361

Red Peril 39
Renault 204, 280
Return On Investment 78, 85, 104, 120, 126, 132, 142, 155
Rover 44, 70, 117, 172
Russia 81, 86, 244, 245, 246

Sarkozy 204
Saturation Point 139
Scrounging 167
Sea power 59
Senna Ayrton 208, 209
Serbian Military 140
Services 61, 74, 76, 78, 89, 135
Shareholders 101, 113, 220
Ships 31, 60, 88, 197
Shop floor 28, 77, 89, 102, 117
Six Sigma 17, 43, 71, 159
Skilled 107, 111, 248, 281, 289
SME 138
Sneakers 145, 158
South America 47, 71, 192, 253
Soviet Union 13, 39, 51, 58, 69
SPC 159
Statistics 48, 90, 103, 120, 184
Sun Tzu 18, 26, 51, 115, 280
Sunderland 117
Supply Chains 23, 42, 72, 94
Sustenance 223
Swindon 116

Tanks 16, 40, 46, 50, 60, 86
Techniques 18, 63, 79, 80, 89
Tectonic 34
Thailand 32, 33, 133, 211
Thatcher 83, 222
Third World 24, 29, 98, 192
Three Dimensional 16, 251, 255
Tiananmen Square 13, 183
Tibbet and Britten 209
Toleman Group 207, 208, 209
Tomahawk 167
Tools 32, 39, 56, 60, 79
Training

Toys 124
Trains 90, 197, 198, 260
Training 67, 71, 99, 104, 120
Transactions 25, 68, 77, 85, 111
Tacchini 208
Transatlantic 27, 29, 31, 32
Transformation 179, 256, 314
Toyota 31, 33, 103, 110, 138, 207

Unbalanced processes 110, 221
United Kingdom 209, 238, 270
United Nations 210, 237
Unorthodox 89, 340, 347, 349
USA 13, 14, 15, 23, 51
UK 209, 238, 270
USSR 285, 300

Vauxhall 117
Vietnam 39, 40, 44, 133, 211

Walmart 133
War footing 72
Warwick 209
Washing Machines 190
Watershed event 34
Waves 34, 37, 49, 60, 81, 230
Weaknesses 120, 142, 158, 203, 222, 250
Weimar republic 84, 284, 307
Welch Jack 43, 44
West 42, 48
Western corporations 41, 44, 89, 200
Western Governments 29, 84, 192, 276
Westernization 146
Winning 15, 52, 90, 252, 261
Work in progress 112, 151, 400
Workforce 18, 72, 103, 125, 128, 361
World economy 21, 25, 31, 40, 47, 303
Worldcom 14, 266, 304, 307

Yield 14, 20, 112, 117, 125, 125

Zimbabwe 84

www.ingramcontent.com/pod-product-compliance
Lightning Source LLC
Chambersburg PA
CBHW051933290426
44110CB00015B/1961